STERLING
Test Prep

AP Biology

Complete Content Review

4th edition

Customer Satisfaction Guarantee

Your feedback is important because we strive to provide the highest quality prep materials. Email us comments or suggestions.

info@sterling–prep.com

We reply to emails – check your spam folder

4   3   2   1

ISBN-13: 978-1-9475563-0-0

Sterling Test Prep materials are available at quantity discounts.

Contact info@sterling–prep.com

Sterling Test Prep
6 Liberty Square #11
Boston, MA 02109

 Printed in the U.S.A.

STERLING
Test Prep

Thousands of students use our study materials to achieve high AP scores.

Scoring well on AP exams is essential to earn placement credits and admission into competitive colleges, positioning you for success. This book provides a thorough review of topics tested on AP Biology, covering the foundations and principles necessary to answer test questions. Understanding key concepts, extracting and analyzing information, and distinguishing between similar answer choices are more effective than mere memorization. This review prepares you to achieve a high score by confidently applying your knowledge when choosing correct answers.

This text is clearly presented and systematically organized to provide targeted AP Biology preparation. Learn the scientific foundations and essential biology topics needed to master the material and answer exam questions. These review chapters teach important principles and relationships and how they apply to questions.

Experienced life sciences instructors analyzed the exam content and developed the material that builds knowledge and skills crucial for success. Our test preparation experts structured the content to match the current College Board curriculum.

Using this book will significantly improve your AP Biology score!

220502gdx

What some students say about this book

★★★★★ *website had great practice material*

I feel much better about class…book helped me understand what we talk about in class. Get the book to have the edge over classmates. The website was very good practice.

Vicky Lowry (Amazon verified purchase)

As a biology teacher, I am always looking for extra prep material for my students. I ordered your AP Biology review book and I am pleased to conclude that it is great for content review and would prepare a student very well for the exam. I will recommend this book to my students so they can get the best possible scores. Thank you!

Mr. Douglas (submitted by email, published with permission)

My teacher recommended this book to the class and I really learned so much. It is very well organized and easy to follow along. The online questions are a good supplementation and practice.

Miriam McGillis (submitted by email, published with permission)

I purchased your book for my son after reviewing several other comparable books and talking with my son's teacher about what he needs to ace the material. He used it all the time while taking the class and he read it again when he was doing self-study before the test. He took the exam and while he didn't receive his score yet, he feels that he did well and that he was well prepared.

Sterling Test Prep customer (*submitted by email, published with permission without name*)

This book has a lot of review material and reflects the curriculum. It covers all the topics tested on the exam. It goes into just enough details to explain each concept, but not too confusing and overwhelming.

Nicole H. (submitted by email, published with permission)

AP Biology Practice Questions provides high-yield practice questions covering topics tested on AP Biology exam. Develop the ability to apply your knowledge and quickly choose the correct answer to increase your test score.

Visit our Amazon store

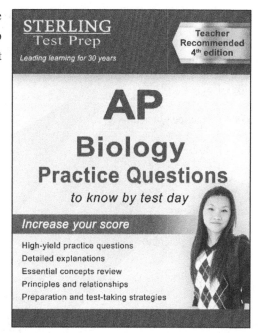

AP Chemistry, Biology and Physics online practice tests

Our advanced online testing platform allows you to take AP practice questions on your computer to generate a Diagnostic Report for each test.

By using our online AP tests and Diagnostic Reports, you will:

Assess your knowledge of subjects and topics to identify your areas of strength and weakness

Learn important scientific topics and concepts for comprehensive test preparation

Improve your test-taking skills

To access AP questions online
at special pricing for book owners, see page 531

Advanced Placement (AP) prep books

Biology Practice Questions

Biology Review

Physics 1 Practice Questions

Physics 1 Review

Physics 2 Practice Questions

Physics 2 Review

Environmental Science

Psychology

U.S. History

World History

European History

U.S. Government and Politics

Comparative Government and Politics

Human Geography

Visit our Amazon store

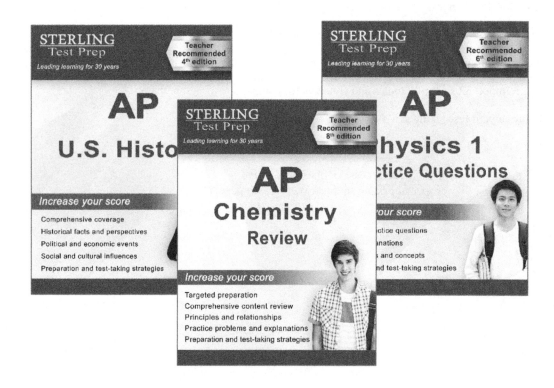

Table of Contents

Table of Contents (*continued*)

Chapter 1

Macromolecules

- Macromolecules

- Proteins

- Nucleotides and Nucleic Acids

- Lipids

- Carbohydrates

- Water

- Nutrients and Human Nutrition

Macromolecules

Biomolecules are the molecules that make up all life on Earth. Except for trace minerals, all biomolecules are *organic molecules*, which are compounds that contain carbon. *Inorganic molecules* such as water and salts are not classified as biomolecules but are major components in the processes of life.

Carbon is the essential element of life because of its bonding capabilities and versatility. It has four valence (outer shell) electrons in the highest energy level of the electron shells that surround the nucleus, allowing it to form up to 4 bonds with other atoms. Other elements can form 4 (or more) bonds, but they are larger and cannot fit into the incredible variety of configurations that carbon atoms can. Along with carbon, the most abundant elements in living organisms are hydrogen, nitrogen, and oxygen. Together these elements comprise 95% of the weight of the human body. Elements such as sulfur, calcium, and potassium make up the remaining 5%.

Monomers are small organic molecules. They are assembled into *polymers,* repeating chains of monomer subunits. Polymers are characterized as *macromolecules,* large organic molecules. Polymers are formed by *dehydration synthesis* (condensation reactions), in which monomers are joined by the removal of H_2O by a hydroxyl group (–OH) from one molecule and a hydrogen from the other.

Therefore, water is a byproduct of dehydration synthesis reactions.

Hydrolysis disassembles polymers into monomers, which involves the addition of water to cleave the long-chain molecule.

There are four major classes of macromolecules:

proteins (comprised of amino acids),

nucleic acids (comprised of nucleotides),

lipids (often comprised of glycerol and fatty acids) and

carbohydrates (comprised of sugars).

Notes for active learning

Proteins

General functions of proteins in the living systems

Proteins are the most abundant macromolecules in living organisms and serve a variety of functions. This includes structural support of cells and tissues, transport of molecules across cell membranes and throughout the body, hormone signaling, movement, and immune defense. Many proteins are *enzymes,* which act as organic catalysts to speed up chemical reactions within cells.

Amino acids – building blocks of proteins

Amino acids are the organic monomers from which proteins are constructed. There are 20 different amino acids commonly found in living organisms. Like all organic molecules, amino acids have a carbon backbone. The *alpha carbon* is bonded to four other groups: a hydrogen atom, a *carboxyl group* (–COOH), an *amino group* (–NH₂), and an *R group.* The R group, a *side chain*, differentiates the amino acids from one another.

The joining of amino acids occurs via dehydration condensation (or dehydration synthesis), when the *amino terminus* (−NH₂) of one amino acid joins with the *carboxyl terminus* (−COOH) of the other, forming a *peptide bond.* Several amino acids linked together by peptide bonds create a polymer, the *polypeptide*. A protein may consist of one or several polypeptides arranged together. The peptide bond has the carbonyl O and H pointed in opposite direction (i.e., up and down). The peptide bond is rigid due to a partial double bond character with the lone pair of electrons on N resonating for the carbonyl carbon.

Peptide bond

Protein Structure

A protein molecule contains carbon, hydrogen, oxygen and nitrogen, and sometimes other elements such as sulfur. Proteins are often structured around other molecules and ions which assist them in their function or maintaining their overall shape.

A functional protein consists of one or more polypeptides that have been twisted, folded and coiled into a unique shape. The order of the amino acids guides the three-dimensional conformation of the protein. Protein shape is an essential component of the protein's function in the organism.

Globular proteins and fibrous proteins are the two main structural classes of proteins. *Globular proteins* fold into a compact, roughly spherical shape. They are somewhat water soluble since they have polar amino acid side chains on their surface.

Nonpolar side chains are arranged in the interior of the protein, away from water.

Globular proteins may act as enzymes, hormones, membrane proteins, transporters, and immune responders. Some globular proteins are assembled into larger protein complexes that have a structural function.

Fibrous proteins are structural proteins with long, thread-like structures that are strong and durable. Fibrous proteins are elongated rather than spherical and, unlike globular proteins, are not water soluble. They provide structure, strength, and flexibility to intracellular and extracellular components. For example, fibrous proteins are used in cell walls and as connective tissue between organs.

Membrane proteins interact with biological membranes, and they are extremely important for the survival of organisms. They move molecules across the membrane or relay signals between the intra- and extracellular environment. *Integral* membrane proteins span the membrane and are permanently attached, while *peripheral* membrane proteins are on one side or the other and are temporarily attached. Pumps, channels, and receptors are all examples of membrane proteins.

Proteins can be modified into *conjugated proteins* by adding non-protein molecules. For example, a *lipoprotein* is a lipid bound to protein, while a *glycoprotein* is a carbohydrate bound to protein. Proteins may be bound as *chromoproteins* (pigment molecules), as *nucleoproteins* (nucleic acids), as *metalloproteins* (metal ions) and many others.

Cofactors are non-protein molecules. Organic cofactors are *coenzymes,* while inorganic cofactors tend to be metal ions. A *prosthetic group* is a cofactor which is tightly bound to the protein. For example, *heme proteins* such as hemoglobin are transporter proteins which require a prosthetic group such as *heme.* This is a small metallorganic compound that helps hemeproteins bind molecules such as oxygen. Because metal is involved, hemeproteins are classified as metalloproteins.

1° (primary) structure of proteins

The *primary structure* of a protein is the linear sequence of amino acids. This is determined by the DNA sequence of the gene that encodes the protein. A change of a single amino acid alters the primary structure and often the function of the protein.

For example, sickle cell anemia is caused by the mutation of a single amino acid (substituting valine for glutamic acid at position 6) in hemoglobin.

A portion of a polypeptide showing the amino acids and corresponding side chains (R groups).
By convention, the amino (NH₃⁺) group is on the left and the carboxyl (COO⁻) group on the right.

2° (secondary) structure of proteins

The *secondary structure* involves the interactions between nearby amino acids in the primary structure. It describes how initial three-dimensional patterns such as coiling and folding arise from these interactions. Secondary structure is dependent on hydrogen bonding between portions of the amino acid backbone. It does not involve covalent or ionic bonds and excludes interactions between the side chains.

The two major secondary structures are alpha helices and beta-pleated sheets. These result from hydrogen bonds between different regions of the peptide chain.

The *alpha helix* is a coiling, cylindrical pattern that forms from hydrogen bonds between the partially positive carbonyl (−C=O) of one amino acid and the partially negative amine (−N−H) of another, four positions away. The number and positioning of the hydrogen bonds gives the α-helix strength and flexibility. The peptide backbone coils around the axis of the helix, while the amino acid side chains (R groups) project outwards.

Alpha helix secondary structure with hydrogen bonds between the amino group of one amino acid and the carbonyl group of another four residues (amino acids) away.

The *beta-pleated sheet* (β sheet) is a pleated ribbon of amino acids. It is planar rather than cylindrical. Hydrogen bonds form between peptide bonds in adjacent regions of the polypeptide chain as *β strands*. This forms an organized network which folds into pleats. Adjacent β strands may be running in the same direction (e.g., both moving from the amino end to the carboxyl end), which are *parallel.* However, β-pleated sheets can be *antiparallel* if the β strands are aligned in opposite directions.

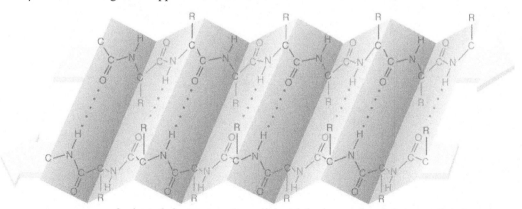

β-pleated sheets as antiparallel with hydrogen bonds between the sheets

When ionic bonds form between side chains, and thus interrupt repetitive hydrogen bonding, irregular regions of *loop conformations* may occur.

3° (tertiary) structure; the role of proline, cysteine, and hydrophobic bonding

Tertiary structure arises when secondary structures interact and form a three-dimensional conformation. Unlike a secondary structure, tertiary structure is due to interactions between side chains of amino acids rather than the peptide backbone. These interactions may be ionic bonds, covalent bonds, hydrophobic interactions, hydrophilic interactions (hydrogen bonds) or van der Waals' forces. The aqueous environment strongly influences the tertiary structure, since it affects hydrophobic and hydrophilic interactions.

Most forces stabilizing tertiary structure are relatively weak except the *disulfide bridges* (covalent bonds). These bonds form between the side chains of two *cysteines,* one of the 20 amino acids. Cysteine has a sulfhydryl group that bonds with another cysteine's sulfhydryl and create a covalent disulfide bridge (−S−S−).

Proline, an amino acid with a ring structure, is another major component in tertiary structure. This amino acid is rigid and does not bend to accommodate other amino acids, causing kinks in the protein chain.

4° (quaternary) structure of proteins

All proteins have a primary structure, and most have a secondary structure and tertiary structure. However, certain large proteins have a *quaternary structure,* the arrangement of multiple protein polypeptide chains into a multi-unit complex. For example, *collagen* is a fibrous protein of three polypeptides that are supercoiled like a rope. This provides structural strength for collagen's role in connective tissue.

In quaternary structure, protein subunits are held together by the same interactions (i.e., hydrophobic, ionic or covalent disulfide bridges) that stabilize the tertiary structure of a single protein. A protein with two subunits is a *dimer*, a protein with three is a *trimer,* and a protein with four is a *tetramer*. The naming of quaternary structures proceeds in this way. Protein polypeptide chains may be identical or different, as in the case of hemoglobin, a tetramer of two alpha chains and two beta chains.

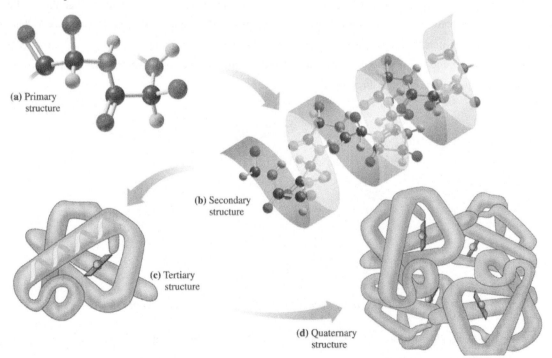

(a) Primary structure

(b) Secondary structure

(c) Tertiary structure

(d) Quaternary structure

Hemoglobin: an example of a four-subunit protein. Proteins have primary, secondary and tertiary structure. Proteins can have 2 or more polypeptide chains (e.g., hemoglobin has 2 alpha and 2 beta chains).

Denaturation of proteins

Denaturation is a process that disrupts the attractive stabilizing forces in the secondary, tertiary or quaternary structure (but not the covalent bonds between individual amino acids or disulfide bonds of −S−S−) of a protein. When a protein is denatured, its primary structure does not change, but its overall structure is unraveled and it becomes dysfunctional. Changes in pH, salt concentration, temperature or other conditions may denature a protein.

For example, most proteins become denatured if they are transferred to an organic solvent such as urea or acetone. This is because organic solvents are hydrophobic, inducing the protein to refold so that its hydrophobic regions now face toward the organic solvent. Heat denatures proteins because it imparts energy to break the weak hydrogen bond interactions that maintain the conformation, which is why organisms strive to maintain stable body temperature. Changes in pH can change the polarity (ionization) of the R groups and disrupt an enzyme's function, or unravel it entirely.

Non-Enzymatic Protein Function

Binding

An essential property of proteins is the ability to bind to other molecules. A *binding site* is a position on a protein that binds to a ligand (molecule associated with the protein). The ligand is usually small and can bind specifically to a protein's shape. Enzymes bind to ligand *substrates* and convert them into products. Proteins may utilize binding for non-enzymatic functions. In this case, the bond between the ligand and the protein is typically non-covalent and reversible. Binding of the ligand usually initiates a conformational change in a protein. *Affinity* is the degree to which a protein binds a particular ligand. Proteins often exhibit high *selectivity* and bind one ligand or class of ligands based on complementary shapes.

Receptor proteins are typically on the outer surface of the plasma membrane where they bind to ligands. The ligand acts as a *signal molecule.* Binding of the ligand induces the release of other molecules (second messengers) inside the cell, which relay the signal and produce a cellular response to the ligand (e.g., peptide hormone).

Membrane transport proteins are transmembrane proteins which coordinate the passive or active movement of certain molecules across the membrane. These proteins allow a certain molecule (or class of molecules) to pass through, contributing to the *selective permeability* of the plasma membrane.

Transmembrane proteins

Membrane transport proteins may be *channel proteins* or *carrier proteins.*

Ligand-gated ion channels are a group of channel proteins that utilize non-enzymatic binding to open their gates. Ligand-gated ion channels are similar to receptor proteins in that they bind a signal molecule, which causes a conformational change in the protein. This change opens the channel and allows ions to pass through the plasma membrane.

Carrier proteins, unlike channel proteins, do not form a continuous pore through the membrane but are open on one side at a time. For example, a ligand which binds at the extracellular side of the carrier protein induces a conformational change that moves the ligand to the intracellular side and closes the extracellular side. The ligand can then be released into the cytoplasm of the cell.

Some transport proteins are free-floating and travel between cells. Hemoglobin, for example, transports oxygen from the lungs to other tissues in the body. *Cytochromes* (often loosely associated with the inner membrane of the mitochondria and chloroplasts) are another group of hemeproteins that carry electrons for various metabolic processes.

Immune system

Antibodies are globular proteins involved in the adaptive immune system, a specialized subset of the immune system which responds to pathogens and antigens (molecules that stimulate an immune response).

Antibodies, *immunoglobulins* (Ig), recognize foreign substances (e.g., viruses) and target them for destruction. They bind to an *antigen* (Ag), a molecule on the invader that signals its identity.

An antibody's secondary structure consists of β-pleated sheets that are bound tightly together. These are arranged into a quaternary structure of four polypeptide subunits. The structure is held together through disulfide bridges between the polypeptide chains as a Y shape.

Antibody structure with ribbon diagram on the left and
detailed view of the four polypeptide chains on the right.
Each antibody has a similar shape with two heavy chains and two light chains.
The binding site for an antigen is in the variable region at the ends (arms of Y shape).

The stem of the Y, which are seen in the image above, is similar in all antibodies and can bind to receptors on a variety of cells in the body. Antibodies bind antigens at the top of each arm of the Y.

These antigen-binding sites are specific to each antibody and depend on the individual amino acids within the antibody protein.

Motor Functions

Motor proteins convert chemical energy into mechanical work and allow for cellular motility by generating forces and torque in the cell. Motor proteins typically have a complex quaternary structure.

Myosin and *actin* are motor proteins found in muscle cells where they drive muscle contraction.

Kinesins and *dyneins* are two common classes of motor proteins, used for transporting materials within a cell and orchestrating chromosome separation during mitosis and meiosis. Dyneins generate the movement of cilia and flagella.

Motor proteins are commonly associated with the *cytoskeleton*, the fibrous network within the cell. They transport molecules by progress along filaments of the cytoskeleton, pulling along vesicles or other proteins. This guided movement is more rapid and targeted than the simple diffusion of the substance within the cytoplasm.

Dynein and kinesin are motor proteins that transport cargo (i.e., vesicles). Dynein transports vesicles towards the negative (–) end, while kinesin transports toward the positive (+) end of the microtubule.

Notes for active learning

Nucleotides and Nucleic Acids

Nucleotides and nucleosides: composition

Nucleotides are the monomers of nucleic acids: *deoxyribonucleic acid* (DNA) and *ribonucleic acid* (RNA). A nucleotide has three components: a nitrogenous base, a pentose sugar and a phosphate group. *Nitrogenous bases* are single or double rings made of carbon, nitrogen, and oxygen. The *pentose sugar* is a five-carbon molecule bonded to the nitrogenous base. In RNA, the pentose sugar is *ribose,* hence the name ribonucleic acid. In DNA, the sugar is devoid of oxygen at the 2' position (*deoxyribose*).

Together, the pentose and nitrogenous bases are a *nucleoside.* Adding a *phosphate group* makes it a *nucleoside monophosphate*, the full name for a nucleotide. If three phosphate groups are added, the nucleoside becomes a *nucleoside triphosphate.* These molecules are not used in nucleic acids but rather for various metabolic processes; *adenosine triphosphate* (ATP) is a well-known example.

A nucleoside has a nitrogenous base and a pentose sugar (either ribose or deoxyribose).
A nucleotide is formed when one or more phosphate groups are added to the nucleoside.

Sugar-phosphate backbone

Nucleotides may be joined to form nucleic acids using dehydration synthesis by linking them with *phosphodiester bonds*. The free 3' hydroxyl group of one nucleotide forms a bond with the 5' phosphate group on the sugar of the next nucleotide. Alternating sugars and phosphate groups form the backbone of nucleic acids. At one end of the nucleic acid is a sugar group and at the other a phosphate group. These terminal groups determine the directionality of the molecule: the sugar is at the *3' end*, and the phosphate is at the *5' end*. During DNA or RNA synthesis, polymerization elongates the molecule from the 5' to 3' end (always adding the next monomer to the 3' end of the growing polymer). As it elongates, a linear nucleic acid begins to twist into a helical shape. It may remain single-stranded (RNA) or be joined to another strand (DNA).

Pyrimidine, purine residues

Nitrogenous bases are either purines or pyrimidines and extend from the sugar-phosphate backbone. *Purines* have a six-membered ring joined to a five-membered ring. The two purines are adenine and guanine. Adenine contains carbon, nitrogen, and hydrogen, while guanine includes double-bonded oxygen. *Pyrimidines* are smaller because they have a single six-membered ring. There are three pyrimidines: cytosine, thymine, and uracil.

Adenine   **Guanine**

Purines

Uracil   **Thymine**   **Cytosine**

Pyrimidines

In double-stranded nucleic acids, purines and pyrimidines are paired by hydrogen bonds.

Guanine always pairs with cytosine (G≡C) for both DNA and RNA.

In DNA adenine is paired with thymine (A=T), while in RNA it is paired with uracil (A=U).

Thymine is only in DNA and uracil only in RNA.

Adenine (A)   Thymine (T)   Guanine (G)   Cytosine (C)

*Adenine and thymine are paired with two hydrogen bonds while guanine and cytosine
are paired with three hydrogen bonds. A purine (A or G) always pairs with a pyrimidine (C, T or U)*

Deoxyribonucleic acid: DNA; double helix

The DNA molecule is responsible for encoding the information that gives rise to the cell's day-to-day activities. DNA controls the direction of its replication, controls RNA synthesis, and has an effect on protein synthesis.

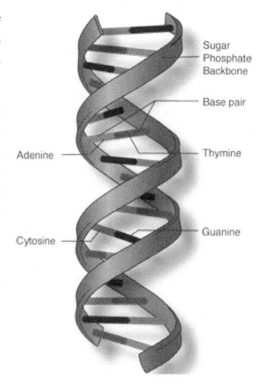

DNA is double-stranded, formed from two separate nucleic acid chains oriented in opposite directions (antiparallel). The 3' end of one strand is aligned to the 5' end of the other. The helices are intertwined and give rise to DNA's shape: the *double helix*. Each nitrogenous base of one strand is paired with a nitrogenous base on the other, *complementary base pairs*. The double helix is held together by hydrogen bonding between their nitrogenous bases.

DNA double helix with two antiparallel strands of DNA. The outside is the sugar-phosphate backbone; bases (A, C, G, T) project inwards with hydrogen bonds to hold the structure as a double helix.

Chemistry

DNA is the genetic code of life due to some chemical and physical properties. The backbone is negatively charged, which allows it to react with positively charged histone proteins and become "supercoiled" into compact chromosomes. This is why DNA that is millions of base pairs long can fit into the nucleus of a cell. In humans, the 23 pairs of chromosomes are in the nucleus of each somatic (i.e., body) cell.

Repulsion forces between stacked base pairs give DNA stability and make it relatively resistant to denaturation. However, each hydrogen bond which links bases is weak and easily broken. This is important, because DNA strands must be separated to replicate (during *S* phase of the cell cycle) new DNA before cell division. Each strand is the template for synthesis of a new strand.

The complementary nature of the strands ensures that each strand carries the same information and serves for the hereditary propagation of genetic material unique to each organism.

Other functions

Transcription is the synthesis of RNA from a DNA template. M*essenger RNA* (mRNA) is transcribed from a template strand of DNA. The mRNA is then *translated* into a protein. After mRNA is encoded with the genetic information found in DNA, it relays the message to *ribosomal RNA* (rRNA). rRNA is unusual because it has enzymatic properties, like an enzymatic protein. rRNA molecules aggregate into a *ribosome* that binds to mRNA and then initiates protein synthesis (translation) in the cytoplasm.

Transfer RNA (tRNA) molecules assist with translation by adding amino acids as dictated by the genetic code carried by the mRNA molecule.

Other RNAs regulate gene expression, splice noncoding (introns) information from mRNA before it is translated, and otherwise modify RNA.

Noncoding DNA sequences have an important role. The majority of DNA is made of *intron* sequences, rather than the *coding* sequences, or *exons*. Both introns and exons are transcribed into mRNA, but the introns are spliced out during processing of mRNA and before export from the nucleus into the cytoplasm for translation into proteins.

Telomeres are repetitive sequences of noncoding DNA that protect the ends of DNA from inevitable degradation with each replication of DNA during mitosis. Additionally, many noncoding regions of DNA regulate gene expression by promoting or inhibiting transcription into RNA.

Centromeres (involved in DNA replication) are other noncoding regions that have a structural function in chromosomes.

The DNA encodes for a primary transcript that is complementary to the DNA sequence.
The mRNA undergoes three steps: removal of introns and joining of exons,
the addition of a 5' cap and a 3' poly-A tail while in the nucleus.
The processed mRNA is then exported to the cytoplasm as the template
for protein synthesis during translation.

Lipids

Lipids are a class of organic molecules that include fats, steroids, oils, and waxes. Unlike other macromolecules, they are not considered polymers, because they are made of subunits arranged in various configurations, not necessarily a chain. Their subunits vary widely and are not classified as monomers. Because lipids are almost exclusively made of nonpolar covalent bonds, they are hydrophobic and have low reactivity.

General functions of lipids in the living systems

Lipids have a variety of functions in the body. Animals and other mammals use them for high capacity energy storage by packing specialized adipose cells with *fats*. These *adipose cells* swell and shrink as fat is taken in and discharged. Fat is used for protection and temperature regulation by cushioning organs and insulating the body against heat loss.

Steroids are a class of lipids used as hormones, the chemical messengers of the body. *Oils* and *waxes* are mixtures of lipids and other chemicals. Many plants and animals secrete them to waterproof and protect cells in the epidermis. Oil produced by mammals lubricates the hair and provides immune defense.

Like proteins, lipids can be conjugated to other groups. Lipids with a phosphate group are *phospholipids* in cell membranes in conjunction with proteins. Membranes include *sphingolipids,* lipids with an amino alcohol. Together these elements are responsible for the shape and fluidity of membranes. *Glycolipids,* lipids with a carbohydrate group, are arranged on the outside of cell membranes for cell recognition. Many other lipid conjugates are important for recognition and signaling.

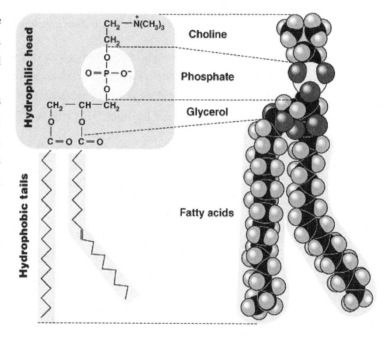

Phospholipids contain a hydrophobic tail and hydrophilic head. The tail may be saturated or unsaturated. The polar head is often modified (i.e., contains phosphate, carbohydrates or choline) with groups attached to one carbon in the three-carbon glycerol backbone.

Fatty acids

Fatty acids are lipids with a carboxyl group that is attached to (often) a 16 to 18 carbon skeleton. Fatty acids differ in length based on the number of carbons they contain and the number and locations of double bonds. If the fatty acid contains no double bonds, it is a *saturated* fatty acid because every carbon is saturated with its maximum number of hydrogens. If any of the carbons form double bonds, the fatty acid becomes *unsaturated.* Saturated fatty acids are straight chains, while unsaturated fatty acids have kinks wherever double bonds are present.

Saturated fatty acids contain all single bonds. They are often solids at room temperature because the chains pack together tightly

Unsaturated fatty acids contain double bonds, and the chain becomes "linked" at the double bond

Free fatty acids are found throughout the body as an energy source since they yield ATP when broken down. However, large quantities of fatty acids are assembled into fats for more long-term storage. In a typical fat molecule, three fatty acids are linked to *glycerol* (three-carbon alcohol). The glycerol is the backbone of the fat, linked to the three fatty acids by ester linkages. This structure is a *triglyceride.*

Glycerol and three fatty acid chains form a triglyceride

Steroids

Steroids are cyclic lipids containing a carbon skeleton of four fused rings. The hundreds of steroid classes are differentiated by the presence of various functional groups on the rings. *Sterols* are steroid alcohols, widely found in animals, plants, and fungi. *Cholesterol* is a sterol found in all animal cell membranes, where it regulates membrane fluidity. Despite its infamous association with cardiovascular disease, cholesterol is vital for building and maintaining cell membranes and is an essential precursor to *steroid hormones.*

Cholesterol

CH_3 CH_2 CH_2 CH_3
CH CH_2 CH
CH_3 CH_3

CH_3

CH_3

HO

Signals / cofactors

Many lipids are intra and extracellular signals, which bind to particular proteins. Steroid hormones travel throughout blood as cell-to-cell messengers. Receptors on a cell membrane may receive a hormonal signal and release *second messengers* inside the cell to relay the message. Derivatives of sphingolipids are commonly used as second messengers and as cell recognition. *Phosphatidylinositol* is another class of lipids that act as intracellular signals.

Some lipids act as cofactors for enzymes (e.g., *fat-soluble vitamins*). Humans must intake these vitamins from food or synthesize them from endogenous lipids.

Fat-soluble vitamins

There are four classes of fat-soluble vitamins (A, D, E and K). Vitamin A has many forms that can be interconverted, such as retinol and beta-carotene. These have anti-inflammatory, antioxidant and immune functions; they function in eye and skin health and are precursors to certain hormones.

Vitamin D has several forms and regulates uptake of minerals in the small intestine, especially calcium and phosphate. Vitamin D is limited in edible foods, so most of it is synthesized from cholesterol in the skin or catalyzed by UV radiation. It is vital for the health of the skeletal and immune systems and functions as a precursor for hormones.

Vitamins E and K are oxidation-reduction cofactors. Vitamin E is an antioxidant that protects other vitamins, as well as cell membranes and free fatty acids, from damage by oxidative stress (free radical damage).

Vitamin K catalyzes the production of blood clotting factors and other essential proteins in the bones and kidneys.

vitamin A

$C_{20}H_{30}O$ part of the visual pigment

vitamin D$_2$ calcium metabolism

$C_{28}H_{44}O$ & bone growth

$C_{29}H_{50}O_2$ **vitamin E** an antioxidant

vitamin K$_1$ a blood clotting factor

$C_{31}H_{46}O_2$

Vitamin A, D, E and K are lipid soluble vitamins and important components of the diet.

Steroid Hormones

Steroid hormones bind to highly specific receptors and trigger changes in gene expression and metabolism. Sex hormones (testosterone, estrogen, and progesterone) are examples of steroid hormones. Another is *cortisol,* produced by the brain's adrenal cortex in response to stress and inflammation. Cortisol is used to digest macromolecules, regulate electrolyte and water balance and promote glucose synthesis in response to low blood sugar.

Aldosterone is a steroid hormone that regulates kidney function.

Prostaglandins (BC)

Prostaglandins are 20-carbon fatty acid derivatives with hormonal functions. They operate within the *paracrine* and *autocrine* systems, which is signaling between adjacent cells and signaling within a single cell, respectively. They are produced locally in response to certain signals and may initiate inflammation, clotting or anti-clotting, vasodilation or vasoconstriction, and smooth muscle movement in the gastrointestinal tract and uterus.

Additionally, they affect the wake-sleep cycle (circadian rhythm), the fever response and the responsiveness of certain tissues to various hormones like glucagon and epinephrine.

Structure of some sample prostaglandin hormones

Notes for active learning

Carbohydrates

Classification

Carbohydrates (saccharides, from the Greek word for sugar) are molecules made of carbon, hydrogen, and oxygen. This composition of elements is different from *hydrocarbons,* the main components of lipids which contain carbon and hydrogen. The empirical formula for carbohydrates is $C_NH_{2N}O_N$ (e.g., glucose is $C_6H_{12}O_6$).

monosaccharide (glucose)

disaccharide (sucrose)

polysaccharide (amylose starch)

Comparison of a monosaccharide (e.g., glucose), disaccharide (e.g., sucrose) and polysaccharide (e.g., amylose starch). Glycosidic (either alpha or beta) bonds link the monomers.

Monosaccharides

Monosaccharides are classified by the number of carbons they contain and the monomers for carbohydrates (simple sugars), from which all carbohydrates are made. They serve as energy and may be used to modify a vast array of other molecules. Monosaccharides function as the raw material for the synthesis of other monomers, including amino acids and fatty acids.

Monosaccharides have the empirical formula of CH_2O. They have a carbonyl group (C=O) and multiple hydroxyl (O−H) groups. Monosaccharides can be classified by the location of the carbonyl group; a carbonyl at one of the terminal carbons is an *aldose*, while a carbonyl at a middle carbon is a *ketose.* They can be classified by the amount of carbon. For example, six-carbon sugars are *hexoses*; five-carbon sugars are *pentoses*, and three-carbon sugars are *trioses.* Every monosaccharide is *chiral*, or asymmetrical, with a "right-handed" and "left-handed" isomer. Organisms use D-glucose (right-handed glucose), not L-glucose. Glucose ($C_6H_{12}O_6$) is the most abundant monosaccharide in animals, and references blood sugar because it is the major monosaccharide in blood. In animals, glucose is an important energy source for the body. Other natural monosaccharides include galactose, fructose, ribose and deoxyribose.

Monosaccharides are metabolized quickly by cells as energy for cellular respiration (produces ATP). However, the cells might not need the energy at once, and therefore stores it. Monosaccharides are stored by polymerizing them into larger carbohydrates (e.g., glycogen).

Disaccharides

Disaccharides are two monosaccharides are joined by dehydration synthesis. *Lactose* is composed of the monosaccharides galactose and glucose and is found in milk. It can be broken into these individual monomers by the *lactase* enzyme. However, some people lack this enzyme and cannot break down lactose, leading to lactose intolerance.

Disaccharides are soluble in water but are too large to pass through cell membranes by diffusion and must be digested into monosaccharides. *Maltose* is composed of two glucose molecules and forms in the digestive tract of humans during digestion of polysaccharides. *Sucrose* is glucose and fructose and is used primarily by plants to transport sugars.

Maltose is a disaccharide of two glucose monomers joined by the β-glycosidic bond

Polysaccharides

Polysaccharides are polymers of monosaccharides that have structural and energy storage functions. *Starch* is a straight chain of glucose molecules with few side branches, formed by plants as carbohydrate storage. *Glycogen* is a highly branched polymer of glucose with many side branches; it is "animal starch" because it is the carbohydrate storage of animals. Glycogen is a short-term energy source that is rapidly mobilized to break into glucose as needed. It is stored in muscles and the liver, but for less than 24 hours, since it takes up a large amount of space. Excess glycogen must be broken down and excreted as waste.

Cellulose is a straight chain of glucose similar to starch, but with glucose, monomers arranged so that they are held together by *beta linkages* (strong cross-linkages). This strength makes cellulose tough, durable and fibrous; it is the primary constituent of plant cell walls. Humans cannot digest cellulose due to the lack of a specific enzyme to cleave the strong β-linkages, but grazing animals have specially adapted digestive systems and symbiotic bacteria which assist the process.

Chitin is a polymer of a nitrogen-containing derivative of glucose. Structurally similar to cellulose, chitin is a primary constituent of the exoskeletons of insects and crustaceans and is a component of certain body parts (e.g., shells and beaks) in other animals.

Functions of carbohydrates in the living systems

Source of energy

Humans ingest carbohydrates (or "carbs") as mono-, di-, and polysaccharides. During digestion, polymers are broken into monosaccharides and then absorbed by the body. These may then be used by the body moments after they are eaten, or polymerized into glycogen for storage. Carbohydrates are soluble in water, making them easy to transport within the body.

Monosaccharides are digested more rapidly than lipids, so they are used when the body requires a quick surge of energy. When an animal requires glucose, it uses blood glucose until exhausted. It may then break glycogen into glucose or synthesize glucose from other biomolecules, such as amino acids.

In animals, the breakdown of carbohydrates begins with digestion into individual *glucose* monomers. Glucose is oxidized by *glycolysis,* forming ATP and other products. Glycolysis is then followed by aerobic (Krebs cycle and electron transport chain) or anaerobic (fermentation) respiration. Aerobic respiration is most efficient, but in the absence of oxygen, as during high-intensity exercise, organisms utilize anaerobic respiration to produce ATP.

Ribose and deoxyribose

Ribose and deoxyribose are five carbon sugars (pentoses) as the backbones of RNA and DNA, respectively. Ribose, found in RNA, is sugar with one hydroxyl group attached to each carbon atom. Deoxyribose, found in DNA, is a modified sugar that lacks one hydroxyl group that is absent at the 2' position. This difference of one oxygen atom is important for the enzymes that recognize DNA and RNA because it allows the two molecules to be differentiated and identified.

Ribose (RNA) sugar is on the left with the presence of the hydroxyl at the 2' position.
Deoxyribose (DNA) sugar is on the right, whereby hydrogen replaces the 2' OH

A table summarizing the characteristics of the four classes of organic molecules.

Polymer	% Dry weight (liver cell)	Monomer	Examples	Function
Proteins	72%	Amino acids	Enzymes, antibodies, peptide hormones	Catalysis, signaling, structure, transport, motility, immunity
Nucleic Acids	8%	Nucleotides	DNA, RNA	Storage and expression of heredity
Lipids	13%	Various subunits (glycerol and fatty acids)	Fatty acids, fats, oils, steroid hormones	Energy, signaling, membranes, insulation
Polysaccharides	7%	Monosaccharides	Simple sugars, carbohydrates	Energy, cell structure

Notes for active learning

Water

Water is vital for all life on Earth but is an inorganic molecule due to its lack of carbon. A molecule of water contains one oxygen atom covalently bonded to two hydrogen atoms in a bent conformation because of the two lone pairs of electrons on the oxygen atom. Due to the electronegativity of oxygen, bonding electrons are concentrated near this central atom, giving oxygen a partial negative charge on oxygen and a partial positive charge on hydrogen. This unequal sharing of electrons makes water a polar molecule.

The significance of water in the living systems

The first cells evolved in water and incorporated water into their living systems; today organisms are 70–90% water. Water is liquid between 0 °C and 100 °C, which is critical since it serves as the solvent of all living organisms. Its polarity allows it to dissolve ionic, polar or semi-polar molecules. This allows for substances such as nutrients to be carried in the blood and is a good medium for metabolic reactions.

The evaporation of water cools plants and animals. These organisms allow heat as energy to break hydrogen bonds, as water molecules evaporate and release energy into the air.

Properties of water

Water is capable of forming four hydrogen bonds: one at each hydrogen atom and two at lone pairs of electrons on the oxygen atom. When water molecules form hydrogen bonds, they create strong intermolecular forces that give the water some characteristic properties.

Physical properties are quantitative measures of a substance that can be measured without permanently altering the substance. For example, the boiling point of water is a physical property because water can be condensed back to the liquid form. *Chemical properties* are not observable without altering a substance in a chemical reaction.

One hydrogen bond (dash line) is between adjacent water molecules.
Two hydrogen bond acceptors form from each lone pair of electrons on partial negative oxygen and two hydrogen bond donors from each partial positive hydrogen.

Physical properties

Water has a high *heat capacity*, as the degree to which a substance changes the temperature in response to the gain or loss of heat. The temperature of a large body of water is stable in response to temperature (average kinetic energy of a molecule) changes of the surrounding air. Since water can hold more heat, its temperature falls more slowly than other liquids; this moderates Earth's surface temperature and protects organisms from rapid temperature changes.

Heat capacity is reflected in the *heat of vaporization,* the amount of energy required to boil a substance (change from liquid to a gaseous state). Water has an unusually high boiling point due to the many strong intermolecular forces (hydrogen bonding). At standard pressure, water boils at 100 °C, because a high amount of heat is needed to break the hydrogen bonds. The high boiling point of water is vital for life on Earth. If the water boiled at a lower temperature, the water in living organisms would start to boil, and the organisms would not survive.

Water has a high *heat of fusion*, the energy required to melt from its solid state. This makes earth's ice caps resistant to sudden and frequent melting. Unlike most other substances, ice exhibits a density lower than liquid water. As water freezes, its hydrogen bonds become more rigid and push apart, expanding the water and settling it into a crystal pattern at 0 °C. The large air spaces between molecules lower the density of ice and allow it to float on liquid water. Because of this property, bodies of water freeze from the top down. If ice were denser than water, it would sink, and ponds would freeze solid. The fact that water becomes less dense as it freezes is beneficial to organisms, as ice forms at the surface and insulates the water underneath, maintaining a hospitable environment for aquatic organisms.

Chemical properties

Water is a universal solvent which dissolves a great number of solutes. This is possible because of its polarity, which causes it to attract charged (or polar substances), associating around the individual molecules and breaking up the aggregation of the solute. Ionized or polar molecules attracted to water are *hydrophilic.* Non-ionized and nonpolar molecules that cannot attract water are *hydrophobic.* Water is a reactant and product in a multitude of chemical reactions, both outside of and within living systems.

Hydrogen bonds are responsible for water's cohesive and adhesive properties. *Cohesion* is water's tendency to stick to itself, due to hydrogen bonding. The strong cohesion between water molecules produces a high *surface tension*, which is measured by how difficult it is to break the surface of a liquid. Water's high surface tension helps cell membranes from collapsing and allows insects to walk on water. *Adhesion* is water's ability to attract other polar molecules. Adhesion and cohesion work together so that water can "climb" against gravity up a thin glass tube, the vascular tissues of a plant or the blood vessels of an animal. This *capillary action* of adhesion is an essential process of life.

Nutrients and Human Nutrition

Nutrition deals with the composition of food, its energy content and synthesized organic molecules. There is a quantitative relationship between nutrients and health. A *balanced diet*, required for good health, includes a properly proportioned variety of foods. Imbalances can cause disease. Nutrition is a major factor in cardiovascular disease, hypertension, and cancer.

Macronutrients are foods required on a large scale each day. These include carbohydrates, lipids, and proteins. Additionally, water is essential because it supports metabolism. Correct water balance is a must for the proper functioning of the body. Monosaccharides, amino acids, and mineral salts are absorbed by transporter-mediated processes, while fatty acid and water diffuse passively.

Carbohydrates

Digestion begins in the mouth by salivary amylase and is completed in the small intestine by pancreatic amylase. Monosaccharides (e.g., glucose, galactose and fructose) are produced by the breakdown of polysaccharides and are transported to the intestinal epithelium by facilitated diffusion or active transport. Facilitated diffusion moves the sugars into the bloodstream.

During the absorptive state, glucose is the major energy source, and some of it is converted to glycogen and stored in skeletal muscle and the liver. In adipose tissue, glucose is transformed and stored as fat. *Glucose sparing* is the reduction of glucose catabolism and the increase in fat utilization by most tissues. Glucose is spared for the brain, resulting in minimization of protein breakdown.

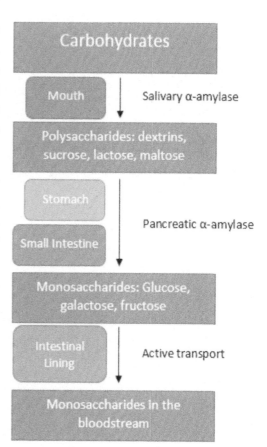

Carbohydrate digestion and absorption

Proteins

Proteins are polymers composed of amino acids. Proteins are found in meat, milk, poultry, fish, cereal grains and beans. They are needed for cellular growth and repair. Twenty common amino acids are found in proteins, of which humans can naturally synthesize eleven. The remaining nine are the essential (must be in the diet) amino acids.

Proteins are not normally used for energy; however, muscle proteins are broken down for energy during starvation. Excess protein can be used for energy or converted to fats. Proteins are broken down to peptide fragments by pepsin in the stomach, and by pancreatic trypsin and chymotrypsin in the small intestine. The fragments are then digested to free amino acids by *carboxypeptidase* from the pancreas and *aminopeptidase* from the intestinal epithelium.

Free amino acids enter the epithelium by secondary active transport and leave it by facilitated diffusion. Small amino acid chains can enter interstitial fluid by endo- and exocytosis. Most amino acids enter cells and are used to synthesize proteins. Any excess amino acids are converted to carbohydrates or fat.

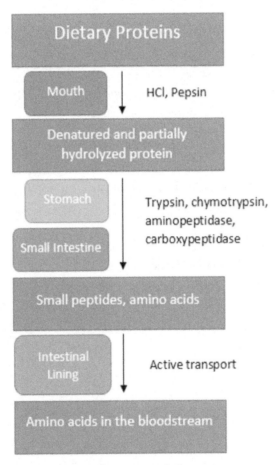

Protein digestion and absorption

Lipids

Lipids generate the greatest energy yield. Therefore, many plants and animals store energy as fats (a type of lipid). Lipids are present in oils, meats, butter and plants (e.g., avocado and peanuts). Some fatty acids, such as linoleic acid, are essential and must be included in the diet. When present in the intestine, lipids promote the uptake of fat-soluble vitamins A, D, E and K.

Fatty acids of plasma chylomicrons are released within the adipose tissue capillaries and form triacylglycerols. Fat digestion occurs by pancreatic lipase in the small intestine, producing a monoglyceride and two fatty acids from this process. Large lipid droplets are first broken down into smaller droplets by a process called emulsification. Emulsification is driven by mechanical disruption (by contractile activity of the GI tract) and by emulsifying agents (amphipathic bile salts). Pancreatic colipase binds the water-soluble lipase to the lipid substrate.

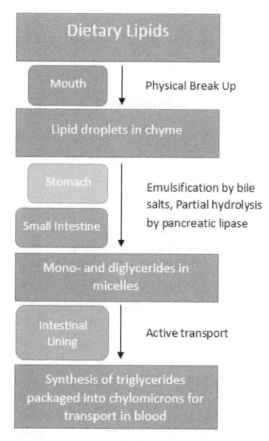

Lipid digestion and absorption

Digested products and bile salts form amphipathic micelles. These micelles keep the insoluble products insoluble aggregates, from which small amounts are released and absorbed by epithelial cells via diffusion. Free fatty acids and monoglycerides then recombine into triacylglycerols at the smooth ER. They are processed in the Golgi and enter the interstitial fluid as chylomicron droplets, which are then taken up by the lacteals in the intestine.

Absorptive and post-absorptive states

The *absorptive state* is when ingested nutrients enter the blood. Some of these nutrients supply the energy need of the body, while the remainder is stored. Carbohydrates and proteins are absorbed into the blood primarily as monosaccharides and amino acids, respectively, while fat is absorbed into the lymph as triacylglycerols.

The *post-absorptive state* is when the GI tract is depleted of nutrients, and the body must supply the required energy. In this state, the net synthesis of glycogen, fat, and protein ceases, and net catabolism of these substances begins. Plasma glucose level is maintained by:

- *Glycogenolysis*, the hydrolysis of glycogen in the liver and skeletal muscles

- *Lipolysis*, catabolism of triacylglycerols into glycerol and fatty acids in adipose tissues. Glycerol reaching the liver is converted to glucose

- *Gluconeogenesis*, catabolism of non-carbohydrate substances to glucose.

Vitamins

Vitamins are necessary organic compounds required for metabolic reactions. They usually cannot be made by the body and are needed in trace amounts. Vitamins may act as enzyme cofactors, known as *coenzymes*. Some vitamins are soluble in fats, while others are soluble in water.

Fat-soluble vitamins are absorbed and stored along with fats. Most water-soluble vitamins are absorbed by diffusion or mediated transport. Fat-soluble vitamins necessitate more complex mechanisms to cross the phospholipid bilayer. For example, due to its large size and charged nature, Vitamin B-12 must first bind to the intrinsic factor protein to be absorbed via endocytosis.

The body is unable to make some vitamins required for metabolic activities. Lack of vitamins results in vitamin deficiencies. The 13 vitamins are divided into fat-soluble (A, D, E, K) and water-soluble vitamins (8 B vitamins and vitamin C). Many vitamins are portions of coenzymes; for example, niacin is part of NAD^+ and riboflavin is a part of a FAD. Coenzymes are needed in small amounts because they are used over and over again. Vitamin A is not a coenzyme but a precursor for the visual pigment that prevents night blindness.

Vitamin A is part of a group of hydrophobic unsaturated nutritional organic compounds that include retinol, retinal, retinoic acid and several carotenoids (e.g., beta-carotene). Vitamin A has multiple functions. It is important for growth and development, for the maintenance of the immune system, and for good vision. Vitamin A is needed by the retina of the eye in the form of retinal, which combines with protein opsin to form rhodopsin (i.e., light-absorbing molecule). Rhodopsin is necessary for low-light (night vision) and color vision.

Skin cells contain a precursor cholesterol molecule converted to vitamin D by UV light exposure. Only a small amount of UV is needed to cause this change. Vitamin D leaves the skin and is modified in the kidneys and then in the liver to become calcitriol. *Calcitriol* circulates throughout the body, regulating calcium uptake and metabolism. It promotes absorption of calcium by the intestines. The lack of vitamin D leads to rickets in children, a condition in which poor mineralization of the skeleton causes bowing of the legs. Most milk is fortified (added during processing) with vitamin D to prevent rickets.

Cell metabolism generates *free radicals*, unstable molecules with an extra electron. O_3^- is a common free radical. Free radicals stabilize by donating electrons to another molecule; however, doing so damages cellular molecules, such as DNA and proteins. This damage may cause plaque in arteries or cancer. Vitamins C, E, and A—abundant in fruits and vegetables—are antioxidants that defend against free radicals. While vitamin supplements can assist in fighting vitamin deficiencies, they do not replace fruits and vegetables, which contain many phytochemicals and other beneficial compounds.

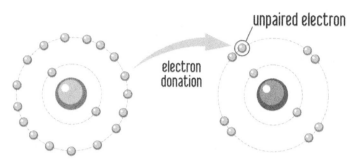

Antioxidants reduce free radicals

Minerals

Minerals are trace elements required for normal metabolism, cell and tissue structure, nerve conduction and muscle contraction. They are essential and can only be obtained from the diet. Iron, iodine, calcium, and sodium are examples of minerals.

Humans require *macrominerals* (e.g., calcium, phosphorus) in amounts of over 100 mg per day. They are constituents of cells and body fluids and are structural components of tissues. Calcium is needed to build bones and tooth enamel, as well as to generate nerve conduction and muscle contraction. Sodium is a key macromineral used to control blood pressure and blood volume and to keep nerves and muscles functioning correctly.

Microminerals are elements (e.g., zinc, iron) recommended in amounts less than 20 mg per day. Microminerals are likely to have specific functions. For example, iron is needed to produce hemoglobin, of which adult females need more due to menstrual blood loss. Iodine is used to produce thyroxin, a hormone of the thyroid glands. Minute amounts of molybdenum, selenium, chromium, nickel, vanadium, silicon and arsenic (among others) are essential to keep the body functioning properly.

Notes for active learning

Notes for active learning

Notes for active learning

Chapter 2

Generalized Eukaryotic Cell

- **Cell Theory**

- **Nucleus and Other Defining Characteristics**

- **Membrane-Bound Organelles**

- **Plasma Membrane**

- **Cytoskeleton**

- **Cell Cycle and Mitosis**

- **Control of Cell Cycle**

- **Gametogenesis by Meiosis**

- **Sperm and Ovum**

Cell Theory

Cell theory, the scientific theory which describes the morphological and biochemical properties of cells, is a fundamental doctrine of biology.

Classical cell theory includes three key tenets derived from the research of early biologists:

1. *All living organisms are composed of one or more cells.*

    Multicellular organisms are composed of many cells, while unicellular organisms, such as bacteria, are composed of one cell.

2. *Cells are the smallest, most basic units of life.*

    Cells are the smallest units of life because they are the smallest structures capable of carrying out the fundamental metabolic process (e.g., reproduce and divide, extract energy from their environment).

3. *Cells may only arise from pre-existing cells and cannot be created from non-living material.*

    The process of creating new cells is cellular division and is involved in both sexual and asexual reproduction.

As the modern understanding of biology evolved, so too did the tenets of cell theory. Modern cell theory adds the following concepts to classical cell theory:

4. *Cells pass on the genetic material during replication in the form of DNA.*

5. *The cells of all organisms are chemically similar.*

6. *Cells are responsible for energy flow and metabolism.*

The tenets of cell theory are somewhat dynamic and, as such, some scientists may omit some of these tenets or include others not mentioned here.

History and development

Robert Hooke first observed the small structural units, which he called "cells," under the light microscope in 1665. However, it was not until nearly 200 years later that significant progress was made in the understanding of these cells. In the 1830s, botanist Matthias Schleiden discovered cells in the tissues of plants and declared that cells are the building blocks of all plants. Simultaneously, Theodor Schwann published his work on cell theory, generalizing it to both plants and animals. Shortly after that, Rudolf Virchow overturned the predominating belief that cells were spontaneously generated from non-living matter. He proclaimed that all cells must arise from other living cells.

From there, cell biology was consistently advanced by new findings in membrane physiology, mitosis and other cellular and molecular processes.

In the 1950s, James Watson and Francis Crick published their discovery of the molecular structure of DNA, which revolutionized the entire field of biology. Other researchers, including Rosalind Franklin, went uncredited for their seminal work on this monumental discovery.

Impact on biology

Cell theory is an important unifying concept which provides biologists with a common understanding from which they can make further discoveries. The relatively slow progress of biology before the mid-1800s demonstrates the difficulties of advancing in a field where the framework is not understood. Once the foundation of cell theory was laid, along with advances in laboratory techniques and instrumentation, scientific progress in the field of biology rapidly accelerated.

By understanding the basics of a single cell, researchers were able to add context to all the life sciences. This is because cells represent the building blocks of all organisms. Multicellular organisms exhibit *emergent properties*, meaning the whole is greater than the sum of its parts. Cells form tissues; tissues form organs, organs form organ systems and organ systems form multicellular organisms. For example, the individual cells in the lungs are not of much use by themselves, but when combined as a working unit, they create a highly sophisticated set of lungs essential for the organism's survival.

Notes for active learning

Notes for active learning

Nucleus and Other Defining Characteristics

Defining characteristics (membrane-bound nucleus, the presence of organelles and mitotic division)

Cells are divided into two taxa: *Eukarya* and *Prokarya*. Prokaryotes may be further divided into the domains Bacteria and Archaea.

The most salient difference between prokaryotes and eukaryotes is that prokaryotes lack a true nucleus with a nuclear membrane or any membrane-bound organelles. The main intracellular components of a prokaryotic cell are its single double-stranded circular DNA molecule, its ribosomes, and its cytoplasm. Prokaryotic cells include a plasma membrane and peptidoglycan cell wall. They are usually much smaller than eukaryotic cells and contain smaller ribosomes (the 30S and 50 S subunits; 70S as assembled).

Eukaryotic cells have linear DNA enclosed in a membrane-bound nucleus, along with many other membrane-bound organelles. Eukaryotic cells replicate via mitosis or meiosis, while prokaryotes replicate via *binary fission*, a form of asexual reproduction.

Many similarities exist between the two cell types. Both prokaryotes and eukaryotes contain cytoplasm, ribosomes, and some form of DNA, and they can be either unicellular or multicellular, although multicellular prokaryotes are rare. Some eukaryotes are capable of asexual reproduction, albeit in a different way than prokaryotes. Furthermore, plants and fungi (eukaryotes) both have cell walls like prokaryotes. Cell walls in fungi are a glucosamine polymer of chitin, plants have cellulose cell walls, while bacteria have peptidoglycan cell walls.

Comparison of prokaryotes to eukaryotes

Prokaryotes	Eukaryotes
Domains: Bacteria and Archaea	Domain: Eukarya
Cell wall present in all prokaryotes	Cell wall in fungi, plants and some protists
No nucleus, circular strand of dsDNA	Membrane-bound nucleus housing dsDNA
Ribosomes (subunits = 30S and 50S; 70S)	Ribosomes (subunits = 40S and 60S; 80S)
No membrane-bound organelles	Membrane-bound organelles

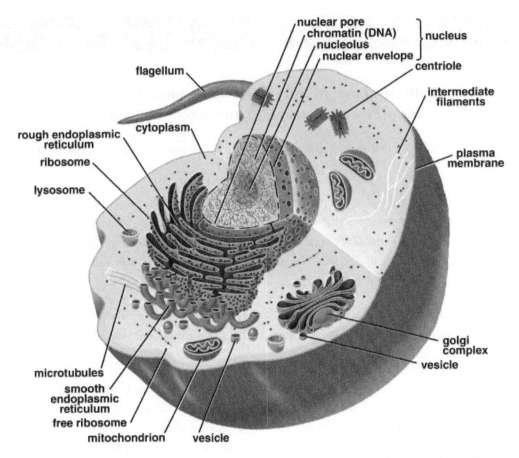

A eukaryotic animal cell with no cell wall or chloroplasts as in eukaryotic plant cells

The cell's metabolic activity describes the many biochemical reactions occurring within the cell. Substances need to be taken into the cell to fuel these reactions, while the waste products of the reactions need to be removed. When the cell increases in size, so do its metabolic activity. The surface area of the cell is vital because it affects the rate at which particles can enter and exit, with a larger surface area resulting in a higher rate of uptake and excretion. However, the volume affects the rate at which materials are made or used within the cell, the chemical activity per unit of time.

As the volume (i.e., chemical activity) of the cell increases, so does the surface area, but not to the same extent. When the cell gets bigger, its surface area-to-volume ratio gets smaller. If the surface area-to-volume ratio gets too small, substances are not able to enter the cell fast enough to fuel the reactions. Waste products are produced faster than they can be excreted, and they accumulate inside the cell. Also, cells are not able to lose heat fast enough and may overheat. It is clear that the surface area-to-volume ratio is important for a cell. It is the physical limitation of the area-to-volume ratio that limits the size of cells.

The nucleus for compartmentalization of genetic information

The *nucleus* is the largest membrane-bound organelle in the center of most eukaryotic cells. It contains the cell's genetic code—its DNA. The function of the nucleus is to direct the cell by storing and transmitting genetic information. Cells can contain multiple nuclei (e.g., skeletal muscle cells), one nucleus or rarely, none at all (e.g., red blood cells).

Inside the nucleus is the *nuclear lamina*, a dense network of filamentous and membranous proteins that associate with the nuclear envelope and its pores. The lamina provides mechanical support and is involved in crucial cell functions, including DNA replication, cell division, and chromatin organization.

The *nucleoplasm* is the semifluid medium of the nucleus, analogous to the cytoplasm of the cell proper. In the nucleoplasm, DNA and proteins interact to form *chromatin*.

A double membrane surrounds the nucleus of the cell with nuclear pores
for select transport of a substance in and out of the nucleus

Nucleolus (location, function)

The *nucleolus* is a region inside the nucleus where ribosomal RNA (rRNA) is transcribed, and ribosomal subunits are assembled. Here, rRNA joins together to form the subunits of a complete ribosome. These subunits are then exported to the cytoplasm for final assembly into the complete ribosome used for translation of mRNA into proteins.

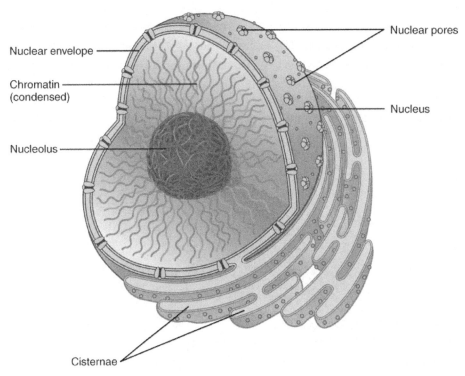

The nucleolus is located within the nucleus and assembles ribosomal subunits in eukaryotic cells

Nuclear envelope, nuclear pores

The nuclear envelope (nuclear membrane) is a double membrane system composed of an outer and inner membrane. The space between these membranes is the *perinuclear space*. Nuclear pores are selective and allow the passage of certain particles through the nuclear envelope, so that essential cell processes and communications can occur. The number of nuclear pores is not static but rather is subject to change based on the needs of the cell. Through the pores, signal molecules, nucleoplasm proteins, nuclear membrane proteins, lipids, and transcription factors can enter the nucleus, while mRNA, rRNA and ribosomal proteins exit into the cytoplasm.

Notes for active learning

Notes for active learning

Membrane-Bound Organelles

The cytoplasm is the cellular material outside the nucleus and within the cell's plasma membrane. It includes the *cytosol*, which is the fluid medium of the cell, and the *organelles*, which are small, usually membrane-bound subunits with specialized functions (ribosomes are not membrane-bound). Among other functions, organelles structurally support the cell, facilitate cell movement, store and transfer energy and exchange products in transport vesicles. Mitochondria in animal cells and chloroplasts in plant cells are organelles that contain their genetic material and replicate independently of the nucleus.

The *endomembrane system* is a series of intracellular membranes that compartmentalize the cell. Vesicles are budding off of the endomembrane system transport molecules within the cell. Products synthesized in the cell pass through at least some portion of the endomembrane system.

A typical pathway through the endomembrane system is:

1. Proteins produced in rough ER (endoplasmic reticulum) and lipids from smooth ER are carried in vesicles to the Golgi apparatus.

2. The Golgi apparatus modifies these products and then sorts and packages them into vesicles that are transported to various cell destinations (e.g., organelles or exported from the cell).

3. Secretory vesicles transport products to organelles or to the membrane, where they are secreted via exocytosis.

Aside from the Golgi apparatus, smooth and rough ER, and secretory vesicles, the endomembrane system includes the membranes of lysosomes, peroxisomes, and all other organelles within the cell.

While most cells have the same organelles, their distribution may differ depending on the cell's function. For example, cells that require a lot of energy for locomotion (e.g., sperm cells) have many mitochondria; cells involved in secretion (e.g., pancreatic islet cells) have many Golgi apparatuses; and cells that primarily serve a transport function (e.g., red blood cells) may have no organelles.

Mitochondria

Mitochondria (sing. mitochondrion) are responsible for aerobic respiration, which is the conversion of chemical energy into ATP (adenosine triphosphate) using oxygen. ATP is used as the major energy source within cells. Mitochondria vary in shape; they may be long and thin or short and broad. Mitochondria can be fixed in one location or form long, moving chains. They have a double membrane, with the outer membrane separating the mitochondria from the cytoplasm. The inner membrane has folds called *cristae*, which project into the inner fluid, the *matrix*. Between the outer and inner membrane is the intermembrane space. This region is high in protons, creating a proton gradient, which drives the synthesis of ATP.

The cristae are dotted with *ATP synthase* protein complexes, which are powered by the proton gradient and convert ADP into ATP. This process is essential to producing the energy that all organisms require for metabolic functions. Thus, cells with higher energy needs require more mitochondria.

Mitochondria are unique in that they have their genome, distinct from the genome within the nucleus. They have circular DNA, inherited exclusively from the mother, which contains the genes for the synthesis of some mitochondrial proteins. Mitochondria can replicate their DNA independently from the nucleus. They have their ribosomes, different from the host cell's ribosomes in both sequence and structure.

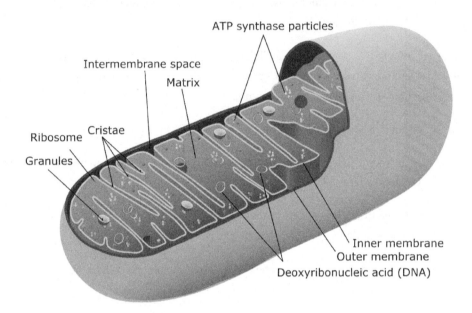

Mitochondria have a double membrane enclosure with ATPase embedded in the inner membrane

The unique characteristics of mitochondria support the *endosymbiosis theory* for the origin of eukaryotic cells. The endosymbiosis theory states that mitochondria were once free-living aerobic prokaryotes that were consumed by a cell about 1.5 billion years ago. Within the cell, the prokaryote (probably a proteobacterium) became an endosymbiont, providing the anaerobic host cell with ATP via aerobic respiration. In return, the host cell provided the endosymbiont with a stable environment and nutrients. Over time, the endosymbiont transferred most of its genes to the host nucleus, to the point that it became obligate (i.e., could no longer survive outside the host cell) and evolved into a mitochondrion.

Biologists largely accept the endosymbiosis theory. One of the most compelling pieces of evidence is the fact that mitochondrial DNA does not encode for its proteins. Rather, many of its genes are in the nuclear DNA; therefore, many proteins must be imported into the mitochondria. Furthermore, mitochondrial DNA, ribosomes, and enzymes are similar to bacterial forms, and mitochondria even replicate by a process similar to binary fission. Additionally, some of the proteins within the plasma membrane of the mitochondria are similar to prokaryotes, which are different from proteins in the eukaryotic plasma membrane.

Chloroplasts, the organelles that conduct photosynthesis, also exhibit strong evidence of an endosymbiotic origin, although they are hypothesized to have descended from cyanobacteria rather than proteobacteria. Chloroplasts and other plastids can undergo secondary and even tertiary endosymbiosis, causing the development of extra membranes.

Lysosomes (vesicles containing hydrolytic enzymes)

Lysosomes, found only in animal cells, are membrane-bound vesicles produced by the Golgi apparatus. These small organelles contain hydrolytic enzymes (low pH) for the digestion of macromolecules: proteins, nucleic acids, carbohydrates, and lipids. These macromolecules may originate from food, from the waste products of cells or foreign agents, such as viruses and bacteria. After these particles enter a cell in vesicles, lysosomes fuse with vesicles and digest their contents by hydrolyzing the macromolecules into their monomers.

Lysosomes are especially important in specialized immune cells. For example, white blood cells that engulf foreign agents use lysosomes to digest the invaders. *Autodigestion* is the process by which lysosomes digest parts of the body's cells, either due to disease or trauma or for immune purposes (e.g., programmed cell death). Mutations in the genes that encode for lysosomal enzymes cause *lysosomal storage disorders*. When a mutation renders certain lysosomal enzymes inefficient (or completely inoperable), waste products accumulate in the cells and cause serious, often incurable complications.

Rough and smooth endoplasmic reticulum

The *endoplasmic reticulum* (ER) is a system of membrane channels, called *cisternae*, that is continuous with the outer membrane of the nuclear envelope. The space enclosed within the cisternae, the *lumen*, is thus continuous with the perinuclear space.

The rough ER, so-called because of its rough appearance, is studded with ribosomes on the cytoplasmic side. Here, proteins are synthesized and enter the ER interior for processing and modification. Modifications may include folding the protein or combining multiple polypeptide chains to form proteins with several subunits.

The smooth ER is usually interconnected with the rough ER but lacks ribosomes, hence its smooth appearance. It is the site of various synthesis, detoxification and storage processes, such as the synthesis of lipids and steroids, and the metabolism of carbohydrates and other molecules.

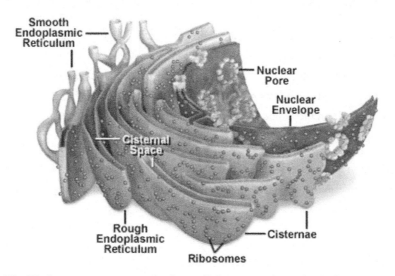

The ER forms transport vesicles for trafficking particles to the Golgi apparatus

RER - site of ribosomes

Ribosomes are organelles composed of proteins and ribosomal RNA (rRNA). They can be found either floating free in the cytoplasm, attached to the surface of the rough ER, or within mitochondria and chloroplasts. They translate messenger RNA (mRNA) to coordinate the assembly of amino acids into polypeptide chains, which then fold into functional proteins.

Ribosomes of eukaryotic cells are 20 to 30 nm in diameter, while those in prokaryotic cells are slightly smaller. They are composed of one large and one small subunit; each with its mix of proteins and rRNA. *Polyribosomes* are several ribosomes simultaneously synthesizing the same protein; they may be attached to ER or floating freely in the cytosol.

Membrane biosynthesis: SER for lipids and RER for transmembrane proteins

The smooth ER and rough ER synthesize key membrane components. The smooth ER synthesizes the major lipids of a membrane: phospholipids, glycolipids, and steroids. Some lipid products are already in the correct form for incorporation into a membrane once secreted by the smooth ER, while others require additional modification by the Golgi apparatus. Either way, lipids synthesized in the smooth ER must pass through the Golgi apparatus before heading to their destination at the plasma membrane or a membrane-bound organelle.

The rough ER synthesizes the protein components of cell membranes. This includes not just the plasma membrane, but the membranes of the ER, Golgi apparatus, lysosomes, and other organelles. Membrane proteins can be divided into several classes (discussed later), but some of their functions include membrane transport, cell-to-cell adhesion, cell signaling, and catalysis. Similarly to lipids synthesized on the smooth ER, proteins synthesized on the rough ER follow a set pathway through the Golgi apparatus towards their final destinations.

RER's role in the biosynthesis of transmembrane and secreted proteins that are cotranslationally targeted to RER by a signal sequence

Proteins destined for the plasma membrane, Golgi apparatus membrane, ER membrane or lysosomal membranes are inserted into the ER membrane immediately after synthesis on the cytosolic side of the rough ER membrane. These proteins are transported as membrane components rather than soluble proteins. ER membrane proteins end their journey here, but the others proceed to the Golgi apparatus. Upon post-translational processing, Golgi membrane proteins remain in the Golgi apparatus, while the remaining proteins (secretory pathway) travel to either lysosome, the plasma membrane or undergo exocytosis to leave the cell.

Proteins for secretion and proteins destined for the *lumen* of the ER or Golgi apparatus are released into the ER lumen following ER synthesis. ER lumen proteins remain in the ER lumen, Golgi lumen proteins travel to the Golgi lumen, and secretory proteins travel to the Golgi and then to the plasma membrane or are secreted out of the cell.

Not all protein synthesis takes place on the rough ER. Free-floating ribosomes synthesize proteins designated for use in the cytosol and some organelles (e.g., nucleus, mitochondria, chloroplasts, and peroxisomes) in the cytosol. After synthesis, cytosolic proteins are released directly into the cytosol, while nuclear, mitochondrial, chloroplastic, and peroxisomal proteins are escorted to their destinations by receptor molecules.

Protein synthesis always begins on free ribosomes. Therefore, proteins that need to be synthesized in the ER must be translocated there. *Posttranslational translocation* to the ER occurs after a free-floating ribosome has fully synthesized a polypeptide. *Cotranslational translocation* is more common in mammalian cells and occurs as the polypeptide is being synthesized.

Cotranslational translocation is facilitated by a *signal sequence* on the growing polypeptide chain. This sequence is a short chain of amino acids, mostly hydrophobic. As soon as the signal sequence emerges on the polypeptide from the ribosome, a protein-RNA complex called a *signal recognition particle* (SRP) recognizes and binds to the signal sequence and ribosome, halting translation. The SRP then targets the ribosome and polypeptide chain to the rough ER membrane, where the SRP binds to an SRP receptor. Binding to the SRP receptor releases the SRP from the ribosome and polypeptide, allowing the ribosome itself to bind to a protein translocation complex next to the SRP receptor called *Sec61*. After binding, the signal sequence is inserted into the Sec61 membrane channel (part of the translocation complex), and polypeptide synthesis resumes. As it grows, the polypeptide chain is translocated through the membrane channel. A *signal peptidase* enzyme cleaves the signal sequence from the rest of the polypeptide, allowing the finished polypeptide to be released into the lumen, where it undergoes folding and modification.

If the polypeptide is a membrane protein that must enter the ER membrane and not the lumen, it is inserted into the ER membrane in a variety of ways. For example, transmembrane proteins may contain a *stop-transfer sequence*, which anchors the polypeptide in the ER membrane partway through synthesis so that the polypeptide is anchored to the ER membrane rather than located in the ER lumen.

Double membrane structure

While most organelles of the eukaryotic cell are composed of a single bilayer membrane, three key organelles have a double membrane: mitochondria, chloroplasts and the nucleus.

Mitochondria have a double membrane structure due to their proposed evolution from an endosymbiotic prokaryote. This double membrane is crucial for creating the proton gradient that drives ATP synthesis. The intermembrane space is high in proton concentration, while the matrix (like cytosol) within the mitochondria is relatively low in proton concentration. This proton gradient powers ATP synthases, with cytochrome proteins dotting the cristae of the inner membrane that combine ADP with Pi and O_2 to form ATP by oxidative phosphorylation.

Chloroplasts, the sites of photosynthesis and ATP synthesis in plant cells, have a double membrane of endosymbiotic origin, the *chloroplast envelope*. The two membranes regulate the passage of particles into and out of the chloroplast. The outer membrane is permeable to ions and metabolites, while the inner membrane is highly specific to transport proteins. Unlike mitochondria, all chloroplasts contain *thylakoids* as additional membrane-bound structures. The thylakoid membranes are analogous to mitochondrial inner membranes, and the spaces within the thylakoids (lumen) are analogous to the mitochondrial intermembrane space. The high proton concentration in the lumen creates the proton gradient that drives the synthesis of ATP on the thylakoid membranes.

A sophisticated, double-membrane nuclear envelope surrounds the nucleus. The highly selective nuclear protein pores dotting the envelope regulate gene expression by controlling the passage of transcription factors, biomolecules, and mRNA into and out of the nucleus. Since the outer membrane is continuous with the rough ER, no vesicle transport is required to transport ER proteins into the nucleus. As a result, the energy requirements of the cell are lower than they would be if transport were required.

Golgi apparatus (general structure; role in packaging, secretion, and modification of glycoprotein carbohydrates)

The *Golgi apparatus*, named for the scientist Camillo Golgi, consists of a stack of many flattened sacs. The Golgi acts as an intermediary in the secretion of biomolecules. The Golgi apparatus receives transport vesicles from the ER and then may further modify their contents before packaging the protein or lipid to be sent in vesicles to its final destination.

Glycosylation is the process by which the Golgi apparatus modifies a protein by adding carbohydrates. Glycosylation affects a protein's structure and function and protects it from degradation. The Golgi apparatus can glycosylate proteins as well as modify existing glycosylations. The finished product of glycosylation is a *glycoprotein* and is a protein with attached saccharides.

Peroxisomes: organelles that collect peroxides

Peroxisomes are membrane-bound vesicles that contain enzymes for a variety of metabolic reactions. They are involved in the catabolism and anabolism of many different macromolecules, including fatty acids, proteins, and carbohydrates. When peroxisomes were first discovered, they were defined as organelles that produce hydrogen peroxide through oxidation reactions. It was believed that peroxisomes use the enzyme catalase to further break down the produced hydrogen peroxide into water and oxygen or use the hydrogen peroxide to oxidize another compound. This process is merely one of their many functions.

Peroxisomes are most abundant in the liver, where they are notable for producing bile salts from cholesterol and metabolizing alcohol. They are believed to be involved in lipid biosynthesis. In germinating seeds, peroxisomes convert oils into sugars to be used as nutrients by growing plants. In leaves, peroxisomes give off CO_2 that can be used in photosynthesis. The functions of peroxisomes are vast and varied, making them a vital part of eukaryotic cells.

Notes for active learning

Notes for active learning

Plasma Membrane

General function in cell containment

The *semi-permeable plasma membrane* separates cell contents from the extracellular environment and regulates the passage of materials into and out of the cell. In plant cells, the outer boundary of the plasma membrane is surrounded by *cellulose* (polysaccharide) cell wall. Fungi and prokaryotes have *cell walls* of alternative polysaccharides. A cell wall gives the cell strength and rigidity but does not interfere with the function of the plasma membrane.

This plasma membrane surrounds the cell, providing support, protection and a boundary from the outside environment. It is primarily composed of lipids and proteins, forming a dynamic bilayer of lipids with membrane proteins. The function and composition of the two layers of a plasma membrane differ; therefore, the membrane is asymmetric.

Lipid components: phospholipids and steroids

Lipids, a large group of naturally occurring hydrophobic molecules, are vital components of the plasma membrane. Lipids in the plasma membrane include phospholipids, steroids, and glycolipids. The foundation of the plasma membrane is the *phospholipid bilayer*. Phospholipids are molecules with a phosphate head and two long hydrocarbon tails. The head is hydrophilic and attracts water and other polar molecules, while the hydrocarbon tails are hydrophobic and repel water molecules.

The special dual nature of phospholipids, *amphipathic*, allows them to align into a bilayer when placed in water spontaneously. In the bilayer, the hydrophilic phosphate heads point out towards the aqueous solution, while the hydrophobic tails point inward towards one another. Thus, the extracellular and intracellular surfaces of a plasma membrane are hydrophilic, while the interior of the membrane is hydrophobic. Hydrophobic interactions in the interior of the membrane hold the entire structure together.

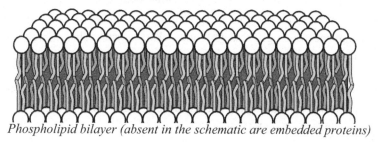

Phospholipid bilayer (absent in the schematic are embedded proteins)

The bilayer not only provides the plasma membrane with stability but with extraordinary flexibility. Lipids exhibit free lateral diffusion about the bilayer, resulting in varying lipid compositions across different sections of the membrane. Generally, cell membranes have a consistency similar to that of olive oil at room temperature. Increasing the concentration of lipids with unsaturated hydrocarbon tails increases membrane fluidity; the addition of saturated hydrocarbon tails makes the membrane more rigid. Cells may regulate membrane fluidity by lengthening phospholipid tails, altering the cytoskeleton, changing their protein composition and adding steroids (e.g., cholesterol).

Steroids are a class of lipids that regulate membrane fluidity by hindering phospholipid movement. Cholesterol, a steroid found in animal plasma membranes, plays a crucial role in maintaining membrane fluidity despite temperature fluctuation. At high temperatures, membranes become dangerously fluid and permeable unless cholesterol interferes with extreme phospholipid movement. At low temperatures, membranes may freeze unless cholesterol prevents phospholipids from becoming stationary due to strong hydrophobic interactions. Cholesterol molecules facilitate cell signaling and vesicle formation.

Glycolipids are lipids modified with a carbohydrate. In the plasma membrane, they assist in various functions and anchor the plasma membrane to the *glycocalyx*, a layer of polysaccharides that are linked to the membrane lipids and proteins. Essentially, the glycocalyx is a carbohydrate coat present on the extracellular surface of the plasma membrane and the extracellular surface of the cell walls of some bacteria. The carbohydrate chains of the glycocalyx face outwards, providing markers for cell recognition and adhesive capabilities to the cell.

Protein components and the fluid mosaic model

In the early 1900s, researchers noted that lipid-soluble molecules entered cells more readily than water-soluble molecules, suggesting that lipids are a component of the plasma membrane. Chemical analysis later revealed that the membrane indeed contained phospholipids. The amount of phospholipid extracted from a red blood cell was just enough to form one bilayer. The analysis suggested that the nonpolar tails were directed inward and polar heads outward. To account for the permeability of the membrane to non-lipid substances, researchers initially proposed a *sandwich model*, describing a phospholipid bilayer in between two layers of protein.

After investigation with an electron microscope, the *unit membrane model* was proposed, which was based on the "trilaminar" appearance of two dark outer lines and a light inner region visible under the electron microscope. The dark outer lines were believed to be protein monolayers, while the inner region was thought to be a phospholipid bilayer. The unit membrane model was essentially in agreement with the sandwich model. However, both of these models failed to explain permeability satisfactorily.

In 1972, Garth L. Nicholson and Seymour J. Singer published the current *fluid-mosaic model*, which describes a plasma membrane as a phospholipid bilayer embedded with proteins. Electron micrographs of the freeze-fractured membrane (and other evidence) supported the fluid-mosaic model. In this model, it is the lipid portion of the plasma membrane which gives it its "fluid" characteristic. Thus, fluidity describes the lipids that diffuse freely throughout the membrane and regulate consistency.

The membrane's protein components contribute to the "mosaic." Protein composition in the plasma membrane is dependent upon the function of the particular cell. Some proteins are held in place by cytoskeletal filaments, but most migrate within the fluid bilayer.

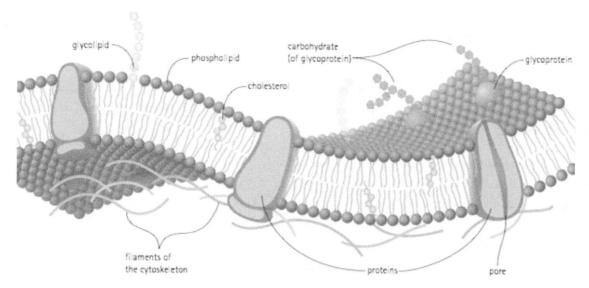

The membrane is a phospholipid bilayer with cholesterol between the hydrophobic lipid tails and embedded proteins – some with modifications (e.g., glycolipid or glycoprotein)

The two classes of proteins embedded in a membrane by location.

Peripheral membrane proteins are on the membrane surface, mainly the intracellular side, that interact with cytoskeletal elements to influence cell shape and motility. These proteins are not amphipathic; they interact with the hydrophilic heads of the membrane. Peripheral membrane proteins can be removed from the membrane with relative ease using high salt or high pH, and therefore are not permanently attached to the membrane.

Integral membrane proteins are permanently attached to the membrane and thus cannot be removed without disrupting the lipid bilayer. They possess hydrophobic domains which are anchored to hydrophobic lipids. Most integral membrane proteins are *transmembrane* proteins, spanning the entire membrane.

Membrane proteins can participate in cell signaling, cell-to-cell adhesion, transport through the membrane, enzymatic activity, and some other activities.

When divided by function, several key classes of membrane proteins emerge.

Receptor proteins provide a binding site for hormones, neurotransmitters, and other signaling molecules. Receptor proteins are usually specific in that they bind to a single molecule or certain class of molecule. Binding of the signal molecule to the receptor triggers a cellular response that corresponds to a specific biochemical pathway.

Adhesion proteins attach cells to neighboring cells for cell-to-cell communication and tissue structure. These proteins generally attach to the cytoskeleton of one cell and extend through the plasma membrane to the extracellular environment, where they bind and interact with the adhesion proteins of another cell.

Transport proteins move materials into and out of the cell. These include *channel proteins* and *carrier proteins.* Channel proteins provide a passageway for large, polar or charged molecules that cannot pass through the lipid bilayer without assistance. These proteins facilitate the passive transport of molecules, that is, they do not require ATP to operate. Carrier proteins, however, may facilitate both passive and active (energy-requiring) transport of molecules. They bind to specific molecules on one side of the cell membrane and then change conformation to release the molecule on the other side of the membrane.

Enzymatic membrane proteins carry out metabolic reactions at the cell membrane. For example, many enzymatic membrane proteins help digest membrane components for recycling. The mitochondrial membrane contains enzymatic proteins (e.g., the protein complexes that are part of the electron transport chain of aerobic cellular respiration).

Recognition proteins are glycoproteins which identify a cell to the body's immune system. They allow immune cells to recognize a substance as either belonging to the body or as an invasive foreign agent to be destroyed. Recognition proteins called antigens are the basis for A, B, and O blood groups in humans. Immune cells recognize the sugars attached to these proteins and attack any red blood cells with foreign sugars, which is why patients of some blood groups cannot donate blood or receive blood from people with other blood groups.

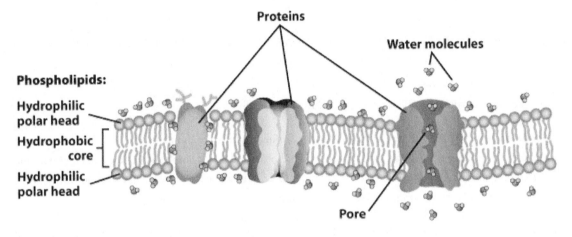

Osmosis: colligative properties and osmotic pressure

All fluids of the body are *solutions*: they contain dissolved substances (solutes) and a fluid (water) in which the substances dissolve (solvent). *Diffusion* is the movement of a solute from an area where it is in higher concentration to an area where it is in lower concentration. *Osmosis* is the diffusion of water from an area of low solute concentration to an area of high solute concentration. Note that solutes diffuse to an area of lower solute concentration, while water (a solvent) diffuses to an area of higher solute concentration. Both solute and solvent work together to offset unequal solute concentration and restore the solution to equilibrium.

The natural inclination of solutes is to diffuse until they are evenly distributed. However, different areas of the body require different concentrations of specific solutes. Separation of these areas is accomplished via the complex system of membrane compartmentalization in organs, tissues, and cells. The body must prevent all body compartments from reaching equilibrium with each other but must allow the passage of certain atoms, ions, and molecules through membranes to the areas where they are needed. To accomplish this, membranes are highly selective and tightly regulated.

Colligative properties of solutions depend on the concentration of a solute in the solution. They do not depend on the chemical nature of the solutes. The most important colligative property for the regulation of body fluids is *osmotic pressure*, the pressure that must be applied to prevent the net flow of water into a solution separated by a membrane (i.e., a measure of water's tendency to flow from one solution to another). This property is related to several other key terms in osmoregulation (the regulation of osmotic pressure). *Osmolarity* is the total solute concentration of a solution and is measured in units of *osmoles*. Osmolarity takes both penetrating and non-penetrating solutes into account and can be used to describe a single solution in addition to comparing different solutions. A *hyperosmotic* solution has a higher osmolarity, while a *hypoosmotic* solution has a relatively low osmolarity. *Isosmotic* solutions have the same osmotic pressure.

Tonicity describes the relative concentration of two solutions separated by a selectively permeable membrane, and explains how diffusion occurs between them (e.g., between intracellular and extracellular fluid). Unlike osmolarity, tonicity refers to non-penetrating solutes (solutes which cannot cross a membrane), and always describes how one solution compares to another. A *hypertonic* solution has a relatively higher concentration of solute. Conversely, a *hypotonic* solution has a relatively lower concentration of solute. Therefore, a cell with a lower concentration of solute than the extracellular fluid is hypotonic to the fluid, while the extracellular fluid is hypertonic to the cell. The reverse is true for a cell with a higher concentration of solute than the extracellular fluid.

A cell placed in a hypertonic solution shrinks through a process of *crenation* (i.e., shrinking of the cells), as water diffuses out of the cell to offset the high concentration of the outside solution. Conversely, a cell in a hypotonic solution swells as water rushes into the cell causing *cytolysis* (i.e., bursting of a cell due to osmotic imbalance caused by excess water entering the cell). Plant cells rely on hypotonic extracellular fluids to keep their cells *turgid* (swollen), maintaining pressure against the cell wall and keeping the entire organism upright. Too much water can enter the cell, resulting in *lysis* (breakage of the cell). An *isotonic* solution has an equal solute concentration as the surrounding solution. In this situation, there is no net water movement.

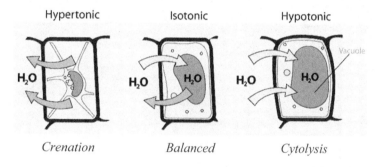

Hypertonic	Isotonic	Hypotonic
Crenation	*Balanced*	*Cytolysis*

Passive transport

The plasma membrane is selectively permeable, meaning certain molecules can pass through. A molecule's ability to diffuse through the plasma membrane depends on the molecule's size, charge, and polarity. The greater the lipid solubility of the diffusing particle, the more easily it passes through the membrane. Generally, smaller particles diffuse more rapidly than larger ones, and hydrophobic particles diffuse more rapidly than hydrophilic particles.

Many particles cannot diffuse through the plasma membrane without assistance. Small, non-charged or non-polar molecules pass through the membrane freely. Large, charged and/or polar molecules usually require assistance to pass through the membrane.

Passive transport enables the movement of molecules across a membrane without the expenditure of energy by the cell. The methods include simple diffusion, osmosis, and facilitated diffusion. Passive transport utilizes a *concentration gradient*, whereby particles diffuse from an area of higher to an area of lower solute concentration.

Simple diffusion is the process by which smaller, lipid-soluble molecules freely diffuse through the phospholipid bilayer unassisted. For example, oxygen and carbon dioxide pass through the membrane via simple diffusion.

While water is a polar molecule, it is small enough that it can diffuse freely across a plasma membrane. *Osmosis* is the passive diffusion of water molecules. Osmosis occurs when water moves from a region of lower solute concentration to a region of higher solute concentration and is facilitated by *aquaporins* as channel proteins. Osmosis is often classified as simple diffusion, despite requiring the transport proteins characteristic of facilitated diffusion.

Facilitated diffusion allows larger, lipid-insoluble molecules which cannot freely pass through the phospholipid bilayer (e.g., sugars, ions, and amino acids) to be transported. During facilitated diffusion, a molecule is transported down its concentration gradient with the assistance of either a carrier protein or channel protein, often as a *uniporter*.

Passive transport includes diffusion and facilitated diffusion
with the expenditure of energy as molecules move down the concentration gradient

Active transport: sodium - potassium pump

Active transport requires cellular energy to move solutes against their concentration gradient. Unlike passive transport, which exploits the natural inclination of molecules to move down their concentration gradient, active transport requires the expenditure of energy to resist this opposing force. Carrier proteins are the transmembrane proteins that mediate movement of molecules that are too polar or too large to move across a membrane by diffusion, thereby governing active transport. During this process, a solute (molecule to be transported) binds to a specific site on a transporter on one surface of the membrane. The transporter then changes shape to expose the bound solute to the opposite side of the membrane. The solute then dissociates from the transporter and is then on the opposite side from which it started. Depending on the membrane and the needs of the cellular environment, many types of transporters may be present with specific binding sites for particular types of substances. *Solute flux magnitude* (i.e., the rate at which the solute flows) through a mediated transport system is positively correlated with the number of transporters, the rate of conformational change in the transporter protein and the overall saturation of transporter binding sites, which depends on the solute concentration and affinity of the transporter.

There are two types of active transport: primary and secondary. *Primary active transport* utilizes energy generated directly from ATP. The carrier proteins for primary active transport are pumps. An example is a sodium-potassium pump, which works by moving 3 Na^+ ions out and 2 K^+ ions into a cell, resulting in a net transfer of positive charge outside the membrane.

For a cell at rest, intracellular K^+ concentration is high, and Na^+ concentration is low, while extracellular K^+ concentration is low and Na^+ concentration is high. These concentration gradients facilitate transport across the plasma membrane and help the cell manage its *membrane potential*, the difference in electrical charge between the outside and inside of the cell.

Cellular sodium and potassium concentrations are maintained via active transport by the sodium-potassium pump (Na^+ / K^+ ATPase). When the intracellular Na^+ concentration is too high, and K^+ concentration is too low, the sodium-potassium pump must pump Na^+ out of the cell and K^+ into the cell to restore the appropriate concentration gradients.

The K^+ / Na^+ pump maintains a cell's membrane potential. Na^+ bind to induce a conformation change in the transmembrane protein and pump Na^+ out of cell up its concentration gradient using ATP

The energy for *secondary active transport* comes from an electrochemical gradient established by the action of primary active transport. Secondary active transporters work via a mechanism of *cotransport*. Cotransport occurs when one molecule moves with (down) its concentration gradient, while another molecule moves against (up) its concentration gradient. The energetically favorable movement of the molecule moving with its concentration gradient powers the movement of the other molecule against its concentration gradient. *Antiporters* (e.g., sodium-calcium exchanger) move molecules in opposite directions, i.e., one is transported out while the other is transported into the cell. *Symporters* move both molecules in the same direction.

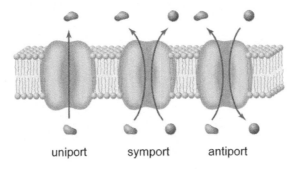

uniport   symport   antiport

One example of a symporter is the sodium-glucose linked transporter (SGLT), which transports sodium *with* its concentration gradient from the exoplasmic space to the cytoplasmic space, and transports glucose *against* its concentration gradient from the exoplasmic space to the cytoplasmic space. These movements are energetically coupled. Note that while both molecules are moving in the same *physical* direction in a symporter, the molecules are moving in opposite directions but are energetically favorable with one process driving the other.

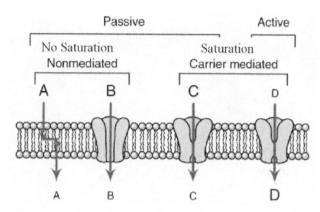

Comparison of passive and active transport: A shows diffusion with movement unaided by a protein,
B shows passive transport down the concentration gradient through a channel (no saturation),
C is passive transport through a carrier protein (saturation),
D is active transport up a concentration gradient (saturation possible and energy needed)

Membrane channels

Membrane channels are transmembrane proteins that allow ions to diffuse across the membrane via passive transport. Different cells have different permeabilities, depending on their membrane channels. The diameter of the channel and the polar groups on the protein subunits forming channel walls determine the permeability of the channels for various ions and molecules.

Porins are a type of channel proteins that are less chemically-specific than many other channel proteins; generally, if a molecule can fit through the porin, it can pass through it. *Ion channels* allow for the passage of ions. Channel gating is the opening and closing of ion channels to the molecules they transport. Changes in membrane potential modulate voltage-gated channels. Ligand-gated channels are modulated by the allosteric or covalent binding of ligands to the channel protein. *Ligands* are small molecules that bind to a protein or receptor, usually to trigger a signal. Mechanically-gated channels are modulated by mechanical stimuli such as stretching, pressure or temperature. Several factors may influence a single channel, and the same ion may pass through several different channels.

Membrane potential

Membrane potential is the electrical potential difference between the intracellular and extracellular environment. Membrane potential is mediated by channels and pumps, which alter electrochemical gradients as needed by each cell. Whenever there is a net separation of electric charges across a cell membrane, a membrane potential exists. The concentration gradient influences all molecules, but ions, because of their charged nature, are influenced by differences in membrane potential. The *electrochemical gradient* is the combined forces of membrane potential and concentration gradient. These forces may oppose one another, work independently from one another or work in conjunction.

The difference in ion concentrations maintains the membrane potential (i.e., voltage)

Nearly all eukaryotic cells maintain a non-zero membrane potential. In animal cells, this value ranges from −40 mV to −80 mV; thus, with respect to the extracellular environment, the inside of the cell has a negative voltage. Membrane potential is especially important for neurons, which have a *resting membrane potential* of about –70 mV. Changes in this resting potential allow for the electrical communications of neurons.

Membrane receptors, cell signaling pathways and second messengers

Cells must communicate with their neighbors as well as their environment. *Cell signaling* is the system by which cells receive, integrate and send signals to communicate information. These signals are sent through the *extracellular matrix*, a collection of polysaccharides and proteins secreted by cells in multicellular organisms. This matrix fills the space between cells, providing structure, facilitating cell signaling and allowing the cells to move and change their shape.

The composition of the extracellular matrix is highly variable depending on tissue type, as different tissues have different functions. For example, the extracellular matrix of bone is highly calcified, while the extracellular matrix of blood is fluid, containing dissolved proteins and other molecules. The most extensive extracellular matrices are of connective tissues, which are found throughout the body and include bone and blood. Connective tissues are largely composed of their extracellular matrix and are sparsely populated with cells.

A typical connective tissue extracellular matrix includes fibrous proteins and *proteoglycans*, glycoproteins that form a packing gel around the fibrous proteins. The primary fibrous proteins are *collagen* and *elastin*, which provide structure and flexibility, along with *fibronectin* and *laminin*, which assist in adhesion and cell migration. Transmembrane proteins such as *integrins* bind to specific proteins in the extracellular matrix and membrane proteins on adjacent cells. Integrins help organize cells into tissues. They are responsible for transmitting signals from the extracellular matrix to the cell interior.

Membrane receptors may be on the plasma membrane or intracellular membranes. Not all signal molecules bind to membrane receptors at the plasma membrane. For example, steroid hormones and gases, diffuse across the plasma membrane and bind to intracellular receptors. Other signal molecules enter the cell via endocytosis. In addition to hormones and gases, signal molecules include neurotransmitters, proteins, and lipids.

Membrane receptors are crucial in the cell-signaling pathways. When a signal molecule binds to a membrane receptor, it may initiate a metabolic response, change the membrane potential or alter gene expression.

Signal transduction is when one signaling molecule triggers a multi-step chain reaction, which indirectly transmits the initial signal to its destination. *Second messengers* are the molecules that relay the signal.

At steps in the signal transduction pathway, second messengers can greatly amplify the strength of the original signal by increasing the number of molecules they activate. For example, one signal molecule at the membrane receptor may produce 10 second messengers, and these 10 second messengers may each produce another 10 second messengers, and so on, amplifying the signal significantly.

Cell signaling is a complex process but is divided into four general categories. *Endocrine signaling* is when a cell secretes a signal that travels to a distant target cell. *Paracrine signaling* is when the target cell is nearby, but not in direct contact. *Juxtacrine signaling* is the signaling of a target cell in direct contact with the secreting cell. *Autocrine signaling* targets the same cell that secreted the signal.

Exocytosis and endocytosis

The fluidity of the plasma membrane allows it to change shape, pinch off and reform. This fluidity enables substances to exit the cell via *exocytosis* and enter the cell via *endocytosis*. Both processes require cellular energy and are therefore considered forms of active transport.

During exocytosis, membrane-bound vesicles in the cytoplasm fuse with the plasma membrane and their contents are released outside the cell. The vesicle then assimilates into the plasma membrane, replenishing portions of the membrane that would otherwise be lost. The process of exocytosis is triggered by stimuli, leading to an increase in cytosolic calcium concentration, which activates proteins required for the vesicle membrane to fuse with the plasma membrane. Exocytosis provides a route for the release of the proteins it produces for extracellular secretion, as well as the proteins and lipids destined for the plasma membrane.

Endocytosis is essentially the opposite process of exocytosis. During endocytosis, extracellular molecules destined for the plasma membrane or the cytoplasm are imported into the cell. In preparation for endocytosis, a region of the outer side of the plasma membrane indents and encloses the material for import. This indentation then folds and pinches off into a membrane-bound vesicle inside the cell. *Pinocytosis* ("cell-drinking" or fluid endocytosis), is a form of endocytosis which cells perform regularly; it is the import of small amounts of extracellular fluid that contain molecules able to be readily absorbed by the cell. The process of pinocytosis may be non-specific or mediated by receptors on the plasma membrane.

Phagocytosis is performed by a few types of specialized cells. Phagocytosis ("cell-eating") involves the import of much larger particulate matter than that imported during pinocytosis. The particulate matter must be broken down before it can be absorbed by the cell. As such, phagocytes digest bacteria, viruses and cell debris as a function of our immune system. Some unicellular eukaryotes, such as amoeba, rely on phagocytosis for nutrient intake.

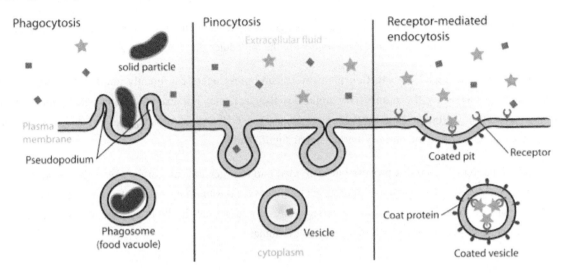

Types of endocytosis with substrates taken into the cell

Intercellular junctions: gap junctions, tight junctions, and desmosomes

Cell junctions are points of contact that physically link neighboring cells. Animal cells have three types of intercellular junctions: gap junctions, tight junctions, and anchoring junctions.

Gap junctions are protein channels that directly link the cytoplasms of adjacent cells. Gap junctions are communicating junctions because they allow for rapid cell-to-cell communication. They are formed by the joining of two membrane channels on adjacent cells, allowing the movement of small molecules and ions between cells, while still preventing their cytoplasms from mixing. Gap junctions are important in tissues such as cardiac muscle, where electrical impulses must be transmitted through cells extremely rapidly so that the muscle fibers contract as a single unit.

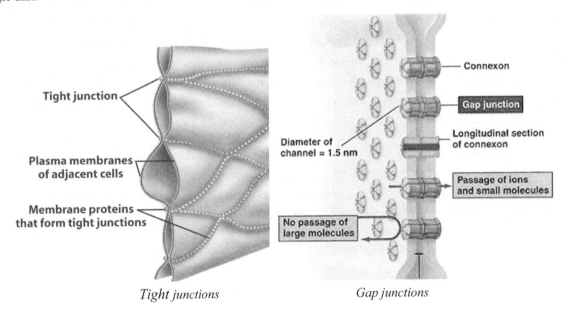

Tight junctions   *Gap junctions*

The *tight junction* has plasma membrane proteins attach in zipper-like fastenings, holding cells together so tightly that the tissues become barriers to molecules. Tight junctions are formed by the physical joining of the extracellular surfaces of two adjacent plasma membranes, producing a seal that prevents the passage of materials between cells. Materials must enter the cells by passive or active transport to pass through the tissue. Tight junctions are important in areas where more control over tissue processes is needed (e.g., the epithelial cells in the intestine involved in nutrient absorption).

Anchoring junctions use proteins extended through the plasma membrane of one cell and attached to another cell. Anchoring junctions are firm but still allow for spaces between adjacent cells. *Desmosomes,* a type of anchoring junction, are created by dense patches of protein on the plasma membranes of two cells. Internally, proteins anchor to the cytoplasm of each cell, while externally the proteins adhere to one another. The purpose and function of desmosomes are to hold adjacent cells firmly in place in tissue areas that are subject to stretching, (e.g., bladder, skin and stomach).

Desmosome

Notes for active learning

Cytoskeleton

The general function of the cytoskeleton in cell support and movement

The *cytoskeleton* is a scaffold of flexible, tubular protein fibers extending between the nucleus to the plasma membrane in eukaryotes. This vast network of fibers maintains the shape of the cell, provides support and facilitates the transport of vesicles. The cytoskeleton is the cellular analogy to the bones and muscles of an animal. It anchors organelles and enzymes to specific regions of the cell to keep them organized in the cytosol.

The cytoskeleton can change shape to facilitate contractility and movement, allowing the cell to divide, migrate or undergo endocytosis and exocytosis. During cell division, the cytoskeletal elements can rapidly assemble and disassemble to form spindles for the organization of chromosomes and to cleave the cell into two daughter cells. The long fibers of the cytoskeleton serve for intracellular transport, upon which vesicles and organelles move via motor proteins (e.g., dynein and kinesin).

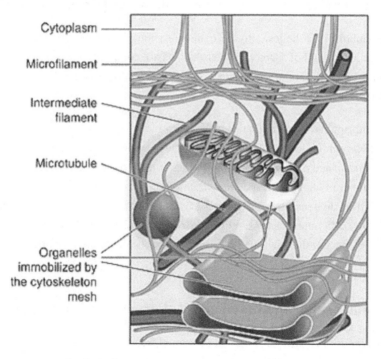

Cytoskeleton as a network of tubular proteins to provide shape and facilitate transport of vesicles

Microfilaments: composition and role in cleavage and contractility

Microfilaments (actin filaments) are the thinnest and most abundant of the cytoskeleton proteins. They are composed of the contractile protein *actin*. These long, thin fibers, about 7 nm in diameter, may be in bundles or meshlike networks. Each microfilament consists of two chains of globular actin subunits twisted to form a helix.

Microfilaments are assembled and disassembled quickly according to the needs of the cell. They are involved in cell motility functions, such as the contraction of muscle cells, the formation of amoeba pseudopodia and cleavage of the cell during cytokinesis. While flexible, microfilaments are strong and prevent deformation of the cell by their tensile strength.

Microfilaments provide tracks for the movement of myosin. Myosin attaches to vesicles (or organelles) and pulls them to their destination along the microfilament track. Additionally, the interaction between microfilaments and myosin is crucial to the function of the cell.

Intermediate filaments: role in support

Intermediate filaments are thicker than microfilaments but thinner than microtubules. Typically, they are 8 to 11 nm in diameter. These rope-like assemblies of fibrous polypeptides are found most extensively in regions of cells that are subjected to stress. Most intermediate filaments are found in the cytoplasm, supporting the plasma membrane and forming cell-to-cell junctions. However, *lamins*, a class of intermediate filaments, are responsible for structural support within the nucleus. Unlike microfilaments and microtubules, intermediate filaments are not capable of rapid disassembly once assembled.

Microtubules: composition and role in support and transport

Microtubules (tubulin) are hollow protein cylinders about 25 nm in diameter and 0.2–25 μm in length. They are the thickest and most rigid of filaments. Microtubules are composed of the globular protein, *tubulin,* which occurs as α tubulin and β tubulin. The microtubule assembly brings these two together as dimers, and the dimers arrange themselves in rows.

The strength and rigidity of microtubules make them ideal for resisting compression of the cell. However, these fibers serve functions similar to microfilaments. Microtubules act as tracks for intracellular transport, but they interact primarily with *kinesin* and *dynein* motor proteins, rather than myosin. The transport function of microtubules is especially important for trafficking neurotransmitters throughout nerve cells. Like microfilaments, microtubules can be rapidly assembled or disassembled. Regulation of microtubule assembly is under control of a *microtubule-organizing center* (MTOC). Microtubules radiate from the MTOC and extend throughout the cytoplasm. During cell division, the centrosome generates the microtubule spindle fibers necessary for chromosome separation.

Composition and function of eukaryotic cilia and flagella

Cilia and *flagella* are two types of microtubule complexes that protrude from the cell body and serve cell motility and sensory functions. In eukaryotes, they are membrane-bounded cylinders that enclose a matrix of nine pairs of microtubules encircling two single microtubules, a *9 + 2 pattern*. Movement occurs when these microtubules slide past one another. At the plasma membrane, a *basal body* anchors the cilium (or flagellum) to the cell body. The basal body is derived from a centriole, which is formed by nine pairs of microtubules without central microtubules, the *9 + 0 pattern*. Eukaryotic cilia and flagella grow by polymerizing (adding) tubulin to their tips.

Cilia are short, hair-like projections. Nearly every human cell has at least one cilium, which is *non-motile* and functions as a sensory antenna important in cell signaling pathways. Non-motile cilia lack the 2 central microtubules and thus are have a 9 + 0 pattern. Many cells are covered with some *motile* cilia, which move in an undulating fashion to transport particles across the cell surface. For example, motile cilia are found in the respiratory tract, where they push mucus and irritants out of the lungs, trachea, and nose.

Essentially, eukaryotic flagella are structurally similar to eukaryotic cilia, so distinctions are often not drawn between the two. Like cilia, they have both sensory and motility functions. However, eukaryotic flagella tend to be longer and move with more of a whip-like motion. An example of a eukaryotic flagellum is the tail of a sperm cell.

Prokaryotic flagella are notably different from their prokaryotic cilia counterparts. These flagella are noted for their long, whip shape and functional differences from cilia.

Centrioles and microtubule organizing centers

The *centrosome* is the main microtubule organizing center at the poles during mitosis and meiosis of the cell. Each centrosome contains a pair of barrel-shaped organelles of *centrioles*. The centrosome has a key role in mitosis when it divides into two centrosomes, which then interact with chromosomes via microtubules to form the mitotic spindle.

Centrosome contains two centrioles oriented at right angles

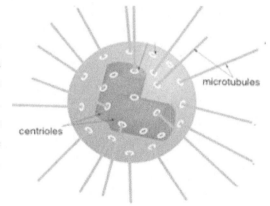

Centrioles are components of the centrosome. Microtubules radiate from these barrel-shaped structures, which are made of microtubules themselves. They are short cylinders with a ring pattern (9 + 0) of microtubule triplets. In animal cells and most protists, a centrosome contains two centrioles oriented at right angles. Plant and fungal cells contain the equivalent of a centrosome, but do not contain centrioles. Centrioles serve as basal bodies for cilia and flagella.

In mitosis, the terms centrioles and centrosomes (some means "body" as in chromosomes) are often used interchangeably because centrioles form the most important parts of a centrosome.

Notes for active learning

...ribes the lifetime of a cell, detailing the life stages from the creation of a new cell to its ...cells. Most of an organism's cells divide throughout their lifetime (i.e., an exception is ...n is the process by which organisms grow, repair tissues and reproduce.

...sis are two types of cell division. *Mitosis* is cell division when new somatic (body) cells ...organisms as they grow, and when tissues are repaired or replaced. When a cell is ...rows larger, the number of organelles doubles and the DNA replicates. *Meiosis* is the ...reproductive cells of egg and sperm) by organisms that reproduce sexually. Meiosis is ...etail.

...produce genetic variations. A daughter cell is identical in chromosome number and ...ent cell. The purpose of mitosis is to distribute identical genetic material to two daughter ...ole is the fidelity with which the DNA is passed along, without dilution or error, from one ...next. All eukaryotes divide by mitosis, but prokaryotes undergo a different mechanism of *binary fission*, a form of asexual reproduction. Binary fission is a simpler process wherein the parent cell replicates its DNA and then divides. Since prokaryotes have a single and circular DNA without a nucleus, there are no complex steps of chromosome formation and separation by mitosis with microtubules between the centromere and centrioles as in eukaryotic cells.

Mitotic process: prophase, metaphase, anaphase, telophase, and interphase

Interphase is the stage before mitosis and represents the majority of a cell's life. This is not a static state but rather a progression towards mitosis. However, in some cases, a cell halts its progress through interphase, either temporarily or permanently. This may be because it is a non-dividing cell (e.g., nerve cell), or because the cell is not healthy enough to perform the growing and replicating functions of interphase.

During interphase ($G_1 \rightarrow S \rightarrow G_2$), the cell prepares to divide by growing, replicating its DNA and many of its organelles, and synthesizing mRNA and proteins. When it has completed all the functions of interphase, the cell exits interphase and enters mitosis.

There are four phases of mitosis: prophase, metaphase, anaphase, and telophase (PMAT).

1. Prophase = *Prepare*: cell *prepares* for mitosis

2. Metaphase = *Middle*: chromosomes align in the *middle* of the cell

3. Anaphase = *Apart*: centromere splits and sister chromatids are pulled *apart* by microtubules to the opposite poles of the cell

4. Telophase = *Two*: two daughter nuclei are re-formed with separate nuclei

Prophase, the first phase of mitosis involves chromatin condensation, nucleolus dissolution, nuclear membrane fragmentation, and centrosome movement. *Chromatin condensation* is the process by which loose euchromatin condenses into chromosomes. At this time, the chromosomes have no particular orientation in the cell. Upon chromatin condensation, the nucleolus dissolves, and the nuclear membrane begins to fragment, exposing the chromosomes to the cytoplasm of the cell. Simultaneously, centrosomes begin to migrate to opposite sides of the cell. Microtubules start to extend from the centrosomes, forming the spindle apparatus.

Prophase

After prophase, the cell enters *metaphase*, when nuclear fragmentation completes and the centrosomes station themselves at opposite poles of the cell. Microtubules emerge from the centrosomes and attach to the chromosomes, aligning them along an imaginary line in the center of the cell, the *metaphase plate*, or *equatorial plate*. This completes the formation of the spindle apparatus. All chromosomes must be attached and lined up along the metaphase plate before the cell can proceed to the next phase.

Metaphase

During *anaphase*, sister chromatids (chromatin strands replicated during S phase of interphase but attached at the centromere) are pulled apart to opposite poles of the cell. The sister chromatids become detached from one another at their centromere and travel towards opposite centrosomes by action of the spindle microtubules. By the end of anaphase, equal numbers of sister chromatids are stationed by both centrosomes.

Anaphase

Telophase is when the cell reverses the actions of prophase and prepares to divide. The spindle apparatus disassembles, and two daughter nuclei reform within the cell. As spindle microtubules disassemble, two regions of identical chromatids are present in the cell. A nuclear envelope develops around each of these regions, forming two daughter nuclei. Within the nuclei, chromosomal DNA uncoils into chromatin, and nucleoli form. The single cell now contains two identical daughter nuclei, and cell division proceeds.

Telophase

Cytokinesis is the division of the cytoplasm to create two daughter cells. This usually coincides with the end of telophase but is *not* a phase of mitosis. Rather, it is a separate event which does not always occur. When mitosis occurs but cytokinesis does not, it results in a multinucleated cell; (often in plants, but in the skeletal muscle cells of animals).

In animal cells, cytokinesis occurs by process of *cleavage*. First, a *cleavage furrow*, a shallow groove between the two daughter nuclei, appears. The cleavage furrow deepens as a band of microfilaments, *contractile ring*, constricts between the two daughter cells. A narrow bridge exists between daughter cells during telophase until constriction completely separates the cytoplasm. The result is two daughter cells enclosed in their plasma membrane and with their own, identical nuclei. Recall that the parent cell replicated its organelles before mitosis; thus, each daughter cell contains a full set of organelles, smaller than the cell size of the parent.

Cytokinesis in plant cells is different because plant cells have rigid cellulose cell walls which do not permit cytokinesis by furrowing. In plants, vesicles containing cellulose move to the middle of the cell. Additional vesicles arrive and coalesce, building a *cell plate* of cellulose (cell wall). When the cell plate is complete, the parent has divided into two separate daughter cells.

Nuclear membrane breakdown and reorganization

Before mitosis begins, the cell's DNA is contained inside the nucleus, inaccessible to the mitotic spindle. During prophase and metaphase, the nucleolus disintegrates, chromatin condenses, and the nuclear membrane breaks down. This process exposes chromosomal DNA to the cell's cytoplasm and allows mitosis to proceed. The nuclear membrane does not reform until telophase when the two daughter nuclei are each enclosed within their nuclear membranes from fragments of the parental cell's nuclear membrane. At this point, chromosomes uncoil into chromatin and the nucleoli reform, making nuclear reorganization complete.

Centrioles, asters, and spindles

As previously discussed, centrioles are the units of the centrosome, the microtubule-organizing centers of the cell. Centrioles are replicated during interphase in preparation for mitosis. During prophase, *polar microtubules* emerge from both pairs of centrioles and centrosomes and push against each other to move the centrosomes to opposite sides of the cell. *Astral microtubules* extend from the centrioles to assist in orienting the mitotic spindle apparatus. At the end of prophase, kinetochore microtubules originate from the centrioles and attach to kinetochores of the chromosomes.

The entire spindle apparatus consists of the two centrosomes (composed of two centrioles each), polar microtubules, astral microtubules (asters), and *kinetochore microtubules* (k-fibers), which attach to the kinetochores on chromosomes.

Like animal cells, plant cells have a spindle apparatus, but many do not have centrioles or astral microtubules. Centrioles are not strictly necessary for mitosis even in animal cells.

Chromatids, centromeres, and kinetochores

As the cell enters metaphase, kinetochore microtubules extend from the centrosomes and attach to *kinetochores* on the chromosomes. Kinetochores are assembled on the *centromere*, the region of a chromosome that links two sister chromatids. Technically, there are two sections of the kinetochore: the inner kinetochore, which associates with the DNA of the centromere, and the outer kinetochore, which interacts with the kinetochore microtubules. During metaphase, these microtubules pull on the chromosomes with equal tension, eventually aligning them at the metaphase plate. Upon successful attachment of all chromosomes to the spindle via the kinetochore and microtubules, proteins are released from the kinetochore, which signals the end of metaphase and the beginning of anaphase.

Mechanisms of chromosome movement

In anaphase, the centromere holding the sister chromatids (S phase of interphase when the chromosome replicated to form two sister chromatids) dissolves, and the sister chromatids are released from their attachment point. The chromosomes are pulled to opposite sides of the cell by shortening of the kinetochore microtubules. Shortening occurs when the motor protein attached to a kinetochore "walks" along the kinetochore-microtubule, dissembling the microtubule into tubulin subunits as it passes. Polar microtubules assist the separation of chromosomes by lengthening the spindle. Wherever the ends of two polar microtubules from opposite poles overlap, motor proteins interact between the fibers and push them in opposite directions, thus pushing the entire spindle apart.

Phases of the cell cycle (G₀, G₁, S, G₂, M)

Interphase is divided into three phases: G_1, S, and G_2. G_0 is another, resting phase when the cell is not dividing nor preparing to divide. G_0 is the static state in which some cells remain permanently (e.g., nerve cells) and others temporarily. A cell can exit G_0 and reenter the active cell cycle upon receipt of suitable signals from *growth factor* proteins. Under a microscope, a cell can be recognized as being in interphase by the lack of visible chromosomes, because the DNA is uncoiled as loose chromatin.

During the *G_1 phase (Gap phase 1)*, the cell continues normal function as it grows larger and replicates its organelles, including ribosomes, mitochondria, and chloroplasts (if a plant cell). The mitochondria generate sufficient storage of energy for the functions of mitosis. In G_1, the cell synthesizes mRNA and proteins in preparation for the *S phase*. In the S phase (*Synthesis*), the cell replicates its DNA to produce two sister chromatids attached at the centromere. During the S phase, any DNA nucleotide damage must be detected and fixed before the cell may proceed.

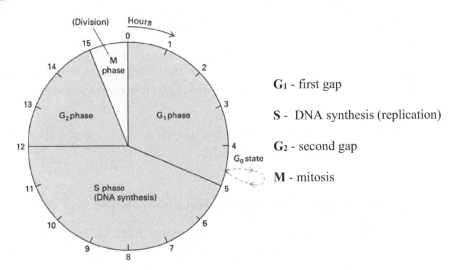

G₁ - first gap

S - DNA synthesis (replication)

G₂ - second gap

M - mitosis

The cell cycle divided between interphase and mitosis

G_2 phase (Gap phase 2) is where the cell continues to grow and synthesize proteins needed for mitosis. Completion of G_2 marks the end of interphase and the beginning of mitosis, often abbreviated as M. In summary, the sequential phases of the cell cycle are:

G_0 = no DNA replication or cell division

G_1 = making of organelles, increase in cell size (growth)

S = DNA replication, complete duplication of chromosomes (sister chromatids)

G_2 = making of organelles, increase in cell size (growth), cell committed to mitosis

M = mitosis (PMAT); prophase, metaphase, anaphase, and telophase

Growth arrest

Cell growth refers to *cell proliferation* (populations) or the growth of an individual cell, whereby biomolecules are synthesized.

Cell proliferation is the ultimate goal of unicellular organisms. These organisms are mostly limited by nutrient availability. However, in multicellular organisms, cell proliferation must be carefully monitored to prevent tumor formation and invasion into nearby tissues. *Contact inhibition*, the tendency for cells to cease dividing when they come into physical contact with their neighbors, regulates this. Therefore, lack of free space signals growth arrest.

The growth of the individual cells regulates cell populations. For individual cell development, growth arrest is *cellular quiescence* or *cell cycle arrest.*

During the cell cycle, the cell encounters checkpoints at which the cell cycle is halted before proceeding. There are three major checkpoints: G_1, G_2, and M:

1. The G_1 Checkpoint – Restriction Point

    Partway through G_1, the cell reaches the restriction point. Here, the cell checks for cell size, nutrients and growth factors. If the cell is not sufficiently healthy and prepared for mitosis, the cycle halts and the cell returns to G_0.

    Additionally, if DNA damage is detected, this triggers *apoptosis* (cell death) if the DNA is not repaired. If everything is as it should be, the cell clears the checkpoint and proceeds toward DNA replication (S phase). G_1 is the only checkpoint mediated by extracellular signals. After this point, only intracellular signals direct the cell cycle to proceed or halt progress.

2. The G_2 Checkpoint – DNA Damage Checkpoint

    At the end of G_2, before the cell proceeds with mitosis, there is another checkpoint. The cell checks for cell size and proper DNA replication. If the DNA is not finished replicating or if DNA has been damaged and requires repair, the cell remains in G_2 until these issues are resolved.

3. The M Checkpoint –Mitotic Spindle Checkpoint

    After the cell has entered mitosis and has reached metaphase, a final checkpoint occurs. The M checkpoint ensures that the proper number of chromosomes are aligned at the mitotic plate and secured to the mitotic spindle. Errors during chromosome segregation can cause defects resulting in genetic conditions (e.g., Down syndrome). The M checkpoint reduces the occurrence of defects by arresting the cell in metaphase until all chromosomes are properly attached to the spindle apparatus and aligned for anaphase.

Notes for active learning

Control of Cell Cycle

The cell cycle is controlled by intracellular and extracellular signals that either stimulate or inhibit metabolic events. Extracellular stimulatory signal molecules are growth factors; these are proteins or hormones that promote cell growth and differentiation. Extracellular inhibitory signal molecules are growth suppressors, or more often *tumor suppressors* because they prevent the rampant growth of cancer cells. Tumor suppressors inhibit growth by halting the cell cycle or directing the cell to destroy itself via apoptosis.

Relative concentrations of cyclin proteins during phases of the cell cycle

Intracellular signaling directs the cell cycle and involves the activation and inactivation of proteins; *cyclin-dependent kinases* (CDKs).

Apoptosis (programmed cell death)

Apoptosis is programmed cell death initiated by the organism. Apoptosis destroys cells which pose a threat to the organism, such as infected cells, cells with DNA damage, cancerous cells, and immune system cells no longer needed and are unnecessarily attacking other body cells. While it may seem paradoxical, apoptosis is important for growth. For example, cells must die to create spaces in the webbed hands of a fetus for the formation of separate digits.

Some internal or external pathways and signals cause cell death, but the morphological changes during apoptosis are consistent whatever the cause. These changes include shrinkage and *blebbing* (bulging) of the plasma membrane, of the nuclear envelope and DNA fragmentation. Engulfment by nearby phagocytic cells ultimately occurs as a result. Apoptotic cells release signals which attract phagocytic cells. The engulfment of fragments of the dying cell prevents viruses or other dangerous cell contents from spilling out of the damaged cell.

Loss of cell cycle controls in cancer cells

Cancer cells are abnormal cells with a variety of dangerous properties, making them a serious threat to the body. They invade and destroy normal tissue, causing serious illness and death. Cancerous cells do not normally respond to the body's control mechanism. They no longer respond to inhibitory growth factors and do not require as many stimulatory growth factors. They may produce the required external growth factor (or override factors) themselves or possess abnormal signal transduction sequences which falsely convey growth signals, thereby bypassing normal growth checks. Due to their irregular growth cycles, if the growth of cancer cells does occur, it does so at random points of the cell cycle.

Cancer can kill the organism because these cells can divide indefinitely if given a continual supply of nutrients. Normally, DNA segments called *telomeres to* form the ends of chromosomes and shorten with each replication, eventually signaling the cell to stop dividing. However, cancer cells produce the enzyme telomerase, which keeps telomeres long and allows the cells to continue dividing. The cell is "*immortal.*"

Unlike normal cells which differentiate, cancer cells are non-specialized. Cancer cells do not exhibit contact inhibition; they do not avoid crowding neighboring cells but rather pile up and grow on one another. This behavior creates the characteristic tissue mass as a tumor.

Not all tumors are necessarily dangerous. A *benign tumor* is encapsulated and does not invade adjacent tissue. However, benign tumors can still compress and damage nearby tissue, and some benign tumors have the potential to become *malignant* (cancerous). Malignancy occurs when new tumors are spread to areas distant from the primary tumor by *metastasis.*

Angiogenesis, the formation of new blood vessels, is a process required for metastasis. Angiogenesis is triggered when cancer cells release a growth factor that causes nearby blood vessels to grow and transport nutrients and oxygen to the tumor. Because of angiogenesis in metastasis, angiogenesis inhibitors are an important class of cancer drugs.

Cancer cells have abnormal nuclei that may be enlarged and have an abnormal number of chromosomes, as some chromosomes are mutated, duplicated or deleted.

When the DNA repair system fails to correct mutations during DNA replication, damage to crucial genes may occur. *Oncogenes* encode growth factor proteins such as Ras, which stimulate the cell cycle, while tumor-suppressor genes encode proteins such as p53 that inhibit the cell cycle. Mutations of oncogenes or tumor suppressor can cause cancer.

Mutation of proto-oncogenes may convert them into *oncogenes*, which are cancer-causing genes. An oncogene can cause cancer by coding for a faulty receptor in the stimulatory pathway, for an abnormal protein product or for abnormally high levels of a normal product that stimulates the cell cycle. About 100 oncogenes have been identified; the *ras* gene family includes variants associated with lung, colon, and pancreatic cancers, as well as leukemia and thyroid cancers.

Mutation of tumor-suppressor genes results in unregulated cell growth. For example, the *p53* tumor-suppressor gene is more frequently mutated in human cancers than any other known gene; it normally functions to trigger cell cycle inhibitors and stimulate apoptosis. However, if it malfunctions due to mutation, cell growth is not suppressed, and cancer may result.

Biosignaling

Rhythmic fluctuations in the abundance and activity of cell-cycle control molecules pace the events of the cell cycle. One example of these control molecules are *kinases*, proteins which activate or deactivate other proteins by phosphorylation. They are responsible for a procession through the G_1 and G_2 checkpoints. To give the signal, the kinases themselves must be activated by a *cyclin* protein. Because of this requirement, these kinases are called cyclin-dependent kinases (CDKs). Cyclins, named for their cycling concentration in the cell, accumulate during the G_1, S, and G_2 phases of the cell cycle. By the G_2 checkpoint, enough cyclin is available to form a complex of cyclin and CDK called the *maturation-promoting factor* (MPF), or the M-Phase-promoting factor. MPF initiates progression from the G_2 to the M phase by phosphorylating key proteins involved in mitosis. Later in mitosis, MPF switches itself off by initiating a process which leads to the destruction of cyclin. Cdk, the non-cyclin component of MPF, persists in the cell in an inactive form until it associates with the new cyclin molecules synthesized during interphase of the next round of the cell cycle.

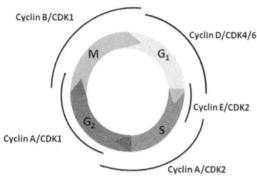

Cyclin-dependent kinases (CDK) and cyclin relationship to regulate the cell cycle

Platelet-derived growth factor (PDGF) is another protein that regulates cell growth and division. PDGF is required for the division of *fibroblasts*, connective tissue cells essential in wound healing. When an injury occurs, platelet blood cells release PDGF, which then binds to fibroblast receptors and activates a signal-transduction pathway that leads to a proliferation of fibroblasts and healing of the wound.

Growth factors released by platelets in wound healing

The extracellular environment has a direct effect on cell division. Cells grown in culture rapidly divide until a single layer of cells is spread over the area of the petri dish. However, if cells are removed, those bordering the open space begin dividing again and continue to do so until the gap is filled. This propensity to avoid division when in contact with neighboring cells is density-dependent inhibition of growth. When a cell population reaches a critical density, the amount of required growth factors and nutrients available to each cell becomes insufficient to allow continued cell growth.

Anchorage is another extracellular factor that controls cell division. For most animal cells to divide, they must be anchored to a substratum, such as the extracellular matrix of a tissue or the inside of a culture plate. Anchorage is signaled via pathways involving membrane proteins and the cytoskeleton.

Notes for active learning

Notes for active learning

Gametogenesis by Meiosis

Gametogenesis is the meiotic cell division that produces eggs (oogenesis) and sperm (spermatogenesis). *Meiosis* is a nuclear division that is broken into two broad stages (meiosis I and meiosis II), which reduces the chromosome number from diploid (2n) to haploid (n). The haploid number is half of the diploid number of chromosomes. Meiosis of one diploid cell results in the production of four haploid cells. These daughter cells, containing half the genetic information, are *gametes.*

Before fertilization, the building blocks to create that cell must be available, so that the initial fertilized cell (zygote) can develop into an embryo, fetus and a mature adult. Developing gametes (egg and sperm) are germ cells, and the first stage in their development is the proliferation of primordial germ cells by mitosis (replication via cell division), in which each daughter cell receives a full set of chromosomes identical to those of the original cell. In females, mitosis activity of germ cells occurs only during embryonic development, while in males it begins at puberty and continues throughout life. For many years, it was believed that at birth, females contain all the egg cells that they will ever have. However, new findings are coming to light with regards to mitotic activity in female gonads, and the idea that females do not produce new eggs during their lifetime is beginning to change with new research.

The next stage of development is meiosis, in which each daughter cell receives half of the chromosomes of the original cell. During meiosis, chromosomes stay in their homologous pairs. In humans, for example, instead of 46 individual chromosomes lining up, there are 23 pairs of chromosomes. Gamete production via meiosis occurs in all sexually reproducing eukaryotes, including animals, plants and fungi.

Sexual reproduction results in the formation of gametes. Human males produce small, motile sperm in the testes, and human females produce a large, immobile, nutrient-laden egg or ovum in the ovarian follicles. These gametes fuse to form a *zygote.* A zygote has the full or diploid (2n) number of chromosomes. If gametes contained the same number of chromosomes as somatic (body) cells, the zygote would have twice the correct number of chromosomes. When the gametes fuse, the chromosomes from both parents naturally combine. Each fertilized egg (zygote) cell has a pair of homologous chromosomes, one 1N homolog from the mother (egg) and one 1N homolog from the father (sperm).

During meiosis, the chromosomes align within the daughter cells in many possible combinations. $(2^{23})^2$ or about 70 trillion combinations are possible without crossing over. This allows for genetic variability in sexually reproducing organisms. Crossing over is the process during meiosis I, where homologous chromosomes are paired with another (synapsis) and can exchange their genetic material to form genetically unique (recombinant) chromosomes. If crossing over occurs once, then $(4^{23})^2$ or 70 trillion squared genetically different zygotes are possible for one couple. Crossing over is unique to prophase I of meiosis.

The Phases of Meiosis

Meiosis I is a reduction stage (2n → 1n), meiosis II separates sister chromatids at the centromere

Both meiosis I and meiosis II have four phases: prophase, metaphase, anaphase, and telophase. Prior to meiosis I, DNA replication occurs in S phase of interphase and each chromosome has a pair of sister chromatids; attached at the centromere (similar to mitosis for somatic cells).

Meiosis I: reduction phase of diploid to haploid (2n → 1n)

In general, during meiosis I, homologous chromosomes come together and line up at the synapsis. During synapsis, the two sets of paired chromosomes lay alongside each other as bivalents (tetrads). Bivalents are a pair of related homologous (one from the mother and one from the father) chromosomes that are held together by a chiasma complex.

Prophase I

1. Nuclear division occurs: nucleolus disappears, nuclear envelope fragments, centrosomes migrate away from each other and spindle fibers assemble.

2. Homologous chromosomes undergo synapsis, forming bivalents; crossing over may occur, in which case sister chromatids exchange genetic material by recombination.

3. Chromatin condenses, and chromosomes become microscopically visible.

Metaphase I

1. During prometaphase, I, bivalents held together by chiasmata move toward the metaphase plate at the equator of the cell.

2. The fully formed spindle aligns the bivalents at the metaphase plate.

3. Kinetochores are proteins associated with centromeres; they attach to *kinetochore spindle fibers* anchored to the centrioles at each pole of the cell.

4. Homologous chromosomes independently align at the metaphase plate.

5. Maternal and paternal homologs may be oriented toward either pole.

Anaphase I

1. The homologs separate and move toward opposite poles.

2. Each chromosome is attached with a centromere and two sister chromatids (replicated previously during S phase).

Telophase I

1. In animals, this occurs at the end of meiosis I.

2. The nuclear envelope reforms and nucleoli reappear.

3. This phase may or may not be accompanied by cytokinesis for portioning the two nuclei with separate plasma membranes (i.e., two daughter cells).

Interkinesis

1. This period between meiosis I and meiosis II is similar to the interphase between mitotic divisions.

2. However, no DNA replication (as in S phase of mitosis) occurs; the chromosomes are 1n (each chromosome has a sister chromatid).

Meiosis II: 1n → 1n

Before meiosis II begins, the DNA does not replicate, and the sister chromatids are still attached by the centromere. During meiosis II, the centromeres split and the sister chromatids separate. Chromosomes in the four daughter cells only contain one chromatid. Counting the number of centromeres verifies the number of chromosomes. Fertilization then restores the diploid number (2n) in the zygote and subsequent somatic cells originating from this zygote.

1. During metaphase II, the haploid chromosomes (with sister chromatids) aligns at the metaphase plate.

2. During anaphase II, sister chromatids separate at the centromeres and the two daughter

chromosomes move toward the poles.

3. Due to crossing over in prophase I, each gamete can contain chromosomes with different gene combinations than either parent.

4. At the end of telophase II and cytokinesis, there are four haploid cells (1 sperm for males and 1 egg and 3 polar bodies for females).

5. In animals, the haploid cells mature and develop into gametes, which may eventually fuse into a zygote (2n) from a 1n sperm and 1n egg.

6. In plants, the daughter cells become spores and divide to produce a haploid adult generation.

7. In some fungi and algae, a zygote results from gamete fusion and immediately undergoes meiosis; therefore, the adult is always haploid.

DNA is replicated only once before both mitosis and meiosis I and II; in mitosis, there is one nuclear division, while in meiosis there are two nuclei divisions between syntheses of DNA.

In humans, meiosis occurs only in reproductive organs to produce gametes, while mitosis occurs in somatic cells (not germline cells) for growth and repair.

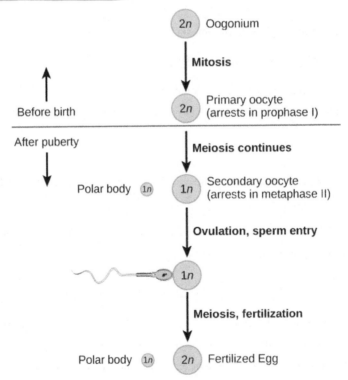

Meiosis generates 4 unique haploid cells while mitosis generates two identical diploid cells.

• During prophase I of meiosis, homologous chromosomes pair for crossing over, which increases genetic variation. Crossing over does not occur during mitosis.

• During metaphase I of meiosis, homologous chromosomes align at the metaphase plate; in mitosis, individual chromosomes align.

- During anaphase I in meiosis, homologous chromosomes, with centromeres intact, separate and move to opposite poles; in mitosis at this stage, sister chromatids separate and move to opposite poles.

- Events of meiosis II are now the same stages as in mitosis; however, the nuclei contain the haploid number of chromosomes in meiosis.

- Mitosis produces two genetically identical diploid daughter cells; meiosis produces four genetically different haploid daughter cells (4 sperm or 1 egg and 3 polar bodies).

Notes for active learning

Sperm and Ovum

In human males, meiosis is part of *spermatogenesis*, the production of sperm, and occurs in the testes. In human females, meiosis is part of *oogenesis*, the production of egg cells, and occurs in the ovaries.

Differences in the formation of the egg and sperm

Spermatogenesis occurs in the seminiferous tubules in the testes and produces sperm from primary spermatocytes. *Spermatogonia* are undifferentiated germ cells that divide by mitosis and differentiate into *primary spermatocytes*. Primary spermatocytes grow and undergo the first meiotic division to form *secondary spermatocytes*. In the secondary spermatocyte stage, cells undergo a second meiotic division to form *spermatids*.

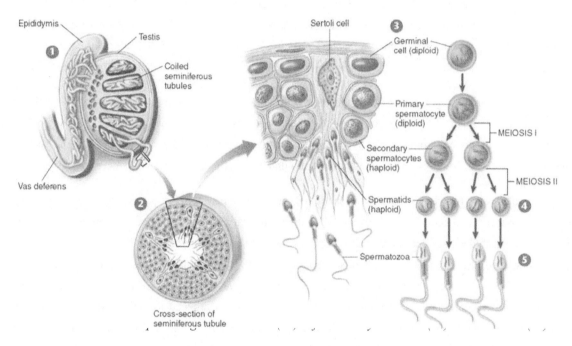

The spermatogonium replicates all of its chromosomes during interphase. It has 46 primary spermatocyte chromosomes, and each chromosome is made of two sister chromatids joined by a centromere. The cell undergoes prophase I, where the homologous chromosomes line up on spindles at the equator. The cell undergoes anaphase I (reduction phase of meiosis), but the centromeres do not divide. Instead, the homologous chromosome pairs separate. During telophase I, two cells are formed. Each cell is a secondary spermatocyte that now contains 23 chromosomes, and each chromosome has two chromatids joined by a centromere. These cells are haploid. Each of these cells then goes through meiosis II: prophase II, metaphase II, anaphase II and telophase II. This second set of divisions DOES resemble mitosis. Chromosomes condense (but do not pair up) during prophase II. The chromosomes align by spindle fibers during metaphase II, and the centromeres divide during anaphase II. The cells finish dividing during telophase II. At the end of meiosis II, there are four haploid cells with 23 chromosomes.

Spermatids, formed from the division of the secondary spermatocytes, develop into mature spermatozoa (sperm). *Sertoli cells* are stimulated by follicle-stimulating hormone (FSH) in the seminiferous tubules and surround and provide nourishment to spermatids during differentiation. They complete maturation (e.g., gain of motility) in the epididymis. *Sertoli cells* also secrete the peptide hormone *inhibin* (acts on the pituitary gland to inhibit FSH release) and *androgen-binding protein* (binds testosterone and acts as an intermediary between germ cells and hormones). The Sertoli cells divide the tubules into compartments with separate environments where different stages of spermatogenesis continue. *Leydig cells* between the tubules produce testosterone in the presence of luteinizing hormone (LH).

Sperm produced in the testes mature within the *epididymides*. These are tightly-coiled tubules outside of the testes. The maturation time in the epididymis is required for sperm to develop the ability to swim. Once sperm has matured, they are propelled into the *vasa deferentia* by muscular contractions. Sperm is stored in the epididymides and the vasa deferentia.

Oogenesis results in the production of a single ovum from a single primary oocyte. Unlike spermatogenesis, the *ovarian cycle* occurs in a monthly rhythm and usually produces only one gamete (egg) per month. Each egg develops in its own bubble-like *follicle*, located primarily in the cortex. Each month, about 20 to 25 *primordial follicles* resume their development. The single layer of squamous follicular cells around the oocyte thicken into cuboidal cells. The follicle is then a *primary follicle*. As the egg enlarges, the follicular cells multiply and pile up into multiple strata; the follicle is then a *secondary follicle*, and the follicular cells are *granulosa cells*.

Oogonia are primitive germ cells that undergo mitosis and develop into *primary oocytes* (with 46 chromosomes), which are the initial cells in oogenesis. Primary oocytes remain in meiotic arrest (i.e., begin first meiotic development but do not complete it). All of the germ cells in a female are believed to be at this developmental stage at birth. However, this is an area currently under investigation by researchers.

Primary oocytes are found in the ovaries of the female reproductive system. Oogenesis occurs on a monthly basis, beginning at puberty and ending at menopause. At puberty, primary oocytes destined for complete ovulation undergo meiosis, and each daughter cell receives 23 chromosomes. Although some primary oocytes undergo *atresia* (immature and degraded) during childhood, there are about 300,000 to 400,000 oocytes at puberty. When the primary oocyte divides, one of the two daughter cells, the *secondary oocyte*, retains most of the cytoplasm. The *first polar body* is the other daughter cell, is nonfunctional and (often) does not proceed to meiosis II. The secondary oocyte proceeds to the metaphase II of meiosis and then suspends. Meiosis II resumes if fertilization occurs. The completion of meiosis II allows the secondary oocyte to become a fertilized egg (2n zygote when fused with the sperm).

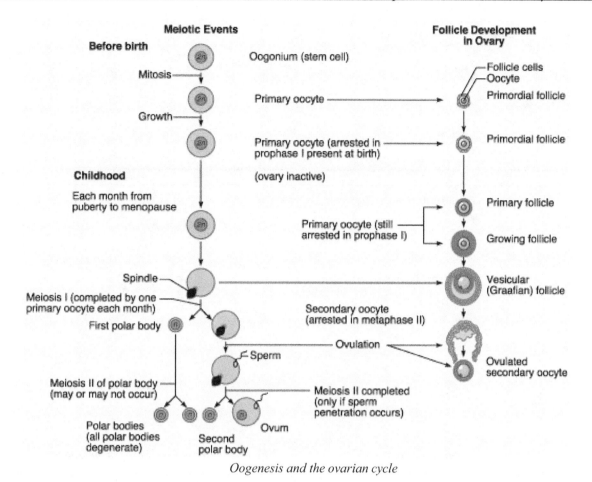

Oogenesis and the ovarian cycle

The meiotic division produces two *second polar bodies* that disintegrate because they receive insufficient cytoplasm. Second polar bodies are ultimately absorbed by the body and serve to retain most of the cytoplasm in the egg. The cytoplasm serves as a source of nutrients for the developing embryo. This is different from spermatogenesis, in which four functional, mature sperm are produced from a single spermatogonium.

A single ovum is produced per month. Normally, only one of the tertiary follicles becomes a fully mature *vesicular* (Graafian) *follicle* or the *tertiary follicle* destined to ovulate. Ovulation occurs around day 14 of a typical cycle. The follicle swells and bursts, releasing the egg and *cumulus oophorus* (a mass of follicular cells surrounding the ovum in the vesicular ovarian follicle) into the mouth of the uterine tube.

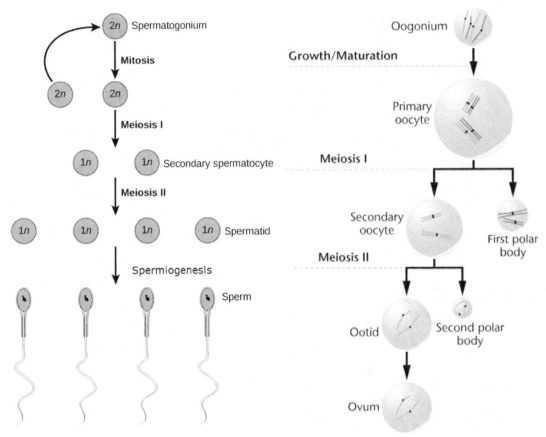

Male spermatogenesis with haploid
secondary spermatocytes (1n) and
spermatids (1n)

Female oogenesis with 1 ovum and (up to)
3 polar bodies

Male and female gametogenesis		
Male	**Female**	**Difference**
Spermatogonium (2n)	Oogonium (2n)	Spermatogonium renews its population by mitosis throughout life. Oogonium stops renewing its population before birth
Primary spermatocyte (1n)	Primary oocyte (1n)	Primary oocyte arrests at prophase I
Secondary spermatocyte (1n)	Secondary oocyte (1n)	Secondary oocyte arrests at metaphase II
Sperm (1n)	Ovum (1n)	Between the secondary spermatocyte and sperm is the spermatid

Differences in morphology

Sperm is compact cells of DNA with flagella that provide motility.

Eggs are non-motile and filled with cytoplasm.

Human spermatozoon with head, midpiece, and tail

Spermatozoa (mature sperm) have three parts. The sperm *head* (haploid with 23 chromosomes), contains a nucleus and DNA covered by an acrosome. The *acrosome* is a cap-like covering over the anterior end of the nucleus that stores enzymes to help the sperm penetrate the several layers of cells and thick membrane enclosing the egg. The *middle piece* contains multiple mitochondria for energy wrapped around microtubules of the flagellum in a $9 + 2$ microtubule array. The *tail* contains microtubules as components of a flagellum for its whip-like movement propelling the sperm. The ejaculate of a human male contains several hundred million sperms. Fewer than 100 ever reach the vicinity of an egg, and usually, only one sperm ultimately enters an egg.

The ovum (egg cell) is the female gamete. Unlike sperm, the egg is not capable of active movement. The egg is also much larger than the sperm (it is visible to the naked eye). Human sperm is about 55 micrometers (μm) in length (head is 5 μm, and flagellum is 50 μm). A mature ovum is between 120-150 μm in diameter. Therefore, the ratio of the length of the sperm to the diameter of the egg is about 1:3. Comparing the width of a sperm cell (~3 μm) to an egg's diameter, the ratio is about 1:50.

The *granulosa cells* produce a glycoprotein gel layer as the *zona pellucida* around the egg; the connective tissue around the granulosa cells condenses into a tough fibrous *theca folliculi*. The granulosa cells secrete *follicular fluid*, which forms small pools. The follicle is then a *tertiary follicle*. The fluid pools eventually coalesce to form a single cavity, the *antrum*. The egg is now held against one side of the antrum by a collection of cells of the *cumulus oophorus*; the innermost layer of these cells is the *corona radiata*.

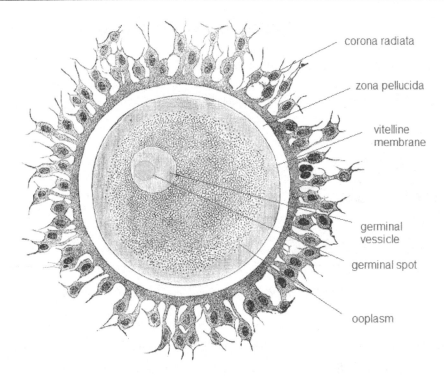

Human ovum with the protective glycoprotein layer of zona pellucida
and inner vitelline membrane enclosing the ooplasm.

The relative contribution to the next generation

Sexual reproduction produces offspring that combine genes from each parent. It entails the union of two gametes (ovum and sperm) to form a zygote (fertilized egg). The gametes, each containing half the genetic information needed to produce the 2n progeny.

Sperm contributes to the chromosomal DNA only, as the egg actively destroys any mitochondria in the sperm. The egg contributes chromosomal DNA and everything else (mitochondria, organelles, and biomolecules within the ooplasm) within the large volume of cytoplasm (i.e., 1 large egg and 3 small, non-functional polar bodies). The egg contains the cytoplasm nutrients and biomolecules needed by a developing embryo.

A diploid zygote (haploid sperm and haploid egg) represents the first stage in the development of a genetically unique organism. The zygote contains the essential components needed for development as the genes of chromosomes. The genes of the zygote are not activated to produce proteins until after several cleavage divisions. During cleavage, the large zygote subdivides into cells of a more conventional size via mitosis. After initial cleavage, blastomeres are the initial cells of an organism's development.

Notes for active learning

Notes for active learning

Chapter 3

Microbiology

- **Virus Structure**

- **Viral Life Cycle**

- **Bacteria Structure**

- **Prokaryotic Cell: Growth and Physiology**

- **Prokaryotic Cell: Genetics**

- **Control of Gene Expression in Prokaryotes**

Virus Structure

In 1884, French microbiologist Louis Pasteur suspected that an infectious agent smaller than bacteria caused the rabies disease. In 1892, Russian biologist Dimitri Ivanovsky confirmed Pasteur's hypothesis about the existence of such agents while working with the tobacco mosaic virus. He showed that passing crushed leaf extracts from infected tobacco plants through a filter with pores smaller than bacteria resulted in a filtered solution that was still infectious. With new technologies, such as the electron microscope (developed in the 1930s), these infectious agents could be visualized for the first time. The term *virus* (Latin term for "poison") was used to name these microscopic agents.

Viruses are believed to have originated from the cells that they infect, implying that their nucleic acids originated from host cell genomes. This hypothesis implies that viruses emerged after cells came into existence. Viruses can mutate and evolve, so a vaccine that is specific for a virus may not always be effective. For example, the flu virus (influenza) mutates regularly and requires the development of new vaccines for protection each year.

Viruses are spread between organisms in several ways. Airborne transmission occurs when viruses in open air infect an organism. Blood-borne transmission occurs when viruses in foreign blood or other bodily fluids enter an organism's circulatory system and cause infection. Additionally, contamination of an organism's water or food supply with viruses can cause transmission.

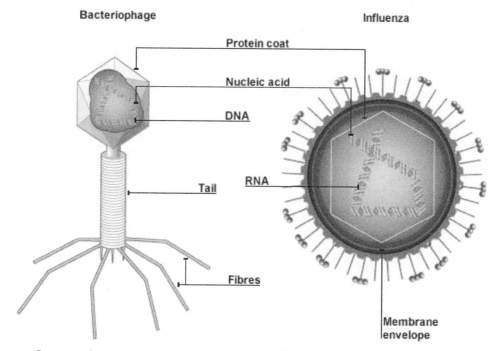

Common elements are an outer protein coat and nucleic acid as the genetic material.

Bacteriophages (or phages) are viruses that infect bacterial cells. The *head* stores the genetic material, the fibers of the *tail* attach to the host bacterium, and the *sheath* provides a passageway for the genetic material to be injected into the host bacterium.

General structural characteristics
(nucleic acid and protein, enveloped and nonenveloped)

Viruses are small particles containing as few as three or as many as several hundred genes. They are host specific and, as a class of particles, can infect virtually any cell type. Viruses have at least two parts: an outer capsid composed of protein subunits and an inner core containing their genetic (DNA or RNA) material.

Their genetic material and structure classify viruses. Their nucleic acid may be DNA or RNA and can exist as either a single-stranded (ssRNA or ssDNA) or double-stranded (dsRNA or dsDNA).

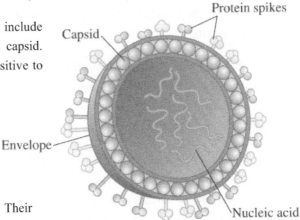

Viruses vary in size and shape, and some viruses include an envelope as an additional layer outside of the protein capsid. Enveloped viruses are generally less virulent and more sensitive to degradation compared to nonenveloped viruses.

Viruses can have surface extensions, molecules extending from the capsid that allow the virus to interact with host cells (cell infected with a virus), such as protein spikes.

Viruses do not contain organelles or a nucleus. Their genetic (RNA or DNA) material is packed inside the protein capsid.

Structure of an enveloped virus with

protein spikes for host specificity

Genomic content (RNA or DNA)

Viruses cannot replicate their nucleic acid (DNA or RNA) or synthesize their proteins. They use host cell machinery for replication, transcription, and translation. Their single-stranded or double-stranded DNA or RNA encodes for the proteins necessary to make new viruses. The viral genome has several hundred genes at most, whereas a human cell contains about 20,000 protein-coding genes.

Although the host cell provides the synthetic machinery needed for viral activity and replication, the viral genomes of some viruses may encode special proteins that they require. For example, a special RNA replicase (RNA-dependent RNA polymerase) replicates viral RNA genomes directly from the RNA template.

Size relative to bacteria and eukaryotic cells

A virus is similar in size to a large protein and is usually under 200 nm in diameter (although some are larger). Viruses are roughly 100 times smaller than bacteria and 1,000 times smaller than most eukaryotic cells.

Notes for active learning

Notes for active learning

Viral Life Cycle

Self-replicating biological units that reproduce within the host cell

The prime directive of all organisms is to reproduce and survive, and this applies to viruses. Viruses are tiny carriers of nucleic acid surrounded by various proteins and a membrane. Due to their size and simplicity, they are unable to replicate outside a living cell. Thus, viruses are *obligate intracellular parasites*. Viruses possess both living and non-living characteristics, but generally, are not considered "living organisms." They are noncellular, cannot metabolize and do not respond to stimuli.

Within a host, viruses need to reproduce before it dies for the infection to propagate. By altering the genetic makeup of a cell, viruses hijack the host cell's synthetic machinery to replicate their genetic material and synthesize their proteins. Viruses multiply inside the cell, and they eventually spread to other cells to repeat the process.

Viruses cause infectious diseases in plants and animals, including humans. Some viruses are specific to human cells (e.g., human papillomavirus and the hepatitis B virus). Some are cancer-producing because they contain *oncogenes*, which are normal genes that mutate to cause cells to undergo repeated divisions.

In humans, viral diseases are controlled by preventing transmission, administering vaccines, and recently through the use of antiviral drugs. Antibiotics are chemicals derived from bacteria or fungi that are harmful to other microorganisms. Antibiotics cannot treat viral infections because viruses use host cell enzymes, not their enzymes, and interfering with the host cell's enzymes would harm the infected organism.

There are over one thousand viruses in plants that cause disease. These viral infections are difficult to distinguish from nutrient deficiencies, and plants generally propagate in a way to avoid viral infection.

Viruses are specific to a type of cell or species because they bind to host cell receptors. The *host range* is the set of all host organisms that a virus can infect. For example:

- Tobacco mosaic virus only infects certain plants
- The rabies virus infects only mammals
- The AIDS virus (HIV-1) infects only white blood cells in humans
- Hepatitis virus invades only liver tissues
- Poliovirus only reproduces in spinal nerve cells

Generalized phage and animal virus life cycles

Viruses have two life cycles: the lytic cycle and lysogenic cycle. The *lytic cycle* involves attachment to and penetration of the host cell, followed by the replication of genetic material, the synthesis of proteins and the release of newly-assembled viruses. The *lysogenic cycle* is essentially a dormant (or latent) stage connected to the lytic cycle. After attachment and penetration, the viral genome integrates into the host genome as a *provirus* (or *prophage* if the host is a bacterium). There it remains inactive for a period, passing to all daughter cells (or *lysogenic cells*) as the host cell divides. Certain stimuli (e.g., UV radiation or nutritional stress) trigger the virus to exit the lysogenic cycle and begin replication and protein synthesis of the lytic cycle.

Formation of a prophage: the virus is shown at the top, attached to the bacterial cell, before injection of the viral genome

Viral life cycles depend on the type of nucleic acid, which influences how replication, transcription, and translation must be carried out.

DNA viruses use the typical DNA-dependent DNA polymerases to replicate their DNA. The DNA can be transcribed into mRNA, which is then translated for viral proteins. The replicated DNA and translated proteins assemble into virions (complete virus particles).

RNA viruses do not have to be immediately transcribed as DNA viruses do. Their RNA serves as the mRNA transcript, which is translated to form the viral proteins. However, they use RNA-dependent RNA polymerase encoded in their genome to replicate their RNA. This replicated RNA and the translated proteins assemble into new virions.

Alternative pathways for RNA virus

Attachment to host cell, penetration of cell and entry of viral material

During *attachment*, portions of the viral capsid adhere to specific sites on the host cell surface. If the virus is enveloped, glycoprotein spikes often serve as ligands for attachment. The attachment step is the basis for host cell specificity (i.e., why viruses that infect one cell type cannot infect another cell type with different characteristics and surface receptors). For bacteria with cell walls, viruses may use an enzyme to digest the rigid peptidoglycan cell wall and allow penetration. Teichoic acids, which provide rigidity in the cell walls of Gram-positive bacteria, are common binding sites.

Penetration is one of many means by which genetic material can enter a host cell. Bacteriophages use a syringe-like mechanism to inject their genetic material; the head and the rest of the protein body remain outside the host cell. Other nonenveloped viruses often enter the cell through *endocytosis*, an engulfing process where the entire virus enters the cell. Enveloped viruses often enter similarly, but they first allow their envelope to fuse with the host membrane before their genetic material and protein coat enter the cell.

Use of host synthetic mechanisms to replicate viral components

The *biosynthesis* stage of viral infection involves the synthesis of viral components. After the virus enters the host cell, the cell is altered to start transcribing the viral genetic material and translating the mRNA into viral protein. Additionally, the expression of host genes that are not necessary for viral replication is decreased. The viral genome replicates to form the genetic material of each new virus. The virus relies heavily on the host cell machinery, using the host's polymerases, ribosomes, tRNA, ATP, deoxyribonucleotide triphosphates (dNTP) and amino acids. Some viruses encode special enzymes (e.g., reverse transcriptase for RNA→DNA) required for their replication.

Self-assembly and release of new viral particles

The newly-produced capsid proteins and viral genetic material assemble into new viruses spontaneously within the host cell; this assembly is the *maturation* of the new viruses. The viruses are then released in one of two major ways. Nonenveloped viruses often exit using *lysis*, which involves the destruction of the host cell membrane for the release of viruses. If the host has a cell wall, the virus may use an enzyme (lysozyme) encoded in its genome to break it down. Enveloped viruses generally exit by *budding*, which involves coating the interior of the host cell membrane with viral proteins and then passing through the membrane. As the virus exits, it takes a piece of host membrane and becomes enveloped by it. Therefore, viral envelopes are derived largely from the host cell's membrane.

The common model of a phage is a nonenveloped virus released by lysis, and the common animal virus model is an enveloped virus that exits by budding. Many of the components of the viral envelope, such as lipids, proteins, and carbohydrates, are obtained from the plasma membrane or nuclear membrane of the host cell.

After exiting, the viruses are free to infect other cells. Viruses are obligate intracellular parasites and must spread extracellularly to find new host cells to infect.

Transduction as the transfer of genetic material by viruses

Transduction transfers DNA from one bacterium to another, using a bacteriophage as a vehicle. First, the bacteriophage introduces viral DNA to the bacterium. Then, during the lytic cycle, when viral DNA is assembled into new viruses, a portion of bacterial (host) DNA is assembled into a new virus with the viral genetic material. When this phage infects another host, the bacterial DNA it carries is introduced. This bacterial DNA in the new host is incorporated by *recombination* with its homologous counterpart in the host cell's DNA.

Retrovirus life cycle, integration into host DNA, reverse transcriptase

A *retrovirus* is a special type of single-stranded RNA virus that uses a DNA encoded intermediate in its life cycle. However, not all single-stranded RNA viruses are retroviruses. Once the RNA of a retrovirus enters the cell, it uses its reverse transcriptase to make a DNA complement of its RNA genome. This newly synthesized double-stranded DNA (complementary DNA or cDNA) is then transcribed to mRNA, which is translated into the viral proteins. The cDNA is integrated into the host genome at a random place by a virally-encoded enzyme (integrase), and this begins a lysogenic cycle, where the integrated DNA is replicated along with the host DNA. External stimuli and other factors cause this retroviral DNA to be transcribed, and new viruses are produced in a lytic cycle. Prophages often exit the host chromosome and reform into virions when they exit the lysogenic cycle. However, integrated retroviral DNA is typically transcribed like other genes in the host genome during the lysogenic cycle.

HIV-1 is a retrovirus that infects humans and is responsible for AIDS (Acquired Immune Deficiency Syndrome). It infects T4 lymphocytes (white blood cells), a component of the human immune system. Depletion of these immune cells reduces a person's ability to fight infections.

Drugs used in the treatment of AIDS attack HIV-1 at the points of reverse transcription and viral protein synthesis. By inactivating processes that are unique to the virus life cycle, damage to the host cell is minimized. Different drugs are used to treat patients with HIV infection.

Nucleoside analogs halt transcription if they are incorporated into viral DNA.

Protease inhibitors prevent viral protein precursors from being processed.

Cell entry drugs block the insertion of viral RNA into the host cell.

Integrase inhibitors prevent incorporation into host DNA.

Prions and viroids are subviral particles

Prions are recently discovered disease agents that are neither viruses nor bacteria. They are proteins with a misfolded tertiary structure that inhibits the function of other proteins. These structures cause other proteins to misfold, leading to the accumulation of large amounts of prions in tissue.

Prions are infective agents that change the shape of some protein in the host

All known prion diseases are untreatable and ultimately fatal, including Creutzfeldt-Jakob disease in humans, as well as scrapie and mad cow disease (bovine spongiform encephalopathy) in cattle.

Viroids are strands of circular RNA without protein coats. Around thirty viroids have been identified, and about a dozen of them cause disease. Viroids do not encode for any protein; rather, they infect a host cell by using the host's RNA polymerase II to catalyze "rolling circle" synthesis of the viroid genome, which is hypothesized to play a role in RNA silencing. Viroids are smaller than other infectious agents.

Structure of a viroid - circular single-stranded RNA with some pairing
between complementary bases and loops where no pairing occurs

Notes for active learning

Bacteria Structure

Prokaryotic domains: Bacteria and Archaea

Prokaryotes include the Bacteria and Archaea domains of life. They were likely the first cells in evolutionary history; fossils of prokaryotes that date 3.5 billion years ago have been found. These fossils indicate that prokaryotes were alone on Earth for 2 billion years, during which time they evolved diverse metabolic capabilities and pathways.

Bacteria are encountered every day—they live inside and on humans and animals. Bacteria were discovered in the seventeenth century when Dutch naturalist Antonie van Leeuwenhoek examined scrapings from his teeth under a microscope. He called these organisms "little animals." At the time, it was believed that organisms could arise spontaneously from inanimate matter. Around 1850, Pasteur refuted the theory of spontaneous generation by showing that contamination was necessary for the growth of microbes. A single spoonful of soil can contain 10^{10} prokaryotic organisms; bacteria are the most numerous life form on Earth.

Classification of bacteria was originally based on metabolism and nutrition, among other characteristics. However, work done by Carl Woese since 1980 has revised the bacterial taxonomy based on similarity with 16S rRNA (genes encoding for the 30S small subunit of the prokaryotic ribosome). Bacteria were initially classified into 12 lineages based on these 16S rRNA sequences, but today the number of phyla has increased to around 52. Bacteria display a wide range of morphologies and live almost everywhere on the planet, including soil, water, hot springs and deep portions of the Earth's crust, and are vital for the recycling of many nutrients. They often live in symbiotic relationships with plants and animals, but some are pathogens that cause disease and even death.

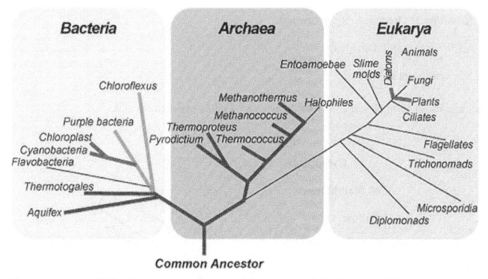

Three domains of life: Bacteria, Archaea and Eukarya and the lineage of their relationships

Archaea are prokaryotes with molecular characteristics that distinguish them from bacteria and eukaryotes. Archaea inhabit extreme environments, such as those with high salt, high temperature or harsh chemicals. Archaea and bacteria are believed to have diverged from a common ancestor about 3.7 billion years ago. The eukaryotes most likely split from archaea at some later time, as suggested by the fact that archaea and eukaryotes share some ribosomal proteins that absent in bacteria. Archaea and eukaryotes initiate transcription in the same manner and have similar types of tRNA.

Archaea come in many shapes, such as spherical, rod-shaped, spiraled, lobed, plate-shaped or irregular. DNA and RNA sequences in archaea are closer to eukaryotes than bacteria. The archaeal cell wall has various polysaccharides but no peptidoglycan, as in bacteria. Additionally, archaea may have unusual lipids in their plasma membranes (glycerol linked to hydrocarbons rather than fatty acids) that allow them to function at high temperatures. Most archaea are chemoautotrophs, and none are photosynthetic, suggesting that chemoautotrophs evolved first. Some exhibit mutualism or commensalism, but none are parasitic or known to cause disease.

There are many types of archaea, including methanogens, halophiles, and thermoacidophiles. *Methanogens* live in anaerobic environments (e.g., marshes), where they produce methane. Methane is produced from hydrogen gas and carbon dioxide, and its production is coupled with ATP formation. Methane released into the atmosphere contributes to the greenhouse effect. Methanogenic archaea produce about 65% of methane found in our atmosphere. *Halophiles* require high salt concentrations (e.g., Great Salt Lake). Their proteins use halorhodopsin (light-gated chloride pump) to synthesize ATP in the presence of light. They usually require salt concentrations of 12-15%; in comparison, ocean water is 3.5% salt. *Thermoacidophiles* thrive in hot, acidic environments (e.g., geysers). They survive best at temperatures around 80 °C, although this varies depending on the species. The metabolism of sulfides forms acidic sulfates, and they generally thrive at a pH between 2–3.

Major classifications:
bacilli (rod-shaped), spirilla (spiral-shaped) and cocci (spherical)

Most bacteria, on average, are 1–1.4 μm wide and 2–6 μm long, making them just visible with light microscopes. They have three basic shapes:

- A *bacillus* is elongated, or rod-shaped.

- A *spirillum* is spiral-shaped.

- A *coccus* is spherical.

Cocci and bacilliform clusters and chains that vary in size between species.

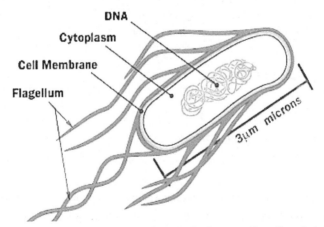

Escherichia coli (E. coli) bacterium with peptidoglycan cell wall and circular DNA

As cells get larger in volume, the ratio of surface area relative to volume decreases, which imposes a limit to how large an actively metabolizing cells can become. The adequate surface area is required for vital processes, such as nutrient exchange across the plasma membrane. If there is too much cell volume and not enough surface area, the exchange rate does not support metabolism. Cells that need a greater surface area-to-volume ratio use modifications, such as folding or microvilli (small projections of the membrane) that increase the surface area while minimizing the additional volume associated with these modifications.

Lack of nuclear membrane and mitotic apparatus

Unlike eukaryotes, all prokaryotic cells lack a nucleus (prokaryote means "before a nucleus"). However, prokaryotes have a dense area where their DNA is concentrated, called the *nucleoid region*. It is irregularly shaped, dense with nucleic acid and not enclosed by any membrane. Prokaryotic DNA is a single, circular, double-stranded DNA chromosome. They do not have histones or associated proteins like eukaryotes. Bacterial cells may have additional *plasmids* or accessory circular DNA molecules. These plasmids, which are smaller than the genomic DNA, may confer additional abilities or characteristics (e.g., genes to encode proteins for antibiotic resistance).

Prokaryotes lack a mitotic apparatus, which is used in eukaryotes to separate chromosomes during mitosis. Instead, prokaryotes use their cytoskeleton to pull the replicated DNA apart during binary fission resulting in cell division.

Lack of typical eukaryotic organelles

Prokaryotic cells lack the membranous organelles of eukaryotic cells. They do not have the Golgi apparatus or endoplasmic reticulum, nor do they have mitochondria or chloroplasts. Their cytoplasm is a semifluid solution with the enzymes needed for essential chemical reactions. Some may have *inclusion bodies*, which are granules that store various substances.

Prokaryotes have thousands of ribosomes for protein synthesis, but they are smaller (the 30S, 50S subunits; 70S assembled) than eukaryotic (40S, 60S subunits; 80S assembled) ribosomes.

Prokaryotes have a cell wall

Like eukaryotes, prokaryotes have a typical plasma membrane with a phospholipid bilayer. The plasma membrane of prokaryotes can form internal pouches, *mesosomes*, that increase surface area for metabolic processes.

Outside the plasma membrane of bacteria, fungi and eukaryotic plant cells is a rigid *cell wall* that keeps the cell from bursting or collapsing due to osmotic changes. The bacterial cell wall is made of peptidoglycan, a polysaccharide-protein molecule that gives the wall much of its strength (archaea have cell wall polysaccharides, but no peptidoglycan). Plant cell walls are made of cellulose (polysaccharide of glucose monomers), and fungi cell walls are made of chitin. The cell wall protects the cell from the outside environment and maintains the shape of the cell. Additionally, some prokaryotes (e.g., Gram-negative bacteria) may have an *outer membrane* (lipopolysaccharide) outside their peptidoglycan cell wall.

Some prokaryotes have another layer of polysaccharides and proteins outside of their cell wall, a *glycocalyx* or *capsule*. The capsule is not easily washed off during experiments. Some prokaryotes may have a *slime layer*, a loose gelatinous sheath conferring some protection from environmental assaults (e.g., antibiotics or dehydration). The slime layer or capsule coverings are especially beneficial for parasitic prokaryotes as protection from host defenses.

Bacteria continuously remodel their peptidoglycan cell walls as they divide, which makes the cell wall a good drug target. β-lactam antibiotics (e.g., penicillin) prevent peptidoglycan cross-links in a bacterium's cell wall by inhibiting the enzyme that catalyzes the formation of these cross-links. This creates an imbalance in cell wall degradation and production, eventually causing the bacterium to lose its cell wall and become susceptible to rupture from osmotic pressure.

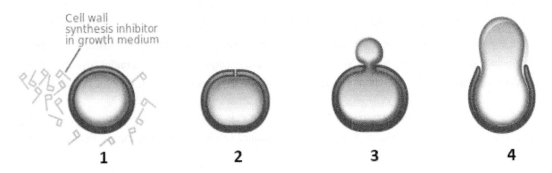

Penicillin's mechanism of action on peptidoglycan cell wall during cell division

The Gram stain procedure (developed in the late 1880s by Hans Christian Gram) differentiates bacteria based on their cell wall. The procedure involves first staining cells with crystal violet dye, washing away the dye, and then recoloring with a pink counterstain dye. Gram-positive bacteria stain purple, while Gram-negative bacteria stain pink.

The different results from the test are due to the differences in their structure. Gram-positive bacteria have a thick peptidoglycan layer and no outer membrane. Their thick peptidoglycan readily takes up the purple dye.

Gram-negative bacteria have a thin peptidoglycan layer surrounded by an outer membrane. They do take up the purple dye, but in the washing step (typically alcohol) their outer membranes are degraded, removing the purple color.

This washing step does not affect the thick peptidoglycan of the Gram-positive bacteria, leaving them purple. The recoloring with a pink dye is done to visualize the Gram-negative bacteria. The pink dye does not affect the purple color of the Gram-positive bacteria.

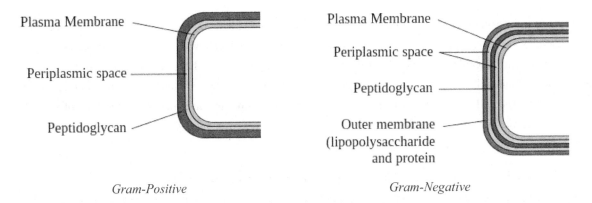

Gram-negative bacteria have a special *lipopolysaccharide* (LPS) in their outer membrane absent in Gram-positive bacteria. This is an *endotoxin*, and it invokes an immune response in humans. This outer membrane provides Gram-negative bacteria with some protection from antibiotics, while Gram-positive bacteria are generally more vulnerable to antibiotics.

Some bacteria in the *Firmicute* phylum (mostly Gram-positive) form resistant *endospores* in response to unfavorable environmental conditions. During spore formation, the bacterium's DNA, ribosomes, dipicolinic acid are encased by several protective spore layers: the exosporium, the spore coat, the spore cortex, and the core wall. The bacterial cell deteriorates, and the endospore is released.

Endospores can survive in the harshest of environments, including desert heat and dehydration, boiling temperatures, polar ice, and extreme ultraviolet radiation. Endospores survive for long periods of time (e.g., 1,300-year-old anthrax spores can cause disease). When environmental conditions are again suitable, the endospore absorbs water and grows out of its spore coat. In a few hours, newly emerged cells become typical bacteria that are capable of reproducing by binary fission. Endospore formation is not reproduction; rather, it is a dormant structure that aids in survival and dispersal to favorable locations.

Flagellar propulsion in bacteria

Some bacteria have *flagella* and are motile. The flagellum is a filament that is composed of three strands of the flagellin protein wound in a helix and inserted into a hook that is anchored by a *basal body*. A basal body is an organelle formed from a centriole and an array of microtubules. It is capable of 360° rotation, which causes the cell to spin and move forward. A motor powered by a proton (or sodium) gradient provides the energy. In contrast, flagella in eukaryotes are made of microtubules and are powered directly by ATP hydrolysis.

Flagellum for a Gram-negative bacteria (left) and Gram-positive bacteria (right)

Prokaryotes may have short, hair-like filaments or appendages *fimbriae*, that extend from their surface, which they can use to attach to another cell or inanimate object. The fimbriae of *Neisseria gonorrhoeae* allow it to attach to host cells and cause the disease gonorrhea.

Pili are similar appendages to fimbriae, but they are thicker and fewer in number. They help bacteria adhere to one another for motility or the exchange of genetic material.

Notes for active learning

Prokaryotic Cell: Growth and Physiology

Reproduction by fission

Prokaryotes reproduce by *binary fission*, a form of *asexual reproduction*, which results in offspring with genetically identical chromosomes.

Binary fission in prokaryotes is similar to mitosis in eukaryotes because both result in daughter cells that are identical to the parent cell. However, in multicellular fungi, plants, and animals, cell division is a routine part of the growth process that produces and repairs cells within the organism. In contrast, binary fission is the method of prokaryotic reproduction. Eukaryotic cells have a spindle apparatus, which is required for distributing chromosomes to daughter cells during mitosis, while prokaryotes divide without microtubules, spindles or centrioles. *E. coli* bacteria can divide in about 20 minutes, while eukaryotic cells may require between an hour and a day to divide.

Binary fission follows the sequence:

1. Before division, the single, circular DNA chromosome is replicated and attached to a special site tethered to the plasma membrane.

2. The two chromosomes separate as the cell enlarges and pulls them apart.

3. When the cell is approximately twice its original length, the plasma membrane grows inward, and a new polysaccharide cell wall (cell plate) bisects the cell and then the plasma membrane forms, dividing the cell into two roughly equal-sized daughter cells.

High degree of genetic adaptability and antibiotic resistance

Prokaryotes have evolved to live in a vast variety of environments because they have a high degree of genetic adaptability, allowing species to differ in how they acquire and utilize energy. There are many sources for genetic variation in prokaryotes. Mutations are generated and distributed through a population more rapidly because prokaryotes have a short generation time. Also, prokaryotes are haploid (single copy of a gene), so mutations are immediately subjected to natural selection. Additionally, plasmids (extrachromosomal circular pieces of DNA) can carry genes for resistance to antibiotics and transfer them between bacteria (e.g., transformation and conjugation), which are described in the chapter.

Exponential growth

The growth of bacteria can be modeled with phases. In the *lag phase*, bacteria adapt to the conditions of their particular environment; the cells are maturing but not yet dividing. In the *log phase*, bacteria grow exponentially in a medium with adequate space and nutrients because of binary fission. The rate of population increase doubles with each consecutive period (e.g., 20-minute intervals). However, this cannot continue indefinitely. The *stationary phase* is when food and space become scarce, growth slows and eventually plateaus. *Death* or *decline phase* is when there is a lack of nutrients or improper conditions, where the bacteria die.

Bacterial growth with a log phase before reaching a stationary phase

Bacteria as anaerobic and aerobic organisms

Bacteria differ in their need for and tolerance of oxygen (O_2). *Obligate anaerobes* are unable to grow in the presence of O_2; this includes the species of anaerobic bacteria of the *Clostridium* genus that cause botulism, gas gangrene, and tetanus. *Obligate aerobes* must have O_2 for growth and die without it. *Facultative anaerobes* can grow in either the presence or absence of gaseous O_2, although they grow better with the O_2 present.

An autotroph (i.e., a "producer") is an organism that is capable of self-nourishment; autotrophic prokaryotes include both photoautotrophs and chemoautotrophs. *Photoautotrophs* are photosynthetic and use light energy to assemble the organic molecules they require. Although the most well-recognized photoautotrophs are plants, many bacteria are in this category. *Primitive photosynthesizing bacteria*, such as green sulfur bacteria and purple sulfur bacteria, use bacteriochlorophyll and hydrogen sulfide (H_2S) as a proton and electron donor instead of H_2O, so they do not release O_2.

Advanced photosynthesizing bacteria, such as cyanobacteria, use bacteriochlorophyll and chlorophylls found in plants. H_2O is used as the proton and electron donor, so they do release O_2. *Chemoautotrophs* make organic molecules by using energy derived from the oxidation of inorganic compounds in the environment. Deep ocean hydrothermal vents provide H_2S and allow for the growth of chemosynthetic bacteria. The methanogens (previously mentioned in the context of archaea) include chemosynthetic bacteria that produce methane (CH_4) from hydrogen gas and CO_2. ATP synthesis and CO_2 reduction are linked to this reaction, and methanogens can even decompose animal wastes to produce electricity as an environmentally-friendly energy source. *Nitrifying bacteria* oxidize ammonia to nitrites (NH_3 to NO_2) and nitrites to nitrates (NO_2 to NO_3).

Heterotrophs cannot synthesize their food. Most free-living bacteria are *chemoheterotrophs* that take in pre-formed organic nutrients. With the existence of numerous *aerobic saprotrophs* (organisms that feed on the dead organic matter and use oxygen), there is probably no organic molecule that cannot be broken down by some prokaryotic species. *Decomposers* are critical in recycling materials in the ecosystem by decomposing dead organic matter and making it available to photosynthesizers.

Parasitic and symbiotic bacteria

Some bacteria are *symbiotic*, forming close, long-term relationships with members of other species, including *mutualistic* (both organisms benefit), *commensalism* (one organism benefits and the other is unaffected), and *parasitic* (one organism benefits while the other is harmed) relationships.

- Mutualistic nitrogen-fixing *Rhizobium* bacteria live in nodules on the roots of soybean, clover, and alfalfa, where they reduce nitrogen to ammonia, which the plant requires. *Rhizobium* bacteria use some of the plant's photosynthetically-produced organic molecules in return.

- Mutualistic bacteria that live in the intestines of humans benefit from partially-digested material and release vitamins K and B_{12}, which humans use to produce blood components.

- Mutualistic prokaryotes, in the stomachs of cows and goats, digest cellulose, which the animal cannot do by itself, and release nutrients that the cow or goat can use. In return, the bacteria get a warm, moist environment and a constant supply of food.

- Mutualistic cyanobacteria provide organic nutrients to fungi, and the fungus protects and supplies inorganic nutrients to the bacteria. This composite symbiotic organism is a *lichen*.

- Commensalistic bacteria live in (or on) organisms of other species and cause them no harm and no benefit, such as some bacterial species that live on the skin of humans.

- Parasitic bacteria (e.g., chlamydia or Cryptosporidium) are responsible for a wide variety of infectious plant and animal diseases.

-

Chemotaxis

Cells can engage in mechanical activities: they can move, and the organelles within them can move. *Cell migration* is the movement of cells from one location to another and is often the response to stimuli. *Chemotaxis* is movement in response to chemicals. For example, bacteria may swim toward the highest concentration of food molecules (positive chemotaxis) and may flee from poisons that they detect in their environment (negative chemotaxis). They can do this by sensing chemical gradients through transmembrane receptors that bind attractants (or repellents), and these receptors stimulate rotation of flagella, causing the bacteria to move.

Prokaryotes may engage in *phototaxis*, which is movable in response to light. Additionally, some prokaryotes can move in response to physical forces in their environment. This ability to respond to force is *mechanotaxis*.

Notes for active learning

Prokaryotic Cell: Genetics

Plasmids as extragenomic DNA

Plasmids are pieces of DNA that exist apart from the genomic DNA and are found in some prokaryotes. They range in size from less than one kilobase pair to several megabase pairs. Plasmids are generally circular, although examples of linear plasmids are known. They usually carry genes that are beneficial but are not always essential for growth and survival. Plasmids replicate independently of the genomic DNA, are inherited, and can be extracted in genetic engineering procedures to be used as vectors to carry foreign DNA into other bacteria. *Episomes* are plasmids that can incorporate themselves into the bacterial chromosome.

Bacterium with chromosomal DNA and plasmids

Conjugation

Conjugation transfers genetic material between bacteria via a sex pilus that temporarily joins a recipient bacterium. *Conjugative pili,* (sex pili) are the tubes specifically used by bacteria during conjugation to pass replicated DNA from one cell to another.

A plasmid is sent from the donor to the recipient through the sex pilus, where it can be incorporated through recombination. Plasmids can contain antibiotic resistance genes so that conjugation may allow the transfer of that resistance. The most well-studied example is the sex pilus of *E. coli* that possesses an F plasmid, which is an episome (e.g., plasmid) that contains the "fertility factor." Since an F plasmid is an episome, genomic DNA may be transferred in some instances. If the F plasmid is transferred to an F⁻ recipient and integrated successfully, the recipient becomes F⁺ and can then create its sex pili. Conjugation can occur between bacteria of the same species, closely related species or distantly related species. It is an important mechanism of horizontal gene transfer, which contributes to the genetic diversity of prokaryotes.

**Formation of sex pilus
that attaches to recipient**

Bacterial conjugation: donor (with plasmid) is on the left, the recipient is on the right

Transformation
(incorporation into the bacterial genome of DNA fragments from external medium)

Transformation is the process of bacteria taking up DNA fragments from outside the cell and incorporating them into their genomes. There are two major sources of these fragments: DNA secreted by live bacteria and DNA released from a bacterium that dies. When a cell lyses (i.e., breaks open), it spills its DNA into the environment. Successful transformation of DNA fragments containing an antibiotic resistant gene (i.e., plasmid) confers antibiotic resistance to the recipient bacterium.

Transposons

Transposons (transposable elements or "jumping genes") are pieces of DNA that can insert themselves into another place in the genome. They exist in both prokaryotes and eukaryotes and can move within or between chromosomes. The changes in the genome caused by transposon relocation in the genome can be advantageous, disadvantageous or neutral.

Some transposons make copies of themselves, and the copies are then inserted into other locations in the genome ("copy and paste"). Other transposons are removed from their original location in the DNA and insert themselves directly into another location ("cut and paste").

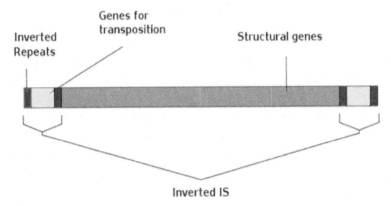

Bacterial DNA transposon flanked by inverted repeats as breakpoints on the DNA

Notes for active learning

Notes for active learning

Control of Gene Expression in Prokaryotes

Coupling of transcription and translation

Gene expression is the processes of *transcription* (DNA → RNA), and *translation* (RNA → proteins). These processes are described in detail in the molecular biology chapter.

There are differences between gene expression in eukaryotes and prokaryotes. Eukaryotes regulate gene expression at all levels (i.e., transcription, post-transcription, translation and post-translation), while prokaryotes regulate gene expression predominantly at the transcription level. In prokaryotes, this regulation largely consists of the actions of *transcription factors*, which are proteins with DNA-binding domains that affect transcription. Eukaryotes have transcription factors, but much of the regulation of gene expression occurs at other levels. For example, *RNA splicing* of the mRNA transcript, which occurs in eukaryotes, can alter the RNA in ways (alternative splicing) to result in the translation of the different protein. RNA splicing does not occur in prokaryotes, because prokaryotes do not have introns.

However, prokaryotes do have some regulation at the translation level. In prokaryotes, mRNA transcripts with a more accurate *Shine-Dalgarno sequence*, which attracts ribosome binding, are translated more readily. Eukaryotes, however, can make additional modifications to the mRNA to regulate translation, such as the 5' cap or 3' poly−A tail (which do not occur in prokaryotic mRNA).

Transcription-translation coupling in prokaryotes occurs during translation as the mRNA is being transcribed. It does not occur in eukaryotes because the modification of the RNA transcripts into mature mRNA occurs in the nucleus and translation occurs in the cytoplasm, requiring transport of the mRNA out of the nucleus before it can be translated. Prokaryotes do not have these restrictions since they have no membrane-enclosed nucleus and no RNA processing, so transcription and translation can occur concurrently.

Attenuation is a form of gene regulation in prokaryotes that uses a transcription-translation coupling. The *attenuator* is a sequence that can cause premature termination of transcription of a gene based on the activity of the ribosome. One example of attenuation is the *trp* operon, a collection of genes that encode for the components used in the synthesis of the amino acid tryptophan. The attenuation mechanism causes transcription to terminate when tryptophan levels are already high, which allows the bacterium to conserve resources.

There is a special sequence early in the *trp* operon that is particularly high in codons that specify tryptophan. When tryptophan levels are high, the ribosome quickly translates along this RNA. Once it translates a certain distance, interactions in the mRNA transcript cause a stem-loop to form, which includes the attenuator sequence. This loop acts as a stop signal; it interacts with the RNA polymerase, causing it to terminate transcription. When tryptophan levels are low, the ribosome stalls translation of the RNA rich in tryptophan codons, since it has difficulty locating tryptophan amino acids for the growing polypeptide. Because the ribosome stalls here, a different stem-loop forms—one that does not involve the attenuator sequence. This stem-loop does not act as a stop signal and allows the RNA polymerase to complete transcription of the operon without being terminated.

High level of tryptophan

Low level of tryptophan

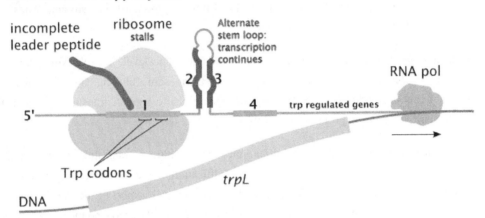

Attenuation in the trp gene; stem-loop formation depends on tryptophan levels

Operon Concept, Jacob–Monod Model

Bacteria do not require the same enzymes all the time, and they produce the enzymes needed at the moment. In 1961, Nobel Prize microbiologists Francois Jacob and Jacques Monod proposed the operon model to explain the regulation of gene expression in prokaryotes. *Operons* are a functional collection of DNA regulatory sequences and genes that work together to regulate transcription. In the operon model, several genes encode for enzymes in the same metabolic pathway and are located in a sequence on a chromosome; expression of these structural genes is controlled by the same regulatory genes, including a single promoter.

Operons consist of the following components:

- *Promoter*: DNA sequence where RNA polymerase attaches to initiate transcription

- *Operator*: a sequence of DNA that can block RNA polymerase when a repressor protein is bound to it

- *Structural genes*: the DNA sequences that encode for the related proteins; operons typically encode for *enzymes* (proteins that act as catalysts) in their structural genes

- *Regulatory genes* (or *regulators*): regions that may be within or outside of the operon region that encodes for repressor proteins or activator proteins, which regulate the attachment of RNA polymerase to the promoter. Activators and repressors are transcription factors. Repressor proteins work by binding to the operator to block RNA polymerase from attaching to the start site of transcription.

Transcription factors are proteins that bind to DNA sequences (*enhancers* or *silencers*) to affect transcription. *Activator* transcription factors bind to enhancers to increase transcription, while *repressor* transcription factors bind to silencers to decrease transcription. Enhancers and silencers in prokaryotes are close to the core promoter (i.e., the minimal portion of the promoter required for initiation of transcription) and are part of the extended promoter (a sequence upstream of the gene with additional regulatory elements). The *operator* in an operon is essentially a silencer because it decreases transcription when a repressor binds it.

The terms co-repressor and co-activator describe molecules that bind to activators and repressors, changing their shape to affect how well they can bind DNA and thus affect transcription. They function either by activating inactive proteins or by inactivating active proteins. They are named for their ultimate effect on transcription: *co-repressors* decrease transcription and *co-activators* increase transcription. When a co-repressor binds to its target, the resulting complex becomes either an active repressor or an inactive activator, which decreases transcription. When a co-activator binds to its target, the resulting complex becomes either an active activator or an inactive repressor, which increases transcription. In the *lac* operon, lactose works as a co-activator by inactivating a repressor. In this example, the lactose molecule is an *inducer*, and the resulting inducer-repressor complex is a *co-inducer*.

Gene repression in bacteria: trp operon

As previously discussed, the *trp* operon in bacteria is responsible for the transcription of the enzymes for tryptophan synthesis. The *trp* operon is organized so that the enzymes are transcribed when tryptophan levels are low and not transcribed when levels are high.

Regulatory genes in the region create the inactive repressor protein. This repressor becomes active when tryptophan binds to it. When tryptophan levels are high, tryptophan synthesis is unnecessary, so tryptophan acts as a co-repressor, and the repressor-co-repressor complex is now an active repressor. This active repressor binds to the operator, preventing RNA polymerase from transcribing the *trp* operon structural genes. Attenuation acts as a second form of repression in this operon.

When tryptophan levels are low, there are not enough tryptophan molecules to be effective as co-repressors, so the RNA polymerase can transcribe the structural genes that lead to tryptophan synthesis. This allows the tryptophan in the cell to be replenished.

Since the *trp* operon exists in the *on* state unless repression specifically acts on it, the enzymes of this operon are *repressible enzymes*. These types of enzymes are typically involved in anabolic pathways that synthesize substances needed by cells. The *trp* operon is repressible while the *lac* operon is inducible.

Trp operon as an example of negative feedback control (attenuation)

Positive control in bacteria: lac operon

The *lac* operon in *E. coli* and a few other species of bacteria control the genes responsible for the breakdown of the lactose sugar. Regulatory genes produce an active repressor that binds the operator and blocks RNA polymerase. When lactose is available in the environment and is ready for the breakdown, allolactose (an isomer of lactose) binds to the active repressor, creating an inactive repressor. The operator is no longer bound, and RNA polymerase can now bind the promoter and transcribe the structural genes.

Structural genes in the *lac* operon are transcribed to metabolize the lactose. Lactose permease facilitates the entry of lactose into the cell. β-galactosidase breaks down lactose into glucose and galactose. Thiogalactoside transacetylase is an accessory in lactose metabolism.

Unlike the *trp* operon, regulatory genes in the *lac* operon create an active repressor. Lactose inactivates the repressor, creating an inactive repressor. The allolactose inducer is a co-inducer or a co-activator, and the enzymes in the structural genes are *inducible enzymes*.

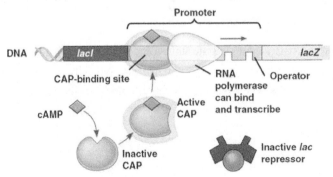

The presence of cAMP-CAP induces the lac operon

E. coli prefer to metabolize glucose over lactose, but it needs to be able to recognize when glucose is absent so that it can consequently turn on the *lac* operon to enable lactose metabolism. When glucose is absent, cyclic adenosine monophosphate (cAMP) accumulates, which then binds to the catabolite activator protein (CAP). This cAMP-CAP complex attaches to a CAP binding site next to the *lac* promoter. The binding of cAMP-CAP bends the DNA in a way that exposes the promoter more effectively to RNA polymerase, which encourages transcription of the *lac* operon structural genes. When glucose is present, there is little cAMP in the cell, leaving CAP inactive and the *lac* operon unable to function maximally. The glucose present is metabolized in preference over lactose.

The negative control is when active repressors inhibit transcription by binding to operon operators. *The positive control* is when transcription is promoted (as in the cAMP-CAP complex, which encourages the RNA polymerase to bind to the promoter). The use of both types of control (positive and negative) allows cells to fine-tune their regulation of metabolism.

Notes for active learning

Notes for active learning

Notes for active learning

Chapter 4

Cell Metabolism and Enzymes

- **Bioenergetics and Thermodynamics**

- **Glycolysis, Gluconeogenesis and the Pentose Phosphate Pathway**

- **Krebs Cycle**

- **Oxidative Phosphorylation**

- **Enzyme Structure and Function**

- **Control of Enzyme Activity**

Bioenergetics and Thermodynamics

Energy is the capacity to do work. Cells continually use energy to develop, grow, reproduce and for biochemical functions. *Kinetic energy* is the energy of motion. Examples of kinetic energy include the beating of cilia, a contracting muscle, and pumping of ions across a plasma membrane.

Potential energy is stored energy. The food contains *chemical energy* within the bonds of the molecule, a type of potential energy. Chemical energy can be transformed into other forms of energy through chemical reactions. For example, when a living organism digests food through a series of chemical reactions, the energy that it obtains from the food is used to move its body; chemical energy is converted to kinetic energy.

Metabolism is the sum of all the biochemical reactions in a cell. Metabolism consists of *anabolism* (synthesis) and *catabolism* (breakdown) of organic molecules required for cell structure and function. Energy obtained during catabolism drives anabolism. The *metabolic pool* is the molecules used for biosynthesis.

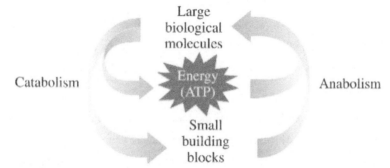

Metabolism includes catabolism for breakdown and anabolism for synthesis

A *metabolic pathway* is an orderly sequence of linked reactions; a specific enzyme catalyzes each step in the pathway. Metabolic pathways begin with a particular *reactant* (a substance that participates in a reaction) and end with a *product* (a substance formed by the reaction). In a reaction A + B → C + D, A and B are reactants, and C and D are products. Since pathways often use the same molecules, one pathway can lead to several others. Metabolic pathways are compartmentalized into different parts of the cell. Within organisms, energy must be transferred in small amounts to minimize the heat released in the process. Reactions that produce energy (exergonic) are coupled with reactions that require energy (endergonic), thereby helping thermoregulation to maintain constant body temperature for homeostasis.

Thermodynamics studies energy transformation and is an important concept in chemical reactions. Chemical reactions involve: (1) the breaking of chemical bonds in the reactants, which requires energy, and (2) the making of new chemical bonds to form products, which releases energy in the form of heat.

There are four laws of thermodynamics.

The *zeroth law of thermodynamics* states that if two systems are in thermal equilibrium with a third system, then they are in thermal equilibrium with each other. This explains the concept of temperature. Another way to understand this law is that two objects placed in contact with each other cause heat energy to transfer from one to the other until they reach thermal equilibrium.

Zeroth law states that objects in contact transfer energy until equal

The *first law of thermodynamics* states that energy can be transferred and transformed, but it can neither be created nor destroyed. The total energy of the universe is constant. In an ecosystem, energy from sunlight is converted by photosynthesis to chemical energy in the form of sugars (e.g., glucose). When an animal consumes the plant, some of the chemical energy in the plant is converted to chemical energy in the animal, which can eventually become kinetic energy or heat loss.

The *second law of thermodynamics* states that energy transfer or transformation increases the entropy (disorder) of the universe (i.e., the trend toward randomness). The tendency to increase disorder is the driving force in spontaneous reactions. To regain order, energy must be invested, which usually releases heat, increasing the entropy elsewhere.

The *third law of thermodynamics* states that the entropy of a system approaches zero as the temperature approaches absolute zero (0 Kelvin). Absolute zero is a theoretical value, and no system has been observed at absolute zero, where the motion of electrons would cease. When the system has a temperature above 0 K, particles start to move, and disorder is generated.

ΔG and K_{eq}: relationship of ΔG and equilibrium constant

Gibbs free energy (G) is a thermodynamic quantity which measures the useful work that a system can do. If the change in Gibbs free energy ΔG for a chemical reaction at a specific temperature T is known, the equilibrium constant (K_{eq}) can be calculated for the process using the equation:

$\Delta G = -RT \ln(K_{eq})$

where $R = 8.314$ J mol^{-1} K^{-1} and T is the temperature in Kelvin.

The equilibrium constant K_{eq} measures the extent to which the reactants are converted to products. When defining the K_{eq} for a chemical reaction, the concentrations of the products are in the numerator, and the concentrations of the reactants are in the denominator. The concentrations are raised to the power of the stoichiometric coefficient for the balanced reaction.

For example, for the balanced reaction $aA + bB \rightleftharpoons cC + dD$, the K_{eq} is:

$K_{eq} = [C]^c[D]^d / [A]^a[B]^b$

Under specified conditions (i.e., same temperature and pH), the K_{eq} is the same for a given reaction. A higher K_{eq} means that a reaction is more likely to occur, while a lower K_{eq} means that a reaction is less likely to occur.

$K_{eq} < 1$: reactants are predominant

$K_{eq} = 0$: both reactants and products are equally favored

$K_{eq} > 1$: products are predominant

Concentration and Le Châtelier's Principle

Le Châtelier's Principle, (Equilibrium Law), describes equilibrium changes when the conditions of a reaction are altered.

When there is a change in pressure, volume, temperature or concentration, the position of equilibrium moves in an attempt to counteract that change.

For the following reaction in equilibrium (i.e., the rate of the forward and reverse reaction are equal):

$$A + B \rightleftharpoons C + D$$

If the concentration of A is increased, the position of equilibrium shifts to counteract the change. Therefore, the position of equilibrium moves toward the products, which increases the concentration of C and D and decreases the concentration of A. If the concentration of A is decreased, the position of equilibrium moves toward the reactants, which increases the concentration of A and decrease the concentration of C and D.

Endothermic and exothermic reactions

Reactions can be classified as endothermic or exothermic, which refer to transfer of heat or changes in enthalpy (ΔH). *Enthalpy* is the heat transferred during a constant pressure process. In an *endothermic* reaction, ΔH is positive, and the reaction absorbs heat, which causes a decrease in the temperature of the surroundings. Examples of endothermic reactions include the melting of ice, cooking an egg and dissolving ammonium chloride in water. All these processes require heat (i.e., it is easier to dissolve a substance in a hot solution).

In an *exothermic* reaction, ΔH is negative, and the reaction gives off heat, which causes an increase in the temperature of the surroundings. Examples of exothermic reactions include freezing water, burning propane and splitting an atom. These processes release heat.

Gibbs free energy: *G*

Free energy, or Gibbs free energy (*G*), is a thermodynamic quantity that represents the amount of energy that is available to do work after a chemical reaction. It is called "free" energy because this is the energy which can perform work, not because there is no energy cost to the system. The change in free energy ΔG refers to the difference between the free energy (relative stability) of the products and the reactants.

It is defined as $\Delta G = \Delta H - T\Delta S$, where ΔH is the change in enthalpy in joules, T is the temperature in Kelvin, and ΔS is the change in entropy. ΔG cannot be measured directly, but ΔH and ΔS can be determined, which allows ΔG to be calculated at a known temperature.

Spontaneous reactions and ΔG

Reactions can be classified as endergonic or exergonic. An *endergonic* reaction has a positive ΔG and requires energy to proceed. Since endergonic reactions require energy, these reactions are not spontaneous. Anabolic reactions, where metabolites combine to form larger molecules, tend to be endergonic ($+\Delta G$).

Exergonic reactions have a negative ΔG and result in a release of energy. These reactions are spontaneous. However, the spontaneous reaction does not necessarily occur rapidly. Catabolic reactions, where larger molecules are broken into smaller metabolites, tend to be exergonic ($-\Delta G$).

Phosphoryl group transfers and ATP:

ATP hydrolysis $\Delta G < 0$ and ATP group transfers

Adenosine triphosphate (ATP) is the energy currency of life. ATP is a nucleotide composed of the base adenine, the 5-carbon sugar ribose, and three phosphate groups. It is a relative of adenine, a nucleotide found in DNA. Adenosine "triphosphate" derives its name from the three phosphates attached to the ribose of the molecule. The phosphate groups are linked by phosphoanhydride bonds, which have a large $-\Delta G$ on hydrolysis, and are therefore "high-energy" bonds. ATP is an unstable molecule because the three phosphates in ATP are negatively charged and repel each other. Compounds with high-energy bonds have high group transfer potential, as chemical groups can easily be removed and transferred to another molecule. Because of the high group transfer potential, the terminal phosphate group on ATP can be spontaneously removed. When the terminal phosphate group is removed via hydrolysis (addition of a water molecule), adenosine diphosphate (ADP), a more stable molecule results.

The change from a less stable ATP molecule to a more stable ADP molecule releases energy ($-\Delta G$)

The conversion of ATP to ADP is an exergonic reaction that releases about 7.3 kcal of energy per mole; this energy can be used for endergonic reactions in the cell that require energy (usually anabolic or synthesis reactions). ATP breakdown is coupled with endergonic reactions to minimize energy loss. For cells to function, ATP must rapidly be regenerated. One muscle cell can consume and regenerate over 10,000,000 ATP per second. If ATP could not be regenerated, humans would have to consume nearly their body weight in ATP each day.

A *coupled reaction* is when energy released by an exergonic reaction is used to drive an endergonic reaction. The endergonic process absorbs the free energy released from the exergonic process. ATP breakdown is coupled with cell reactions that require energy.

It is possible for both of the high-energy phosphoanhydride linkages in ATP to be cleaved by hydrolysis. When two phosphate groups are removed, the resulting molecule is adenosine monophosphate (AMP), which serves as an energy sensor and regulator of metabolism. When there is a deficiency in the amount of ATP being produced, a higher proportion of the cell's adenine is in the form of AMP, and AMP stimulates the pathways that generate more ATP.

The synthesis of ATP involves endergonic reactions that require energy. The pathways of cellular respiration allow energy in glucose to be released slowly; therefore, ATP is produced gradually. In contrast, rapid breakdown of glucose would result in the loss of most energy as unusable heat.

ATP can have three functions: (1) chemical work, where ATP supplies energy to synthesize molecules for the cell, (2) transport work, where ATP supplies energy to pump substances across the plasma membrane, and (3) mechanical work, where ATP supplies energy to perform muscle contraction, propel cilia, etc.

Biological oxidation-reduction:
half-reactions, soluble electron carriers, and flavoproteins

Oxidation-reduction reactions (redox reactions) involve the transfer of electrons. *Oxidation* is the loss of electrons, and *reduction* is the gain of electrons. Use the acronym "OIL RIG" (Oxidation Is Loss, Reduction Is Gain). Although the focus of oxidation-reduction reactions is the transfer of electrons, other factors identify whether a reaction involves oxidation or reduction: oxidation frequently involves gaining oxygen or losing hydrogen, while reduction frequently involves losing oxygen or gaining hydrogen.

An oxidation reaction and its corresponding reduction reaction occur at the same time because one molecule accepts the electrons that are given up by another molecule. A *half-reaction* is either the oxidation or reduction component of a redox reaction. In a half-reaction, the change in oxidation states in an individual substance is considered.

An example of an oxidation-reduction reaction is the reaction between fluorine and hydrogen, where fluorine is reduced (gaining electrons) and hydrogen is oxidized (losing electrons).

$$H_2 + F_2 \rightarrow 2\ HF$$

This redox reaction can be written as two half-reactions. The oxidation reaction is:

$$H_2 \rightarrow 2\,H^+ + 2\,e^-$$

The reduction reaction is:

$$F_2 + 2\,e^- \rightarrow 2\,F^-$$

In biological systems, electron carriers are usually required to transport electrons from one molecule to another. The *electron donor* is the molecule that electron carriers accept electrons from, and the *electron acceptor* is the molecule that electron carriers give electrons to. There are two major electron carriers in cells. One is nicotinamide adenine dinucleotide (NAD^+). When NAD^+ (the oxidized form) accepts a hydrogen ion (H^+) and two electrons ($2\,e^-$), it becomes reduced to $NADH + H^+$. The other important electron carrier is flavin adenine dinucleotide (FAD), which is a flavoprotein (it contains a nucleic acid derivative of riboflavin). FAD (the oxidized form) can accept two hydrogen ions ($2\,H^+$) and two electrons ($2\,e^-$) so that it is reduced to $FADH_2$. Both of these electron carriers are soluble in water.

Notes for active learning

Notes for active learning

Glycolysis, Gluconeogenesis and the Pentose Phosphate Pathway

Glycolysis (aerobic), substrates and products; feeder pathways: glycogen and starch metabolism

In *cellular respiration*, cells release the energy in chemical bonds of food molecules and transfer this energy to ATP molecules, which allows for efficient use of an organism's energy. The ATP generated during cellular respiration is then used for life's essential processes.

Cellular respiration can be *aerobic* (with oxygen) or *anaerobic* (without oxygen). *Glycolysis* (glycol for sugar, lysis for breaking) is the first step in cellular respiration and is the same in both aerobic and anaerobic cells because glycolysis does not require oxygen. Glycolysis occurs in the cytosol of the cell and catabolizes a six-carbon glucose molecule into two three-carbon pyruvate molecules. During glycolysis, energy is transferred through phosphate groups undergoing hydrolysis reactions (breaking) and condensation (joining).

The overall reaction of glycolysis is:

D-Glucose   *Pyruvate*

From the reaction above, glycolysis yields two ATP molecules and two NADH molecules per molecule of glucose. The ten steps of glycolysis are below. However, the summary of the steps is:

1. The glucose molecule goes through several enzymatically regulated reactions and becomes a double-phosphorylated fructose molecule.

2. The 6-carbon fructose molecule is cleaved into two glyceraldehyde 3-phosphate molecules (3-carbon molecules with a phosphate group), abbreviated GA3P (or PGAL). This transformation requires 2 ATP.

3. Hydrogen and water are removed from the two PGAL, leaving two pyruvate molecules. This creates 2 NADH and 4 ATP (net ATP production is 2 ATP).

	Reaction 1, Phosphorylation — First ATP invested: Glucose is converted to glucose-6-phosphate when ATP is hydrolyzed to ADP. The reaction is catalyzed by hexokinase.

Glucose-6-phosphate

Phosphoglucoisomerase

P = phosphate group

Reaction 2, Isomerization:

The enzyme phosphoglucoisomerase converts glucose-6-phosphate (an aldose) to its isomer fructose-6-phosphate (a ketose).

Fructose-6-phosphate

ATP
Phosphofructokinase
ADP

Fructose-1,6-bisphosphate

Reaction 3, Phosphorylation — the Second ATP is invested:

A second ATP is hydrolyzed to ADP, and the phosphate is transferred to fructose-6-phosphate forming fructose-1,6-bisphosphate. "Bisphosphate" indicates two phosphates. This reaction is catalyzed by phosphofructokinase.

Aldolase

Dihydroxyacetone phosphate

Glyceraldehyde-3-phosphate

Triosephosphate isomerase

Glyceraldehyde-3-phosphate

Reaction 4, Cleavage — Two trioses are formed:

Fructose-1,6-bisphosphate is cleaved into two triose phosphates (dihydroxyacetone phosphate and glyceraldehyde-3-phosphate), catalyzed by aldolase.

Reaction 5, Isomerization of a triose:

Triosephosphate isomerase converts one of the triose products (hydroxyacetone phosphate) to the other (glyceraldehyde-3-phosphate). Now, all six carbon atoms from glucose are in two identical 3-carbon triose phosphates.

O ‖ C—H | H—C—OH | CH₂O — P Glyceraldehyde-3-phosphate P_i + NAD⁺ ⟍⟋ Glyceraldehyde- NADH + H⁺ ⟍⟋ 3-phosphate dehydrogenase O ‖ C—O — P | H—C—OH | CH₂O — P	*Reaction 6, First energy production yields NADH:* The aldehyde group of glyceraldehyde-3-phosphate is oxidized and phosphorylated by the enzyme glyceraldehyde-3-phosphate dehydrogenase. The coenzyme NAD⁺ is reduced to the high-energy compound NADH (and H⁺) in the process.
1,3-Bisphosphoglycerate ADP ⟍⟋ Phosphoglycerate ATP ⟍⟋ kinase O ‖ C—O⁻ | H—C—OH | CH₂O — P	*Reaction 7, Next energy production yields ATP:* The energy-rich 1,3-bisphosphoglycerate drives the formation of ATP when phosphoglycerate kinase transfers one phosphate from 1,3-bisphosphoglycerate to ADP.
3-Phosphoglycerate ‖ Phosphoglycerate mutase O ‖ C—O⁻ | H—C—O — P | CH₂OH	*Reaction 8, Formation of 2-phosphoglycerate:* A phosphoglycerate mutase transfers the phosphate group from carbon 3 to carbon 2 to yield 2-phosphoglycerate.
2-Phosphoglycerate H_2O ⟍⟋ Enolase O ‖ C—O⁻ | C—O — P ‖ CH₂	*Reaction 9, Removal of water makes a high-energy enol:* Enolase catalyzes the removal of water to yield phosphoenolpyruvate, a high-energy compound that transfers its phosphate in the next step.
Phosphoenolpyruvate ADP ⟍⟋ Pyruvate ATP ⟍⟋ kinase O ‖ C—O⁻ | C=O | CH₃ Pyruvate	*Reaction 10, Third energy production yields a second ATP:* ATP is generated in this final reaction when the phosphate from phosphoenolpyruvate is transferred. The pyruvate kinase catalyzes the reaction.

Glucose is not always immediately available, as it is often stored in skeletal muscles and the liver as the polysaccharide glycogen. Hormones control whether glucose enters the anabolic pathway to form glycogen or the catabolic pathway to undergo glycolysis to form pyruvate. If the signals for the catabolic pathway are initiated, cellular respiration begins (glycolysis → Krebs → electron transport chain).

With the help of glycogen phosphorylase, glycogen can be converted into glucose 6-phosphate, and enter the second step in the ten-step pathway of glycolysis. Fructose can undergo glycolysis. In the liver, fructose catabolism is unregulated and can produce excess products that become stored in the body as fat. In the muscles, fructose is converted to fructose-6-phosphate, entering glycolysis at step 3. In the liver, it is converted to the trioses used in step 5 of glycolysis.

Starch (amylose and amylopectin) begins to be digested in the mouth by enzymes in the saliva. The enzyme α-amylase hydrolyzes some of the α-glycosidic bonds in the starch molecules, producing glucose, disaccharide maltose, and oligosaccharides. Only monosaccharides are small enough to be transported from the gastrointestinal system into the bloodstream. To complete the digestion of starch, enzymes in the small intestine hydrolyze starch and disaccharides into monosaccharides.

The most important regulatory step in glycolysis is step 3. The enzyme phosphofructokinase, which catalyzes the phosphorylation of fructose-6-phosphate to fructose-1,6-bisphosphate, is tightly regulated by the cells because this step is irreversible and commits the pathway to glycolysis. ATP acts as an inhibitor of phosphofructokinase, so if cells have sufficient ATP levels, glycolysis slows down. If there is not much ATP, then glycolysis continues. The step after glycolysis depends on the type of respiration (i.e., aerobic or anaerobic).

Fermentation (anaerobic glycolysis)

Glycolysis produces two pyruvate molecules, two NADH molecules, and two ATP molecules. At this point, it is possible to either begin the aerobic part of the cellular respiration (Krebs Cycle) or to continue with anaerobic respiration. *Fermentation* is the next step in anaerobic (i.e., without oxygen) cellular respiration, which takes place in the cytoplasm. It predominantly occurs in yeast and bacteria but occurs in oxygen-starved muscle cells of vertebrates.

The goal of fermentation reactions is to oxidize NADH produced in glycolysis back to NAD^+ by reducing the pyruvate. Then, the NAD^+ molecules are used in another round of glycolysis to produce two more ATP and two more NADHs. It is clear that fermentation is a slow and inefficient method of making ATP, since two ATP are produced in each cycle (compared to ~36 ATP that are produced in each complete cycle of aerobic respiration).

There are two types of fermentation. *Lactic acid fermentation* produces two molecules of lactate (or lactic acid as the acidic form of the molecule) and occurs in bacteria and some types of fungi. It is used in the production of some foods (e.g., yogurt). *Lactobacillus* is one genus of bacteria known for lactic acid fermentation. Lactic acid fermentation occurs in the muscle cells of humans and other mammals during demanding physical activities (e.g., sprinting), when the rate of demand for energy is high; lactic acid fermentation provides a quick burst of energy via ATP synthesis needed for the muscular activity.

Lactic acid is toxic to mammals; this is the "burn" felt when undergoing strenuous activity. When blood cannot remove all of the lactate from muscles, this decreases the pH, causing muscle fatigue. *Oxygen debt* is the oxygen that the body needed, but that was not delivered to the cell. At this point, oxygen is needed to restore ATP levels and rid the body of lactate (thus "repaying" the oxygen debt), which is one reason why a person might breathe harder after exercise. Recovery occurs after lactate is sent to the liver, where it is converted into pyruvate; some pyruvate is then respired or converted into glucose.

During lactic acid fermentation, the middle carbonyl (C=O) in pyruvate is reduced (i.e., hydrogen is added) to an OH group, and lactate is formed, as catalyzed by lactate dehydrogenase. The hydrogen (and energy) required for this reaction is supplied by NADH, producing NAD^+. NADH passes its electrons to pyruvate, and NAD^+ then returns to the glycolysis pathway to receive more electrons. In lactic acid fermentation, pyruvate is the final electron acceptor.

Alcoholic fermentation is the production of two ethanol molecules and two carbon dioxide molecules. Yeasts and some types of bacteria perform alcoholic fermentation. Some yeasts perform aerobic cellular respiration when oxygen is available, and only utilize alcoholic fermentation in anaerobic environments. However, many yeasts prefer fermentation, even if oxygen is available. These yeasts are utilized in the production of bread and alcoholic beverages. *Saccharomyces cerevisiae,* the yeast used in baking, consumes sugars in the dough of bread (converting glucose to pyruvate during glycolysis) and then reduces the pyruvate, creating carbon dioxide and ethanol as waste products. The carbon dioxide causes the dough to rise, and the ethanol evaporates when the bread is baked. *S. cerevisiae* is used in the production of beer. This yeast consumes the grain starches during glycolysis, and the carbon dioxide that is produced along with the ethanol during alcoholic fermentation is carbonation in the beer. Just as lactic acid is toxic to mammals, ethanol is toxic to the microorganisms that produce it.

Unlike lactic acid fermentation, where the pyruvate directly accepts electrons from NADH, there is an intermediate compound in alcoholic fermentation. The two pyruvate molecules are first converted into two molecules of acetaldehyde, catalyzed by pyruvate decarboxylase. The byproduct is carbon dioxide. The acetaldehyde is the final electron acceptor (from NADH). Then, the two acetaldehyde molecules are converted into two molecules of ethanol, catalyzed by the enzyme alcohol dehydrogenase.

$$CH_3-\overset{\overset{O}{\|}}{C}-\overset{\overset{O}{\|}}{C}-O^- + NADH + 2H^+ \longrightarrow CH_3-\overset{\overset{HO}{|}}{\underset{\underset{H}{|}}{C}}-H + CO_2 + NAD^+ + e^-$$

Pyruvate   *Ethanol*

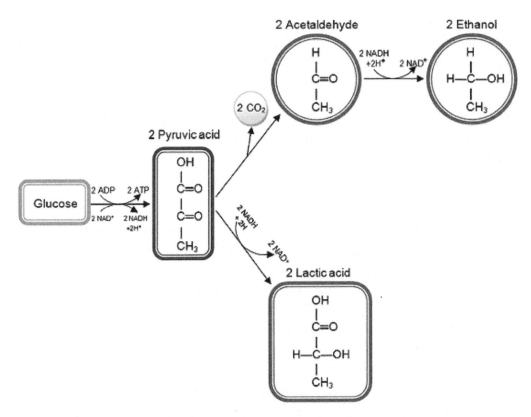

*Alcoholic fermentation for ethanol production and
lactic acid fermentation pathways to regenerate NAD$^+$*

Gluconeogenesis

In addition to catabolizing glucose, many organisms can produce it from non-carbohydrate substances, as *gluconeogenesis*. Gluconeogenesis occurs in the mitochondria and cytoplasm of many organisms, including animals, plants, fungi, and bacteria. In vertebrates, gluconeogenesis occurs primarily in the liver and, to a limited extent, in the kidneys. This process helps maintain the glucose concentration in blood.

A variety of non-carbohydrate carbon substrates, including pyruvate, glycerol, lactate, and certain amino acids, can be used as the starting molecule in gluconeogenesis. If the starting molecule is not pyruvate, the first step in gluconeogenesis is to convert the precursor (e.g., lactate) to pyruvate. It is possible for an amino acid precursor to enter the gluconeogenesis metabolic pathway at oxaloacetate or later in the pathway (for glycerol).

The steps of gluconeogenesis are displayed below, along with enzymes that catalyze each step. The entire metabolic pathway of gluconeogenesis uses two ATP, two GTPs and one NADH. As seen from the similarity of the two pathways, gluconeogenesis can be thought of as "reverse glycolysis." However, three of the enzymes used in the two pathways are different, so the energy cost of gluconeogenesis is not too great to be energetically favorable for the organism. Instead of using hexokinase, phosphofructokinase and pyruvate kinase (used in glycolysis), gluconeogenesis uses glucose-6-phosphatase, fructose-1,6-bisphosphatase and PEP carboxykinase/pyruvate carboxylase. This replaces three highly endergonic reactions in glycolysis with reactions that are exergonic and therefore favorable.

Glucose is produced via gluconeogenesis

In addition to building up glucose from carbon substrates (i.e., gluconeogenesis), organisms derive glucose by breaking down stored energy sources, such as the polysaccharides of starch and glycogen, with hormones controlling these processes. The hormone glucagon promotes glycogen degradation and inhibits glycolysis in the liver, which causes the glycolytic intermediates to be used in gluconeogenesis. Glucagon does this by inhibiting the phosphofructokinase (PFK) enzyme, since PFK is integral to glycolysis, to increase the concentration of glucose in the blood. Conversely, insulin inhibits gluconeogenesis by activating the PFK enzyme, so that the concentration of glucose in the blood is reduced.

Pentose phosphate pathway

The *pentose phosphate pathway* is a metabolic pathway that produces nicotinamide adenine dinucleotide phosphate (NADPH) and five-carbon sugars. In most organisms, it takes place in the cytosol, the exception being plants where it occurs in plastids. This pathway can be thought of as "parallel" to glycolysis, but rather than as a catabolic pathway, the pentose phosphate pathway is anabolic, since it synthesizes five-carbon pentose sugars.

The first phase of the pentose phosphate pathway is the oxidative phase, where two $NADP^+$ molecules are reduced to two NADPH molecules, and glucose-6-phosphate is oxidized to ribulose-5-phosphate. The production of NADPH in the pentose phosphate pathway is vital because it is the primary source of NADPH in non-photosynthetic organisms.

The oxidative phase of the pentose phosphate pathway

1: glucose-6-phosphate

2: 6-phosphogluconolactone

3: 6-phosphogluconate

4: ribulose 5-phosphate

The second phase of the pentose phosphate pathway is the non-oxidative phase, where other types of pentoses are synthesized from ribulose-5-phosphate. One of these pentoses is ribose-5-phosphate, which is used to synthesize nucleic acids. Another type of pentose is erythrose-4-phosphate, which is used to generate aromatic amino acids. The pentose phosphate pathway is important, as it enables the biosynthesis of the biomolecules as the building blocks of life.

The second phase of the pentose phosphate pathway with ribose-5-phosphate (nucleic acids) and erythrose-4-phosphate. Note the spelling of phosphate should include an -e ending

Net molecular and energetic results of respiration processes

From fermentation, the two ATP produced per glucose molecule is equivalent to 14.6 kcal. The ATP is produced via substrate-level phosphorylation as the direct enzymatic transfer of a phosphate to ADP, no extraneous carriers needed. Complete glucose breakdown to CO_2 and H_2O during aerobic cellular respiration represents a possible yield of 686 kcal of energy. Therefore, efficiency for fermentation is 14.6 / 686, or about 2.1% – much less efficient than aerobic respiration. Thus, the presence of an oxygen-rich atmosphere, which facilitated the evolution of aerobic respiration, is crucial in the complexity and diversification of life.

Notes for active learning

Krebs Cycle

Cellular respiration is the controlled release of energy from organic compounds in cells to produce ATP. Aerobic cellular respiration includes the anaerobic process of glycolysis, as well as the aerobic processes that occur in the mitochondria of eukaryotes. These three processes within the mitochondria are pyruvate decarboxylation, the Krebs cycle (the citric acid cycle or TCA) and oxidative phosphorylation via the electron transport chain (ETC).

Cellular respiration outlining the sequence of glycolysis, Krebs cycle and electron transport chain

Acetyl-CoA production

Pyruvate decarboxylation follows glycolysis in aerobic respiration. Pyruvate decarboxylation is a link reaction as the intermediate step after glycolysis and before the Krebs cycle, thereby linking the two metabolic pathways. In eukaryotes, pyruvate decarboxylation occurs in the mitochondrial matrix (cytosol of mitochondria). In prokaryotes, it occurs in the cytoplasm and at the plasma membrane. It converts pyruvate into acetyl coenzyme A (acetyl-CoA) and is catalyzed by the pyruvate dehydrogenase complex (PDC), a complex of three enzymes. From two pyruvate molecules (one original molecule of glucose), two acetyl-CoA are created, and two NAD^+ are reduced to NADH. Additionally, two molecules of CO_2 are released.

Coenzyme A (CoA) is an important energy exchanger that contains adenosine, three phosphates, and a pantothenic acid-derived (vitamin B_5) portion. The two forms are acetyl-CoA (high energy) and CoA (low energy). Energy is released from acetyl-CoA when the C–S bond in the thioester group is hydrolyzed, producing an acetyl group and CoA.

Coenzyme A exists in a low energy form as CoA or high energy form as acetyl-CoA

In addition to glucose breakdown, there are other ways that acetyl-CoA can be produced for use in the Krebs cycle. Fat breaks down into glycerol and fatty acids. Glycerol is converted to PGAL, a metabolite in glycolysis. Beta oxidation is when the fatty acids can be broken down to generate acetyl-CoA. An 18-carbon fatty acid can be converted to nine acetyl-CoA molecules that each enter the Krebs cycle. Acetyl-CoA can be produced by degrading the carbon skeletons of ketogenic amino acids. However, regardless of whether acetyl-CoA is produced from carbohydrates, fats or proteins, the subsequent step for this molecule is the same: the acetyl-CoA proceeds to the Krebs cycle as the next phase of aerobic respiration.

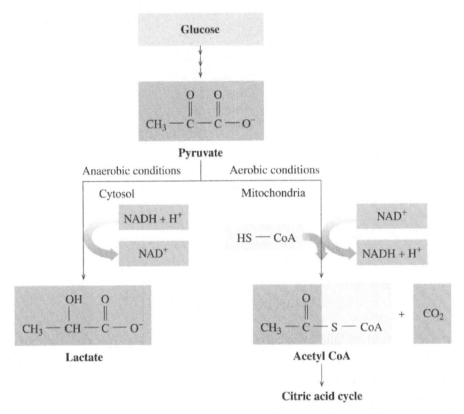

Pyruvate is the product of glycolysis that proceeds into the citric acid (Krebs) cycle or fermentation when oxygen is absent

Reactions of the Krebs cycle, substrates, and products

The *Krebs cycle* takes place in the fluid matrix of the cristae compartments of the mitochondria. The cycle is named after Sir Hans Krebs, who received the Nobel Prize for identifying these reactions. It is called the citric acid cycle or the tricarboxylic acid cycle (TCA) cycle because of the intermediate acids in the cycle. The Krebs cycle removes energy, carbon dioxide, and hydrogen from acetyl-CoA via enzyme-mediated reactions of organic acids. It begins by combining acetyl-CoA (two carbons) with oxaloacetate (four carbons), producing citric acid (six carbons). Citric acid undergoes several oxidations, decarboxylation, dehydrogenation, and hydration, yielding two CO_2, one GTP, three NADH, and one $FADH_2$ for each turn of the cycle. One original glucose is split into two pyruvates during glycolysis. Therefore, one glucose undergoes two turns of the Krebs cycle. The products for one glucose are four CO_2, two GTP, six NADH, and two $FADH_2$. GTP readily converts to ATP in the cell. The cycle regenerates oxaloacetate to begin again. The oxidations release energy, which is stored by the nucleotide carriers (NADH and $FADH_2$) when they accept the hydrogen electrons. This stored energy in NADH and $FADH_2$ is used by cytochromes in the electron transport chain to produce ATP by oxidative phosphorylation.

The details of the Krebs cycle are outlined here:

Reaction 1, Formation of Citrate: The acetyl group from acetyl-CoA (two carbons) combines with oxaloacetate (four carbons), forming citrate (six carbons) and CoA.

Reaction 2, Isomerization to Isocitrate: The OH and one of the H atoms are exchanged in citrate to form isocitrate. This rearrangement is necessary because isocitrate is oxidized in the next reaction.

Reaction 3, First Oxidative Decarboxylation (Release of CO_2): An alcohol undergoes oxidation (electron and two hydrogens are removed) to the ketone α-ketoglutarate and NAD^+ is reduced to NADH, accepting the proton and electrons removed during the oxidation. The six-carbon isocitrate is decarboxylated (release of CO_2) to the five-carbon α-ketoglutarate.

Reaction 4, Second Oxidative Decarboxylation: The thiol group of CoA is oxidized (loses an electron), and another NAD^+ is reduced (gains electron) to NADH. α-ketoglutarate (five carbons) is decarboxylated into a succinyl group (four carbons). The CoA is bonded to the succinyl group, thus producing succinyl CoA.

Reaction 5, Hydrolysis of Succinyl CoA: Succinyl CoA undergoes hydrolysis to yield succinate and CoA. The resulting energy produces the high-energy nucleotide GTP (guanosine triphosphate) from GDP and P_i. The GTP is converted to ATP in the cell.

Reaction 6, Dehydrogenation of Succinate: One hydrogen is eliminated from each of the two central carbons of succinate, forming a *trans* C=C bond, thus producing fumarate. The coenzyme FAD is reduced to $FADH_2$.

Reaction 7, Hydration of Fumarate: Water adds to the *trans* double bond of fumarate as H and OH to form malate.

Reaction 8, Oxidation of Malate: As in reaction 3, the secondary alcohol of malate is oxidized to a ketone, forming oxaloacetate and providing protons and electrons for reducing the coenzyme NAD^+ to NADH.

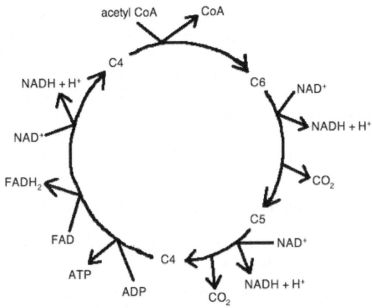

Krebs cycle is showing the reactants and products. GTP is equivalent to ATP.

Net molecular and energetic results of respiration processes

The two pyruvate molecules produced during glycolysis are converted into two acetyl-CoA molecules in the link reaction. The acetyl-CoA then enters the Krebs cycle, which turns twice because two acetyl-CoA molecules enter the cycle per original glucose molecule. The final products of the Krebs cycle are oxaloacetic acid (to further drive the cycle), 2 ATP (converted from GTP), 6 NADH, 2 $FADH_2$, and 4 CO_2. The high-energy molecules NADH and $FADH_2$ are used in the final step of aerobic respiration, oxidative phosphorylation.

The equation for one turn of the Krebs cycle:

$$\text{Acetyl-CoA} + 3\ NAD^+ + FAD + GDP + P_i + 2\ H_2O \rightarrow 2\ CO_2 +\ 3\ NADH + 2\ H^+ + FADH_2 + CoA + GTP$$

The net production in cellular respiration from glycolysis through the Krebs cycle is 8 NADH, 2 $FADH_2$, 2 ATP, and 6 CO_2.

To summarize, the Krebs cycle degrades two carbon acetyl groups from acetyl CoA into CO_2, and the carbon dioxide is released in two reactions (as a waste product exhaled in animals). GTP is produced in one of the reactions and is converted into ATP. Hydrogen is removed in four reactions. NAD^+ accepts two electrons and the proton in three of these reactions, creating three NADH. FAD accepts two electrons and the proton in one reaction, creating one $FADH_2$.

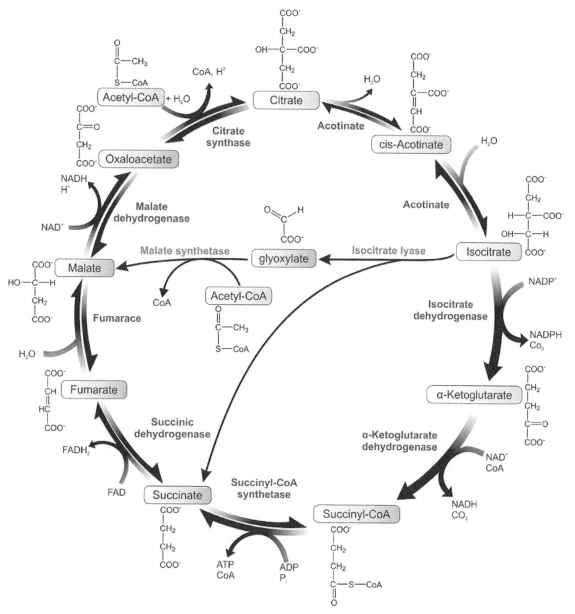

Krebs cycle with structures, enzymes and produces

Regulation of the cycle

The Krebs cycle must be carefully regulated so that the proper amount of ATP is generated. Although oxygen is not directly used in the Krebs cycle, the cycle can only occur under aerobic conditions, because FAD and NAD^+ can only be regenerated when oxygen is present. If the availability of oxygen is drastically reduced, respiration may drop to the point where it may ultimately lead to death. Low oxygen concentrations divert aerobic cellular respiration from the Krebs cycle to anaerobic fermentation.

The Krebs cycle is mainly regulated by substrate availability, product inhibition, and competitive feedback inhibition. During the cycle, ADP (a substrate) is converted to ATP, and a decreased amount of ADP reduces the rate of the cycle. This leads to an accumulation of NADH, decreasing the amount of NAD^+ available for the cycle. NADH can allosterically inhibit the enzymes in the Krebs cycle, including the pyruvate dehydrogenase complex (PDC), which catalyzes the link reaction (i.e., pyruvate decarboxylation to produce acetyl-CoA). Acetyl-CoA inhibits the PDC as an example of end product inhibition (or feedback inhibition) because acetyl-CoA is the product of the reaction catalyzed by the PDC.

Acetyl-CoA can enter the Krebs cycle from sources other than glycolysis, such as the breakdown of fatty acids. Calcium is an activator of the PDC and activates other dehydrogenase enzymes that catalyze reactions in the Krebs cycle. AMP (adenosine monophosphate) activates the PDC. Citrate, the first compound in the Krebs cycle (formed from acetyl-CoA joining oxaloacetate), is used for feedback inhibition. Citrate inhibits phosphofructokinase, an important enzyme used in glycolysis. When high quantities of citrate accumulate, the rate of the respiration pathway is reduced to prevent the overproduction of ATP.

Notes for active learning

Notes for active learning

Oxidative Phosphorylation

Electron transport chain and oxidative phosphorylation, substrates and products, and general features of the pathway

Oxidative phosphorylation is the next step in aerobic cell respiration, which includes the electron transport chain (ETC). This final step produces the majority of ATP. This is done by the oxidation (loss of electrons) by high-energy intermediates (NADH and $FADH_2$) which causes H^+ to be pumped into the intermembrane space (between inner and outer membranes) of the mitochondria. The reactions of the electron transport chain occur at the *cristae*, which are the folds of the inner mitochondrial membrane that increase the surface area for the electron transport chain. During this process, a gradient across the mitochondrial membrane is created to drive the production of ATP. Depending on cell conditions and if the prokaryotic or eukaryotic organism is present, about 32 to 34 molecules of ATP are produced by oxidative phosphorylation per glucose molecule.

The *electron transport chain* uses the NADH and $FADH_2$ from the Krebs cycle for a series of protein complexes that extract energy and pump protons across the inner mitochondrial membrane. Energy is released as the hydrogen and electrons from the NAD^+, and FAD^+ carrier molecules flow into the system. When the electrons reach the end of the chain, they are accepted by oxygen (the final electron acceptor), and water is released when oxygen combines with the electrons and protons.

Chemiosmosis is the mechanism of ATP generation that occurs when energy is stored in the form of a proton concentration gradient across a membrane. ATP is produced by oxidative phosphorylation during the action of the electron transport chain. When H^+ molecules from the carrier molecules are transported from the matrix to the intermembrane space, a pH and electric charge gradient are created. The ATP synthase enzyme uses the potential energy on this gradient to create ATP when the protons flow through the ATPase channel in the membrane back into the matrix.

Note: A common question about this topic concerns pH changes from these processes. Remember that an *increase* in H^+ concentration means a *decrease* in pH.

Within the inner membrane of the mitochondria, there are four enzyme complexes (numbered I – IV). ATP synthase is sometimes referred to as complex V. The electron carriers' coenzyme Q (CoQ), and cytochrome c are not firmly attached to any complex and shuttle electrons between the complexes. CoQ (i.e., ubiquinone) is a fat-soluble carrier dissolved in the membrane. It can be fully reduced, fully oxidized or somewhere in between. This property enables it to perform in the electron transport chain. CoQ carries electrons from Complex I and Complex II to Complex III. Like all coenzymes, CoQ has a vitamin-like structure. *Cytochrome c* is a water-soluble protein that transfers electrons between Complex III and Complex IV. There is a central iron atom in this molecule; it is surrounded by heme protein. Cytochrome c is highly conserved across species, and it is often used to study evolutionary relationships between organisms.

The details of the electron transport chain are outlined below.

Complex I, NADH Dehydrogenase: NADH enters the electron transport chain. During its oxidation, two electrons and two protons are transferred to the electron transporter CoQ, reducing its two ketone groups to alcohols. NAD^+ is regenerated and returns to a catabolic pathway, as in the Krebs cycle. The reaction at Complex I is $NADH + H^+ + Q \rightarrow NAD^+ + QH$.

Complex II, Succinate Dehydrogenase: $FADH_2$ enters electron transport after the reduced nucleotide is produced in the conversion of succinate to fumarate in the Krebs cycle. Two electrons and two protons from $FADH_2$ are transferred to CoQ to yield QH_2. The reaction at Complex II is $FADH_2 + Q \rightarrow FAD + QH_2$.

Complex III, Coenzyme Q–Cytochrome c Reductase: The reduced coenzyme Q (QH_2) molecules are reoxidized to ubiquinone (Q). The electrons pass through a series of electron acceptors until they arrive at cytochrome c, which moves the electrons from Complex III to Complex IV.

Complex IV, Cytochrome c Oxidase: Single electrons are transferred from cytochrome c through another set of electron acceptors to combine with hydrogen ions and oxygen as the final electron accepts to form water. The reaction is $4 H^+ + 4 e^- + O_2 \rightarrow 2 H_2O$.

Three of the complexes (I, III and IV) span the inner membrane and pump protons out of the matrix and into the intermembrane space as electrons are shuttled through the complexes. The complex that does not pump protons is Complex II.

The formation of the chemiosmotic (proton) gradient across the inner mitochondrial membrane provides the energy for ATP synthesis. Protons move back into the matrix through the transmembrane ATP synthase enzyme, and the resulting release of potential energy from the chemiosmotic gradient drives the synthesis of ATP by oxidative phosphorylation as protons and electrons join $\frac{1}{2}O_2$.

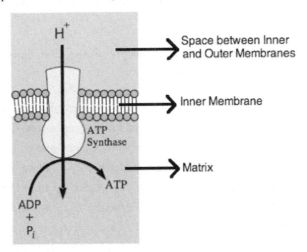

Oxidative phosphorylation with protons passing through the ATP synthase

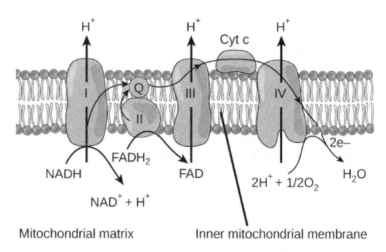

Intermembrane space

Electron transport chain showing the membrane-bound cytochromes as electrons move down their reduction potential towards O_2 as the final electron acceptor

Electron transfer in mitochondria: NADH, NADPH, flavoproteins, and cytochromes

The coenzymes nicotinamide adenine dinucleotide (NAD^+) and flavin adenine dinucleotide (FAD) are energy-transferring compounds that exist in different redox states. NAD^+ (low-energy oxidized form) accepts two electrons and proton to become NADH (high-energy reduced form). FAD (low-energy oxidized form) accepts two electrons and two protons to become $FADH_2$ (high-energy reduced form). The active end of each coenzyme contains a vitamin component. Nicotinamide is derived from the niacin (B_3) vitamin, and riboflavin (B_2) vitamin is found in FAD. The FAD is, therefore, a type of flavoprotein.

Electrons received by NAD^+ and FAD can then be carried to cytochrome protein of the electron transport chain. NAD^+ and FAD are coenzymes of oxidation-reduction since they both accept and donate electrons. Only a small amount of these coenzymes are needed in cells because the exchange of electrons regenerates each molecule. For example, once NADH delivers electrons to the electron transport chain, it becomes oxidized to NAD^+ and then can be reduced with electrons and protons. Recycling NAD^+, FAD, and ADP eliminate the need to synthesize them de novo continuously.

NAD^+ is converted into nicotinamide adenine dinucleotide phosphate ($NADP^+$). $NADP^+$ is similar in structure to NAD^+ but has an additional phosphate group, and it can be reduced to NADPH. In non-photosynthetic organisms, the production of $NADP^+$ generally occurs through the pentose phosphate pathway. In plants, however, it is produced during the last step of the electron transport chain (across the thylakoid membrane) in the light reactions of photosynthesis. In general, NAD^+, $NADP^+$ and FAD are reduced during catabolic processes; their reduced forms (NADH, NADPH, and $FADH_2$) are oxidized during anabolic processes.

For each NADH formed within the mitochondrion (during the link reaction and the Krebs cycle), three ATP are produced. For each $FADH_2$ formed by the Krebs cycle, two ATP are produced. This is because $FADH_2$

delivers electrons after NADH (Complex II vs. Complex I). Therefore, NADH yields more energy than $FADH_2$, because more H^+ is pumped across the membrane per NADH (3:2 ratio). However, an exception occurs for NADH formed outside the mitochondrion (by glycolysis) in the cytoplasm. The NADH formed by glycolysis is the same molecule as the NADH formed in the mitochondria but yields two ATP (equivalent to ATP production by FADH during the Krebs cycle) instead of three ATP. One ATP is consumed to transport the NADH of glycolysis from the cytoplasm into the mitochondrion, resulting in a net gain of two ATP.

ATP synthase and chemiosmotic coupling; proton motive force

The movement of protons from the mitochondrial matrix into the intermembrane space creates a concentration gradient. The *proton motive force* is the energy used to pump these protons across the inner membrane, and it comes from the energy released by the electrons passing through the electron transport chain. Remember that three out of four enzyme complexes in the electron transport chain can pump protons into the intermembrane space: complexes I, III and IV. The protons create a concentration gradient (lowering the pH) as they move into the intermembrane space.

Chemiosmosis is ATP production tied to an electrochemical (H^+) gradient across a membrane. There is now a high concentration of protons in the intermembrane space and a low concentration of protons in the mitochondrial matrix. The protons then move down the concentration gradient from the intermembrane space back into the matrix. However, the inner membrane is impervious to protons, and they can move back into the matrix via the ATP synthase, an enzyme embedded in the inner membrane. ATP synthase complexes span the membrane and are channel proteins that serve as enzymes for ATP synthesis.

As the protons are transported back into the matrix through the channels of ATP synthase, they release energy, which is then used by ATP synthase to convert ADP into ATP by the addition of an inorganic phosphate (P_i). This process is oxidative phosphorylation, because the electrons come from previous oxidation reactions of cell respiration, and the ATP synthase uses ½O_2 to accept the electrons to catalyze the phosphorylation of ADP into ATP. Once formed, ATP molecules diffuse out of the mitochondrial matrix through channel proteins and become available for use by the cell.

Tests confirmed the chemiosmotic nature of ATP synthesis with respiratory poisons (i.e., poisons that inhibit ATP synthesis), where these poisons caused the H^+ concentration gradient to increase. British biochemist Peter Mitchell received the 1978 Nobel Prize for his chemiosmotic theory of ATP production, which occurs in the membranes of both mitochondria in animal cells and chloroplasts in plant cells.

The exergonic flow of electrons is generally coupled with the endergonic pumping of protons across the cristae membrane of the mitochondria. When electron flow and proton transport are uncoupled, the energy in the proton gradient is released as heat. This assists in maintaining body temperature through *thermogenesis*, which occurs primarily in warm-blooded animals.

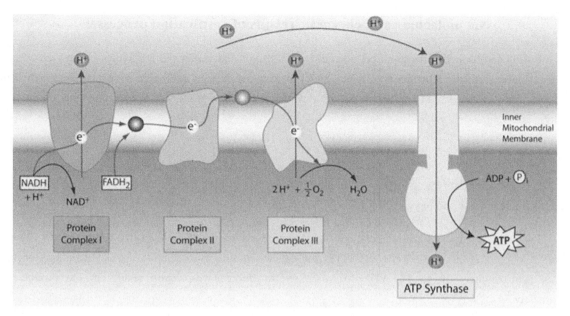

Inner membrane contains cytochromes that pass electrons. ATP synthase produces ATP by oxidative phosphorylation when protons pass down the concentration gradient into the matrix

Aerobic cellular respiration showing precursor molecules used during glycolysis, citric acid cycle (Krebs) and electron transport chain

Net molecular and energetic results of respiration processes

During aerobic cellular respiration, glucose breakdown provides energy for a hydrogen ion gradient across the inner membrane of the mitochondria, which couples proton flow with ATP formation. At the end of cellular respiration, glucose is oxidized to carbon dioxide and water, and ATP is produced. The overall equation for aerobic respiration is:

$$C_6H_{12}O_6 + 6\ O_2 \rightarrow 6\ CO_2 + 6\ H_2O + energy$$

It is the reverse of the equation for photosynthesis, which uses carbon dioxide, water, and energy from sunlight to create glucose and oxygen.

The primary purpose of cellular respiration is the production of ATP for the cell's energy needs. Glycolysis produces 2 ATP, the Krebs cycle produces 2 ATP, and the electron transport chain (i.e., oxidative phosphorylation) produces approximately 30 to 32 ATP. In total, aerobic cellular respiration results in the production of approximately 34 to 36 ATP.

The energy yield can be calculated using the energy content of glucose and ATP. Glucose contains 686 kcal/molecule, while ATP contains 7.5 kcal/molecule.

$$7.5 \times 34 = 255\ kcal/mol\ for\ all\ ATP\ produced$$

$$255\ /\ 686 = 37.2\%\ energy\ recovered\ from\ aerobic\ respiration$$

Therefore, the ~36 resulting ATP molecules represent approximately 37% of the energy in one molecule of glucose. Aerobic respiration is almost twenty times as efficient as anaerobic respiration, which has a net of 2 ATP and efficiency of approximately 2%.

Overall, cellular respiration is an exergonic process ($\Delta G = -686$ kcal/mole).

Regulation of oxidative phosphorylation

The movement of electrons through the electron transport chain is regulated by the proton motive force (PMF). When the magnitude of the PMF is high (i.e., a high H^+ concentration gradient), the rate of electron flow through the electron transport chain is lower. When the magnitude of the PMF is low, the rate of electron flow is greater to increase the H^+ concentration gradient.

The energy demands of the cell directly influence the regulation of oxidative phosphorylation. During resting conditions, the demand for ATP is low, and there is a low rate of proton movement from the intermembrane space through the ATP synthase in the inner mitochondrial membrane. However, when the demand for energy is high (e.g., during vigorous activity), protons flow more quickly through the ATP synthase due to an increased concentration of ADP in the mitochondria. The level of ADP is the primary factor in determining the rate of oxidative phosphorylation. If protons are not flowing through the ATP synthases and thus allowing ADP to be phosphorylated into ATP, electrons do not flow through the cytochromes of the electron transport chain to oxygen, the terminal electron acceptor.

Oxygen is another important regulator of oxidative phosphorylation. If there is insufficient oxygen, then electrons cannot pass through the electron transport chain and NADH, and $FADH_2$ cannot be oxidized to NAD^+ and FAD. Eventually, NAD^+ and FAD are depleted, and the link reaction and Krebs cycle are suspended. By measuring oxygen consumption, the rate of the electron transport chain can be calculated (i.e., elevated oxygen consumption indicates faster electron transport). The rate of electron transport is the cellular respiratory rate.

Several compounds inhibit oxidative phosphorylation by preventing electron transport. One example is antimycin A, which inhibits cytochrome b in the coenzyme Q–cytochrome c Reductase (Complex III). Other inhibitors, such as Rotenone and Amytal, block the use of NADH as a substrate in NADH dehydrogenase (Complex I). The inhibitors cyanide, carbon monoxide, and azide prevent electron flow in Cytochrome c Oxidase (Complex IV).

Some compounds can inhibit oxidative phosphorylation by acting as uncoupling agents. These include 2,4-dinitrophenol (DNP) and pentachlorophenol (acidic aromatic compounds). The protons in the intermembrane space of the mitochondria pass through the membrane with the protons attached, and then the uncoupling agent releases the protein once inside the mitochondrial matrix. This dissipates the proton motive force and allows protons to bypass the ATP synthases embedded in the membrane, preventing the production of ATP. This uncoupling of oxidative phosphorylation is a way for organisms to generate heat, (i.e., thermogenesis).

Additionally, the enzyme inhibitors oligomycin and dicyclohexylcarbodiimide can directly inhibit the ATP synthase by preventing the influx of protons.

Mitochondria, apoptosis and oxidative stress

Mitochondria are the organelles involved in energy production. A mitochondrion (powerhouse of the cell) has a double membrane with an intermembrane space between the outer and inner membrane. The matrix is a watery substance that contains ribosomes and many enzymes. Enzymes in the matrix and inner membrane catalyze the oxidation of carbohydrates, fats, and amino acids. These enzymes are vital for the link reaction and the Krebs cycle.

The inner membrane is where the electron transport chain and ATP synthase are located, and where oxidative phosphorylation takes place. The space between the inner and outer membranes is a small volume space into which protons are pumped. Due to its small volume, a high concentration gradient can be reached quickly, which is vital for chemiosmosis. The outer membrane is a membrane that separates the contents of the mitochondrion from the rest of the cell, creating the ideal environment for cell respiration. The cristae are tubular projections of the inner membrane that increase the surface area for oxidative phosphorylation.

Three parts of aerobic cellular respiration take place in the mitochondria: the link reaction, the Krebs cycle, and oxidative phosphorylation. During these processes, the pyruvate from glycolysis is broken down completely to CO_2 and H_2O, which is why aerobic respiration is thought of as glucose breakdown. CO_2 and ATP are transported out of the mitochondria into the cytoplasm. CO_2 enters the bloodstream for transport to the lungs and is expelled during expiration. H_2O can remain or enter the blood and be excreted by the kidneys.

Apoptosis is the programmed cell death that occurs in multicellular organisms. It occurs in both developing tissue (e.g., in embryonic development where parts of tissues are no longer needed) and adult tissue (where cell death balances cell division). When a cell dies by apoptosis, its cytoskeleton collapses, and its nucleus is fragmented, and its chromatin irreversibly condenses. After apoptosis, certain neighboring cells (e.g., macrophages) recognize alterations in the surface of the dead cell and phagocytize the cell before its contents are leaked, which allows for efficient recycling of the cell's biomolecules.

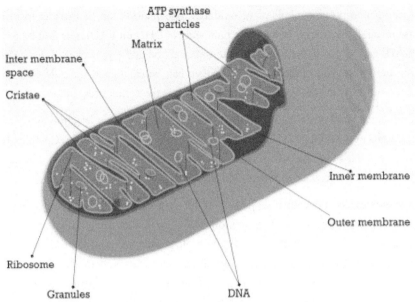

Mitochondrion with cellular compartments and select biomolecules

The machinery for apoptosis depends on an intracellular proteolytic cascade (which involves the breaking of peptide bonds within proteins). Target proteins (both enzymes and structural proteins) are cleaved by proteases, leading to the activation of more proteases. Eventually, this leads to the degradation of all the cell's organelles. However, before this cascade begins, signals must cause the initiation of the apoptosis pathway. Apoptosis usually begins in response to stress; nuclear receptors recognize many stress factors including nutrient deprivation, heat, viral infection, radiation and lack of oxygen. These stress factors lead to the release of intracellular apoptotic signals that cause proteins to initiate the apoptotic pathway.

Mitochondria are the target of some apoptotic proteins. These proteins may create pores in the mitochondrial membrane and cause swelling, or they may change the permeability of the mitochondrial membrane. When the mitochondrial membrane is made more permeable, apoptotic effectors can leak out and activate the proteins of the apoptotic pathway.

Oxidative stress describes an imbalance between reactive oxygen species (i.e., free radicals) and the organism's ability to detoxify these harmful effects. *Free radicals* are atoms or molecules that have an unpaired electron, and thus an odd number of electrons. Free radicals, such as the hydroxyl radical (HO•), are highly reactive, and if they react with important cellular components such as the cell membrane or DNA, the cell can be severely damaged. The extent of the damage can be extensive, because when a free radical abstracts an electron from a cell component, the cell component must then take an electron from another cell component, leading to a chain of free radical reactions. The creation of a free radical could disrupt cellular signaling if the original molecule was a cellular messenger. Oxidative stress is involved in many diseases including cancer, Alzheimer's disease, and Parkinson's disease. However, oxidative stress can be useful, (e.g., when it attacks pathogens rather than the host's cells).

Antioxidants are molecules that donate electrons to free radicals without becoming destabilized, and they are the primary method by which the reactive oxygen species are counteracted. Oxidative stress can be caused by a decrease in antioxidant levels, an increase in free radical levels, or both. Sometimes, oxidative stress can trigger apoptosis or necrosis (cell injury leading to premature cell death).

Notes for active learning

Notes for active learning

Regulation of metabolic pathways: maintenance of a dynamic steady state

Metabolism refers to the biochemical reactions that occur in the cells of living organisms, including the reactions that allow the cell to grow, reproduce and function. Because organisms are usually in environments that are constantly changing, metabolism must be tightly regulated so that the internal conditions of the cell remain constant; this property is *homeostasis* and can be thought of as a "dynamic steady state." Homeostatic processes act at multiple levels, from the cell or the tissue to the whole organism. Examples include the regulation of pH, blood glucose and internal body temperature.

Both catabolic (breaking down) and anabolic (building up) pathways are extensively regulated. During the metabolic reactions that occur in steady-state conditions, the substrate is being converted to the product as efficiently as possible.

Regulation of glycolysis and gluconeogenesis

Glycolysis, the breakdown of glucose into two pyruvate molecules, is universal to biological organisms. Glycolysis is tightly regulated. The three most important steps in the pathway—the reactions catalyzed by phosphofructokinase (phosphorylation of fructose-6-phosphate), hexokinase (phosphorylation of glucose), and pyruvate kinase (phosphate transfer from phosphoenolpyruvate to ADP)—are the most closely regulated because these three steps are essentially irreversible due to a large $-\Delta G$. The production of these three enzymes is regulated by hormones that control the rate of transcription (DNA→mRNA). For more immediate action, allosteric effectors bind to these enzymes reversibly, or the enzymes can be covalently modified to inhibit activity permanently.

Phosphofructokinase is the most important enzyme for glycolysis regulation. High ATP levels allosterically inhibit phosphofructokinase, meaning that the ATP binds to an allosteric site distinct from the catalytic active site. ATP inhibits the key reaction in glycolysis because if there are high levels of ATP, there is no need for more to be produced. Citrate, one of the early intermediates in the Krebs cycle, inhibits phosphofructokinase. It does this by enhancing ATP's inhibitory effect. When there are high levels of citrate, there is no need for additional glucose breakdown.

Some compounds activate phosphofructokinase. For example, the activator AMP reverses ATP's inhibitory action and allows the catalytic activity of phosphofructokinase to resume. Fructose 2,6-bisphosphate, another allosteric activator, reduces ATP's inhibitory effect and increases the enzyme's affinity for fructose-6-phosphate. The concentration of fructose 2,6-bisphosphate is controlled by two enzymes: phosphofructokinase 2 (different than phosphofructokinase) and fructose bisphosphate 2.

These *bifunctional enzymes* are present in a single polypeptide chain. The activity of this bifunctional enzyme is controlled by the phosphorylation of a serine residue in the polypeptide chain. The phosphorylation of this residue, which occurs when glucose levels are low, leads to a reduction in fructose 2,6-biphosphate production and thus a reduction in the rate of glycolysis, thereby conserving glucose. However, when glucose is abundant, dephosphorylation of the serine residue occurs, leading to an increase in fructose 2,6-biphosphate production and thus an increase in the rate of glycolysis. This regulation modulates the levels of glucose, so it is available when needed without being degraded.

Hexokinase, another important regulatory enzyme in glycolysis, is inhibited by its product, glucose-6-phosphate. Since glucose-6-phosphate is in equilibrium with fructose 6-phosphate (the reactant of phosphofructokinase), the inhibition of phosphofructokinase results in the inhibition of hexokinase. This further suggests that phosphofructokinase is the key enzyme in glycolysis regulation.

Pyruvate kinase controls outflow from the glycolysis pathway and is thus important in regulation. It is activated by fructose 1,6-bisphosphate, as an example of *feedforward stimulation*, since fructose 1,6-bisphosphate is an earlier intermediate in the pathway that enables pyruvate kinase to keep up with the oncoming flux of intermediates. Pyruvate kinase is allosterically inhibited by ATP (which signals that energy is abundant) and alanine (which signals that building blocks are abundant).

Transcription of the enzymes used in glycolysis is controlled by hormones, which allows for coordination between different organs and tissues. These hormones regulate the rate of gluconeogenesis (glucose from non-carbohydrate substrates). Gluconeogenesis and glycolysis are "reciprocally regulated," meaning that one pathway is active while the other is inactive. This prevents the occurrence of a *futile cycle*, where ATP is hydrolyzed without useful metabolic work, resulting in chemical energy dissipating as heat and being wasted.

As discussed earlier, gluconeogenesis uses the enzymes glucose-6-phosphatase, fructose-1,6-bisphosphatase and PEP carboxykinase/pyruvate carboxylase, replacing three strongly endergonic reactions with reactions that are more exergonic (and therefore more favorable). These replacements allow for the reciprocal regulation of these two pathways; i.e., the same compounds that activate one enzyme in glycolysis may inhibit the replacement enzyme in gluconeogenesis.

For example, phosphofructokinase in glycolysis is activated by AMP and inhibited by ATP and citrate; fructose-1,6-bisphosphatase, however, is inhibited by AMP and activated by ATP and citrate. Since gluconeogenesis consumes ATP while glycolysis produces ATP, high levels of ATP promote gluconeogenesis (by activation of fructose-1,6,-bisphosphate) and reduce the rate of glycolysis (by inhibition of phosphofructokinase).

Acetyl-CoA is an important activator of gluconeogenesis. It activates pyruvate carboxylase to catalyze the first reaction in gluconeogenesis. Conversely, it inhibits the enzyme pyruvate kinase in glycolysis, demonstrating the reciprocal control of the two pathways.

Metabolism of glycogen

Glycogen is a large, branched polysaccharide made of glucose residues, linked primarily by α-1,4-glycosidic bonds, although one of every ten bonds is an α-1,6-glycosidic bond.

Glycogen with α-1,4-glycosidic and α-1,6-glycosidic bonds

It is the main form of stored glucose in the body (mostly stored in the liver and skeletal muscles) because it can easily be broken down when energy is needed, allowing monomers of glucose to be released when levels are low. When glycogen is metabolized in the liver, it can be slowly released into the bloodstream (e.g., between meals). When it is metabolized in muscle, it can provide a quick burst of glucose for energy production of ATP for aerobic or anaerobic activity. Oxygen is not required for glycogen breakdown.

Glycogenolysis is the breakdown of glycogen in the following reaction:

$$\text{glycogen}_{(n\ residues)} + P_i \rightleftarrows \text{glycogen}_{(n-1\ residues)} + \text{glucose 1-phosphate}$$

There are three main steps in glycogen metabolism. The first step is the release of a glucose-1-phosphate molecule from glycogen, which is catalyzed by glycogen phosphorylase. It is a phosphorolysis reaction (breakdown by the addition of a phosphate molecule). Glycogen phosphorylase only acts on non-reducing ends of a glycogen polymer that are five or more glucose residues away from a branch point (see figure above).

In the second step, the glycogen is remodeled for further breakdown of the polysaccharide. When there are only four glucose residues before a branching point, a glycogen debranching enzyme (a type of transferase) transfers three of the remaining four units of glucose (a trisaccharide) from the 1,6 branch to an adjacent 1,4 branch. This exposes the 1,6 branching point for hydrolysis by α-1,6-glucosidase. The final glucose molecule is removed, and the branch is eliminated, thus allowing the phosphorolysis of glycogen by glycogen phosphorylase to continue.

The third step of glycogen metabolism is the conversion of glucose-1-phosphate to glucose-6-phosphate by the enzyme phosphoglucomutase, which uses a phosphoserine to remove a phosphoryl group.

At this point, there are three possibilities for the glucose-6-phosphate molecule resulting from the glycogen breakdown: (1) enter the glycolysis pathway for the production of ATP, (2) enter the pentose phosphate pathway for the production of NADPH and ribose derivatives, or (3) become dephosphorylated and converted into free glucose for release into the bloodstream by the enzyme glucose 6-phosphatase (i.e., the final step in gluconeogenesis).

Regulation of glycogen synthesis and breakdown: allosteric and hormonal control

The regulation of glycogen anabolism and catabolism is complex. If both pathways were to occur at the same time, it would be a futile cycle, so the simultaneous action of these pathways must be avoided. Like glucose synthesis or breakdown, glycogen synthesis and breakdown are reciprocally regulated. Many of the enzymes involved in these processes are controlled allosterically, and they respond to metabolites that signal the cell's energy needs. The enzyme activity is adjusted so that the demands for energy are met. Glycogen phosphorylase is inhibited by high-energy molecules such as ATP, glucose-6-phosphate, and glucose, and is activated by low-energy molecules such as AMP.

In addition to allosteric control, hormones regulate glycogen synthesis and breakdown. Hormones trigger a cAMP (cyclic AMP) cascade, which is a signaling pathway that can act through the enzyme protein kinase A (PKA). PKA can activate phosphorylase kinase and deactivate glycogen synthase (through the addition of a phosphoryl group), which prevents glycogen synthesis and catabolism from occurring simultaneously. Conversely, protein phosphatase 1 reverses the regulatory effects of PKA. Insulin activates protein phosphatase 1, which stimulates the synthesis of glycogen. Hormonally-stimulated cascades allow the rate of glycogen synthesis or catabolism to be adjusted by the needs of both cells and the entire organism.

Analysis of metabolic control

Metabolic *regulation* refers to the changes that signaling molecules cause on the activity of enzymes that catalyze reactions in metabolic pathways, while metabolic *control* refers to how these changes in enzyme activity control the flux (i.e., the overall rate) of the pathway. These two concepts are closely linked.

There are multiple levels of metabolic control. *Intrinsic control* occurs when the reactions in metabolic pathways are self-regulated, meaning that they respond to changes in the levels of products and substrates. For example, the product of glycogen phosphorylase is glucose-6-phosphate, and it is inhibited by glucose-6-phosphate (feedback inhibition or negative feedback). Positive feedback occurs when the product of a reaction amplifies the reaction rate (e.g., blood clotting).

Extrinsic control occurs when a cell in a multicellular organism alters its metabolism in response to a signal sent from another cell. These signals are usually hormones or growth factors, and they are detected by receptors on the surface of the affected cell, which then leads to a transmission of signals within the cell (second messenger system). An example of extrinsic control is the hormone-triggered phosphorylation cascade that reduces the rate of glycogen synthesis (described earlier).

Extrinsic control systems allow for maintenance of homeostasis at the whole-organism level. There are three components to homeostatic control mechanisms that enable this to happen. The *receptor* is the first component, which senses environmental stimuli. The receptor sends a signal to the second component, the *control center* (e.g., brain). Then, the control center sends a signal to the third component, the *effector*, which responds to the stimuli.

Notes for active learning

Notes for active learning

Metabolism of Fatty Acids and Proteins

When glucose supply is low, the body uses other energy sources in the priority order of: other carbohydrates, fats, and proteins. First, these molecules are converted to glucose or glucose intermediates; then they are degraded in glycolysis or by the Krebs cycle.

Monosaccharides and amino acids travel directly through the bloodstream to the cells for absorption. Triglycerides are packaged into lipoproteins (chylomicrons) for delivery.

Description of fatty acids

Fatty acids are a family of molecules classified as lipids, which are usually ingested and stored as triglycerides. A *triglyceride* (triacylglycerol) consists of a three-carbon glycerol backbone with three fatty acids connected to it, as displayed below.

glycerol   **three fatty acids**

Glycerol and three fatty acids are each joined by a phosphodiester bond

Saturated fats have hydrogens that occupy all possible bonds and have only single bonds. *Unsaturated* fats do not have hydrogen atoms at all positions, and there is at least one double bond.

Fatty acids are an important source of energy, because they are reduced and anhydrous (hydrophobic), which allows for a higher energy yield. Carbohydrates are more hydrated, so the amount of energy that can be stored per unit mass is much lower than fatty acids. For this reason, it is ideal for an organism to store energy as fat in adipose tissue when a large quantity of energy needs to be kept in reserve for later use (e.g., hibernating bear).

Cholesterol is a four fused ring structure   *Cis and trans unsaturated fatty acids*

Digestion, mobilization, and transport of fats

The pancreatic enzyme lipase breaks down triglycerides into free fatty acids and monoglycerides (3-carbon glycerol and fatty acid) by hydrolyzing the ester bond, because triglycerides cannot be absorbed by the duodenum (first segment of the small intestine). Pancreatic lipase forms a complex with the protein colipase, which is essential for its activity, and this complex works at a water-fat interface because dietary fats are nonpolar molecules.

Bile is excreted from the gallbladder into the stomach to assist in digestion. Bile contains *bile salts*, which are *amphipathic* (i.e., having both hydrophilic and hydrophobic parts) to orient their nonpolar face toward the dietary fats and their polar face toward the water, forming *micelles*, which are spherical lipid droplets. *Emulsification* is the breaking of larger nonpolar globules into micelles. The micelles move the dietary fats closer to the intestinal cell wall so that cholesterol can be absorbed across the intestinal wall and triglycerides can be hydrolyzed.

Once across the intestinal wall, free fatty acids and monoglycerides are reassembled as triglycerides, while the cholesterol is linked to another free fatty acid, forming a cholesterol ester. These are repackaged as chylomicrons, lipoproteins that transport triglycerides in the bloodstream and then the tissues, where they are used for energy production or are stored. The liver is an important organ for fatty acid metabolism.

Adipocytes are cells where the majority of body fat is stored, as the entire cytoplasm is filled with a single fat droplet. Adipocytes synthesize and store triglycerides during food uptake and cluster to form adipose tissue, most of which is located beneath the skin and around internal organs.

     Copyright © Sterling Test Prep.

Oxidation of fatty acids (saturated and unsaturated fats)

Fatty acids can be degraded to produce ATP when glucose supplies are low. For fatty acids to undergo catabolism, they first must be activated. Catalysis by the enzyme fatty acyl-CoA synthase links fatty acids to coenzyme A, forming activated fatty acyl-CoA. Then, the fatty acyl-CoA is transported to the mitochondrial matrix with the help of the enzymes: carnitine acyltransferase I (which conjugates fatty acyl-CoA to carnitine), carnitine-acylcarnitine translocase (which shuttles carnitine and acylcarnitine inside the mitochondria), and carnitine acyltransferase II (which liberates the carnitine and turns the molecule back into fatty acyl-CoA). However, this applies to long-chain fatty acids; short-chain fatty acids can diffuse directly into the mitochondrial membrane with no need for the carnitine carrier system.

The molecule then undergoes β oxidation (beta carbon of the fatty acid is oxidized to a carbonyl group). In this process, fatty acyl-CoA undergoes oxidation by repeatedly cleaving two-carbon molecules, each time producing a new fatty acyl-CoA that is two carbons shorter, along with one molecule of acetyl-CoA. The details of β oxidation, including the enzymes that catalyze each step of the process, are in the figure below.

Each turn of β oxidation produces one NADH and one FADH$_2$,
which are later used in the electron transport chain for the production of ATP

β oxidation works best for even-numbered saturated fatty acids due to the repetitive cleaving of two carbons from the chain. Saturated fatty acids produce one NADH and one FADH$_2$ for every cut into two carbons.

The acetyl-CoA produced during β oxidation enters the Krebs cycle, and the typical progression of aerobic cellular respiration occurs. A short eight-carbon fatty acid can produce four acetyl-CoAs. Each acetyl-CoA yields 12 ATP (3 NADP, 1 FADH$_2$, and 1 ATP). Therefore, this eight-carbon fatty acid nets 48 ATP, and fat with three chains of this length produces 144 ATP, illustrating why fats are such a good source of energy. Fats provide 9 calories per gram, while carbohydrates and proteins each provide 4 calories per gram.

For odd-numbered saturated fatty acids in the lipids of some marine organisms and plants, the products of β oxidation are propionyl-CoA and acetyl-CoA. With the help of three enzymes and the vitamins cobalamin and biotin, the propionyl-CoA undergoes carboxylation and molecular rearrangement to form succinyl-CoA. The succinyl-CoA then enters the Krebs cycle.

Unsaturated fatty acids require additional enzymes for β oxidation because the double bonds in the fatty acid are usually in a *cis* configuration, which causes steric hindrance. First, β oxidation of the unsaturated fatty acid occurs normally, but when the presence of a *cis* bond interferes with the ability of acyl-CoA dehydrogenase or enoyl-CoA hydratase to catalyze the necessary reaction, the *cis* bond must be converted into a *trans* bond. Odd-numbered *cis* bonds are transformed by enoyl-CoA isomerase, which changes the *cis* bond to a *trans* bond. Even-numbered *cis* bonds are transformed by 2,4-dienoyl-CoA reductase, which creates an odd-numbered bond, and the enoyl CoA isomerase can then act. Unsaturated fatty acids yield one less FADH$_2$ per double bond compared to saturated fatty acids because they are already partially oxidized, thus reducing total ATP production.

The glycerol that was originally part of the stored triglyceride is converted to glyceraldehyde phosphate and enters glycolysis or gluconeogenesis (depending on the cell's needs at the time). However, it must be converted to glyceraldehyde-3-phosphate (PGAL) before it can enter either of these pathways.

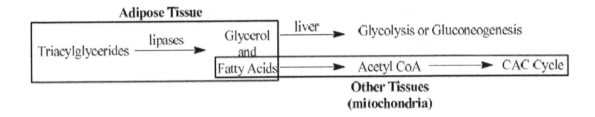

Ketone bodies

Sometimes there is an insufficient supply of glucose in the body (e.g., during periods of low food intake), and once the cellular carbohydrate stores have been depleted, it is necessary for the organism to find another way to obtain energy. *Ketogenesis* is the production of ketone derivatives of acetyl-CoA groups, as another form of fatty acid breakdown and occurs in the mitochondria of the liver.

The oxidation of large amounts of fatty acids can cause acetyl-CoA to accumulate in the liver, and if the quantities of acetyl-CoA are high, it may exceed the processing capacity of the Krebs cycle. This can occur when excess deaminated ketogenic amino acids are degraded, causing acetyl-CoA buildup. In cases of high acetyl-CoA accumulation, the ketogenesis pathway is initiated. In ketogenesis, the two carbon acetyl units condense in the liver, forming the following four carbon ketone molecules: β-hydroxybutyrate, acetoacetate, and acetone. These are collectively referred to as *ketone bodies* and the figure below illustrates how ketone bodies are produced.

These ketone bodies are transferred from the liver to the heart, brain, and muscles. In these organs, β-hydroxybutyrate and acetoacetate can be reconverted to acetyl-CoA for entry into the Krebs cycle. Acetone is converted to pyruvate, lactate, and acetate, or excreted as waste if it is not used quickly.

Conversion of acetyl-CoA to ketones (acetone) and β-hydroxybutyrate

Ketosis occurs when an excessive amount of ketone bodies is present in the body. In this metabolic state, the majority of energy comes from ketone bodies in the blood. It can occur during fasting or low-carbohydrate diets and is "fat-burning mode." Because acetoacetate and *β*-hydroxybutyrate are acidic, the excessive formation of ketone bodies can cause *ketoacidosis* or *metabolic acidosis,* a condition where blood pH is drastically decreased, sometimes to fatal levels. This occurs if the body fails to regulate ketone production properly.

Anabolism of fats

When there are excess dietary carbohydrates, the molecules must be converted to fat for storage. The anabolism of fats primarily occurs in the cytoplasm and the endoplasmic reticulum of liver cells, in contrast with fatty acid breakdown, which occurs in the mitochondria. *Lipogenesis* is the process whereby fats are produced from acetyl-CoA and malonyl-CoA precursors by fatty acid synthases that polymerize and reduce acetyl groups.

Lipogenesis is stimulated by insulin because insulin activates pyruvate dehydrogenase (an enzyme that catalyzes the formation of acetyl-CoA) and acetyl-CoA carboxylase (an enzyme that catalyzes the formation of malonyl-CoA). Then the synthesized fatty acids are esterified with glycerol to create triglycerides, and the triglycerides are packaged into lipoproteins and secreted from the liver.

Synthesis of palmitate, the primary fatty acid synthesized in the human body

As seen in the diagram above, ATP and NADPH are required for fatty acid synthesis. During the process, these molecules are oxidized to ADP and $NADP^+$, respectively.

For the synthesis of an unsaturated fatty acid, a desaturation reaction introduces a double bond into the fatty acyl chain (usually requiring a desaturase enzyme).

Essential fatty acids cannot be synthesized in mammalian tissue and are required in the diet. The essential fatty acids for humans are linolenic acid (omega-3 fatty acid) and linoleic acid (omega-6 fatty acid). If these are not consumed in the diet, health problems develop from a deficiency of these essential fatty acids (from diet).

Non-template synthesis: biosynthesis of lipids and polysaccharides

Lipids are a group of molecules that include triglycerides, fat-soluble vitamins, waxes, sterols, and phospholipids. Polysaccharides (carbohydrate polymers) are synthesized by non-template *de novo* synthesis. For *de novo* synthesis, there is no template as there is in the synthesis of nucleic acids or proteins; rather, the synthesis of carbohydrate polymers is based solely on gene expression and enzyme specificity.

Additionally, other molecules are synthesized *de novo*. Terpenes, a class of lipids that exists in all organisms are created by the assembly and modification of isoprene units. These molecules can then be used to create sterols (e.g., cholesterol).

Isoprene as a component of carotenoids, steroids, etc.

Glycogen is a polysaccharide that is synthesized *de novo*, constructed by joining units of uracil-diphosphate-glucose by the enzyme glycogenin, which acts as a primer. Glycogen synthase adds glucose monomers to the existing chain, and the glycogen branching enzyme creates branches.

Metabolism of proteins

When carbohydrates and fats are unavailable, proteins are then used as an energy source. Proteins are the least desirable form of energy for the body because a large amount of energy is required for protein breakdown. *Proteolysis* (protein catabolism) requires proteases to break the peptide bonds of proteins via hydrolysis for the release of smaller polypeptides or amino acids. Amino acids can provide intermediates for a variety of other molecules. Most amino acids are deaminated (the amino group is removed) in the liver and are then converted to pyruvate, acetyl-CoA or other Krebs cycle intermediates. Depending on the specific amino acid, these intermediates enter cellular respiration at various points.

From dietary intake, protein digestion begins in the stomach, where proteins are denatured (unfolded) by the acidic digestive juices. Digestive enzymes like pepsin, trypsin, and chymotrypsin hydrolyze covalent peptide bonds. Amino acids are absorbed in the small intestine into the bloodstream for delivery to the tissues. Amino acids can produce ATP when other fuel supplies are low, and the cell does not require other nitrogen-containing compounds. For this process, the amino group of amino acid must either be removed by oxidative deamination to produce a keto acid and NH_3 or transferred to a keto acid by *transamination* (transfer of an amino acid group to an organic acid).

The keto acid enters the glycolytic pathway or the synthetic pathways for glucose and fat. The nitrogen from the amino group can be used to synthesize important nitrogen-containing molecules such as purines and pyrimidines. The toxic NH_3 (ammonia) passes into the bloodstream through the plasma membrane and is transported to the liver, where it is linked with CO_2 to form, in mammals, the relatively non-toxic urea, which is excreted by the kidneys. In fish, insects, and birds, the ammonia is converted to uric acid rather than urea.

Amino acids may replenish the intermediates in the Krebs cycle. Three-carbon amino acids (e.g., alanine) enter the pathways as pyruvate. Four-carbon amino acids (e.g., aspartate) are converted to oxaloacetate. Five-carbon amino acids (e.g., valine) are converted to α-ketoglutarate. Some amino acids can enter at more than one point, depending on cellular requirements.

Plants synthesize all the amino acids they need; animals lack some enzymes needed to make some amino acids. Humans synthesize eleven of the twenty necessary amino acids. The diet must provide the remaining nine amino acids as *essential amino acids*.

Total free amino acid pool in the body is derived from (1) ingested protein degraded to amino acids during digestion, (2) synthesis of non-essential amino acids from keto acids and (3) the breakdown of body proteins. The amino acids in these pools can be used for protein biosynthesis.

Notes for active learning

Notes for active learning

Hormonal Regulation and Integration of Metabolism

Higher level integration of hormone structure and function

Hormones are signaling molecules produced by glands in multicellular organisms and travel in the bloodstream to their target cell, organ or tissue. These molecules play an important role in the regulation of cell metabolism, as is evident from the several examples of hormonal regulation throughout this chapter. There are three main categories of hormones, based on their chemical structure: peptide hormones, steroid hormones, and modified amino acid hormones.

Peptide hormones range from three amino acids to folded proteins with subunit structure. When they have longer amino acid chain lengths, they are protein hormones. These hormones, which include insulin and parathyroid hormone, are initially produced in endocrine tissue as large products, and then undergo extensive processing before they are stored in vesicles or granules in preparation for release.

Peptide hormones have short half-lives in the bloodstream, so they are only released at the precise moment they are needed. The response is rapid because these hormones are stored in large quantities. When they are released, peptide hormones target protein and glycoprotein receptors embedded in cell membranes. The binding of the hormone to the receptor on the surface of the cell can initiate a signal transduction cascade within the cell, which may have any number of effects. These include increasing uptake of a molecule, phosphorylation or dephosphorylation of target molecules within the cell, triggering secretion or activating mitosis.

Steroid hormones, such as glucocorticoids and progestins, are synthesized from cholesterol, usually in the adrenal glands and the gonads. The synthesis of these hormones occurs in the mitochondria and smooth endoplasmic reticulum, where a series of enzymatic reactions convert cholesterol into the specified steroid hormone. Unlike polypeptide hormones, steroid hormones are not stored in large quantities. Most hydrophobic steroid hormones circulating in the bloodstream are bound to carrier proteins, and the unbound steroid hormones are the steroid molecules entering the target cells.

Steroid hormones easily pass through cell membranes, because they are hydrophobic and fat-soluble. Inside the cell, they bind to intracellular receptors, causing a conformational change in a transcriptional complex. This either increases or decreases the rate of transcription (DNA→RNA) of specific genes and consequently affects the rate at which certain proteins are produced. An example is glucocorticoids that bind to the glucocorticoid receptor complex, which inhibit the action of pro-inflammatory transcription factors, thus having an anti-inflammatory effect.

Modified amino acid hormones are the third category of hormones. Examples are norepinephrine, epinephrine, and the thyroid hormones thyroxine (T_4) and triiodothyronine (T_3). The chemical modifications that occur to create modified amino acid hormones include methylation, decarboxylation or hydroxylation. Modified amino acid hormones may have a long half-life like steroid hormones or may have a short half-life like peptide hormones. Depending on the hormone, they may bind to receptors on the cell-surface (like peptide hormone) or to intracellular receptors (like steroid hormone). They are a varied, yet important, group of hormones that can have a significant effect on cell metabolism.

Tissue-specific metabolism

Each tissue of the human body has a particular specialized function reflected in its anatomy, presence of biomolecules and metabolic activity. Skeletal muscle tissue, for instance, allows for directed motion, while adipose tissue stores and releases energy in the form of fat. The brain pumps ions across the plasma membranes of neurons to produce electrical signals. The liver processes and converts nutrients that include carbohydrates, fats and proteins, and distributes them to the appropriate locations.

The liver detoxifies foreign compounds like drugs, preservatives, and food additives. The liver is responsible for synthesizing fats. The process of lipogenesis, where acetyl-CoA is converted to fatty acids through the addition of two carbon units, occurs in the cytoplasm. Most of the enzymes involved in fatty acid synthesis are arranged into a multienzyme complex as fatty acid synthetase. In animals and humans, fatty acids are usually stored in adipose tissue and the liver as triglyceride.

The hormone insulin is an indicator of blood sugar levels. The level of insulin increases as blood glucose levels increase. Insulin increases the rate of storage pathways (e.g., lipogenesis) by stimulating the pyruvate dehydrogenase complex (PDC), leading to the formation of acetyl-CoA and acetyl-CoA carboxylase (ACC), which forms malonyl-CoA from acetyl-CoA. As insulin levels increase, the levels of malonyl-CoA increase; this is important because the synthesis of malonyl-CoA is the first committed step in the fatty acid synthesis. Insulin affects ACC in a way similar to PDC; dephosphorylation leads to the activation of the enzyme. Glucagon has an agonist effect and increases phosphorylation, which inhibits ACC, thus slowing fat synthesis.

Muscle tissue is involved in mechanical movements of the body. Additionally, muscle tissue, which consumes large quantities of oxygen, is considered an ATP generator. Muscular activity releases epinephrine from the adrenal medulla; epinephrine binds to a receptor on the muscle cell membrane and initiates adenyl cyclase in the membrane, triggering the cAMP cascade (described previously). Epinephrine is involved in glycogen breakdown in the muscles and occasionally in the liver.

The protein kinase, activated by cAMP, causes phosphorylations on a series of enzymes to produce glucose-1-phosphate, later converted to glucose-6-phosphate. Simultaneously, enzymes activate glycogen breakdown (glycogenolysis), while other enzymes such as glycogen synthetase are inactivated to inhibit glycogenesis.

The two hormones involved in the control of glycogenolysis are the peptide hormone glucagon (released from the pancreas when blood glucose levels are low) and the catecholamine epinephrine (released from the adrenal glands in response to a threat or stress). Both glucagon and epinephrine activate enzymes to initiate glycogen phosphorylase to start glycogenolysis, and they inhibit glycogen synthetase.

The stimulation by epinephrine and other hormones results in the production of glucose-6-phosphate, which may proceed through glycolysis; this can occur in a muscle cell. However, if it happened to a liver cell stimulated by glucagon, glucose-6-phosphate would be converted to glucose and released into the bloodstream. During muscle contractions, ATP is constantly being used to supply energy.

The *Cori cycle* involves recycling lactic acid in the liver and muscles. In this cycle, lactate goes through gluconeogenesis, producing glucose. If muscular activity continues in the body, the amount of oxygen at the end of the electron transport chain becomes the limiting factor, and soon the oxygen supply is completely exhausted. When this occurs, the Krebs cycle is inhibited, and pyruvate starts to accumulate. Epinephrine stimulates the enzymes involved in glycogenolysis, and more glucose-6-phosphate is produced.

When the cells become anaerobic, the process of glycolysis continues as pyruvic acid is converted to lactic acid, which shifts part of the metabolic burden to the liver. The formation of lactic acid requires NADH from glycolysis and produces NAD^+ to allow the glycolysis pathway to perpetuate. If, however, strenuous muscle activity has stopped, glucose activity can be utilized to rebuild supplies of glycogen through glycogenesis. During this time, the oxygen debt is eliminated as O_2 is replenished. For lactic acid to be converted to glucose, some of it must be transformed into pyruvic acid and then to acetyl-CoA. The Krebs cycle and electron transport chain is initiated, which produces ATP to give energy for glycogenesis of the remaining lactic acid to glucose.

Hormonal regulation of fuel metabolism

Thyroid hormones are important for controlling metabolism and play a permissive role in the development and maintenance of the nervous system. Thyroid hormones are the most important determinant of basal metabolic rate (BMR). They can increase BMR by increasing oxygen consumption, and heat-production in most body tissues termed a *calorigenic effect*.

Blood glucose concentration levels fluctuate throughout the day. Homeostasis targets plasma blood glucose levels around 80 to 120 mg/dl. Through negative feedback, certain target organs can affect the rate at which glucose is taken up from the blood or released into the blood.

When glucose levels are too high (above the homeostasis set point), β cells in the pancreatic islets produce insulin, which stimulates muscle cells and liver cells to take up glucose from the blood and convert it into glycogen. Glycogen is then stored as granules in the cytoplasm. Some cells are stimulated to take up glucose and use it immediately for cell respiration. These processes all lower the levels of glucose in the blood.

When glucose levels are too low (below the homeostasis set point), α cells in the pancreatic islets produce glucagon. Glucagon stimulates the liver cells to convert glycogen back into glucose and release this glucose into the blood, thereby raising the blood glucose level.

Cholesterol in the body comes from both the diet and from *hepatic synthesis* (synthesis by the liver). The liver excretes cholesterol by adding it to bile. The homeostatic control that keeps the plasma cholesterol level constant mainly involves hepatic synthesis.

The ingestion of saturated fatty acids (animal fats) raises plasma cholesterol levels, while the ingestion of unsaturated fatty acids (vegetable fats) lowers it. Low-density lipoproteins (LDL) deliver cholesterol to cells throughout the body, while high-density lipoproteins (HDL) remove excess cholesterol from blood and tissue and deliver it to the liver for excretion. The ratio of LDL to HDL is important, and the lower the ratio, the lower the deposition of extra cholesterol in the blood vessels.

Obesity and regulation of body mass

Diabetes mellitus, commonly called diabetes, is a disease where body cells are unable to metabolize sugar. Blood glucose levels become high enough for the kidneys to excrete glucose, which can be tested in a urine sample. The liver cannot store glucose as glycogen, and cells are unable to utilize glucose for energy. Since carbohydrates are not being metabolized, the body breaks down protein and fat for energy. *Ketones*, a class of chemicals produced from the fat breakdown, then build up in the blood, resulting in reduced blood volume and acidosis (lower pH). This can lead to coma and death. In *type 1 diabetes*, usually diagnosed in children and young adults, the pancreas does not produce insulin. A viral infection may cause cytotoxic T cells to destroy pancreatic islets. This condition of diabetics is treated with a daily administration of insulin; an overdose of insulin or lack of eating results in hypoglycemia. The brain has constant sugar requirements; low blood sugar can result in unconsciousness. An immediate intake of sugar is an effective treatment for hypoglycemia.

Of the 26 million diabetics in the U.S., the vast majority have *type 2 diabetes*. This form usually occurs in obese individuals and can occur at any age, although it generally appears later in life. Obesity can be caused by inactivity, an unhealthy diet, lack of sleep (may cause hormonal changes), medical problems, or a combination of these. In type 2 diabetes, the pancreas does produce insulin. However, liver and muscle cells do not respond to it because they lack sufficient receptors for insulin. Untreated, type 2 diabetes can have serious consequences, including blindness, kidney disease, circulatory disorders, and strokes. A healthy diet avoiding processed carbohydrates (low glycemic index) and regular exercise can help control the disease, and oral drugs can make cells more sensitive to insulin or stimulate the pancreas to produce higher levels of insulin, in an attempt to overcome insulin resistance.

Type 1 diabetes	Type 2 diabetes
The onset is usually early, sometime during childhood.	The onset is usually late, sometime after childhood.
β cells do not produce enough insulin.	Target cells become insensitive to insulin.
Diet by itself cannot be used to control the condition. Insulin injections are needed to control glucose levels.	Insulin injections are not mandatory. A low-fat diet can control the condition, but oral medications may be necessary.

Notes for active learning

Notes for active learning

Enzyme Structure and Function

The function of enzymes in catalyzing biological reactions

Enzymes assist almost all chemical reactions that occur in living organisms. Enzymes are biological molecules that act as catalysts by increasing the rate of chemical reactions. The vast majority of enzymes are proteins, although RNA molecules (ribozymes) can catalyze reactions. An enzyme cannot force a reaction to occur if it would not normally occur (i.e., products are less stable than reactants); it makes a reaction occur faster. Enzymes are highly specific in their action and catalyze a single reaction or class of reactios. Enzymes are not consumed in a reaction, so only small amounts of enzymes are needed in a cell. The overall 3D shape (tertiary structure) of an enzyme plays an important role in the enzyme's function.

Enzymes are often named for their substrates by adding the suffix "–*ase*." For example, ribonuclease, abbreviated as RNase, is an enzyme that catalyzes the degradation of ribonucleic acid (RNA) into smaller components.

For example, the enzyme hexokinase is written above or below the reaction arrow. The reactants (starting material) upon which an enzyme acts, written to the left of the reaction arrow, are substrates. An enzyme may bind to one or more substrates (a molecule that enzymes act upon).

In the example below, there are two substrates: glucose and adenosine triphosphate (ATP). The products (to the right of the reaction arrow) are glucose-6-phosphate and adenosine diphosphate (ADP). Intermediates (not pictured in this example) are compounds temporarily formed between initial reactants and final products.

The substrates glucose and ATP are catalyzed by hexokinase to form glucose-6-phosphate and ADP. The hexokinase is not consumed in the reaction and continues the process with new substrates.

Reduction of activation energy

Reactants must reach a certain energy level before the reaction can proceed to convert the substrate(s) to the product(s). This energy is the *activation energy* (E_a) and is needed to break bonds within the reactants and thus enable them to react to form products. At a later stage in the reaction, energy is released as new bonds form within the product.

Enzymes decrease the activation energy of a reaction by lowering the energy of the transition state. The *transition state* (bond making and bond breaking state) is where the reactants are in an activated complex. As shown in the image below, the transition state corresponds to the highest energy level—the activation energy.

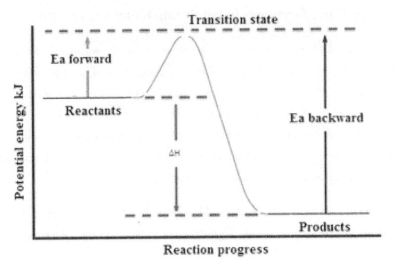

The energy is on the y-axis and time is shown on the x-axis. The products are lower in energy than reactants, and the reaction is spontaneous. The enzyme speeds the rate of spontaneous reactions.

Activation energy is an energy barrier to the reaction, in which the reactants must overcome before they can be converted into products. This can be accomplished non-enzymatically by increasing the temperature, which increases molecular collisions between reactants. However, homeostasis means the body temperature is maintained within narrow ranges in many organisms. The same enzyme may lower the activation energy barrier for both the forward and reverse reaction, increasing both rates of reaction, or another enzyme catalyzes each reaction separately.

In the graph, the enzyme makes it easier for reactions to occur by lowering the required activation energy, but it does not alter the net energy release, ΔG (Gibbs free energy).

The enzyme provides an alternate pathway for reactants to form products. The lowering of the activation energy, which is accomplished during the formation of the enzyme-substrate complex, occurs in several ways:

Proximity: When the enzyme-substrate complex forms, the substrates are nearby, and therefore do not have to find each other as in a solution, thereby lowering the entropy (i.e., the disorder) of the reactants.

Optimizing orientation: The enzyme holds the substrates in the correct alignment and at the appropriate distance, usually by aligning active chemical groups. This lowers the entropy of the reactants.

Modifying bond energy: While binding to the substrate, the enzyme may stretch or distort a bond and weaken them so that less energy is needed to break the bond.

Electrostatic catalysis. Acidic or basic amino acids in the active site of the enzyme (a portion of the enzyme where the substrate binds) may form ionic bonds with the intermediate, which stabilize the transition state and lower the activation energy.

Substrates and enzyme specificity

When an enzyme binds to one or more substrates, it forms an enzyme-substrate complex, which is held together by hydrogen or ionic bonds. While bound, the catalytic action of the enzyme converts the substrate(s) to the product(s).

The substrate binds to active site of the enzyme with hydrogen or ionic bonds

An enzyme can distinguish its substrate from similar molecules and even isomers (same molecular formula but different molecules) of the same molecule. This enzyme-substrate *stereospecificity* refers to an enzyme's ability to distinguish between stereoisomers (different shapes) of the same molecule. For example, hexokinase binds D-glucose but not its stereoisomer L-glucose.

Enzyme classification by reaction type

While the names of some enzymes such as RNase describe their function, many enzymes have common names that do not refer to the substrate that they bind. Scientists created an enzyme classification system based on reaction type, with six main classes of enzymes. Note that within these six categories there are many subcategories. Knowing the reaction that a particular enzyme catalyzes is essential to categorization.

Oxidoreductases catalyze reactions that transfer electrons (oxidation-reduction or redox reactions). Common names for enzymes in this category are dehydrogenase, reductase, and oxidase.

Transferases catalyze group transfer reactions, whereby a group is transferred from a donor to an acceptor molecule. Hexokinase is a transferase that catalyzes the transfer of a phosphate group from ATP to glucose.

Hydrolases catalyze hydrolysis, in which water is used to break a bond (hydrolysis). Hydrolases transfer a functional group from a donor molecule to water (acceptor) and therefore are a specific type of transferase. An example is the digestive enzyme chymotrypsin, which can hydrolyze amide (amino acids) and ester (fatty acids) bonds.

Lyases catalyze the breakage of bonds using mechanisms other than hydrolysis (water) and oxidation (electron transfer). Lyases cleave double bonds by the addition of functional groups along with the reverse reaction (i.e., double bond formation via the removal of functional groups). Examples of lyases include fumarase (removes water), and adenosine deaminase (removes ammonia).

Isomerases produce isomeric forms (same atoms but the different connection between atoms) by transferring functional groups within a molecule, which allows for geometric or structural changes. For example, phosphoglucose isomerase converts glucose 6-phosphate to fructose 6-phosphate.

Ligases form covalent bonds by joining two molecules. A linkage reaction is usually coupled with an energy-producing reaction, such as the breakdown of ATP to ADP. An example is DNA ligase, which catalyzes the formation of a phosphodiester bond by joining DNA nucleotides together during replication of the genetic material.

Active Site Model

Every enzyme has an active site, which is a region on the surface of the enzyme where it binds to the substrate, orients it and facilitates the reaction. There are two prominent hypotheses on how substrates bind to the enzyme's active site. The *lock and key model* proposes that there is only one rigid active site that precisely fits the reactants, and the substrate fits inside its active site as a key fits into a lock. In this model, there is no modification of the enzyme after the substrate binds to the active site.

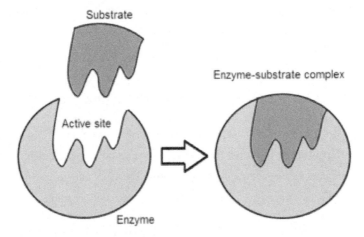

Lock and key model proposes that the enzyme has a shape matching the substrate and enzyme shape is static

Induced Fit Model

As an alternative to the lock and key model, the more recently developed *induced fit model* proposes that there is not a perfect match between the active site of an enzyme and the substrate that it binds. In this model, a small conformation (rotation) change occurs as the enzyme and substrate come together, which allows the active site to bind more precisely with the substrate. The induced fit model hypothesizes that certain amino acid residues (i.e., side-chains) in the active site facilitate the enzyme finding the proper substrate. The initial interaction between the enzyme and substrate is weak, but these weak interactions cause conformational changes in the enzyme that strengthen binding. The energy barrier is lower in the "closed" form of the enzyme, where the active site fits snugly around the substrate.

Think of a handshake where the fingers move to more tightly grasp the other hand. The induced fit is the favored model of enzyme-substrate binding.

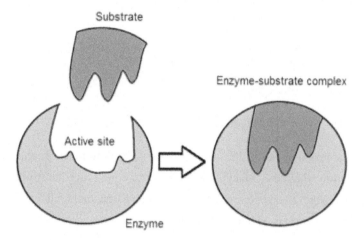

The induced fit model proposes that conformational changes resulting from rotation around single bonds in the enzyme increase the interactions between enzyme and substrate.

Mechanism of catalysis (cofactors, coenzymes, and water-soluble vitamins)

When the enzyme and the substrate form the enzyme-substrate complex, the R-groups (i.e., side chains) of the amino acids in the active site catalyze the reaction. They often pull or contort the substrate, temporarily weakening bonds or altering the substrate's conformation. In reactions with two or more substrates, the side chains form a template to guide the substrates into the most energy-efficient conformation.

Some enzymes require *cofactors*, which are non-protein molecules that assist in chemical reactions that cannot be performed by the active site alone. Not all organisms can produce the cofactors needed, so they are required (essential) in the diet. Cofactors may be inorganic trace elements or metal ions, such as Cu^{2+}, Fe^{3+} or Zn^{2+} (electron carriers), or organic molecules as coenzymes.

Coenzymes are small, complex organic molecules, usually derived from vitamins, which facilitate enzymatic reactions. Vitamins can be fat-soluble (A, D, E and K) or water-soluble (B and C), and it is the water-soluble vitamins that generally act as precursors to coenzymes. Vitamin deficiency may lead to the lack of a specific coenzyme and thus a lack of enzymatic action. Coenzymes may be loosely or tightly bound to the enzyme. Loosely-bound coenzymes are *cosubstrates*. Some coenzymes are so tightly bound to their enzyme that they cannot be removed without denaturing the enzyme and a coenzyme is a *prosthetic group*. Prosthetic groups may be attached to enzymes with covalent bonds. However, the division between loosely and tightly-bound coenzymes is not always clear. For example, NAD^+ can be loosely bound in some enzymes but tightly bound in other enzymes.

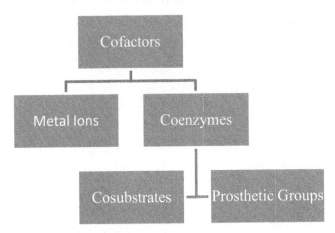

The relationship among molecules required by some enzymes

An *apoenzyme* is an enzyme missing the cofactor that it requires to function, and the enzyme is inactive. A *holoenzyme* is an active form in which the cofactor and enzyme are bound together. Cofactors must be regenerated (i.e., returned to their original state) to complete the catalytic cycle. Cofactors, unlike enzymes, may change during the course of the reaction and therefore need to be replenished.

Effects of local conditions on enzyme activity

Many factors can affect enzyme activity, including substrate concentration, pH, temperature and the presence of modulators.

At a constant enzyme concentration, an increase in the substrate concentration increases the enzyme's activity by increasing the number of random collisions between the substrate and the active site on the enzyme. However, at some point, all available active sites are bound, and increasing the substrate concentration has no further effect on enzyme activity, a state known as *saturation*. The substrate in a cell is regulated by an organism's diet, rates of absorption in the intestine, the permeability of the plasma membrane or changes in intracellular breakdown and synthesis of the substrate.

Enzymes have an optimum pH at which they work most efficiently. At this pH, the enzyme maintains its tertiary structure and, therefore, its active site. As the pH diverges from the optimum, enzyme activity decreases and may cease altogether.

Additionally, changes in pH may change the nature of an amino acid side chain. If an enzyme requires a carboxylate ion (COO⁻), lowering the pH could convert the carboxylate ion to a carboxylic acid (COOH), which would cause enzyme activity to decrease.

An enzyme's pH optimum depends on the location of the enzyme. Enzymes in the stomach function at a much lower pH because of the stomach's acidic environment.

Enzyme	Location	Substrate	pH Optimum
Pepsin	Stomach	Peptide bonds	2
Sucrase	Small intestine	Sucrose	6.2
Urease	Liver	Urea	7.4
Hexokinase	All tissues	Glucose	7.5
Trypsin	Small intestine	Peptide bonds	8
Arginase	Liver	Arginine	9.7

Sometimes, the active site of an enzyme functions as a microenvironment more conducible to the reaction, such as providing a pocket of low pH in an otherwise neutral cell.

There is usually a temperature optimum at which an enzyme exhibits peak activity. Like the pH optimum, it is dependent on the environment in which the enzyme normally operates. For example, a DNA polymerase of a human has a lower temperature optimum than a DNA polymerase of a thermophilic bacterium. For most human enzymes, the temperature optimum is body temperature (37 °C).

As temperature increases, molecules move faster, with more random collisions between enzymes and substrates. Within the upper-temperature limit range, enzyme activity generally doubles with every 10-degree increase.

However, as with pH, at a certain point, the temperature gets too high, and bonds maintaining the 2°, 3° and 4° structure of the protein dissociate. This causes the enzyme's active site to become unstable, leading to a loss of function. A *denatured* protein changes its three-dimensional shape. Denaturation alters the structure of an enzyme or another organic molecule so that the enzyme cannot carry out its intended function. The enzymes in bacteria are often denatured by high temperatures in processes like boiling contaminated drinking water and heat-sterilizing medical and scientific equipment. However, enzyme activity is decreased by low temperatures, as when food is stored in a refrigerator or freezer. Enzymes are major participants in food spoilage, but low temperatures can significantly slow the spoilage process.

Modulators are compounds that modify the binding site of an enzyme, either inhibiting or enhancing the enzyme's activity. Modulators can have a strong effect on enzyme activity through either covalent (irreversible) or non-covalent (reversible) interactions between modulators and an enzyme. Modulators are products of other chemical reactions or are activated by chemical signals. If modulators are required for enzymes to catalyze the reaction, they are cofactors. Modulators that increase an enzyme's catalytic activity are enzyme activators, enhancers or inducers; modulators that decrease or eliminate an enzyme's catalytic activity are enzyme inhibitors.

Notes for active learning

Control of Enzyme Activity

Kinetics: general (catalysis), Michaelis–Menten and cooperativity

Enzyme activity is studied using the principles of *enzyme kinetics*, which describe the rates of reactions and the effects of varying the conditions of a reaction. The *Michaelis-Menten kinetics* model of a single-substrate reaction is shown below.

Enzymes become saturated when substrates occupy all of the active sites

The graph shows that the rate of enzyme-catalyzed reactions is not linearly correlated with substrate concentration; this is because as the substrate concentration becomes higher, the enzyme becomes saturated with the substrate and approaches its maximum rate, V_{max}. K_m indicates an enzyme's affinity for a substrate. A low K_m reflects a high affinity for the substrate, while a high K_m reflects a low affinity. The Michaelis constant K_m is the substrate concentration at which the reaction rate is half of V_{max}.

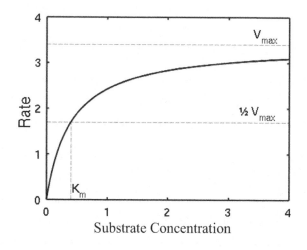

At V_{max} (maximum activity) the enzyme is operating in its optimum conditions, the steady state. Under steady state conditions, the substrate is converted to the product at maximum efficiently.

In the *reaction rate* $= k\,[A]\cdot[B]$, the enzymes' rate depends on the constant k which is a property of the enzyme. A higher k increases the speed of the reaction. Enzymes do not change ΔG, the net change in free energy between the products and reactants. Therefore, enzymes affect the kinetics (i.e., rate) of a reaction, but not the thermodynamics (relative stability).

Cooperativity can occur in enzymes with multiple binding sites. When one or more of these sites become activated (or deactivated), it affects the other binding sites on the enzyme, either by a conformational change of the enzyme or chemical alteration within the protein. Positive cooperativity causes an increase in the affinity of the other binding sites for a substrate. Negative cooperativity is the decrease in affinity of the other binding sites for a substrate.

Feedback regulation

Negative feedback (feedback inhibition) occurs when the product of a reaction deactivates an enzyme in the process. In feedback inhibition, the enzyme typically has one or more *allosteric sites* (regions other than the active site), where the reaction product can bind. When the reaction product binds, the enzyme is spatially rearranged or chemically modified and can no longer bind to the original substrate, halting the reaction. This can be done to prevent overproduction of a product, or to avoid consuming too many molecules that are energy sources for the cell. For example, hexokinase, the first enzyme in glycolysis (first pathway in cell respiration), is inhibited by its product, glucose-6-phosphate. This prevents the glucose substrate from being depleted. It is an example of negative feedback because the product is used as a signal to decrease the further output of the product.

Positive feedback (feedforward) is when a product is used as a signal to increase the further output of the product. An example is blood clotting, which is a catalytic cascade process. The cascade begins with an initial factor, such as catalyzing proteases, and additional steps follow, each step amplifying the preceding. Positive feedback is much less common than negative feedback.

Inhibition types: competitive, uncompetitive, non-competitive, and mixed

Inhibitors are molecules that reduce enzyme function. There are several types of behaviors that inhibitors may display. Some inhibitors are irreversible; they cause the enzyme to lose activity permanently because they become covalently bound to the enzyme and cannot be easily removed.

An irreversible inhibitor covalently bonds with amino acid side chains in the active site of the enzyme, excluding the substrate and thus blocking the catalytic reaction. Since blocking the activity of a particular enzyme can deactivate a pathogen or correct a metabolic imbalance, many medications are enzyme inhibitors. Penicillin is an example of an irreversible inhibitor of medical applications. Penicillin binds to the active site of an enzyme that bacteria use to synthesize cell walls. When the bacterial enzyme covalently bonds with penicillin, the enzyme loses its catalytic activity, and the growth of the bacterial cell wall slows. Without a proper cell wall for protection, the bacteria cannot survive, and the bacterial infection is alleviated.

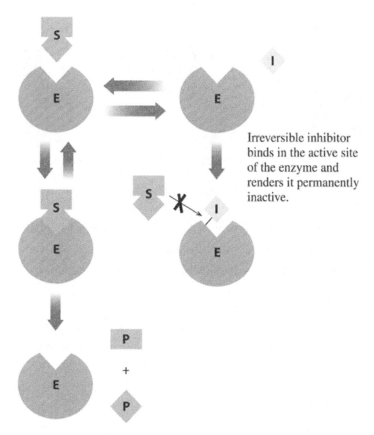

Irreversible inhibitors often bind to the active site with covalent bonds

Other inhibitors are reversible, which use hydrogen bonds, hydrophobic interactions or ionic bonds, and cause the enzyme to lose activity temporarily. In reversible inhibition, the inhibitor causes the enzyme to lose catalytic activity, but if the inhibitor is removed, the enzyme becomes functional again. There are four types of reversible inhibitors: competitive, uncompetitive, non-competitive and mixed.

Competitive inhibitors are structurally similar to the substrate and bind to the enzyme's active site. When a competitive inhibitor binds to the active site, it prevents the substrate from binding to the same site. Only when the inhibitor has been released from the active site can the substrate bind. The inhibitor directly competes with the substrate for the active site.

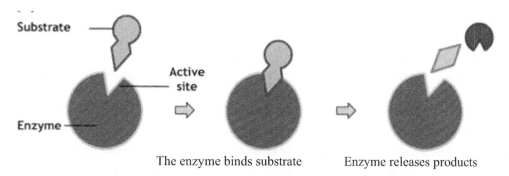

The substrate binds to the enzyme at the active site to form a product

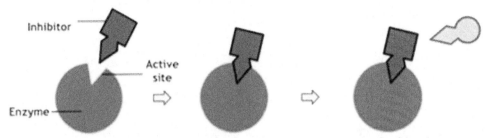

The enzyme binds inhibitor   Inhibitor competes with substrate

Competitive inhibition where the inhibitor binds to enzyme's active site

Competitive inhibitors usually bind directly to the active site. In other examples, they competitively may bind close to the active site in a way that blocks the active site. The definition of competitive inhibition is that the binding of the competitive inhibitor and binding of the substrate are mutually exclusive.

Malonate is an example of a competitive inhibitor. It is structurally similar to succinate, a substrate in the Krebs cycle of aerobic respiration which binds to the active site of a dehydrogenase enzyme. Malonate can compete with succinate for the active site and prevent succinate from binding, thereby inhibiting oxidation.

Competitive inhibition is when another molecule has a similar shape as the substrate and binds to the active site

The effects of competitive inhibition can be *reduced* by increasing the substrate concentration. The substrate can then outcompete the inhibitor for binding to the active site. As in the graph below, it is possible to reach the maximum rate of reaction V_{max} (or a rate close) in the presence of a competitive inhibitor. However, note that K_m increases because more substrate is needed to reach K_m (substrate concentration equal to $\frac{1}{2}V_{max}$), indicating lowered binding affinity of the substrate.

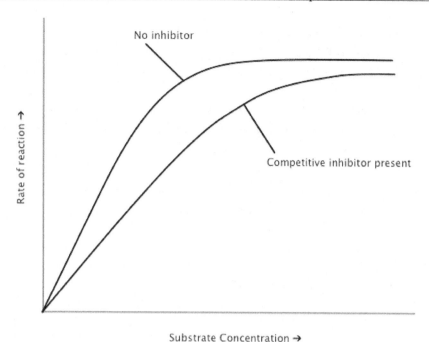

The effect of increasing substrate concentration on a competitive inhibitor where substrate outcompetes the competitor for enzyme binding

Uncompetitive inhibitors bind to the enzyme-substrate complex and render it ineffective. The uncompetitive inhibitor can only bind once the enzyme-substrate complex is fully formed. This type of inhibition is most effective when the substrate concentration is high. An uncompetitive inhibitor does not have to resemble the substrate of the reaction that it is inhibiting. Uncompetitive inhibition decreases V_{max} because it takes longer for the substrate or product to leave the active site, which decreases K_m. The decrease in K_m indicates a higher binding affinity of the substrate to the enzyme.

The uncompetitive inhibitor binds after the enzyme-substrate complex is formed

Non-competitive inhibitors are not structurally similar to the substrate, and they bind to an allosteric site (not the active site) of the enzyme. This binding changes the conformation (shape) of the enzyme, thereby reducing the affinity of the substrate to the active site. For this inhibition, the substrate may still be able to bind to the active site; however, the enzyme is not able to catalyze the reaction or does so at a slower rate. Non-competitive inhibitors bind equally well to either the enzyme or enzyme-substrate complex, with no preference for either state. Increasing the substrate concentration cannot prevent a non-competitive inhibitor from binding to the enzyme. Therefore, some enzymes are inhibited when a non-competitive inhibitor is present, regardless of substrate concentration.

An example of a non-competitive inhibitor involves ATP. When ATP accumulates within the cell, it binds to an allosteric site on the phosphofructokinase-1 enzyme. When bound, it changes the enzyme conformation and lowers the rate of reaction so that less ATP is produced. This is an example of negative feedback inhibition.

The maximum rate of reaction V_{max} is lower in the presence of a non-competitive inhibitor, while the K_m remains unchanged because the substrate concentration to achieve $\frac{1}{2}V_{max}$ of both reactions is the same.

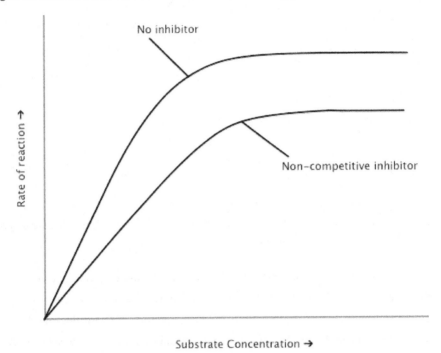

A non-competitive inhibitor binds to an allosteric site, increasing substrate concentration cannot restore V_{max}

Mixed inhibitors, like non-competitive inhibitors, can bind to the enzyme at the same time as the substrate, but the binding of the substrate affects the binding of the inhibitor, and vice versa. Although the inhibitor can bind to the enzyme whether or not the substrate is bound, the inhibitor has a greater affinity for one of the states. Mixed inhibition affects the rate between that of competitive and uncompetitive inhibition.

Mixed inhibition is often grouped with non-competitive inhibition because both can bind to either the enzyme or enzyme-substrate complex. However, non-competitive inhibitors have an equal preference for either state, while mixed inhibitors prefer one state. Furthermore, while non-competitive inhibition is allosteric, it is possible for mixed inhibitors to bind at the active site, although they usually bind allosterically.

Increasing the concentration of the substrate can reduce the rate for mixed inhibition but cannot entirely overcome it. Mixed inhibition results in a decreased V_{max}, and can result in either an increase or decrease in K_m, depending if the inhibitor binds to the free enzyme or the enzyme-substrate complex.

Inhibition Type

	Competitive	Uncompetitive	Non-competitive	Mixed
Molecule(s) which bind	Enzyme	Enzyme-substrate complex	Enzyme-substrate complex or enzyme	Enzyme enzyme other)
V_{max} effect	Unchanged	Decrease	Decrease	Decrease
K_m effect	Increase	Decrease	Unchanged	Increase or decrease
Mechanism of inhibition	Blocks substrate binding	Blocks substrate and enzyme from forming a product	Allosterically changes enzyme conformation	Allosterically blocks substrate binding or changes enzyme conformation

Regulatory enzymes:
allosteric enzymes, covalently-modified enzymes, and zymogens

There is a vast array of enzymes in organisms, but only regulatory enzymes undergo inhibition or activation. The initial mechanism by which enzymes are regulated is the expression of enzyme-encoding genes. However, enzymes can be part of the regulatory mechanism. In cells, groups of enzymes can work together for metabolic processes; such as an *enzyme system*. The enzymes often act in successive pathways, where the product of one enzyme becomes the substrate of the next enzyme in the sequence. A sequence of enzyme-mediated reactions generally contains a rate-limiting reaction (the slowest step) and regulates the rate of the entire pathway.

Regulatory enzymes display increased (or decreased) activity in response to different signals. This is ideal for the production of molecules that may be needed in different amounts at different times (e.g., hormones). The most efficient position for the regulatory enzyme is the first enzyme in the pathway so that the intermediate products of the pathway are not unnecessarily synthesized, which wastes biomolecules and cellular energy. There are two classes of regulatory enzymes in metabolic pathways: allosteric enzymes and covalently-modified enzymes. However, it is possible for an enzyme to use both types of regulation.

Allosteric enzymes, which are usually larger and more complex than simple non-regulatory enzymes, change their conformation when a *modulator* (effector) non-covalently binds to an allosteric site. The binding of the effector causes a change in the enzyme's conformation, which leads to a reversible change in the binding affinity at the enzyme's active site. This is an example of cooperativity. The allosteric effector can be either an activator that increases the enzyme's affinity for its substrates (positive cooperativity, positive allosteric modulation or allosteric activation) or an inhibitor that decreases the enzyme's affinity for its substrates (negative cooperativity, negative allosteric modulation or allosteric inhibition). Due to the complex cooperative interactions between protein subunits, allosteric enzymes usually do not follow the typical hyperbolic Michaelis-Menten behavior of other enzymes. Instead, they display sigmoid kinetic behavior.

Allosteric enzymes show a sigmoidal (S-shaped) profile on a velocity vs. substrate concentration graph. They are proteins with quaternary structure involving two or more polypeptide chains (e.g., hemoglobin).

One example of allostery is when the end product of a pathway binds at an allosteric site on the first enzyme of the pathway, shutting down the pathway. This is negative feedback (feedback inhibition); more specifically, it is *end-product inhibition*. When there is an excess of the end product, the whole metabolic pathway ceases as the end product inhibits the first enzyme of the pathway. This decreases the formation of intermediates and the end product. When the levels of the end product decrease to a particular level, the end products that are bound to allosteric sites on the enzyme are released, and the enzymes become active again, turning on the metabolic pathway. In this example, the allosteric effector is an inhibitor. Allostery may be observed in competitive, non-competitive, uncompetitive or mixed inhibition.

Allostery and the types of inhibition are often confused with one another. The types of inhibition are broad terms which describe how the inhibitor affects the V_{max} and K_m of an enzyme. Allostery is a specific way that inhibition (or activation) can be accomplished, by binding at a site other than the active site, which causes a conformational change and alters the shape of the active site and the enzyme's activity. Inhibitors may exhibit allosteric behavior, but not all allosteric behavior is necessarily a part of inhibition or any enzyme regulation.

There are two classic models of allosteric regulation. Both of these hypothesize that enzyme subunits exist in either a relaxed state (higher affinity for a substrate) or a tensed state, (lower affinity for a substrate). The *concerted model*, (symmetry model) states that all subunits in an enzyme must exist in the same conformation, either relaxed or tense, and the binding of an allosteric effector shift the conformation of the various sites from relaxed to tense, or vice versa. The *sequential model* states that subunits are not necessarily all in the same conformation, and when an effector binds to an allosteric site, it does not propagate a conformational change to the other subunits; rather, it slightly alters the structure of the active binding sites so that they are either more or less receptive to a substrate.

Homotropic allosteric modulators are the substrates for the enzymes that they bind to. When a homotropic allosteric modulator binds to one active site of the enzyme, it alters binding affinity or catalytic activity at other active sites. Homotropic allosteric modulators are usually activators and an example of positive feedback. *Heterotropic* allosteric modulators are more common, whereby most allosteric modulators are not both a substrate and modulator of the same enzyme. They can be either activators or inhibitors.

Allosteric enzymes are not the only regulatory enzymes that the body utilizes. Enzymes can be regulated by the addition or removal of chemical groups that are covalently bound to the enzyme. This changes the chemical properties of the active site, thus changing the enzyme's catalytic activity. The covalent addition of chemical groups activates some enzymes and inactivates others. Many chemical groups can function as covalent modifiers, including phosphoryl, methyl, and uridyl. The covalent modification can be either reversible or irreversible.

A common covalent modification is phosphorylation (adding a phosphate group) or dephosphorylation (removing a phosphate group) of an enzyme's amino acid side chains because these are relatively easy biochemical processes. *Kinases* catalyze the addition of a phosphate group (i.e., phosphorylation), while *phosphatases* catalyze the removal of a phosphate group (i.e., dephosphorylation). Phosphorylation is important in regulatory pathways; an attached phosphate group gives an additional negative charge to the protein, which can be a source of electrostatic interactions that change the enzyme's conformation. This changes its capacity to form hydrogen bonds and alters its affinity for a substrate. Phosphorylation can greatly amplify a signal, because one kinase may create an exponential effect, phosphorylation cascade.

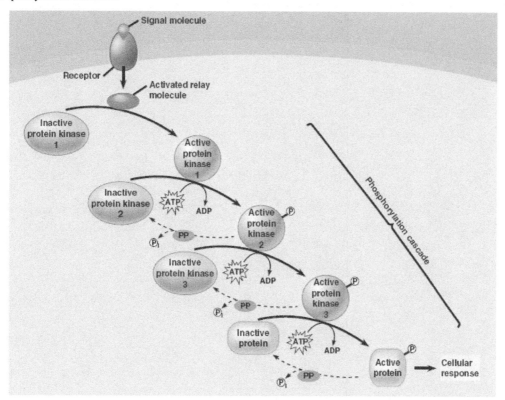

Proteolysis is another common covalent modification, by which specific peptide bonds in a protein are cleaved in a hydrolysis reaction. Proteolysis is often accomplished by protease enzymes but can be affected by other enzymes or non-enzymatic methods. *Zymogen* (a proenzyme) is an enzyme that must undergo proteolysis to be activated. To form the final active enzyme, the zymogen requires a biochemical change such as proteolysis. For example, the proteins involved in blood clotting circulate in the bloodstream as zymogens. Tissue damage or trauma activates enzymes that cleave the zymogens to make them active enzymes, which then cleave other enzymes, creating a cascade of clotting factor formation. The last step is the cleavage of the protein fibrinogen into fibrin, which causes blood to clot. Proteolysis is irreversible, so if the enzyme has to be deactivated, enzyme inhibitors are required.

Notes for active learning

Notes for active learning

Notes for active learning

Chapter 5

Photosynthesis

- **Photosynthetic Organisms**

- **Photosynthetic Reactions**

- **Types of Photosynthesis**

Photosynthetic Organisms

Photosynthesis is the conversion of solar energy into chemical energy, which is then used to assemble the organic molecules which fuel an organism's metabolic activities. Photosynthesis includes the *light-dependent reactions*, when solar energy is captured, and the *Calvin cycle* (light-independent or "dark" reactions) when carbohydrates are synthesized. Only plants, algae, and certain bacteria are capable of carrying out photosynthesis, but all organisms perform cellular respiration (i.e., the breakdown of nutrients into energy). In eukaryotes, photosynthesis occurs in chloroplasts, while cellular respiration occurs in mitochondria. Photosynthesis is considered a "backbone process" as it is crucial for life on Earth.

Photosynthesis is a complex metabolic pathway, but can be expressed as:

light energy + carbon dioxide + water $\rightarrow$ carbohydrate + oxygen + water

light energy + 6 CO_2 + 12 H_2O $\rightarrow$ $C_6H_{12}O_6$ + 6 O_2 + 6 H_2O

Cellular respiration breaks down carbohydrates (e.g., glucose) produced from photosynthesis into energy (ATP) to fuel metabolic activities:

carbohydrate + oxygen $\rightarrow$ carbon dioxide + water + energy

$C_6H_{12}O_6$ + 6 O_2 $\rightarrow$ 6 CO_2 + 6 H_2O + ~34 ATP

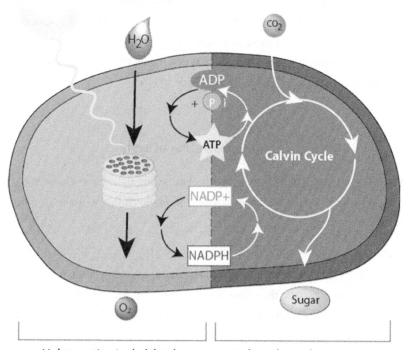

Light reaction in thylakoid   Light-independent in stroma

Light-dependent and light-independent reactions during photosynthesis

Photosynthesis as the transformation of solar energy

Solar radiation is composed of a range of wavelengths, most of which are filtered out as they pass through the atmosphere. 42% of the total light from the sun that hits the earth's atmosphere reaches the surface. The ozone layer filters the high-energy wavelengths (e.g., gamma rays, x-rays, and UV radiation). Many of the low-energy wavelengths (e.g., radio waves, microwaves and some infrared radiation) are also filtered. Visible light is the majority of solar radiation reaching Earth's surface.

Einstein named *photons* as the discrete particles of light. Today, a photon is considered both a particle and a wave, as it exhibits properties of both. The energy of photons varies with their wavelength. Longer wavelength light has lower energy, while shorter wavelength light has higher energy. *Excitation* is when a molecule absorbs light energy, and the energy levels of its electrons are elevated. *Fluorescence* is when the energy is emitted immediately upon absorption. If it is emitted after a delay, then the effect is *phosphorescence*. Light energy may be converted into many forms; a property exploited by photosynthesis.

Primary producers (autotrophs) are organisms that transform inorganic elements of their surroundings into organic compounds. Nearly all primary producers are *photosynthetic autotrophs* that use light energy to create carbohydrates. Other producers are *chemosynthetic autotrophs* that use inorganic chemical reactions to create organic compounds. Except for the rare life based on chemosynthetic autotrophs, all food chains rely on the photosynthesizing organisms. The organic molecules created by photosynthesis fuel both the primary producers and all organisms above them in the food chain.

The rate of photosynthesis by an organism can be determined by measuring oxygen production and carbon dioxide uptake, or indirectly by an increase in biomass. For example, the oxygen bubbles released by aquatic plants during photosynthesis can be collected and measured to determine oxygen production. Measuring the uptake of carbon dioxide is more difficult and is usually done indirectly. When plants absorb carbon dioxide from water, the pH of the water rises, so measuring pH levels indicate carbon dioxide uptake.

Abiotic factors of photosynthesis

There are four abiotic (nonliving) factors necessary for photosynthesis: carbon dioxide (CO_2), water (H_2O), light and temperature. These elements influence the efficiency of photosynthesis. Usually, one of these is the *limiting factor* in a plant at a given time.

Earth's atmosphere contains approximately 78% nitrogen and 21% oxygen, with the remaining 1% being a mixture of gases such as carbon dioxide. CO_2 in the atmosphere reaches photosynthetic tissues via *stomata* (openings) on the underside of plant leaves. Carbon dioxide then dissolves in a thin film of water that covers the outside of leaf cells and diffuses through the cell walls to reach the chloroplasts. The rate of photosynthesis increases with CO_2 concentration but eventually levels off at high concentrations.

Another abiotic factor, water, may or may not be plentiful at the location of an individual plant. In hot, dry climates, plants often close their stomata to conserve water, although this reduces the CO_2 supply to the chloroplasts. Less than 1% of the water that is absorbed by plants is used in photosynthesis; the remainder is either *transpired* (evaporated from leaves) or incorporated into cell components. The water utilized in photosynthesis is the source of the O_2 gas byproduct.

Light is a crucial component of photosynthesis. Light wavelengths within the visible light spectrum, which ranges from the red light at 780 nm to violet light at 390 nm, are the only forms of solar radiation useful for photosynthesis.

Mnemonic ROY G BIV (red, orange, yellow, green, blue, indigo, violet) describes the order of colors according to decreasing wavelength (or increasing energy). Wavelength and energy are inversely proportional. In the visible spectrum, red has the longest wavelength but the lowest energy.

Of the visible light that reaches a leaf, approximately 80% is absorbed. Light intensity may vary widely depending on the time of day, temperature, season, altitude, latitude and other atmospheric conditions. While photosynthetic pigments utilize the entire spectrum of visible light, the rate of photosynthesis varies across different wavelengths. Violet-blue light (400 to 525 nm) and orange-red light (625 to 700 nm) are the wavelengths most often absorbed for photosynthesis. Light intensity is a limiting factor because if there is no sunlight, then *photolysis* (splitting of water by photons) cannot occur during the light-dependent reactions. This results in a shortage of ATP and NADPH, products of the light-dependent reactions necessary for the Calvin cycle. At low and medium light intensity, the rate of photosynthesis is directly proportional to the light intensity. However, high-intensity light is not necessarily beneficial for plants, as it can decrease photosynthetic efficiency.

Temperature, like the other abiotic factors, has an optimum range. At low temperatures, the enzymes involved in photosynthesis work slowly and therefore less efficiently. As temperature increases, the rate of photosynthesis increases steeply until the optimum temperature is reached. If temperature increases beyond this point, then the rate of photosynthesis begins to decrease rapidly.

Plants as photosynthesizers

Plant photosynthesis requires the intake of CO_2 and H_2O. Absorption of water is primarily handled by roots which move the water up through vascular tissue in the stem until it reaches the leaves. Within the leaves are specialized *mesophyll cells*, where photosynthesis takes place. The exchange of O_2 and CO_2, as well as some water, occurs through the stomata. These pores are opened and closed by special *guard cells*. The density of stomata is dependent upon ecological conditions like humidity and CO_2 concentration.

The plant's leaves, composed of the *lamina* (blade) and the *petiole* (stalk), are its primary photosynthetic organs and typically have a large surface area to maximize light harvesting. A *simple leaf* has one lamina, while a *compound leaf* has many distinct laminae. Leaves can be highly variable in shape and are usually thin so that light can penetrate to cells on the underside. The underside of leaves is often covered with hairs called *trichomes*, which serve to catch water, reduce airflow and produce wax. The waxy cuticle covers the outer epidermis of the leaf to prevent water loss but has the tradeoff of limiting gas exchange.

The upper and lower epidermises of the leaf feature the stomata and serve a protective function, while loosely arranged *spongy mesophyll* tissue creates air spaces. *Palisade mesophyll* is more tightly packed and contains the highest concentration of chloroplasts. Chloroplasts usually remain near the cell wall, since this arrangement guarantees optimal use of light.

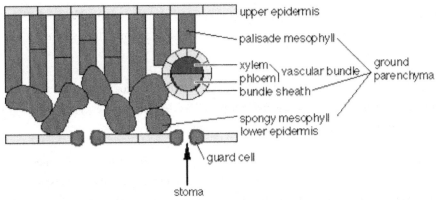

Cross section of a typical (C4) plant's leaf

Once CO_2 and H_2O have entered a mesophyll cell, they diffuse into the chloroplasts, the site of both the light-dependent reactions and the Calvin cycle. A chloroplast is a double-membraned organelle known as a *plastid*, each of which has its ribosomes and identical copies of a double-stranded, circular DNA molecule unique to the cell's DNA.

The membrane structure of a chloroplast includes an outer plasma membrane, an intermembrane space, and an inner plasma membrane. Within the inner membrane, a fluid-filled space called the *stroma* serves as the site of the Calvin cycle. *Thylakoids* are flattened disc-like sacs, which are often organized into stacks known as *grana,* also reside in the stroma. The light-dependent reactions occur in the thylakoids. These structures have a large surface area for light absorption and an inner *lumen* where protons accumulate. The accumulation of protons in the thylakoid lumen creates an electrochemical gradient used in photosynthesis. Chlorophyll and other pigments involved in the absorption of solar energy are embedded in the thylakoid membranes.

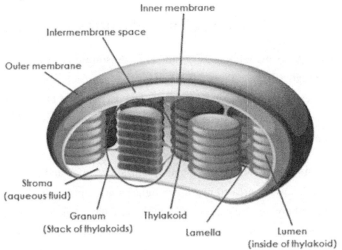

Structure of chloroplast as a double-membered structure showing stroma as the site of the Calvin cycle

Photosynthetic Pigments

Every pigment molecule has a distinctive *absorption spectrum* for light absorption. A graph of the percent of light absorbed at each wavelength is used to visualize this spectrum. Photosynthetic activity under different wavelengths of light can be plotted on an *action spectrum* graph. Action spectrums, which resemble absorption spectrums, indicate that chlorophyll is the main pigment involved in photosynthesis. It is the most abundant photosynthetic pigment in plants, which is why the rate of photosynthesis is highest at the low wavelengths of visible light (400 to 525 nm). These wavelengths, which comprise violet and blue light, are the most readily absorbed by chlorophyll. Chlorophyll absorbs an appreciable portion of red and orange light, which is why the significant photosynthetic activity is found there.

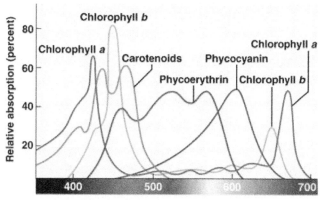

Relative absorption of visible light wavelengths (nm) by plant pigments

Very little light is absorbed by chlorophyll at wavelengths of yellow and green light (525 to 625 nm) and most is reflected, giving plants their green color. Photosynthetic organisms that are not green utilize alternate photosynthetic pigments. For example, red algae use *phycobilins,* which absorb blue, yellow and green light and reflect red light.

Chlorophyll exists in several forms which differ slightly in molecular structure. All chlorophyll molecules have a long lipid tail that anchors them in the lipid layers of thylakoid membranes, a *porphyrin ring* of alternating double and single bonds, and a single atom of magnesium in the center. Chlorophyll is analogous to *heme,* the iron-containing pigment in hemoglobin protein within the red blood cells which carries O_2.

Chlorophyll a and *chlorophyll b* are the most common forms, with chlorophyll *a* generally being three times as abundant as chlorophyll *b*. Chlorophyll *a,* a bluish-green pigment, has the formula $C_{55}H_{72}MgN_4O_5$ while chlorophyll *b*, which is yellow-green, is $C_{55}H_{70}MgN_4O_6$. The main role of chlorophyll *b* is to broaden the spectrum of light available for photosynthesis. It absorbs light energy and transfers the energy to a chlorophyll *a* molecule.

Green plants contain other pigments that contribute to photosynthesis. *Carotenoids* are yellow-orange pigments that absorb light in the violet, blue and green ranges of the spectrum. When chlorophyll breaks down in the autumn, plant leaves turn yellow, orange and red as carotenoids become visible. Even though carotenoids are present in small amounts, they allow a low rate of photosynthesis to occur at wavelengths of light that chlorophyll cannot absorb. *Accessory pigments* (antenna pigments) are the light-absorbing pigments that aid chlorophyll *a*, including chlorophyll *b*, *c*, *d*, and carotenoids.

Light-harvesting complexes (antenna complexes) contain 250 to 400 antenna pigment molecules and other compounds. They surround the *reaction center,* a pair of special chlorophyll *a* molecules. Together, the antenna complexes and reaction center make up a *photosystem*. In the chloroplasts of green plants, two photosystems, *Photosystem I* (PS I) and *Photosystem II* (PS II), operate together to initiate the first phase of photosynthesis. There are countless numbers of these two photosystems throughout the grana of the chloroplasts.

Notes for active learning

Photosynthetic Reactions

Light-dependent reactions require solar energy as energy-capturing reactions. The primary function of the light-dependent reactions is to trap solar energy and store it as chemical energy as ATP or NADPH. These reactions begin with light striking the chlorophyll molecules. Subsequent reactions result in the conversion of some light energy to chemical energy.

When solar energy excites electrons in the antenna complex, it is *photoactivated*. The energized electrons then pass from one pigment molecule to the next until they reach the special chlorophyll *a* pair at the reaction center. The reaction center then passes on the excited electron to the first in a chain of electron carriers called the *electron transport chain* (ETC). These excited electrons in the chlorophyll are unstable and re-emit absorbed energy as they travel from molecule to molecule along the electron transport chain. The result is the production of ATP and NADPH. The light-reactions comprise all events from initial photoactivation of a photosystem to ATP and NADPH synthesis. This process is constant during daylight hours as the plant produces ATP and NADPH for the Calvin cycle.

Two photosystems play critical roles in the light-dependent reactions of photosynthesis. Photosystem I (PS I) is best excited by light at about 700 nm, while Photosystem II (PS II) cannot use photons of wavelengths longer than 680 nm. Each photosystem has an antenna complex composed of chlorophyll, carotenoids, accessory proteins and cofactors such as magnesium and calcium.

Photosynthesis then proceeds to the Calvin cycle reactions in the stroma, where the NADPH and ATP created by the light-dependent reactions is used to reduce CO_2 into carbohydrates. Oxidation-reduction reactions are found throughout the processes of photosynthesis and respiration. Oxidation results in the net loss of an electron or electrons, while reduction results in the net gain of an electron or electrons. The mnemonic device "OIL RIG" stands for <u>O</u>xidation <u>I</u>s <u>L</u>oss and <u>R</u>eduction <u>I</u>s <u>G</u>ain.

carbohydrates, other complex molecules

Examples of oxidation-reduction reactions in photosynthesis:

- Overall, photosynthesis is a redox reaction: water is oxidized to oxygen and CO2 is reduced to sugar and water

- During photolysis, water is oxidized by the energy of photons into oxygen, protons, and electrons

- During the electron transport chain, each molecule in the chain is reduced (gain an electron) as it receives an electron and is then oxidized (loses an electron) as it passes the electron to the next

- At the end of the electron transport chain, $NADP^+$ is reduced to NADPH

- During the Calvin cycle, CO_2 is reduced into sugar and water

Light-Dependent Reactions

There are two sets of reactions in the thylakoid membrane: the *noncyclic electron pathway* and the *cyclic electron pathway*. Both are light-dependent reactions. Each pathway produces ATP, but only the noncyclic electron pathway also produces NADPH. *Photophosphorylation* is ATP production via photosynthesis, so the two pathways are the *cyclic* and *noncyclic photophosphorylation*.

Light-dependent reactions within the chloroplast

Noncyclic Electron Pathway

The noncyclic electron pathway is a light-dependent reaction in thylakoid membranes and requires the participation of both PS I and PS II. Despite their names, the pathway begins at PS II, which contains chlorophyll *a*, a carotenoid called *beta-carotene*, several electron-carrier proteins and numerous cofactors. The reaction center of PS II is a special pair of chlorophyll *a* molecules known as *P680*. The noncyclic electron pathway begins when a photon of light strikes accessory pigments surrounding P680 near the inner surface of a thylakoid membrane. The light energy excites the electrons of these pigments, which transfer their energy to the reaction center to excite electrons in P680. This is an unstable reaction, and thus most of the energy is lost to heat. Up to four photons at a time may strike PS II, but P680 only accepts one electron at a time.

Once excited, the electron leaves the chlorophyll and passes from one molecule to the next along the electron transport chain. The first molecule in this chain, the primary electron acceptor, is *pheophytin*. Pheophytin accepts the excited electron and transfers it to the next acceptor, the *plastoquinone complex*. Plastoquinone then delivers the electron to the *cytochrome complex*, which is passed to *plastocyanin*, and finally PS I.

The electrons are passed through a chain of oxidation-reduction reactions. After each molecule in the electron transport chain passes an electron to the next, it is reoxidized, readying it to accept a new electron from the molecule behind it in the chain. However, for P680 to continually send electrons down the chain, it must be resupplied. The splitting of water accomplishes this by photons (i.e., photolysis). Photolysis occurs in the *oxygen evolving complex* (OEC), which contains manganese and an enzyme complex. Photolysis produces 4 electrons, 4 protons, and O_2. The 4 electrons are transferred to P680; the protons remain in the thylakoid lumen. The O_2 is released into the atmosphere as a waste product of this process.

As electrons are traveling along the electron transport chain, protons (H^+ ions) are pumped across the thylakoid membrane into the thylakoid lumen, creating a proton gradient. The protons can travel back across the membrane, down their concentration gradient, but to do so, they must pass through ATP synthase, generating ATP. The synthesis of ATP via the noncyclic electron pathway is noncyclic photophosphorylation.

The activity occurring at PS I resembles that of PS II, with chlorophyll *a*, beta-carotene, electron carriers, and cofactors. The PS I reaction center is *P700*. It is a special pair of chlorophyll *a* molecules. Like PS II, pigments in PS I are capable of absorbing photons, but only the reaction center molecules can truly utilize the light energy. The other pigments are accessory molecules which help harvest light energy and transmit it to the reaction center.

Just as in PS II, after a photon of light strikes PS I, it excites electrons in P700. The excited electrons are passed along the electron transport chain. The electrons continually resupply P700 shuttled along the electron transport chain before it. The primary electron acceptor after P700 is a series of iron-sulfur molecules called *4Fe-4S*. 4Fe-4S then passes the electrons to the next acceptor molecule, *ferredoxin* (NADP). Ferredoxin releases the electrons to an enzyme called *ferredoxin-NADP reductase* (FNR), which catalyzes the reduction of $NADP^+$ to NADPH. This process requires two electrons and one proton ($NADP^+ + 2e^- + H^+ \rightarrow NADPH$). NADPH is integral in providing hydrogen ions to the second series of major photosynthetic reactions: the Calvin cycle or *carbon-fixing reactions*.

The flow of electrons in the noncyclic pathway is linear:

Photon strikes antenna complex of PS II → 4 electrons are released → P680 → Pheophytin → Plastoquinone → Cytochrome complex → Plastocyanin → P700 → 4Fe-4S → Ferredoxin → 2 NADPH

Light-dependent reaction with photosystem II and photosystem I as reactive centers to absorb electrons

Cyclic Electron Pathway

Sometimes an organism has the reductive power (NADPH) that it needs to synthesize new carbon structures, but still needs ATP to power other activities in the chloroplast. If the light intensity is not a limiting factor, there usually is a shortage of $NADP^+$ as NADPH accumulates within the stroma. $NADP^+$ is needed for the normal flow of electrons in the thylakoid membranes, as it is the final electron acceptor. If $NADP^+$ is not available, then the normal flow of electrons is inhibited. This promotes the *cyclic electron pathway*, which bypasses NADPH production in favor of ATP synthesis only.

The cyclic electron pathway begins when P700 receives an electron from plastocyanin and passes it to ferredoxin. However, because $NADP^+$ is not available in this case, ferredoxin does not pass electrons onward to $NADP^+$. Rather, it returns the electrons to the cytochrome complex. This causes the cytochrome complex to pump protons across the thylakoid membrane and create a proton gradient to drive ATP synthesis. The electrons are then returned to P700 via plastocyanin, and the process repeats.

The process is cyclic because the electrons return to PS I rather than move on to $NADP^+$; in this case PS I produces only ATP. In the cyclic electron pathway, PS I receives an electron not from PS II but from itself. The electron must be recycled continuously. The role of PS I as ATP producer may seem counterintuitive, since in the noncyclic electron pathway it is responsible for NADPH production, while PS II produces ATP. However, PS I is excellent at transferring an electron, as it is a powerful reducing agent (electron donor) and passes an electron to ferredoxin rather than $NADP^+$ to produce ATP when NADPH levels are high.

Chemiosmosis

Both the noncyclic and cyclic electron pathways produce ATP by generating a proton gradient across the thylakoid membrane. The movement of protons down their concentration gradient across the membrane is *chemiosmosis.* Chemiosmosis drives ATP synthesis.

Chemiosmotic gradient comparison for cellular respiration (mitochondria) and photosynthesis (chloroplast)

Cyclic photophosphorylation is driven by the events along the cyclic pathway between PS I and cytochrome. The proton-motive force produced as electrons travel from P700 to ferredoxin to cytochrome causes cytochromes to pump protons into the lumen. The thylakoid lumen acts as a reservoir for H^+ ions. The concentration gradient created by the accumulation of H+ in the lumen causes the H^+ to move back across the thylakoid membrane to the stroma, down the concentration gradient. From chemiosmosis, ATP synthase uses the energy released from the movement of hydrogen ions down their concentration gradient to synthesize ATP from ADP and inorganic phosphate.

Noncyclic photophosphorylation is a more complex process. Hydrogen ions enter the thylakoid lumen at two points along the noncyclic electron pathway. The first occurs during photolysis when 2 H_2O are split into O_2, 2 electrons, and 2 H^+. The O_2 is a waste product and is released into the atmosphere. The electrons are donated to P680, which resides in the transmembrane PS II complex. Meanwhile, the H^+ are released into the thylakoid lumen.

The electrons travel from P680 to pheophytin to plastoquinone and then reach the cytochrome complex. The electron transfers from plastoquinone to cytochrome, via an intermediate carrier molecule, creates energy which pumps more H^+ from the stroma into the thylakoid lumen. As in cyclic photophosphorylation, the protons move down their concentration gradient and drive ATP synthase. The hydrogen ions return to the stroma to synthesize NADPH from $NADP^+$ and 2 electrons from PS I.

The Calvin Cycle Reactions

Both ATP and NADPH are important products of light-dependent reactions, and both are used in the synthesis of carbohydrates from atmospheric CO_2. The reactions that accomplish this have historically been known as light-independent (or dark) reactions. Despite their names, these reactions do not typically occur at nighttime. They indirectly require light, because they rely on light-dependent reactions which only take place during daylight. For this reason, the term "dark reactions" is no longer used, and some scientists even claim that "light-independent" is a misnomer. In recent years, the term *carbon-fixing reactions* have emerged as a more apt description of the Calvin cycle.

These reactions take place in the stroma of chloroplasts and occur if the end products of the light-dependent reactions are available. Depending on the plant involved, the carbon-fixing reactions may progress in different ways. Commonly, CO_2 from the atmosphere is combined with a 5-carbon sugar called *ribulose-1,5-bisphosphate* (RuBP). The CO_2 and RuBP are converted via several steps into a 6-carbon sugar such as glucose. Some of the sugars are further combined into polysaccharides for storage within the plant.

Calvin cycle (light-independent) synthesizes sugars from CO_2

The Calvin cycle has three stages: (1) carboxylation, (2) reduction, (3) regeneration.

1) Carboxylation or Fixation of Carbon Dioxide: CO_2 + RuBP ⇒ PGA

   Carboxylation is the attachment of CO_2 to 5-carbon RuBP to form an unstable 6-carbon intermediate. The enzyme *ribulose-1,5-bisphosphate carboxylase/oxygenase* (RuBisCO) catalyzes this reaction. RuBisCO comprises 20–50% of the protein content of chloroplasts. Its ubiquity most likely makes it the most common protein in the world. As soon as the 6-carbon intermediate is formed, it splits to form two molecules of the 3-carbon compound *3-Phosphoglyceric acid* (3-PG, 3-PGA, or PGA). 3-Phosphoglyceric acid is *glycerate 3-phosphate*.

2) Reduction of 3-Phosphoglyceric acid: PGA + ATP + NADPH $\Rightarrow$ G3P + ADP + Pi + NADP+

Using ATP produced by light-dependent reactions, each PGA is phosphorylated to form an intermediate. The intermediate is then reduced by NADPH, the other product of light-dependent reactions, to form *glyceraldehyde 3-phosphate*. This is a 3-carbon compound, just like PGA. Glyceraldehyde 3-phosphate (G3P, GP, GA3P, or GAP) is also *triose phosphate* (TP) and *3-phosphoglyceraldehyde* (PGAL). Along with each G3P, the reduction produces ADP, inorganic phosphate (Pi) and $NADP^+$.

G3P can be converted into many useful molecules, such as glucose. Glucose can be combined with fructose to form sucrose, an important plant carbohydrate. Glucose is the starting point for the synthesis of polysaccharides (i.e., starch and cellulose).

3) Regeneration of RuBP: G3P + ATP $\Rightarrow$ RuBP + ADP + Pi

However, only one G3P can be used for conversion into glucose. The remaining G3P is used to regenerate RuBP, which is essential for carbon fixation to continue. These G3P are met with a carbon acceptor and undergo a series of reactions, requiring energy from ATP, which convert them into RuBP. At this point, the cycle begins again.

While this description followed the fate of one original RuBP molecule, in reality, the process uses six RuBP and six CO_2 for each cycle.

Carboxylation converts six 5-carbon RuBP and six CO_2 into six 6-carbon unstable intermediates. The six intermediates then break down into twelve 3-carbon PGA.

$$6 \text{ RuBP} + 6 \text{ } CO_2 \rightarrow 12 \text{ PGA}$$

During reduction, the 12 PGA plus 12 ATP and 12 NADPH are converted into 12 3-carbon G3P, 12 ADP, 12 Pi, and 12 $NADP^+$. Two of the G3P create glucose phosphate.

$$12 \text{ PGA} + 12 \text{ ATP} + 12 \text{ NADPH} \rightarrow 12 \text{ G3P} + 12 \text{ ADP} + 12 \text{ Pi} + 12 \text{ } NADP^+$$

Finally, during regeneration the other 10 G3P, using 6 ATP, are remade into 6 RuBP, producing 6 ADP and 4 Pi as a result.

$$10 \text{ G3P} + 6 \text{ ATP} \rightarrow 6 \text{ RuBP} + 6 \text{ ADP} + 4 \text{ Pi}$$

Notes for active learning

Types of Photosynthesis

Not all plants perform the Calvin cycle. The terms C_3, C_4, and *CAM plant* describe the ways in which plants perform photosynthesis. C_3 and C_4 refer to the carbon length of the first photosynthetic carbohydrate product. C_3 plants produce a 3-carbon molecule, 3-phosphoglyceric acid (PGA), and C_4 plants produce a 4-carbon molecule, *oxaloacetate* (OAA). Like C_4 plants, CAM plants also produce oxaloacetate but undergo photosynthesis differently.

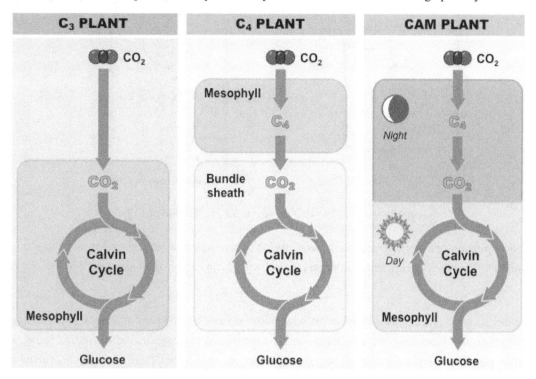

Comparison of C_3, C_4 and CAM plants for the synthesis of glucose

C3 Photosynthesis

More than 90% of all angiosperms are C_3 plants. In C_3 plants, the Calvin cycle proceeds as described, in which CO_2 is fixed directly into the 3-carbon molecule PGA.

In hot weather, stomata close to save water, but this has the disadvantage of decreasing CO_2 concentration in leaves while increasing O_2 concentration. High O_2 concentration is a disadvantage because RuBisCO can use O_2 in the Calvin cycle rather than CO_2. Using O_2 in this way is *photorespiration* because it involves intake of O_2 and production of CO_2, like cellular respiration. During photorespiration, RuBP reacts with O_2 to create CO_2, in contrast to photosynthesis, when RuBP reacts with CO_2 to form carbohydrates. The former is an oxygenation reaction, while the latter is a carboxylation reaction. RuBisCO performs oxygenation rather than carboxylation around 25% of the time, and this may be promoted by low CO_2, high O_2 or high temperature.

Photorespiration results in the production of one PGA and one *phosphoglycolate*. Phosphoglycolate is of little use in the plant and inhibits normal carboxylation, so the plant must spend energy to convert the phosphoglycolate back to a useful molecule and reclaim the two carbons. Peroxisomes break down the products of this process.

Comparison of C_3 (left) and C_4 plants for the fixation of CO_2

Photorespiration is a wasteful and inefficient process that results in a net energy loss for the plant. Plants must spend up to 40% of their energy stored in sugars to deal with the inevitable damage created by the oxygenation reaction.

The oxygenation reaction developed as an adaptation to Earth's early atmosphere. When photosynthesis first evolved billions of years ago, the concentration of atmospheric O_2 was low compared to today, making photorespiration rare. Photorespiration grew to be a great inconvenience to plants. Plants have since evolved ways to reduce the damage caused by O_2 in the Calvin cycle.

Humans have attempted to circumvent the issues created by the oxygenation reaction. Molecular genetics has been used to modify the properties of RuBisCO to eliminate the oxygenation reaction while retaining the carboxylation reaction. Results so far indicate that the two reactions cannot be separated, because modifications in RuBisCO that reduce oxygenase activity reduce carboxylase activity. Nature developed a system to avoid photorespiration.

The comparison of the anatomy of C_3 (left) and C_4 plants.
C_4 photosynthesis uses carbon concentration to improve the efficiency of photosynthetic carbon fixation.
The leaves of most C_4 plants have a Kranz leaf anatomy consisting of bundle sheath and mesophyll cells.

C4 Photosynthesis

C_4 *photosynthesis* is found in less than 5% of plants, mostly in hot, dry climates. It is especially well represented in the grasses. Corn and sugar cane, two of the most important crops, are C4 plants. Because C4 plants avoid photorespiration, their net photosynthetic rate may be 2 to 3 times that of a C3 plant. However, in moist or cold environments, C3 plants are more efficient. C_4 photosynthesis has evolved from C3 plants independently many times in the evolutionary timeline. All of the enzymes that were co-opted for C_4 photosynthesis were already present in the C3 plants from which they evolved. Researchers are currently attempting to artificially convert certain C3 plants into C4 plants to maximize crop yields and allow agriculture in more hostile environments.

While C3 plants have chloroplasts in their mesophyll cells, C4 plants have additional chloroplasts in special *bundle sheath cells*. These cells surround the veins of the leaves; an arrangement called *Kranz anatomy*. In the leaves of a C4 plant, mesophyll cells are arranged concentrically around the bundle sheath cells. The light-independent reactions are split between both cell types, with preliminary carbon fixation occurring in the mesophyll cells and the Calvin cycle occurring in the bundle sheath cells. Rather than RuBisCO, the mesophyll cells contain alternate *phosphoenolpyruvate* (PEP) enzyme. RuBisCO is in the bundle sheath cells.

When CO_2 enters the leaves of a C4 plant, it is first absorbed by mesophyll cells, as in a C3 plant. However, rather than being fixed by RuBisCO into PGA, the CO_2 is combined with PEP to form 4-carbon *oxaloacetate* (OAA). This reaction is catalyzed by the enzyme *PEP carboxylase* (PEP-C or PEPCase). PEPCase has no affinity for O_2, unlike RuBisCO, and has a higher affinity for CO_2 at high temperatures than does RuBisCO. PEPCase assimilates carbon more efficiently while avoiding photorespiration.

Oxaloacetate is then usually converted to *malate,* a reduced form of oxaloacetate, and pumped into the bundle sheath cells. Some plant species reduce oxaloacetate to aspartate rather than malate, and many do not alter oxaloacetate before shuttling it to the bundle sheath cells.

Once in the bundle sheath cells, the malate is converted back to oxaloacetate and then decarboxylated (CO_2 is removed) to form 3-carbon *pyruvate*. The CO_2 remains in the bundle sheath cells to begin the Calvin cycle, while the pyruvate is returned to the mesophyll cells to be regenerated into PEP using ATP and its efficiency is lost in cooler temperatures.

The initial fixed carbon form, whether oxaloacetate, malate or aspartate, does not substitute for any of the carbon compounds of the Calvin cycle, such as RuBP or PGA. These acids merely serve as sources of CO_2 for the conventional Calvin cycle in the bundle sheath cells. CO_2 is fixed into RuBP as normal and then proceed throughout the cycle. In this regard, C_4 plants fix carbon twice: once in the mesophyll and once in the bundle sheath.

CAM Photosynthesis

CAM (Crassulacean acid metabolism) *photosynthesis* is another alternative to the C3 strategy, found almost exclusively in plants from dry environments. Some CAM plants include cacti, stonecrops (family Crassulaceae, for which the strategy is named), orchids, bromeliads, and succulents. Like C4 plants, CAM plants use PEPcase to fix CO_2 into oxaloacetate and separate this step from the Calvin cycle. However, while C4 plants separate them spatially, with the former occurring in mesophyll cells and the latter in bundle sheath cells, CAM plants separate them temporally. In this case, both steps proceed in the mesophyll cells, but initial CO_2 takes place at night, while the Calvin cycle is during the day.

In a CAM plant, stomata are opened only at night, when CO_2 is taken up into the plant and incorporated into the mesophyll. They proceed to use PEPCase to react CO_2 and PEP to form oxaloacetate, which they then convert into malate and store as the malic acid in large vacuoles in the mesophyll cells. During the day, malic acid is returned to the chloroplasts for conversion into oxaloacetate, then decarboxylated into pyruvate and CO_2. The CO_2 is then introduced into the Calvin cycle, while the pyruvate is used to regenerate PEP.

No CO_2 intake occurs during the daytime, as stomata are closed to avoid transpiration. The CAM strategy was evolved mainly to avoid transpiration rather than to reduce the effects of photorespiration, although a benefit as well. The major advantage of a CAM strategy over a C4 strategy is the ability to conserve water by closing stomata during the day greatly. Photosynthesis in a CAM plant is minimal due to the limited amount of CO_2 fixed at night, but this does allow them to live under stressful conditions.

Notes for active learning

Notes for active learning

Chapter 6

Specialized Eukaryotic Cells and Tissues

- **Neuron**

- **Muscle Cell**

- **Electrochemistry**

- **Biosignaling**

- **Tissues Formed from Eukaryotic Cells**

Neuron

Neurons (nerve cells) generate electric signals that pass from one end of the cell to the other. Neurons release chemical messengers, *neurotransmitters*, to communicate with other cells. A neuron conducting signals toward a synapse (the junction where a neuron communicates with a target cell) is a *presynaptic neuron*, while a neuron conducting signals away from a synapse is a *postsynaptic neuron*. Neurotrophic factors are proteins that guide the development of neurons.

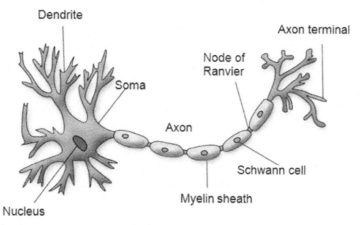

Neurons contain dendrites to receive signals that propagate along the axon toward the axon terminal

Neurons outside the central nervous system (CNS) can repair themselves, but neurons within the CNS cannot. In the autonomic nervous system, the transmission of an impulse involves the interaction between at least two different neurons. The first neuron is the *preganglionic neuron*, and the second is the *postganglionic neuron*. Neurons vary in size and shape, but all have three parts: cell body, dendrites, and axon.

A motor neuron relays signals from the brain or spinal cord to a muscle or gland

Cell body: site of nucleus and organelles

Because nerve cells are specialized for signal transmission and pathway-formation, the form of neurons reflects their function. The cell body contributes much to a neuron's density. The cell body houses the neuron's organelles, such as the nucleus and mitochondria. The cell body has a well-developed, rough endoplasmic reticulum and a Golgi apparatus for synthesis and modification of important proteins for proper neuronal function. This part of the neuron is similar in form to most somatic cells, except for the dendrites.

Dendrites: structure and function

Dendrites are the branched receptive areas of a neuron that extend from the cell body. They receive information and conduct impulses toward the cell body. The branching of dendrites increases the surface area for reception. The number of dendrites depends on the function of the neuron. For example, *unipolar neurons* have one dendrite.

Axon: structure and function

The *axon* is one key feature that differentiates neurons from other cells. The axon is crucial in the neuron's impulse generation and is responsible for carrying outgoing messages from the cell. A long axon is a *nerve fiber*. A nerve fiber is a single axon, while a nerve is a bundle of axons bound together by connective tissue. This axon can originate from the CNS and extend to the body's extremities. This effectively provides a pathway for messages from the CNS to the periphery. Axons conduct impulses away from the cell body to stimulate or inhibit a neuron, muscle or gland.

Axon terminals, secretory regions of the nerve, are located at the end of the axon, away from the neuron's cell body. Other names for the axon terminal are the synaptic knob or synaptic bouton. The neuron's axon terminal is the site of signal transmission toward the receptor of another cell.

Glial cells and neuroglia

Nervous tissue is made of neurons and neuroglia. *Neuroglia* support and nourish the neurons. *Glial cells* are nervous tissue support cells capable of cellular division. Oligodendroglia and Schwann cells are glial cells that support neurons physically and metabolically. *Astroglia* regulates the composition of the extracellular fluid in CNS. *Microglia* perform immune functions. Other glial cells include ependymal cells (use cilia to circulate cerebrospinal fluid), satellite cells (support ganglia) and astrocytes (provide physical support to neurons of CNS; maintain mineral and nutrient balance).

Myelin sheath, Schwann cells, oligodendrocytes for insulation of axon

The *myelin sheath* is a phospholipid layer that surrounds a neuron's axon. The myelin sheath insulates the axon, increasing the conductivity of the electrical messages sent through a nerve cell. Myelin is a good insulator because it is fatty and does not contain channels. By preventing leakage of charge, myelin increases the speed of propagation, enabling axons to be thinner. It is formed by the membranes of highly-specialized, tightly-spiraled *neuroglia cells*. These neuroglia cells are either Schwann cells or oligodendrocytes.

Schwann cell sheath is a phospholipid coat growing around a nerve axon

In the peripheral nervous system (PNS), the *Schwann cells* produce myelin for nerve cells. Many of these specialized cells wrap myelin around the neuron's axon, providing an insulating sheath that prevents the loss of signal transmission. *Oligodendrocytes* are the central nervous system analog of Schwann cells. They make myelin sheaths (insulation) around CNS axons. Insulation occurs at intervals, punctuated by opening, which exposes the plasma membrane of the axon, causing an action potential to jump along nodes of Ranvier.

Only vertebrates have myelinated axons. Myelinated axons appear as white matter, while neuronal cell bodies appear as gray matter.

Many neurodegenerative autoimmune diseases result from a lack of myelin sheath. For instance, in multiple sclerosis, the lack of insulation from a myelin sheath slows or leaks the conductivity of signals across neural pathways, severely decreasing the efficiency of the patient's nervous system.

Nodes of Ranvier: role in the propagation of nerve impulse along an axon

The spaces between adjacent sections of myelin where the plasma membrane of the axon is exposed to extracellular fluid are *nodes of Ranvier* (neurofibril nodes). The myelin sheath prevents the flow of ions between intracellular and extracellular compartments. Therefore, action potentials occur at the non-insulated nodes of Ranvier; *saltatory conduction* is this jump of action potentials from one node to another.

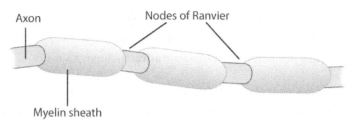

Nodes of Ranvier for saltatory conduction occurring at exposed sections of plasma membrane

Synapse as the site of impulse propagation between cells

Synapse is the space between the axon bulb and the dendritic receptor of the next neuron. A synapse is a junction between two neurons that permits a neuron to pass an electrical (or chemical) signal to another cell. A synapse consists of a *presynaptic membrane*, a *synaptic cleft*, and the *postsynaptic membrane.* In a synapse, the electrical activity in the presynaptic neuron influences the electrical activity in the postsynaptic neuron. The influence can be either excitatory (positive response) or inhibitory (negative response).

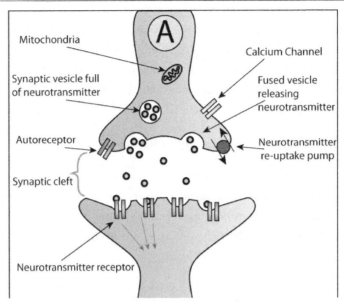

The synaptic cleft between two neurons

Between the presynaptic membrane and the postsynaptic membrane, there is a narrow fluid-filled space of the synaptic cleft. Neurotransmitters are released into synaptic vesicles from the presynaptic neuron's axon terminal and into the synaptic cleft. The vesicles migrate the synaptic cleft and travel toward the postsynaptic neuron, binding to postsynaptic receptors.

In *convergence*, many presynaptic neurons affect a single postsynaptic neuron. This allows information from many sources to influence the activity of one cell. In *divergence*, a single presynaptic nerve cell affects many postsynaptic nerve cells, allowing one information source to affect multiple pathways.

The nervous system uses several types of synapses to create complex pathways for relaying information. *Axodendritic synapses* exist between the axon terminal of one presynaptic neuron and one dendrite of the postsynaptic neuron. An *axosomatic synapse* resides between the axon terminal of the presynaptic neuron and the cell body of the postsynaptic neuron. *Axoaxonic synapses*, while rare, can exist between the presynaptic and postsynaptic axon terminals.

At *electric synapses*, the presynaptic and postsynaptic cells are joined by *gap junctions*, allowing action potentials to flow directly across the junction. Due to the short distance and the direct, physical link between the two neurons, these junctions provide an incredibly fast transmission of signals. Since chemical synapses are usually fast enough for signal transmission, electrical synapses are relatively rare.

At a *chemical synapse*, the axon of the presynaptic neuron ends in swelling as the axon terminal. An extracellular space of the synaptic cleft separates the presynaptic and postsynaptic neurons, preventing a direct propagation of current. Chemical synapses are unidirectional; a signal can be transmitted from presynaptic to the postsynaptic neuron.

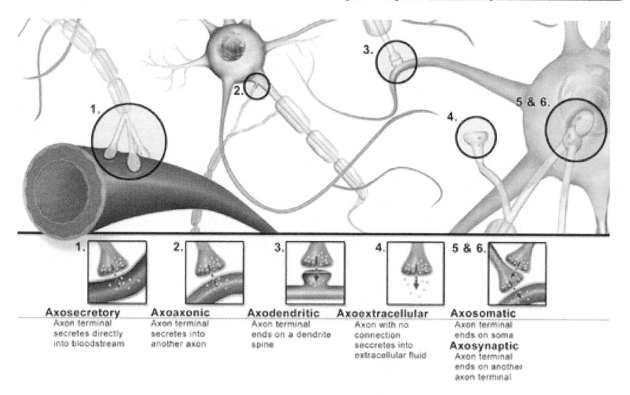

Axosecretory
Axon terminal
secretes directly
into bloodstream

Axoaxonic
Axon terminal
secretes into
another axon

Axodendritic
Axon terminal
ends on a dendrite
spine

Axoextracellular
Axon with no
connection
seccretes into
extracellular fluid

Axosomatic
Axon terminal
ends on soma

Axosynaptic
Axon terminal
ends on another
axon terminal

Synapse types

Synaptic activity: transmitter molecules, synaptic knobs, fatigue and propagation between cells without resistance loss

An action potential travels along the axon and reaches the end of the presynaptic neuron. The depolarization of the presynaptic membrane results in the opening of voltage-gated calcium channels. Calcium ions flow into the presynaptic neuron, causing vesicles with neurotransmitters inside the neuron to fuse with the plasma membrane.

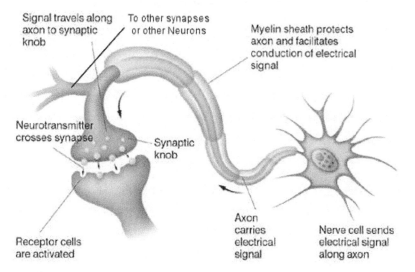

Signal travels along axon to synaptic knob

To other synapses or other Neurons

Myelin sheath protects axon and facilitates conduction of electrical signal

Neurotransmitter crosses synapse

Synaptic knob

Receptor cells are activated

Axon carries electrical signal

Nerve cell sends electrical signal along axon

Dendrites receive stimuli, propagate impulse with diminution along the axon and release neurotransmitter into the synaptic cleft toward the postsynaptic neuron

The Ca^{2+} ions induce reactions that allow the vesicles holding neurotransmitters to fuse with the plasma membrane and liberate their contents into the synaptic cleft by exocytosis. These synaptic vesicles store neurotransmitters that diffuse across the synapse towards the postsynaptic membrane. When an action potential arrives at the presynaptic axon bulb, synaptic vesicles merge with the presynaptic membrane. When vesicles merge with the neuron's plasma membrane, neurotransmitters are discharged into the synaptic cleft. Neurotransmitter molecules diffuse across the synaptic cleft to the postsynaptic membrane where they bind with specific receptors.

The neurotransmitters are then released into the synaptic cleft via exocytosis. These neurotransmitters then diffuse via Brownian motion (a type of irregular motion) and bind within the synaptic cleft to specific receptors located on the postsynaptic plasma membrane. The receptors are ligand-gated ion channels, which open and let sodium and other positively charged ions into the postsynaptic neuron. As these positively charged ions enter the postsynaptic neuron, they cause the neuron's membrane to depolarize, which results in an action potential, which moves down the postsynaptic neuron. The calcium ions are pumped back into the synaptic cleft from inside the presynaptic neuron. Finally, the neurotransmitters are degraded and recycled by enzymes in the synaptic cleft.

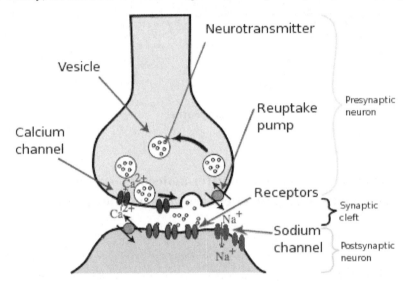

Synaptic transmission with Ca^+ causing the release of the neurotransmitter from the presynaptic membrane into the cleft

Neurotransmitters are chemicals that cross the synapse between two neurons, or between the neuron and a muscle or gland. After an action potential has traveled down the axon, it induces the release of neurotransmitters from the presynaptic neuron's axon terminal into the synapse. The axon terminal, or synaptic knob, contains vesicles of neurotransmitters waiting to be exocytosed. An action potential reaching the synaptic knob causes an influx of calcium, which signals the vesicles to fuse with cell membranes (exocytosis) to release the neurotransmitters into the synaptic cleft.

Once the postsynaptic membrane receives the neurotransmitter, the chemicals bind to a receptor (usually on the dendrite) and open ion channels. This causes a change in the membrane potential of the postsynaptic neuron. If this *graded potential* stimulus is large enough, it triggers an *all-or-none response*, inducing the propagation of the signal down the axon of the postsynaptic neuron. Enzymes quickly degrade these neurotransmitters or are taken up by the presynaptic terminal so that they do not persistently stimulate the postsynaptic neuron.

At least 25 different neurotransmitters have been identified. *Acetylcholine* (ACh) and *norepinephrine* (NE) are two common neurotransmitters. *Cholinergic fibers* release ACh. In some synapses, the postsynaptic membrane contains enzymes that rapidly inactivate the neurotransmitter. For example, acetylcholinesterase degrades acetylcholine. Once a neurotransmitter is released into a synaptic cleft, it initiates a response and is then removed from the cleft. *Biogenic amines* are neurotransmitters containing an amino group such as *catecholamines* (e.g., dopamine, norepinephrine, epinephrine and serotonin). Nerve fibers that release epinephrine and norepinephrine are adrenergic and noradrenergic fibers, respectively. Amino acid neurotransmitters are the most prevalent neurotransmitters in the CNS. These include glutamate, aspartate, GABA (gamma-aminobutyric acid) and glycine.

Neuropeptides are composed of two or more amino acids. Neurons that release neuropeptides are peptidergic (e.g., beta-endorphin, dynorphin and enkephalin groups). Nitric oxide, ATP and adenine act as neurotransmitters. Many neurons of the PNS end at neuroeffector junctions on muscle and gland cells. Neurotransmitters released by these efferent neurons then activate the target cell. In other synapses, the presynaptic membrane reabsorbs neurotransmitters for repackaging in synaptic vesicles or for the molecular breakdown. The short existence of neurotransmitters in a synapse prevents continuous stimulation (or inhibition) of postsynaptic membranes. Many drugs that affect the nervous system act by interfering with (or potentiating) the action potentials of neurotransmitters.

Resting potential and electrochemical gradient

Luigi Galvani discovered in 1786 that an electric current stimulates a nerve. An impulse is too slow to be caused by an electric current in an axon. Julius Bernstein proposed that the impulse is the movement of unequally distributed ions on either side of an axon-membrane, the plasma membrane of the axon. The 1963 Nobel Prize went to the British researchers A. L. Hodgkin and A. F. Huxley, who confirmed this theory.

Hodgkin, Huxley and other researchers inserted a tiny electrode into the giant axon of a squid. The electrode was attached to a voltmeter and an oscilloscope to trace the change in voltage. The voltmeter measured the difference in the electrical potential between the inside and the outside of the membrane. The oscilloscope indicated any changes in polarity. Since the plasma membrane is more permeable to potassium ions than to sodium ions, there are always more positive ions outside the cell; this accounts for some polarity. The large, negatively charged proteins in the cytoplasm (e.g., Cl−) contribute to the resting potential of − 70 mV.

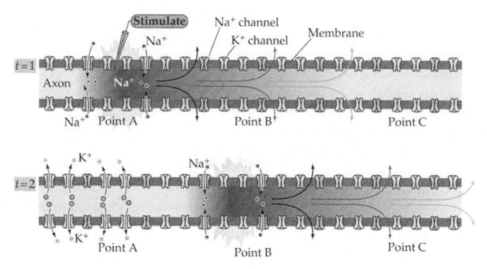

Movement of ions along a synapse changes the voltage across the membrane

When an axon is not conducting an impulse, an oscilloscope records a membrane potential of –70 mV, indicating that the inside of the neuron is more negative than the outside. *Resting potential* is the electrical potential across the plasma membrane of a cell's axon that is not conducting an impulse. This polarization is due to the difference in electrical charge on either side of the axon membrane.

The magnitude of the voltage potential is determined by the differences in specific ion concentrations between the intracellular and extracellular fluids, as well as the differences in membrane permeability of different ions as a function of the number of open ion channels for these ions. Na^+ and K^+ are the most important ions in generating the resting membrane potential. At rest in a living cell, Na^+ is greater outside the cell, while K^+ is greater inside the cell. The ions flow about the *electrochemical gradient*, which is the combined electrical and chemical concentration differences on each side of a membrane. This difference is attributed to the net flow of charge across the nerve cell's membrane.

The *sodium-potassium pump* moves three Na^+ ions to the outside of the membrane for every 2 K^+ ions it moves into the cell along with Cl^- ions inside the cell and creates a net negative charge inside the cell. Additionally, the plasma membrane is more permeable to K^+ ions as K^+ moves out of the cell more easily than Na^+ moves into the cell, accentuating the relatively negative resting potential inside the neuron. In general, K^+ moves out of the cell and Na^+ moves into the cell down their concentration gradients. However, the intracellular concentration of these two ions are kept constant by an active transport system that pumps Na^+ out of the cell and K^+ into it.

Action potential: threshold, all-or-none, sodium-potassium pump

Action potentials are large, rapid alterations in membrane potential. It is the reversal and restoration of the electrical potential across the plasma membrane of a cell, as an electrical impulse passes (i.e., depolarization and repolarization). Membranes capable of producing action potentials are excitable membranes (e.g., membranes of nerve and muscle cells).

When the membrane becomes depolarized, sodium channels open and positive sodium ions rush inside. During *depolarization*, the ion concentration is opposite from resting potential. Sodium ions dominate the inside, while potassium ions dominate the outside. In response, the membrane potential moves in a positive direction. The membrane potential goes from –70 mV at resting potential to +30 mV in the depolarization phase.

During *repolarization*, potassium channels open and sodium channels close. The positive potassium ions rush outside, and the membrane potential drops down. Now, sodium ion concentration is higher on the inside, while potassium ion concentration is higher on the outside. This is the opposite of the resting state. Thus, the membrane potential returns to its resting value, and the potential returns to   −70 mV again in the repolarization phase.

A *hyperpolarization* is an event in potential axon propagation where potassium channels do not close fast enough. Consequently, the membrane potential briefly drops below the normal resting potential, to around −80 mV.

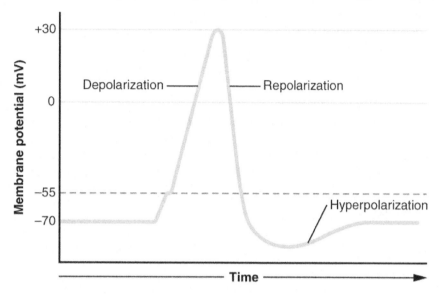

Action potential and voltage changes; depolarization occurs when Na⁺ rushes in, and K⁺ exits the cell; hyperpolarization restores the resting potential with the Na⁺ / K⁺ pump

After an action potential is propagated along the axon of a neuron, there is a period when a second stimulus does not produce a second action potential. This is the *absolute refractory period* and occurs because once the voltage-gated Na^+ channels close, the membrane needs to repolarize before the channels can open again. The sodium-potassium pump works to re-establish the original resting state (i.e., potassium inside and sodium outside). It maintains this unequal distribution of Na^+ and K^+ ions. The sodium-potassium (Na^+ / K^+) pump is an active transport system that moves Na^+ ions out and K^+ ions into the axon. The pump is always working because the membrane is permeable to these ions and they diffuse toward the lesser concentration.

Until the resting potential of −70 mV is restored, the neuron cannot generate another action potential. Following the absolute refractory period, a second action potential can be produced only if the stimulus strength is greater than usual. This is the *relative refractory period* and results from hyperpolarization. The relative refractory period begins after hyperpolarization and lasts until the resting potential is re-established. The refractory period prevents an action potential from reversing direction, even though theoretically ions are rushing in and diffusing in both directions.

In local anesthetics, Na^+ ion channels are blocked, and pain signaling is absent.

Since a neuron is a long cell, it gets depolarized part-by-part and not all at once. The area of the membrane that gets depolarized has a difference in potential with the adjacent area of the membrane that is still at resting potential, thereby causing a local current. This current then depolarizes the adjacent resting membrane, and an action potential continues onward. Since depolarization of an area is followed by a refractory period, the action potential moves unidirectionally.

Sufficient depolarization greater than threshold leads to an action potential

Similar to water flow through a pipe, the velocity of an action potential across an axon is positively correlated with fiber diameter; a larger fiber offers less resistance. Thus, the greater the axon's diameter allows, the less resistance to the flow of ions. Myelination of the neuron's axon increases efficiency by preventing ions from escaping, referred to as "charge leakage."

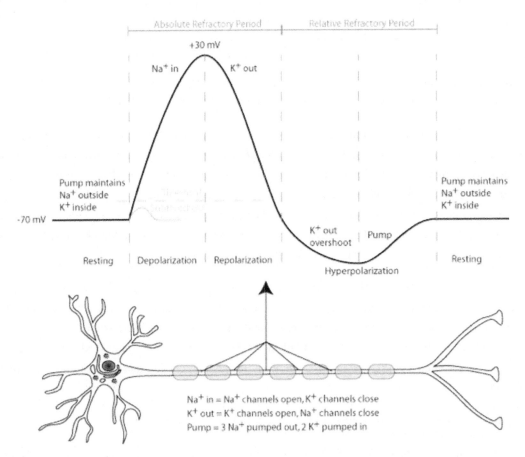

The direction of impulse through a neuron is: dendrite → cell body → axon.

In summary, an action potential is all-or-none. This means that if neurotransmitters cause the postsynaptic cell to reach a certain threshold potential, the action potential induced is just as large as the presynaptic action potential. Propagation between cells involves no resistance loss because the postsynaptic action potential is as large as the presynaptic potential.

Excitatory and inhibitory nerve fibers and summation

Graded potentials are changes in membrane potential confined to a small region of the plasma membrane. The magnitude of these potentials is related to the magnitude of the initiating stimulus. When a stimulus (graded potential) depolarizes above a threshold value, an action potential (AP) occurs, initiating a signal. If one graded potential barely makes the threshold value and another overshoots it a lot, both cause the same action potential. A graded potential is an all-or-none response. From –70 mV up to the threshold of ~ –55 mV (or –70 downward), the graded potential cannot travel, but it can potentially (if it surpasses threshold) open the voltage-gated channels. If the threshold is exceeded, the action potential travels down the axon by opening other voltage-gated channels. The other gated types cannot spread unless they trigger this AP. Since the AP is an all-or-none response, the strength of a neural signal is based on other factors (frequency of AP firing or how many nerve cells contribute APs, etc.).

Most synapse interactions are either excitatory or inhibitory. Whether the response is excitatory or inhibitory depends on the type of neurotransmitter or receptor. *Excitatory neurotransmitters* use gated ion channels and are fast acting. *Inhibitory neurotransmitters* affect the metabolism of the postsynaptic cells and are slower. *Neuromodulators* modify the postsynaptic cell's response to neurotransmitters by changing the presynaptic cell's synthesis, or by releasing or metabolizing the neurotransmitter. Neurotransmitters may be taken back into the nerve terminal (active transport), be degraded by synaptic cleft enzymes (recycled back to presynaptic neuron), or diffuse out of the synapse.

Excitatory chemical synapses occur when the activated receptor on the postsynaptic membrane opens Na^+ channels. Na^+ ions move into the cell, resulting in depolarization. This potential change in the postsynaptic neuron is an *excitatory postsynaptic potential* (EPSP). EPSPs are graded potentials. *Inhibitory chemical synapses* occur when the activated receptor on the postsynaptic membrane opens Cl^- channels. Cl^- ions move into the cell, resulting in hyperpolarization. The potential change in the postsynaptic neuron is an *inhibitory postsynaptic potential* (IPSP). Like EPSP, IPSP are graded potentials.

Integration is the summing up of excitatory and inhibitory signals. If a neuron receives many excitatory signals from one synapse (consecutive neuron firing), the axon probably transmits a nerve impulse. If both excitatory and inhibitory signals are received, the summing may prohibit the axon from firing.

In most neurons, one EPSP is not enough to cross the threshold in the postsynaptic neuron. Only the combined effects of many excitatory synapses can exceed the threshold and initiate an action potential. *Temporal summation* is when the number of EPSP arriving at different times creates a depolarization. *Spatial summation* is when the number of EPSPs arriving at different locations creates a depolarization. IPSP also show similar summations, but the effect is a hyperpolarization and the inhibition of an action potential.

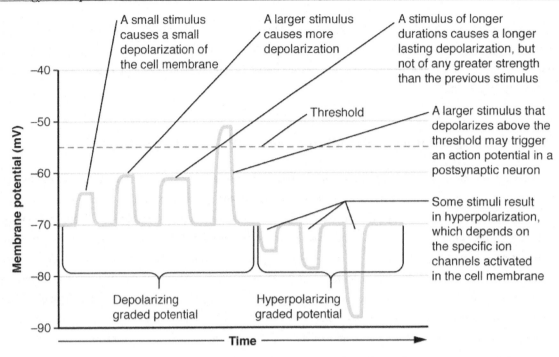

Graded potential includes temporal and spatial summation. Stimuli can be excitatory or inhibitory

Interneurons

Interneurons (association neurons) are typically located within the structures that make up the central nervous system (i.e., the spinal cord and brain). They account for 99% of all neurons in the human body. Interneurons are multipolar, consisting of many dendrites used for receiving information and a single axon to send the collected information toward the synapse.

Interneurons form complex brain pathways throughout the central nervous system, transmit signals to the periphery via motor neurons and act as integrators to evaluate impulses for the appropriate response. Generally, the term interneuron is used to refer to small neurons that connect to other nearby neurons (as opposed to *projection neurons* that can connect over long distances). Interneuron pathways play important roles in human survival and advancement, accounting for phenomena such as memory and language. Interneurons are usually inhibitory, although excitatory interneurons do exist.

CNS and PNS structures with the direction of propagation shown for afferent sensory neurons (receptors → CNS) and efferent motor neurons (CNS → effectors)

Sensory and Effector neurons

Afferent neurons (sensory neurons) send impulses from the PNS towards the CNS. Afferent neurons are unipolar, as a single dendrite collects information and transmits it through one axon. A sensory receptor at a dendrite of an afferent neuron conveys signals from tissues and organs to the brain and spine.

Receptors are specialized endings of afferent neurons or separate cells that affect ends of afferent neurons. They collect information about the external and internal environment in various energy forms. This stimulus energy is first transformed into a graded potential (receptor potential). *Stimulus transduction* is the process by which a stimulus is transformed into an electrical response. The initial depolarization in afferent neurons is achieved by either a *receptor potential* (in receptors) or by a spontaneous change in the neuron membrane potential as a *pacemaker potential*.

Efferent neurons (motor neurons) carry signals away from the CNS to cells of muscles or glands in the peripheral system. In total, 43 main nerves are branching off the CNS to the peripheral nervous system. Efferent neurons are structurally multipolar and stimulate *effectors*, which are target cells that elicit a response. For example, neurons may stimulate effector cells in the stomach to secrete gastrin.

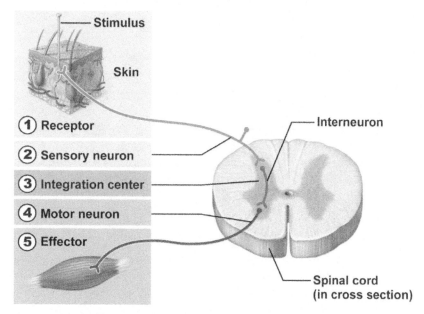

A stimulus is processed through a sensory neuron to the spinal column.
An interneuron communicates the information to a motor neuron for a response at the effector

Notes for active learning

Muscle Cell

Muscular Cell Structure

A muscle consists of muscle cells bound together by connective tissue. A single muscle fiber is a multinucleated cell formed from myoblasts during development. Muscle cells contain several parallel *myofibrils*, each of which is composed of *myofilaments* (primarily actin and myosin). These myofibrils contain the *sarcomeres*, which are the basic units of the contraction in the skeletal muscle. Myofibrils are packed together within the multinucleated skeletal muscle cells. The *sarcolemma* (plasma membrane) of the muscle cell contains the myofibrils and keeps them packed together. The nuclei of the muscle fibers are located at the edges of the diameter of the fiber, adjacent to the sarcolemma.

The *sarcoplasm* is the cytoplasm of muscle fibers and contains numerous mitochondria that produce ATP for muscle contraction. The *sarcoplasmic reticulum* is similar to the smooth endoplasmic reticulum; it extends throughout the sarcoplasm of the muscle cell and is involved in storing calcium ions used in muscle contraction.

Muscle is attached to a bone by collagen bundles called tendons. After infancy, new fibers are formed from undifferentiated satellite cells and generally do not undergo mitosis to create new muscle cells after development, called *hyperplasia*. However, muscle cells increase in size and thus increase the overall volume of the muscle, *hypertrophy*. In adulthood, any compensation for lost muscles occurs mostly through an increase in the size of fibers.

The function unit of a muscle cell is the sarcomere

Transverse tubules (*T-tubules*) are tunnel-like extensions of the sarcolemma that pass through muscle cells from one side of the cell to another, forming a network around myofibrils. They are referred to as transverse because of the way they are oriented. The transverse tubules play a vital role in muscle contraction. A muscle action potential, which is the movement of electrical charge, travels along the transverse tubules and stimulates the release of calcium ions from the sarcoplasmic reticulum. This allows the calcium ions to flood back into the sarcoplasm and binds to troponin.

Calcium triggers the movement of various protein filaments (including *actin, myosin,* and *tropomyosin*) within the myofibrils, which results in muscle contraction. The general function of the T-tubules is to conduct impulses from the surface of the cell to the sarcoplasmic reticulum where Ca is released.

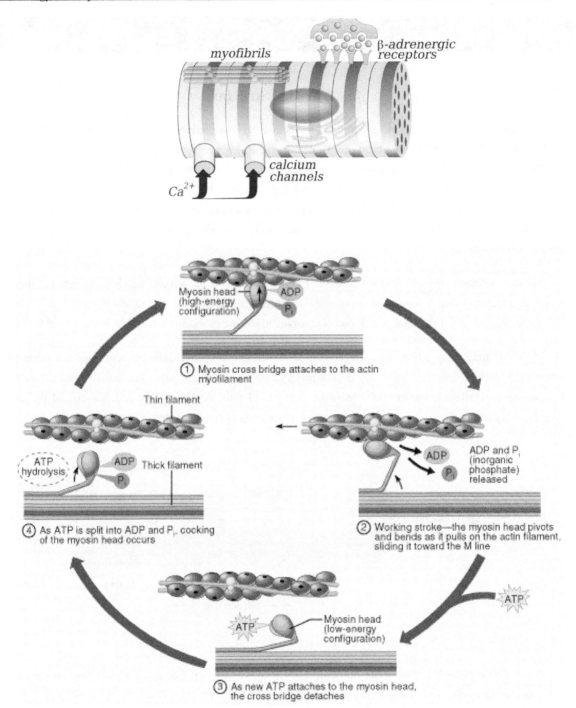

*Calcium binds to troponin to cause a conformational change in tropomyosin
and expose the myosin binding sites on the actin myofilament (step 1)*

The sarcoplasm in muscle cells is equivalent to the cytoplasm of other cells. The sarcoplasmic reticulum in muscle cells is homologous to the endoplasmic reticulum. Unlike the endoplasmic reticulum, the sarcoplasmic reticulum stores and secretes Ca⁺, the ion essential in muscle contraction.

The sarcoplasmic reticulum forms a sleeve around each myofibril, with enlarged *lateral sacs* that store Ca^{2+}. It is abundant in skeletal muscle cells and related to myofibrils. The membrane of the sarcoplasmic reticulum contains active pumps involved in moving calcium into the sarcoplasmic reticulum from the sarcoplasm. The sarcoplasmic reticulum contains specialized gates for calcium. Action potentials lead to depolarization of the sarcoplasmic reticulum membrane, leading to depolarization of the T-tubules. This opens the Ca^{2+} channels of the lateral sacs, causing the contraction to begin. To end contraction, Ca^{2+} is pumped back into the lateral sacs by active transport proteins, called plasma membrane Ca^{2+} ATPase (PMCA).

Sarcomeres with I and A bands, M and Z lines, and the H zone

Skeletal muscle cells have longitudinal bundles called myofibrils. Each myofibril consists of thin (actin) and thick (myosin) filaments, which repeat along the myofibril in units called sarcomeres. Organelles within the sarcomeres resemble the form and function of other types of eukaryotic cells. In the *H zone*, the central region of the sarcomere, there is no overlap between thin and thick filaments. The *M line*, in center of the H zone, links the center regions of thick filaments and divides the sarcomere vertically.

Sarcomere with associated regions

Each sarcomere has a band of thick filaments in the middle called the *A band*. Sarcomeres are flanked on both sides by thin filaments. Vertical borders between sarcomeres are *Z lines*, which anchor thin filaments.

I bands represent thin actin filaments, and *H bands* represent thick myosin filaments. Titin protein fibers from the Z line are linked to the M line and the thick filaments. Due to the banded pattern provided by thin and thick filaments, skeletal muscle is striated muscle.

Fiber type

Fibers within muscle tissue can be organized into fast and slow fibers. *Fast fibers* contain myosin with high ATPase activity and have high shortening velocity. *Slow fibers* contain myosin with low ATPase activity and have low shortening velocity. Fast fibers fatigue rapidly, while slow fibers fatigue gradually.

Oxidative fibers have numerous mitochondria and therefore a high capacity for oxidative phosphorylation. ATP production is dependent on oxygen. Oxidative fibers contain myoglobin, an oxygen-binding protein, which increases the rate of oxygen diffusion into the fiber. Myoglobin gives oxidative fibers a red color, as red muscle fibers.

Glycolytic fibers have few mitochondria but a high concentration of glycolytic enzymes and glycogen. Therefore, it is glycolysis, rather than oxidative phosphorylation, which fuels the contractions. These fibers are white muscle fibers due to their pale color. Glycolytic fibers can develop more tension than oxidative fibers because they are larger and contain more filaments, both thick and thin. However, they fatigue rapidly.

The three major types of skeletal muscle fibers, determined by their myosin ATPase activity and energy source, are 1) slow oxidative, 2) fast oxidative / glycolytic, and 3) fast glycolytic. Most muscles contain all three fiber types.

Slow oxidative fibers are one of the two main skeletal muscle fibers with abundant mitochondria and myoglobin. They generate energy predominantly through the aerobic conditions. Slow oxidative fibers twitch at a slow rate and are resistant to fatigue. The peak force exerted by these muscles is low. Slow muscle fibers have a lot of oxidative enzymes but are low in ATP activity.

Fast oxidative / glycolytic fibers can contract at a fast rate and produce a large peak force while being resistant to tiring even after many cycles. These fibers have a large amount of ATP activity and are high in oxidative and glycolytic enzymes. They are used for anaerobic activities that need to be sustained for a prolonged time.

Fast glycolytic fibers can exert a large force and contract at a fast rate. However, this comes at the expense of the fibers tiring easily. After a small amount of exertion, the muscle requires rest to recover. These fibers have low oxidative capacity while ATP and glycolytic activity is high. These fibers are used during anaerobic activity for short durations of time.

Abundant mitochondria in red muscle cells as ATP source

Mitochondria are abundant in muscle cells because of the need for a quick source of energy at any time. However, certain types of muscles have more mitochondria than others. *Type I muscle* (slow twitch or red muscle) contains more mitochondria than other types of muscle. Type I muscles are desirable for long-distance running. This type of muscle uses mitochondria to produce ATP from oxygen aerobically.

Type IIB muscles are common in weightlifters. These types of muscles require short bursts of energy and therefore are not as dependent on mitochondria. Type IIB muscles are mitochondria-poor and appear white. These types of muscles are more reliant on short bursts of glycolysis and therefore have greater stores of glycogen. While they can generate greater force than type I muscles, type IIB muscles experience muscle fatigue at a much faster rate.

Type IIA muscles are those intermediate between types I and IIB. They have fewer mitochondria than type I, but more than type IIB. Type IIA muscles fatigue less easily than type IIB but cannot replenish ATP as efficiently as type I. Type IIA muscle is often pink.

Long-distance runners typically have a greater percentage of red fibers than white fibers. Short-distance runners typically have a greater percentage of white than red fibers.

Red muscle (type I)	White muscle (type IIB)
High endurance, but slow	*Fast, but fatigue easily*
• Predominantly aerobic respiration	• Anaerobic respiration (glycolysis)
• Many mitochondria because red muscles undergo aerobic respiration	• Few mitochondria because white muscles mainly undergo glycolysis
• Equipped to receive abundant oxygen supply: many capillaries and much myoglobin	• Equipped for short bursts of glycolysis: store high amounts of glycogen

Many muscle cells rely on ATP to perform their function. Muscle cells contain myoglobin, which stores oxygen. Cellular respiration does not immediately supply the ATP needed. Since ATP availability is essential, the body has adapted additional mechanisms than glycolysis to generate it. For example, when in need of ATP, muscle fibers rely on *creatine phosphate* (phosphocreatine), a stored form of high energy phosphate. Creatine phosphate does not directly participate in muscle contraction; however, it contributes by regenerating ATP rapidly: Creatine – P + ADP → ATP + Creatine.

When all creatine phosphate is depleted, and O_2 is limited, fermentation produces a small amount of ATP to compensate. Over time, however, this results in a buildup of lactic acid that leads to muscle fatigue due to oxygen debt. Lactic acid is transported to the liver, where 20% is broken down to CO_2 and H_2O via aerobic respiration. The ATP gained from this respiration is then used to reconvert 80% of the lactate to glucose. For example, those that train for marathons increase the number of mitochondria, allowing aerobic respiration for longer periods of time. Rigor mortis, the stiffness seen in a recently deceased corpse, occurs because nonliving organisms do not produce ATP. Therefore, the mechanisms behind muscle contraction are unable to allow the muscles to relax; muscles remain contracted until the enzymatic breakdown of cross-linking of actin and myosin filaments occurs.

Increased amounts of contractile activity (exercise) increases the size (hypertrophy) of muscle fibers and capacity for ATP production. Low-intensity exercise affects oxidative fibers, increasing the number of mitochondria and capillaries. High-intensity exercise affects glycolytic fibers, increasing their diameter by an increased synthesis of actin, myosin filaments, and glycolytic enzymes.

Muscle glycogen is the major fuel in the initial stages of exercise. After the initial stages, blood glucose and fatty acids are used. Muscle fiber generates ATP by one phosphorylation of ADP with the use of creatine phosphate, which is the source of ATP during the initial phase of contraction. This is followed by the slower pathways of second oxidative phosphorylation in mitochondria, or by glycolysis in the cytosol. At the end of muscle activity, creatine phosphate and glycogen levels are restored by energy-dependent processes, leading to a continued elevated level of oxygen consumption, *oxygen debt*, even after exercise finishes.

Notes for active learning

Electrochemistry

Concentration cell: the direction of electron flow and Nernst equation

Electrochemistry is the field that relates electricity to chemical reactions. In electrochemical reactions (e.g., batteries), free electrons are produced or consumed by reduction-oxidation mechanisms (i.e., the electrons move from one molecule to another).

The *cell potential* refers to the potential difference between the electrodes of a cell. If the cell potential is positive, the reaction proceeds to the right (products). The standard cell potential E° is related to the standard free energy $G°$ by the following equation:

$$\Delta G° = -nFE°$$

By using the relationship between the free energy G and the change of free energy ΔG, the equation can be substituted and rearranged to determine the relationship between the cell potential E (i.e., the total voltage of the cell) and standard cell potential E°, giving the *Nernst equation:*

$$E = E° - (RT / nF) \cdot [\ln(Q)]$$

where R is the universal gas constant, T is the absolute temperature, n is the moles of electrons transferred, F is the Faraday constant, and Q is the reaction quotient.

The Nernst equation describes how a cell membrane can develop an electrical charge and how the concentration of a substance affects the cell potential.

Notes for active learning

Biosignaling

Cells communicate with adjacent, neighboring cells, whereby one cell secretes a signal molecule into the extracellular fluid, which is picked up by the target cells. An example is the release of neurotransmitters at the synapse between two neurons.

Hormonal signaling is used by plant and animal cells to communicate to other cells in the organism that are a great distance away. One cell secrets a signal molecule (hormone) into the blood system (if an animal) or into the extracellular fluid (if a plant). The signal molecule travels throughout the body until it reaches the target cells that have the receptors necessary to bind the hormone and elicit the response.

While neurons use the nervous system to interpret the environment, other cells communicate via complex cascades, called signal transduction pathways (STPs). While certain chemical structures (e.g., nonpolar steroid hormones) can transverse the phospholipid bilayer, larger or polar molecules (e.g., peptide hormones) require signal transduction pathways to initiate the intended cellular response. These molecular circuits involve a plethora of intermediate steps and molecules.

Signal transduction pathways transmit chemical messages between different cells. These pathways are essential for appropriate bodily function and environmental response. They are highly conserved in a wide range of organisms. STPs use the interpreted information and induce advanced responses, such as alteration of enzymatic activity or gene expression.

The different signal transduction pathways are:

(1) Pathways with intracellular receptors

(2) Pathways with extracellular receptors

(3) Receptors that function as ion channels

(4) Receptors that function as enzymes

(5) Receptors that interact with cytoplasmic proteins

(6) Receptors that interact with G proteins

(7) Receptors that act as transcription factors

If there are two chemical messengers involved in the signal transduction pathway, the one that binds to a specific receptor on the plasma membrane is the first messenger, and the chemical messenger that is enzymatically generated by receptor activation and enters the cytoplasm is the second messenger. Ca^{2+} frequently acts as a second messenger.

The transduction pathways stop when the concentration of the first messenger decreases due to diffusion or degradation. Additionally, receptors either become chemically altered, decreasing their affinity for the first messenger, or they are removed when the messenger-receptor complex is taken inside the cell by endocytosis.

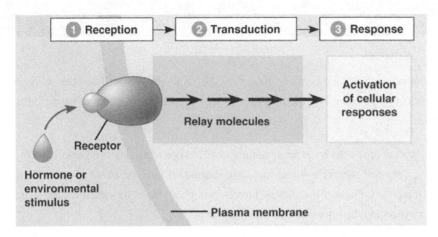

Signal transduction involves three key steps: reception, transduction, and response

First, the environmental stimuli received by receptors on the cell membrane must bind to a receptor. The combination of messengers with receptors causes a change in conformation of the receptor, *receptor activation*. This leads to changes in (1) permeability, transport properties or the electrical state of the plasma membrane, (2) the metabolism of the cell, (3) the secretory activity of the cell, (4) the rate of proliferation and differentiation of the cell and (5) the contractile activity of the cell.

In *transduction*, the signal must be communicated to the inside of the cell without the ligand (large or polar molecule) entering. This is accomplished by a receptor protein, which binds the ligand so that the signal is transduced across the cell membrane, beginning a cascade involving multiple secondary messenger molecules (e.g., cyclic AMP). These secondary messenger molecules have more freedom to move throughout the cell, allowing them to have a wide range of effects depending on the original chemical signal. Often, the effect is the phosphorylation or dephosphorylation of molecules in the cytoplasm. Secondary messengers are capable of signal amplification, which accentuates the cellular response. There is usually an amplification of the signal (e.g., one hormone can elicit the response of over 10^8 molecules).

While secondary messenger systems provide an excellent method of producing a cellular response, they can instigate problems. If multiple signal transduction pathways occur simultaneously, signals can be slowed or disrupted, leading to inappropriate cellular responses. *Cellular response* is the final step in signal transduction pathways. This response can include activating an enzyme, rearranging the cytoskeleton or transcribing a gene. The activation of a gene can lead to further cellular effects, triggering a signal transduction cascade. When genes are expressed, physiological changes that affect the whole organism can occur (e.g., an increase in the uptake of glucose from the bloodstream).

Gated ion channels: voltage-gated and ligand-gated channel

Ion channels are membrane proteins that play an important role in cellular signaling. Due to their ability to form pores (openings) across the cell membrane, ion channels are involved in a variety of essential signaling mechanisms. In the nervous system, ion channels are used to regulate neurotransmitter release and the rate of electrical propagation. While many types of ion transporters exist in cellular systems, ion channels are characterized by two special features. First is the high rate of movement of ions through ion channels (10 million ions per second). Second, ion channels operate by passive transport. Based on a concentration gradient, no ATP or other energy is required to move ions through the channel. Voltage-gated and ligand-gated are the two types of gated ion channels.

Gated ion channels in specialized receptor membranes allow for fluctuations in ion concentrations across the membrane, generating a graded receptor potential. The magnitude of the receptor potential is determined by stimulus strength, the summation of receptor potentials and receptor sensitivity. The graded potential may initiate an action potential. The magnitude of the graded potential determines the frequency of the action potential.

Changes in charge influence voltage-gated ion channels. In a neuron, voltage-gated ion channels on the axon are responsible for the cell's action potential. These proteins transverse the membrane of the cell, opening and closing in response to fluctuations in electrical membrane potential. The activation of these ion-specific channels depends on the concentration of ions on either side of the membrane. These ions collectively influence the net charge inside and outside the neuron. Appropriate regulation of these charges is essential for effective impulse transmission. Examples of voltage-gated ion channels include calcium ion-specific channels (important in neurotransmitter release) and the sodium/ potassium channels in nerve cells.

Voltage-gated Na⁺ channels. 1) channel is closed at resting potential, 2) channel opens in response to a nerve impulse, and Na⁺ enters the cell and 3) briefly after activation, the channel does not open in response to a new signal

Ligand-gated ion channels respond to *ligands*, signal-triggering molecules. When a ligand reaches the channel's binding domain, the transmembrane domain of the ligand "opens," allowing ions to transverse the membrane. Ligand-gated ion channels are less selective than voltage-gated ion channels because a variety of ions can cross the membrane. For example, once the correct ligand binds to the extracellular domain, sodium, potassium, calcium and chlorine ions may all pass through the same ligand-gated ion channel.

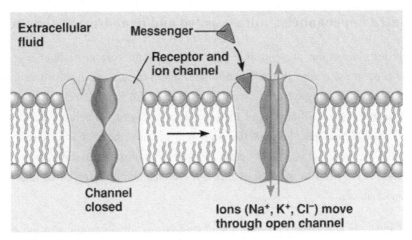

The ligand binds to the receptor on the extracellular side of the side and opens an ion channel

Ligand-gated ion channels are seen at the synapse. Here, neurotransmitters function as the ligands, binding to the channel, opening the channel ion transport and propagating a desired cellular response. Alternatively, the binding domain of these channels can exist on the intracellular surface of the neuron. In this example, the channel would respond to chemicals inside the cell, such as secondary messengers, to initiate a response by channeling ions to the outside. This mechanism is responsible for the conversion of chemical information to electrical information. Chemical signals are interpreted by cells and then passed on to the nervous system to be interpreted as electrical information by the brain.

Receptor enzymes

Tyrosine kinase receptors, an important family of receptors with a complex structure, exemplify a type of signal transduction pathway in cells. The receptor spans the cell membrane and consists of two important domains: the hormone-binding domain on the outside and the tyrosine kinase domain on the inside of the cell.

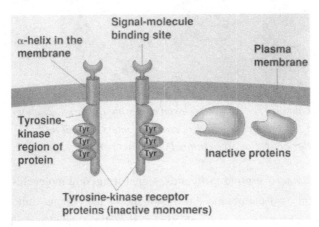

Tyrosine-kinase receptor with two transmembrane proteins separated

The tyrosine kinase receptor is activated when two signal molecules, often hormones, bind to the extracellular receptors. The receptors aggregate, forming an activated *dimer* (a structure formed from two similar transmembrane subunits). The activation of the tyrosine kinase phosphorylates the intracellular tyrosine residues, forming binding sites for relay proteins with specific domains. When these proteins bind to the phosphorylated portion of the receptor, a conformational change occurs, activating various proteins. This activation leads to a *kinase cascade*, a series of phosphorylations and activations of molecules within the cytoplasm. The cascade eventually reaches its target: transcription factors. Once phosphorylated, the active transcription factors influence DNA, altering gene transcription.

Progression of tyrosine kinase cascade (from top left) through the response(s) within the cell

Once activated, a tyrosine kinase dimer can activate over ten different relay proteins, each of which triggers a different response. The ability of one ligand-binding event to elicit so many response pathways is a key difference between these receptors and G-protein-linked receptors, which are described in the following section. Abnormal tyrosine kinase receptors that aggregate without the binding of a ligand have been linked with some forms of cancer.

G protein-coupled receptors

G protein-coupled receptors are a large family of receptor proteins that activate signal transduction pathways within a cell. They are especially important in human embryonic development, vision, and smell. Over 60% of modern medications exert their effects by influencing G protein pathways. G protein-coupled receptors are capable of recognizing a wide range of chemical signals, including nucleotides, photons, and peptides.

The structure of these proteins is highly conserved across all the eukaryotic organisms that have them. G protein-coupled receptors have an extracellular domain that binds a ligand, seven transmembrane alpha-helices that integrate the cell membrane and a G protein-interacting site on the inside of the cell. While inactive, this G protein exists in a trimeric state (an alpha component bound to a GDP molecule and a beta-gamma dimer component).

G protein activation involves three steps: binding, changing conformation and signaling. After the ligand binds to the G protein-binding domain, the chemical signal transverses the receptor's convoluted channel. On the cytoplasmic side of the cell, this signal induces the G protein's alpha segment to exchange GDP for GTP, a molecule readily available in the cytosol. This exchange of GDP for GTP causes the G protein to undergo a conformational change.

The conformational change causes the G protein's beta-gamma dimer to disassociate from the G protein-coupled receptor complex, activating other proteins. The recruitment of other proteins amplifies the signal by the bound ligand via a cascade mechanism. The signal becomes inhibited when the GTP is exchanged for GDP on the original G protein. Regulator G protein-signaling molecules can assist in this process.

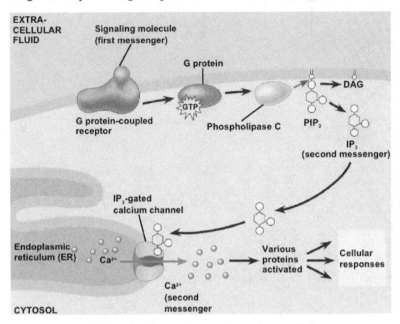

G-protein and cascade of second messengers for a cellular response
by the binding of the signaling molecule

Notes for active learning

Notes for active learning

Tissues Formed from Eukaryotic Cells

Epithelial cells: simple epithelium and stratified epithelium

Epithelial cells make up epithelial tissues, which are surfaces that line structures throughout the body, particularly organs and blood vessels. Several types of epithelial cells perform a variety of functions. *Squamous epithelial cells* appear flat, *cuboidal epithelial cells* are cube-shaped and *columnar epithelial cells* are column-shaped.

Types of epithelium

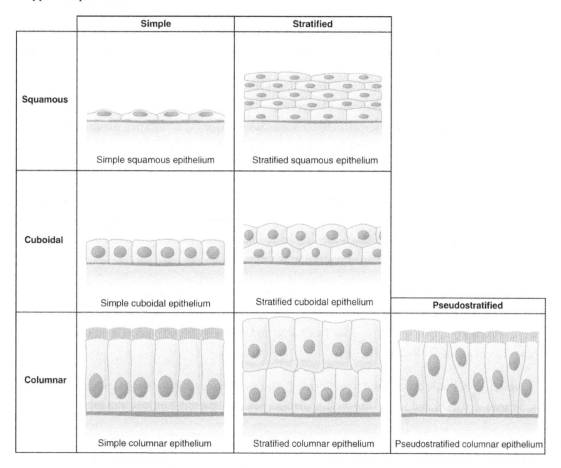

Simple epithelium is a single layer of epithelial cells connected by tight junctions. The function of the simple epithelial layer is highly dependent on the types of epithelial cells involved. Simple squamous layers are often involved in passive diffusion, lining surfaces such as the alveoli during oxygen exchange. Simple cuboidal layers are involved in secretion and absorption (e.g., gland ducts and kidney tubules). Simple columnar epithelial layers form a protective layer in the stomach and gut.

Epithelial cells can form layers as *stratified epithelium*. Layered epithelial layers allow for more protection and complex function. For example, stratified columnar epithelium lines the vas deferens, protecting the glands and assisting in secrction. Stratified columnar and cuboidal epithelium is rarely seen in human anatomy; stratified squamous covers the entire body as the skin.

Endothelial cells

The *endothelium* is a layer of simple squamous cells that forms the interior lining of lymphatic vessels and blood vessels. It acts as a semi-selective barrier that controls the passage of materials. *Lymphatic endothelial cells* are in direct contact with lymph. *Vascular endothelial cells* are in direct contact with blood, and line every part of the circulatory system, from the tiniest capillaries, to larger arteries, veins and to the heart itself. These endothelial cells have many functions, including blood clotting, the formation of new blood vessels, blood pressure control and inflammation control. Endothelial cells have a strong capacity for cell division and movement, and they proliferate quickly.

Connective tissue cells:
major tissues and cell types, loose fiber vs. dense fiber and extracellular matrix

Connective tissue holds structures of the body together. It consists of specialized cells, ground substance, and fibers. The cells in connective tissue secrete the extracellular matrix, which is held together by ground substance. The fibers, made mainly of collagen, give the matrix its strength. Several types of connective tissue cells exist, making up bone, fat, tendons, ligaments, cartilage and blood. For example, chondroblasts make cartilage, fibroblasts make collagen, and hematopoietic stem cells make blood.

The nomenclature of the numerous types of cells in connective tissue helps to differentiate their function. Cells that contain the suffix *blast* describe a stem cell that actively produces a matrix, while the suffix *cyte* describes a mature cell. For example, while osteoblasts are specialized connective tissue cells that build the matrix in bone, osteocytes are mature, immobile osteoblasts involved in bone maintenance.

Various types of fiber make up connective tissue. The most common protein fiber is collagen or *collagenous fibers*. These coiled fibers give collagen its rigidity. There are many collagenous fibers, including *elastic fibers*, which give connective tissue its flexibility, and *reticular fibers*, which mainly join one connective tissue to an adjacent organ or blood vessel.

Connective tissue is either "loose" or "dense." The *loose connective tissue* has a higher concentration of ground substance and cells and fewer fibers. It provides protective padding around the internal organs, as well as fat.

The *dense connective tissue* has a higher concentration of collagenous fibers than loose connective tissue and is needed in anatomical structures that require great strength (e.g., ligaments and tendons).

Cartilage is a connective tissue that is produced and maintained by chondrocytes. Cartilage can absorb shock and is seen on the ends of bones and in the spinal disks. Since it is more flexible than bone, cartilage is advantageous for structures that do not require as much protection, such as the nose or ears.

The *extracellular matrix* (ECM) exists outside of cells. Cells secrete molecules that make up the matrix, which include proteins and polysaccharides. In connective tissue, the ECM gives surrounding cells a support system both physically and chemically.

Dense Connective Tissue

Adipose Tissue (Connective Tissue)

Areolar Tissue (Connective Tissue)

Compact Bone (Connective Tissue)

Blood (Connective Tissue)

Notes for active learning

Notes for active learning

Notes for active learning

Chapter 7

Genetics

- **Mendelian Concepts**

- **Meiosis and Genetic Variability**

- **Analytic Methods**

Mendelian Concepts

Gregor Mendel (1822-1884) was an Austrian monk whose experiments with plant breeding in the mid-1800s formed the basis of modern genetics. Mendel was a friar at the monastery of St. Thomas in Brunn, Austria, while teaching part-time at a local secondary school. Mendel's goal was to have firm scientific evidence for how genetic information is passed from parents to offspring. He focused on how plant offspring acquired traits from their parents. He traced the inheritance of individual traits and kept careful records of numbers, then used his understanding of probability to interpret the results.

Unfortunately, Mendel's results, published in 1865 and 1869 in the *Proceedings of the Society of Natural History of Brunn*, went mostly unnoticed until 1900. Three independent investigators, Carl Correns (Germany), Hugo De Vries (Holland) and Erich Von Tschermak (Austria), conducted similar experiments and reached the same conclusions as Mendel. After researching the literature, the three researchers gave credit to Mendel. This rediscovery and confirmation of Mendel's work launched the field of modern genetics.

Mendel chose to study the *Pisum sativum* (garden pea), as it was easy to cultivate, had a short generation time, and could be cross-pollinated by hand. Mendel chose 22 of the many pea varieties for his experiments. Concerning certain traits, all the plants used in the experiment had to be *true breeding* (progeny identical to parents). He chose this approach to ensure accuracy and simplicity in his studies.

Inbreeding genetically similar individuals obtain true-bred organisms for many generations. Pea plants can be *self-pollinated*, an effective form of inbreeding. The process eliminates genetic variation from the gene pool and results in a strain with certain identical traits in all individuals.

Mendel studied seven simple traits: seed shape, seed color, flower position, flower color, pod shape, pod color, and plant height. He correctly hypothesized that the pattern of inheritance of these traits from generation to generation was because the genetic information was being passed from their parents. He terms this *hereditary factors*. The *particulate theory of inheritance* proposed by Mendel stated that these factors, or "discrete particles," do not blend. This is in contrast to the *blending theory of inheritance*, now discredited, which stated that offspring have traits that are a blend of the parents. For example, red and white flowers would produce pink flowers. This is observed in nature, but the pink offspring then self-fertilize and produce several all-red and all-white offspring. Proponents of the blending theory dismissed this as mere instability in genetic material. Charles Darwin wanted to develop a theory of evolution based on hereditary principles, but the blending theory did not account for genetic variation and species diversity.

Mendel's particulate theory properly accounts for Charles Darwin's theory of evolution, although he never knew this because he did not live to see Mendel's work rediscovered. A *particulate inheritance theory* is essential for Darwin's theory of *natural selection*. Otherwise, any selectively favored trait would be blended away as soon as the selected individual reproduced with one of a different trait.

Mendel's explanation of heredity was remarkable, since it was based solely on the interpretation of breeding experiments, and it was done long before scientists understood cell division and molecular biology. During the early part of the 20th century, the processes of mitosis and meiosis were discovered by the microscopic examination of cells. Researchers found that Mendel's hereditary factors were not free-floating particles, but rather were located on chromosomes in the nucleus. The hereditary factors were given the name genes.

Gene

A *gene* is a stretch of DNA that encodes for a specific trait (or characteristic). On a molecular level, each gene encodes for a protein which produces a particular trait. An organism's *genome* includes its entire set of genes.

The *chromosomal theory of inheritance* states that genes are located on chromosomes and that inheritance patterns can be explained by the specific locations of genes on chromosomes. Chromosomes can be classified as autosomes and allosomes. *Autosomes* are non-sex chromosomes that are the same number and kind in all sexes. *Allosomes* are sex chromosomes (e.g., X or Y). Humans have 22 pairs of autosomes (44 total), and 1 pair of allosomes (2 total). *Diploidy* is the characteristic of having pairs of chromosomes. One member of each pair is from the mother, and the other is from the father. *Homologous chromosomes* are similar but not identical copies.

Locus

A *locus* is a specific location of a gene or segment of DNA on a chromosome. Loci can be mapped by their physical position on the chromosome, or by their relative distance from each other.

The loci of two homologous chromosomes are identical in their placement and align during meiosis.

Allele: single and multiple

Loci are identical, but the gene at each locus may be in different forms (e.g., brown eyes or blue eyes) as *alleles*. An allele is an alternative form of the gene and differs from another allele by one or more nucleotide bases that encode a different protein. Diploid organisms have two similar versions of each chromosome so that an individual can have a maximum of two alleles for each gene, one on each chromosome. One allele comes from the mother, and one comes from the father. Traits exhibited by an organism are determined based on the alleles an individual has inherited.

Although each diploid organism inherits two alleles, there are usually more than two possible alleles of each gene in the population. *Multiple alleles* are when more than two types of alleles can encode for a particular characteristic. A classic example is blood type in humans. There are three blood group alleles: I^A, I^B and i. Each can have two alleles, so the possible combinations are $I^A I^A$, I^Ai, $I^B I^B$, I^Bi, $I^A I^B$ and ii. An organism's combination of alleles is its *genotype*.

Blood type comparison of genotype and phenotype:

Genotype	Blood type (phenotype)
$I^A I^A$ or I^Ai	A
$I^B I^B$ or I^Bi	B
$I^A I^B$	AB
ii	O

Homozygosity and heterozygosity

Zygosity is the similarity of the alleles at any given locus. An individual is *homozygous* for a gene when the two alleles that the individual carries are identical. In the blood type example, individuals with the genotype I^AI^A, I^BI^B and ii are homozygous, since they have two identical alleles. A *heterozygous* individual has two different alleles, as the genotypes I^Ai, I^Bi, and I^AI^B.

Wild-type

The *wild-type allele* is the most prevalent and most dominant version of the allele, with some exceptions. *Mutant alleles* are the product of changes in the nucleotide sequence within DNA (mutation) and are generally less common in a population. For example, red eyes are a wild-type trait in Drosophila (fruit fly), while white eyes are the mutant trait. However, alleles often do not fit into either of these categories with additional variation.

Recessiveness

When an allele is *recessive,* the individual must inherit two copies of this allele to express the trait. The *dominant* allele is when a single copy is needed for it to be observed. A dominant allele masks or hides expression of a recessive allele. For example, the allele for attached earlobes in humans is recessive, and the allele for unattached earlobes is dominant. An individual must inherit two attached earlobe alleles to express this trait. If she inherits one attached allele and one unattached allele, the unattached allele dominates the other, leading to unattached earlobes.

By convention, the dominant allele is an uppercase letter, and the recessive allele is a lower case letter. The letter may be the first letter of either the dominant or recessive allele (by convention). For example, in Mendel's pea plants the alleles for seed shape are named R for the dominant round allele. The recessive allele, wrinkled, is denoted *r.* However, in fruit flies, the alleles for wing size are named for the recessive allele, vestigial wings. Therefore, the dominant allele (normal wings) is denoted V and the recessive allele as v. In many cases, the locus is given one letter, and the alleles are superscripts of the letter. For example, with sex chromosomes (e.g., X^AX^a). Other, more complex naming schemes are often seen in the case of multiple alleles (e.g., blood types) and co-dominant or incompletely dominant alleles, as discussed later.

Genotype and phenotype:
definitions, probability calculations, and pedigree analysis

Genotype is the alleles received when an organism is conceived. The *phenotype* describes the observable traits which are expressed. Due to recessiveness and dominance, zygosity cannot be deduced by observation of phenotype. Two organisms with different allele combinations can have the same phenotype. For example, if a homozygous individual has the alleles I^AI^A and a heterozygous individual has the alleles I^Ai, they have different genotypes, but the same phenotype and both exhibit blood type A since I^A is a dominant allele. Its presence overshadows the i allele in the heterozygous individual.

Mendel inferred genotype from observable phenotype by performing breeding experiments that revealed how traits emerge, disappear and re-emerge over generations. Traits are *characters,* and their expression in an individual is a *character state*. Mendel was able to streamline his experiments by using character states that were *discontinuous* (no intermediates). Discontinuous traits have discrete, distinct categories; the trait is either there or not. Mendel could quantify his results by counting the two different phenotypes among the offspring of each experimental cross. Mendel's knowledge of statistics enabled him to recognize that his results followed theoretical probability calculations, even though his small sample size resulted in slight deviations from the expected ratios.

Probability is the likelihood that a given event occurs by random chance. With each coin flip, there is a 50% chance of heads and a 50% chance of tails. In Mendelian genetics, the chance of inheriting one of two alleles from the parent is 50%.

The *multiplicative law of probability* states that the chance of two or more independent events occurring together is the product of the probability of the events occurring separately. If two parents that are heterozygous for unattached earlobes (genotype Ee) have a child, the probability of the child's genotype can be calculated using probability.

In half (½) of cases, the mother passes an E allele to the child, and in the other half of the cases, she passes an e allele. The same is true for the father. The possible combinations for the child's genotype, where one allele is inherited from the mother and another from the father:

$$EE = \frac{1}{2} \times \frac{1}{2} = \frac{1}{4}, \quad eE = \frac{1}{2} \times \frac{1}{2} = \frac{1}{4} \quad Ee = \frac{1}{2} \times \frac{1}{2} = \frac{1}{4} \quad ee = \frac{1}{2} \times \frac{1}{2} = \frac{1}{4}$$

The *additive law of probability* calculates the probability of an event that occurs in two or more independent ways; it is the sum of individual probabilities of each way an event can occur. In the example, the chance that the child is a heterozygote is the sum of the probability of having the genotype eE (¼) or Ee (¼) = ½, or a 50% chance. The probability of having unattached earlobes is the sum of the probabilities of inheriting at least one E (dominant) allele. This sum is ¼ + ¼ + ¼ = ¾, or a 75% chance.

These laws of probability were used in creating a method that predicts the genotypic results of genetic crosses: the *Punnett square,* introduced by R. C. Punnett. For example, in a Punnett square, all possible types of alleles from the father's gametes may be aligned vertically, and all possible alleles from the mother's gametes may be aligned horizontally; possible combinations of offspring are placed in squares. The Punnett square predicts the chance of each child's genotype and corresponding phenotype.

In genetics, probability depends on independent, mutually exclusive events. For example, the odds of a couple having a boy or a girl is always 50%. Using the multiplicative law of probability, it is overall unlikely that a couple has five boys: ½ × ½ × ½ × ½ × ½ = 1/32, or 3.125%. However, this probability has no bearing on another event. Even if the couple has four boys, there is still a 50% chance their fifth child is a boy or a girl. Each fertilization is an independent event. In the Punnett square below, note that the mother has two copies of the X allele, while the father has one X allele and one Y allele. In 50% of cases, the child inherits an X from the mother and an X from the father, while in the other 50% of cases the child inherits an X from the mother and a Y from the father.

Mother

	X	X
X	XX (Girl)	XX (Girl)
Y	XY (Boy)	XY (Boy)

Father (to the left)   X (to the right)

Punnett square for the probability that parents have a girl (XX) or boy (XY). Probability is 50%.

Mendel began his experiments by creating true-breeding plants and then *crossing* (mating), two strains that were true breeding for different alleles of the same trait. An example is to cross a true breeding pea plant with round seeds with another plant with wrinkled seeds; these two individuals constitute the *parental (P) generation*. Crossbreeding is accomplished by removing the pollen-producing male organs from a "father" plant and using them to fertilize the ovary of another because pea plants are *monoecious* (both male and female reproductive organs). Mendel had to remove the male organs from the "mother" plant to prevent it from self-pollinating.

The *first filial* (F1) generation is the hybrid offspring produced by this cross. These individuals breed with one another to produce the *second filial* (F2) generation. This is a *monohybrid cross* because it is between two individuals that are heterozygous for a single trait, e.g., Rr × Rr. This produces F2 offspring in a phenotypic ratio of 3:1 round to wrinkled seeds.

Example using true-breeding plants with round seeds and true-breeding plants with wrinkled seeds. Compare results to genotype to observed phenotype ratios. The proportions of a test cross with a homozygous dominant:

P generation:	homozygous round (RR) × homozygous wrinkled (rr)
F1 generation:	100% heterozygous round (Rr)
F2 generation:	25% homozygous round (RR)
	50% heterozygous round (Rr)
	25% homozygous wrinkled (rr)
	Genotypic ratio: 1:2:1 RR to Rr to rr
	Phenotypic ratio: 3:1 round-seeded to wrinkle-seeded

The F2 offspring ratio is conceptualized using a Punnett square of the F1 generation cross, Rr × Rr:

Parent 1 gametes

		R	r
Parent 2 gametes	R	RR	Rr
	r	Rr	rr

When Mendel performed this experiment with the six other traits of pea plants, he obtained similar results. He recognized a pattern of 3:1 phenotypic ratio in the F2 generation. Mendel extended his experimental results through inductive reasoning to claim that all discontinuous traits, no matter what animal or plant species is studied, would follow the same pattern. This was how he developed the notion that each distinct phenotypic trait in an individual is controlled by two "hereditary factors" (now called alleles). The alternative hypothesis that each trait is controlled by one factor was not a viable explanation, because it could not explain the reappearance of wrinkled seeds in the F2 generation. These observations led him to develop the principles of dominance and recessiveness since he understood that the factor for round seeds masked the factor for wrinkled seeds.

Notice that he could have hypothesized that there are more than two hereditary factors in each individual, but he used the principle of *parsimony*, which states that the simplest explanation for observation is likely the most accurate.

From these conclusions, Mendel was able to deduce his first law of inheritance: *the law of segregation*. Each organism contains two alleles for each trait, which segregate during the formation of gametes for one allele in each gamete. During fertilization, gametes from two individuals are united, giving the offspring a complete set of alleles for each trait.

Although Mendel did not understand meiosis when he formulated his theories, he correctly outlined its principles in this law. He understood that if two alleles control each distinct phenotype, it then follows that one is passed on to an offspring by each parent. Otherwise, the number of alleles would double with each generation. Mendel's law of segregation is consistent with the particulate theory of inheritance because many individual "discrete particles" of inheritance are passed on from generation to generation.

Mendel then performed a *dihybrid cross* between two organisms that are heterozygous for two traits rather than just one. A dihybrid cross is achieved by first crossing parent organisms that are true breeding for different forms of two traits; it produces F1 offspring that are heterozygous for both traits (dihybrids). Mendel performed a dihybrid cross of the F1 individuals with one another. He expected that the dihybrids would produce two types of gametes: dominant (RY) gametes and recessive (ry) gametes. He thought he would see a phenotypic ratio of 3:1 in the F2 generation, as with his monohybrid crosses. This would mean that 75% of the F2 individuals would be round and yellow and 25% would be wrinkled and green.

Mendel's expected Punnett square for his F1 dihybrid cross:

	RY	**ry**
RY	RRYY	RrYy
ry	RrYy	rryy

P generation:	homozygous round yellow (RRYY) × homozygous wrinkled green (rryy)
F1 generation:	100% heterozygous round yellow offspring (RrYy)
F2 generation:	25% homozygous round, homozygous yellow (RRYY)
	50% heterozygous round, heterozygous yellow (RrYy)
	25% homozygous wrinkled, homozygous green (rryy)
	Genotypic ratio: 1:2:1 RRYY to RrYy to rryy
	Phenotypic ratio: 3:1 round yellow to wrinkled green offspring

However, Mendel observed the following results from the dihybrid cross.

Parents' genotype	RRYY	× rryy
Parents' gametes	RY	ry

F1 generation	RrYy
F1 gametes	RY rY Ry ry

Punnett square of gametes produced

	RY	Ry	rY	ry
RY	RRYY	RRYy	RrYY	RrYy
Ry	RRYy	RRyy	RrYy	Rryy
rY	RrYY	RrYy	rrYY	rrYy
ry	RrYy	Rryy	rrYy	rryy

☐ Round and yellow phenotype   ▨ Wrinkled and yellow phenotype

▨ Round and green phenotype   ☐ Wrinkled and green phenotype

The offspring from that cross produced a phenotypic ratio of 9:3:3:1 (of round and yellow, round and green, wrinkled and yellow, and wrinkled and green). It was not predicted that the offspring could have the dominant form of one phenotype and the recessive form of the other. He deduced that dihybrids produce not two types of gametes (RY and ry) but *four:* RY, Ry, rY, and ry. He realized that dominant alleles do not have to be shuffled into the same gametes as other dominant alleles, nor do recessive alleles.

Mendel's law of independent assortment states that alleles assort independently from other alleles and that a parent's gametes contain all possible combinations of alleles. This leads to a phenotypic ratio of 9:3:3:1 in dihybrid crosses. However, the ratio often breaks down in more complex cases, patterns of *non-Mendelian inheritance* (do not follow Mendel's laws), for reasons that would not be understood until the 20th century.

Humans cannot be bred like pea plants, so their genetic relationships are studied using pedigrees. *Pedigrees* are charts that portray family histories by including phenotypes and family relationships. In a pedigree chart, squares represent males, circles represent females, and diamonds represent individuals of unspecified sex. If an individual displays a trait studied, their shape is filled. Heterozygotes are half-filled (if the disorder is autosomal) or have a shaded dot inside the symbol (if the disorder is sex-linked). If the trait of interest is a disease, heterozygotes are *carriers.* However, it is often not known if an individual is heterozygous, since this may not be visible phenotypically.

Lines between individuals denote relationships. Horizontal lines connect mating couples, and a vertical line connects to their offspring. Siblings are grouped under a horizontal line that branches from this vertical one, with the oldest sibling on the left and the youngest on the right. If the offspring are twins, they are connected by a triangle. If an individual dies, its symbol is crossed out. If it is stillborn or aborted, it is indicated by a small circle.

The generations are shown using Roman numerals (I, II, III, etc.), and each from the same generation is indicated by Arabic numbers (1, 2, 3, etc.). The pattern of inheritance of a particular trait can be determined by analyzing pedigrees. Often, the trait in question is a genetic disease. These are typically recessive traits, which can be seen by the way the disorder skips generations, passed by carriers. The first family member known to seek treatment for the disease is called the *proband* and may be indicated by an arrow. The proband serves as the starting point for the pedigree, and researchers may work both backward and forward from there.

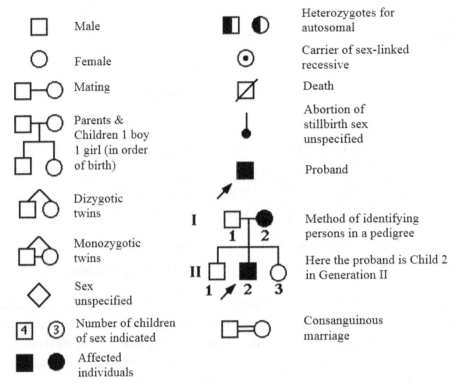

Pedigree chart convention specifying relationships and observed phenotypes

Complete dominance

Dominance is a relationship between alleles of one gene, in which one allele is expressed over a second allele at the same locus. Thus far, only *complete dominance* of alleles has been discussed. This occurs when only one dominant allele is needed to express a trait since it masks the recessive allele. The traits of Mendel's pea plants had complete dominance, with a round seed shape completely dominates a wrinkled seed shape.

Genotype	Phenotype
RR	Dominant - round
Rr	Dominant - round
rr	Recessive - wrinkled

The homozygous dominant and heterozygous individual exhibit the "dominant phenotype," but the heterozygote has a recessive allele, though not observed.

Co-dominance

In *co-dominance*, two or more alleles are equally dominant, so a heterozygote expresses the phenotypes associated with both alleles. The most famous example in humans is the ABO blood type system, a multiple allele system. The locus is named "I." A person with genotype $I^A I^A$ or $I^A i$ expresses the A blood type; a person with $I^B I^B$ or $I^B i$ expresses the B blood type; and a person with $I^A I^B$ expresses roughly equal amounts of both "A" and "B" antigens, giving the blood type AB. Thus, I^A and I^B are co-dominant. Note that allele i represents the absence of any antigens. Therefore it is recessive and must be homozygous to express type O blood.

Blood groups with genotype and phenotype:

Genotype	Phenotype
$I^A I^A$	*A*
$I^A I^O$	*A*
$I^A I^B$	Both *A* and *B*
$I^B I^B$	*B*
$I^B I^O$	*B*
$I^O I^O$	*O*

Incomplete dominance, expressivity, and penetrance

Although Mendel completely dismissed the notion that traits "blend." *Incomplete dominance* (partial dominance) occurs when the phenotype of a heterozygote is an intermediate of the phenotypes of the homozygotes. For example, true-breeding red and white-flowered four-o'clock plants produce pink-flowered offspring. The red allele is partially dominant to the white allele, so its effect is weakened and it appears pink. This does not support a blending theory of inheritance since the red and white parental phenotypes reappear in the F2 generation.

P   true breeding red × true breeding white; $(C^R C^R) \times (C^W C^W)$

F1   All pink offspring; $(C^R C^W)$

If these F1 individuals are crossed, the results are:

pink × pink; $(C^R C^W) \times (C^R C^W)$

F2   1 red: 2 pink: 1 white; $1(C^R C^R) \times 2(C^R C^W) \times (C^W C^W)$

Another example of incomplete dominance is *sickle-cell anemia*, a blood disorder controlled by incompletely dominant alleles. Homozygous dominant individuals $(Hb^A Hb^A)$ are asymptomatic and healthy. Homozygous recessive individuals $(Hb^S Hb^S)$ are afflicted with sickle-cell anemia. Their red blood cells are irregular in shape (sickle-shaped) rather than biconcave, due to abnormal hemoglobin. Sickle-shaped red blood cells clog vessels and break down, which results in poor circulation, anemia, low resistance to infection, hemorrhaging, damage to organs, jaundice and pain in the abdomen and the joints. This is an example of *pleiotropy,* where one gene affects many traits.

Incomplete dominance is heterozygous individuals ($Hb^A Hb^S$) since they do not have the full-blown disease but have some sickled cells and minor health problems. This is the *sickle-cell trait*. In regions prone to malaria (e.g., Africa) being heterozygous for the sickle-cell allele confers an advantage, because the malaria parasite dies as potassium leaks from sickle cells. *Heterozygote advantage* describes the case where the heterozygous condition bears a greater advantage than either homozygous condition.

Penetrance is the frequency by which a particular genotype results in a corresponding phenotype. For example, Mendel's pea plants had 100% penetrance for seed color. A plant with genotype Yy or YY always had yellow seeds, and a plant with genotype yy always had green seeds. However, many genes have *incomplete penetrance*. For example, the BRCA gene (breast cancer) for women with this mutation have an 80% lifetime risk of developing cancer. Certain people may have a gene that predisposes them to lung cancer, but due to their lifestyle habits and random chance, they may never develop cancer. This means that in some cases, a given genotype does not guarantee that the expected phenotype is expressed.

Phenotypes can exhibit *expressivity* (variation in the presentation). This is different from penetrance, which is a question of whether or not the phenotype is expressed. Expressivity refers to individuals that express their phenotype, but to varying degrees. In the case of *constant expressivity*, individuals with the same genotype have the same phenotype. For example, if pea plants are homozygous recessive for flower color (pp), they are all approximately the same shade of white. Discontinuous traits typically exhibit fairly constant expressivity. However, a trait like a polydactyly (extra digits) in humans is prone to *variable expressivity,* when a phenotype is expressed in different degrees from the same genotype. Although a single gene controls polydactyly, afflicted individuals may have extra fingers or toes. The expressivity varies from person to person.

Crossing individuals with different alleles of a continuously varying phenotype do not produce the discrete ratios that enabled Mendel to discover the laws of inheritance. The genetics of *continuous variation* is far more complex than that of discontinuous variation (e.g., pea plants). Such traits follow a bell-shaped curve when the number of individuals is plotted against the range of the variable trait.

Continuous variation for height distribution in a population

With continuous variation, there is a phenotype in between any two chosen for comparison, because the distribution of phenotypes in the population varies along a continuum; individuals differ by small degrees. Mendel's theory explains both discontinuous and continuous patterns of individual variation. With continuous variation, however, many different genes typically influence the same trait, not just one, as Mendel proposed.

Traits such as height and weight are not due to variable expressivity of a single gene but due to *polygenic inheritance*. Polygenic inheritance is when two or more genes govern one trait. Often, the genes have an additive effect, with each dominant allele adding to the "intensity" of the phenotype. The more genes involved, the more continuous the variation in phenotypes, resulting in a bell-shaped curve.

A human example of polygenic inheritance is skin color. Many genes control skin pigment and the more dominant alleles that an individual has the darker their skin. Parents with intermediate skin color can have offspring with light or dark skin.

Albinism, a condition where the eyes, skin, and hair have little to no color due to lack of pigment production, is an example of *epistasis*, a phenomenon where one gene interferes with other genes in the expression of a phenotype. It does not matter if an individual has other genes which would otherwise give her dark skin; if the individual is homozygous recessive for the albinism gene, this shuts off pigment production and prevents the other genes from being expressed.

Traits such as height and weight have a polygenic component but are heavily influenced by outside factors, such as environment, exercise, and nutrition (nature vs. nurture).

Hybridization and viability of offspring

Leakage is gene flow from one species to another, which occurs when individuals of two related species mate and produce *hybrid* offspring. The hybrid now has genetic information from both species and may mate with either one, causing genes to "leak" from each gene pool and flow into the other.

A hybrid is the product of parents that are true breeding for different forms of one trait. The parents may be of different breeds of a single species or a different species altogether. When hybrids are created from two different species, they may not always be *fertile* (capable of producing offspring). This may be because the hybrid is infertile or it dies before reproductive age. Even if the hybrid is fertile and able to reproduce, the offspring may prove not to be viable (able to survive until reproduction), a *hybrid breakdown*.

Hybrid vigor (heterosis) is when the hybrid has the best qualities of both species or strains. The hybrid's superior quality is due to the suppression of recessive alleles and the increase in heterozygotic traits, leading to heterozygote advantage. Hybrids are bred with the intention to create new breeds that are healthier or more desirable than either parent breed.

Outbreeding is the mating of genetically dissimilar individuals and is a powerful agent of genetic diversity. Inbreeding tends to promote harmful recessive alleles and decrease the number of alleles in the population.

Gene pool

Population genetics studies the variation of alleles within a population. The *gene pool* is the total of all genetic information in the population, described by gene frequencies.

Demes are local gene pools, consisting of individuals who are likely to breed with each other. A great deal of evolutionary change occurs in these groups. Modern biologists view each as a temporary vessel housing a small fraction of the gene pool. Thus, the concept of a gene pool is an abstract pooling of all genetic variation in the population; it does not exist apart from the individuals themselves.

Notes for active learning

There are several sources of genetic variability in nature, some of which are random, while others are the result of selective processes. These sources include mutation, sexual reproduction, diploidy, outbreeding and balanced polymorphisms.

Significance of meiosis

Meiosis is essential to sexual reproduction, diploidy, and genetic diversity. Asexual organisms produce offspring that are genetic clones of themselves, but sexual reproduction creates offspring that are both similar to and unique from either parent. Meiosis creates haploid gametes that fuse together and form a diploid zygote. Meiosis provides several opportunities to promote variability in the gene pool and allow for new combinations of alleles.

Important differences between mitosis and meiosis

Mitosis and meiosis begin similarly with a somatic cell in G1 of interphase, which has 46 total chromosomes. Each chromosome has a homologous structure that originated from the other parent; there are 23 homologous pairs, and each chromosome is scattered randomly within the nucleus. During S phase, each chromosome duplicates. Each duplicate is renamed a sister chromatid, and together, two sister chromatids comprise one chromosome. Sister chromatids are chromatin strands attached at the centromere, which are identical copies (except for low-frequency mutations of nucleotides) of the same chromosome (not homologous). One chromosome (a pair of sister chromatids) has another chromosome, its homolog.

During prophase / metaphase of mitosis, the chromosomes do not attempt to locate their homolog. Each chromosome lines up along the metaphase plate individually. During anaphase, the sister chromatids of each chromosome are separated so that one chromatid (resulting as a single strand separated at centromere) is partitioned into a daughter cell. The result is two diploid daughter cells with identical genetic makeup.

However, during prophase I and metaphase I of meiosis, homologs do pair into a *tetrad* (bivalent). The tetrad consists of two homologous chromosomes or four sister chromatids in total. Tetrads line up on the metaphase plate so that one homologous chromosome is on one side, and the other homolog is on the other side of the midline. During anaphase I, the tetrad is separated, and one chromosome is pulled into one pole, while the second is pulled toward the other pole. The result of meiosis I is that two daughter cells have a different genetic makeup; one has half of the organism's genome and the second cell has the other half.

A key difference is that mitosis involves one set of cell divisions, in which the chromatids of each chromosome separate. In meiosis, there are two sets of cell divisions. During the first division, the chromosome of each tetrad separates (chromosome has 2 strands attached at the centromere). In the second division, the centromere splits and the sister chromatids of each chromosome separate.

During meiosis, when the homologous pairs are arranged into tetrads, their ends overlap and cause *recombination* (exchange of genetic material). Homologous chromosomes exchange some DNA so that once they are separated, the maternal chromosome has some paternal DNA, and vice versa. Gametes are unique from the organism's genome.

Mitosis	*Meiosis*
One set of divisions	Two sets of divisions
Occurs in the body (somatic) cells	Occurs in the testes or ovaries (gametes)
Two identical daughter cells	Four unique daughter cells (four sperm cells or one egg with up to three polar bodies)
Daughter cells are diploid $2n \rightarrow 2$ cells with 2n	Daughter cells are haploid $2n \rightarrow 4$ cells with 1n
No crossing over occurs	Crossing over (tetrad) during prophase I creates genetic variability

Segregation of genes

Mendel understood that different genes are segregated into different gametes despite being unaware of meiosis. His first *law of segregation* supports the conclusion that each diploid individual has two alleles but passes one to its offspring. Segregation of genes and diploidy are important concepts for explaining the genetic variability.

Independent assortment

Mendel's second law, the *law of independent assortment*, states that any gamete may have any combination of alleles. In the era of molecular biology, it is known that this occurs during meiosis. During metaphase I of meiosis, homologous chromosomes pair as tetrads along the metaphase plate in a random orientation. They have then pulled apart so that some homologous chromosomes from each parent end up in one daughter cell and some in another. The law of independent assortment requires that homologous chromosomes line up randomly during metaphase. The segregation of alleles of one gene does not affect the segregation of alleles of another gene. Mendel initially thought that a dihybrid (e.g., AaBb) would produce the gametes AB and ab. However, he realized that the A alleles and the B alleles are not linked; they can segregate into gametes in four combinations: AB, aB, Ab and ab. He noted that these gametes are produced in equal numbers; no one combination is favored over another.

Mendel's research was based on simplistic traits of pea plants. He sometimes encountered puzzling phenotypic ratios, which suggested that some allele combinations were more frequent than others. If Mendel chose two phenotypic traits controlled by two tightly linked loci for his dihybrid cross, he would have obtained two types of gametes due to the *linkage.*

Linkage

Mendel's law of independent assortment does not apply to linkage (genes on the same chromosome), whereby some genes are located on the same chromosome and are therefore inherited together. Because of this, his law of independent assortment is applied to chromosomes rather than genes; chromosomes assort independently, but alleles do not. *Linked genes* are found close on the same chromosome, while those found far apart or on different chromosomes altogether are *unlinked genes.*

Genes on separate chromosomes are unlinked and can segregate independently, but genes on the same chromosome must often be inherited together as a *linkage group.* However, this is not always the case. *Crossing over* allows genes on the same chromosome to become unlinked due to the probability that the genes undergo recombination in the region between them.

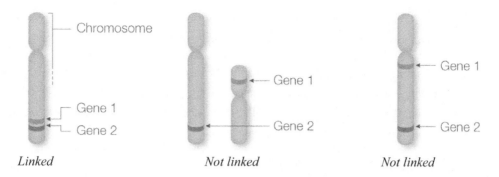

Linked   Not linked   Not linked

Recombination

Genetic recombination introduces genetic diversity into the gametes during meiosis. It includes both independent assortment and crossing over. Crossing over occurs during prophase I of meiosis when homologous chromosomes are paired together into tetrads. The pairing of tetrads is *synapsis* and is facilitated by a protein structure of the *synaptonemal complex*. It is thought that the synaptonemal complex functions primarily as a scaffold to allow interacting chromatids to complete their crossover activities.

During prophase I, synapsis links the four sister chromatids (4 strands with 2 chromosomes) of a pair of homologous chromosomes. The ends of different chromatids often overlap and make contact at sites, as *chiasmata*, between loci. Both chromatids cut at the same locus, allowing them to bind where they are cut (chiasma) and swap their DNA. In this way, an individual can create gametes with some chromatids that are different from the chromatids they inherited. *Recombinant* are chromatids which have undergone recombination, and those which did not are *parental*. Once crossing over is finished, the homologous chromosomes are no longer tightly linked, and the homologous chromosomes are independent. However, the recombinant chromatids remain connected by their chiasma until anaphase, when the centromeres divide and liberate each sister chromatid strand, which becomes a chromosome.

Sex-linked characteristics

In a human, the normal chromosome complement is 46, two of which are sex chromosomes. A human female has two X chromosomes, while a human male has an X and a Y chromosome. The sex chromosomes carry genes that determine the sex of an organism and various unrelated traits that are *sex-linked*. Because the Y chromosome is small, the X chromosome essentially carries all sex-linked traits as X-linked traits. The alleles are designated as superscripts to the letter X.

In females, one of the duplicate X chromosomes is deactivated during embryonic development, resulting in an unused chromosome, a *Barr body*. This is random for each cell, so in one cell the paternal X chromosome may become the Barr body, while in the other the maternal X chromosome becomes the Barr body.

In males, chromosomes X and Y do not make a homologous pair since they are of different sizes and contain different genes. The X chromosome in humans is much longer than the Y chromosome and contains many more genes. In a male, the smaller Y chromosome has no opposing alleles to those found on the X chromosome. Males are *hemizygous* for X-linked traits, meaning they have one allele since they have one X chromosome. In the pairing seen below, all genes on the X chromosome with an arrow pointing to them are dominant, because they have no opposition from the Y chromosome. Note that there are some genes with loci on both X and Y chromosomes.

Males are more prone to certain genetic diseases due to this characteristic. A female who inherits a sex-linked recessive allele that encodes for a genetic disease may inherit the dominant allele on the other X chromosome. She then is unafflicted (in the case of complete dominance) or has minor afflictions (incomplete or co-dominance). A male, however, has no such mitigating protection.

The number of genes on the Y chromosome

The Y chromosome is significantly smaller than the X chromosome and contains a much lower density of genes, perhaps 50 to 60. However, these few genes do have an important impact on sex determination and male characteristics. Genes on the Y chromosomes that do not recombine are passed from father to son and are not present in females. The lack of recombination weakens the effectiveness of natural selection to reduce the frequency of disadvantaged variants and select for favorable ones.

Sex determination

Humans have an *XY sex-determination system*. Most other mammals, along with some insects and fish, follow this as well. Every female produces gamete with a single X chromosome, while sperm from the male can contain either a Y chromosome or an X chromosome. There is a 50% chance that a gamete contains either chromosome. Therefore, when the gametes fuse during fertilization, there is a 50% chance of a female (or male) sex.

The maternal gamete is *homogametic* because all its cells possess the XX sex chromosomes. Sperm gametes are the variable factor and are thus *heterogametic* because around half contain the X chromosome, and the other half possess the Y chromosome.

In the absence of a Y chromosome, genes on the X chromosomes direct a fetus to produce female sex hormones and develop internal and external female sex organs. However, if a Y chromosome is present, its *SRY gene* inhibits the development of female sex organs and promotes male sex organs. The SRY gene is so powerful since it controls the activity of many other genes, which direct the development of internal and external male characteristics. Mutations in this gene can cause the fetus to develop nonfunctional testes or even ovaries. In some cases, errors during the male production of gametes attach the SRY gene to an X chromosome instead. This results in a female fetus developing male characteristics.

Note that many other organisms have different sex determination schemes. For example, in an *X0 sex determination system* females have two X chromosomes, and males have one. In a *ZW sex-determination system* (e.g., birds, reptiles, and many other organisms), the males have two Z chromosomes, while females have a Z and a W chromosome. Several other sex-determination systems involve different chromosomes, often more than two; for example, platypuses each have ten sex chromosomes.

In many reptiles and invertebrates, sex is determined not by genetics but by environmental factors (e.g., temperature). Some species can change sex throughout their lifetime.

Cytoplasmic and extranuclear inheritance

Extranuclear inheritance, also *cytoplasmic inheritance,* is the inheritance of genetic material found outside the nucleus. Carl Correns discovered this in 1908. The two most prevalent examples are the inheritance of mitochondria and chloroplasts in many eukaryotes. Along with the nuclear chromosomes, DNA from the mitochondria (and chloroplasts for plants) are transferred in the cytoplasm of the maternal gamete. Sperm contains these organelles as well, but they either do not enter the egg during fertilization or do enter but are destroyed by the egg. Therefore, extranuclear DNA is always passed along the maternal line, making it useful for certain genetic testing.

Mutation

Mutations are changes in the DNA nucleotide sequence that arise by means other than recombination. Mutant genes may produce abnormalities in structure and function, leading to disease. Cystic fibrosis, sickle-cell anemia, hemophilia, and muscular dystrophy are *single gene diseases* because they arise from mutations that occur in a single gene. *Polygenic diseases,* such as diabetes, cancer, cleft lip and schizophrenia, result from several defective genes that have little effect on their own, but collectively can have significant effects. Many genetic disorders, physical features, and behavioral traits are greatly influenced by the environment.

Genetic mutations can be beneficial, neutral or harmful. Beneficial or *advantageous mutations* provide an improvement to the fitness of the organism. *Deleterious mutations* disrupt gene function and result in a harmful effect to the fitness of the organism. It is possible for mutations to be harmful in one situation but advantageous in another.

Neutral mutations have a negligible effect on fitness, considered neither harmful nor beneficial. Mutations may not affect the phenotype as *silent mutations,* or the effect does not arise until later generations.

Types of mutations: random, transcription error, translation error, base substitution, deletion, insertion, frameshift and mispairing

Random mutations are changes in DNA sequence that occur at any time, due to radiation, chemicals, replication errors or other chance events. *Transcription errors* occur specifically during transcription of DNA into mRNA. This results in mRNA with some RNA nucleotide sequences that do not accurately correspond to the original DNA code. *Translation errors* occur during translation of mRNA into a protein with a mutant amino acid sequence.

Their structural effects may classify mutations. *Base substitutions* are when another replaces one or more nucleotides. They range from advantageous to fatal (as with many mutations), but most base substitutions are minor. Nucleotide base substitutions may cause a stop codon to halt transcription, a *nonsense mutation.* Substitutions could cause a different amino acid to be transcribed in the final protein, causing a *missense mutation.* Even a single amino acid change may change the protein's function or render it inoperable. However, since some mRNA codons can encode for the same amino acid (i.e., code is degenerative), sometimes base substitutions may not result in a different amino acid sequence. *Silent mutations* do not affect the phenotype.

Deletions involve a base (or several bases) being removed from the DNA or mRNA sequence, while *insertions* involve the addition of one (or more) bases. One or two insertions (or deletions) result in *frameshift mutations* since they shift the reading frame of the three-base codons.

For example, the mRNA sequence AUGUUGACUGCCAAU is meant to be read:

AUG - UU<u>G</u> - ACU - GCC – A ...

Met - Leu - Thr - Ala - ...

If the 6th base (guanine) is deleted, a frameshift mutation changes the transcribed amino acids.

AUG - UUA - CUG - CCA - ...

Met - Leu - Leu - Pro - ...

The first codon is unaffected and still encodes for methionine. The second codon *is* changed, but since this codon encodes for the same amino acid (leucine), it is a silent mutation. However, the third and fourth codons are changed so that they encode for entirely different amino acids. It is assumed that many other amino acids in the sequence are changed. This is a serious mutation that often renders the protein inoperable. However, deletions and insertions of nucleotides that involve multiples of threes do not cause a frameshift, since they remove an entire codon (i.e., three nucleotides that encode an amino acid). The reading frame remains intact, but the absence of the single amino acid may be a serious issue.

Slipped-strand mispairing is a mutation that occurs during transcription, translation or DNA replication. After DNA strands are denatured during replication, the template or replicated strand may slip (become temporarily dislodged) and cause incorrect pairing of complementary bases. This is believed to have led to the evolution of many repetitive DNA sequences found in the human genome.

Portions of the chromosome are subject to deletion, especially during meiosis. Chromosomal deletion may be severe and even render the gamete incapable of fertilization or spontaneous abortion.

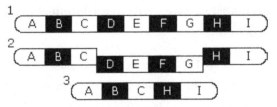

Chromosomal deletion where sections D, E, F, and G are absent after deletion

Chromosomal rearrangements: inversion and translocation

Along with base mutations, the entire structure of the chromosome is subject to rearrangement, especially during meiosis. Chromosomal mutations may be severe and even fatal, terminating the fetus before birth.

Inversions involve a stretch of DNA breaking and reattaching in the opposite orientation. There are two types of inversions: paracentric and pericentric. *Paracentric inversions* do not involve the centromere; they occur when a piece of the arm of a chromosome breaks, inverts and reattaches. A *pericentric inversion* includes the centromere; the breakpoint is on either arm of the chromosome.

Chromosomal inversion

The organism experiencing the newly inverted sequence may not be viable if it includes a necessary region of the chromosome. The mutation could be advantageous. However, inversions usually do not affect the phenotype of the organism and go undetected. Their greatest impact is on the production of gametes since they are often marked by loops in the chromosome that affects recombination. An individual with a chromosomal inversion may generate some gametes with altered linkage relationships or abnormal chromatids. The former case is likely harmless, while the latter case usually yields inviable gametes.

Translocation is when a segment of one chromosome separates and binds to the other. This is a drastic rearrangement that is often lethal. An individual inheriting a chromosome that has been altered due to translocation has extra alleles or too few alleles, leading to a variety of defects. This may occur in both autosomal and sex chromosomes, where it leads to infertility issues and other genetic disorders. *XX male syndrome* occurs when the portion of the Y chromosome containing the SRY gene is translocated to an X chromosome during a male's production of gametes. If the sperm cell containing the mutant X chromosome fertilizes an egg, a female fetus develops that has male secondary sex characteristics and genitalia.

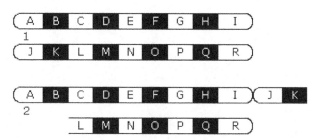

Chromosomal translocation where section J and K join the other chromosome

Although there are safeguards in place to ensure chromosomes properly separate during meiosis, these checks sometimes fail. Failure of proper chromosome separation causes *nondisjunction errors,* in which three chromosomes of a tetrad are pulled to one side of the spindle, and one is pulled to the other side. This results in some gametes having an extra chromosome and some gametes lack a chromosome. A chromosome with three copies is a *trisomy*, while a chromosome with one copy is *monosomy*. Both examples of gamete formation by nondisjunction usually lead to an inviable zygote.

Down syndrome is a common nonlethal autosomal trisomy, involving chromosome 21. In general, the chance of a woman having a Down syndrome child increases with age. This disorder leads to faster aging, moderate to severe developmental issues and a higher risk of health complications in the child.

Many nonlethal nondisjunction errors involve the sex chromosomes. Females with *Turner syndrome* have one X sex chromosome. This results in nonfunctional ovaries and the absence of puberty. Afflicted females have somewhat masculine characteristics and are sterile, but they usually have no cognitive issues and use hormone therapy.

Klinefelter syndrome occurs when a zygote receives one Y chromosome and two (or more) X chromosomes. Presence of the Y chromosome makes affected individuals identifiably male, but they have underdeveloped sex organs and are sterile. The extra X chromosomes cause the development of breasts, lack of facial hair, and may result in developmental delay. Males with Klinefelter syndrome have one or more Barr bodies due to the extra X chromosomes.

Females with *Poly-X syndrome* have extra X chromosomes and therefore extra Barr bodies. They do not exhibit enhanced feminine characteristics and usually appear physically normal. Some experience menstrual irregularities but most have regular menstruation and are fertile. Females with three X chromosomes are not developmentally delayed but have some impaired cognitive skills. However, four X chromosomes cause severe cognitive impairment.

Jacob's syndrome is the condition of one X chromosome and two Y chromosomes. Although it was previously believed that individuals with Jacob's syndrome were more likely to be aggressive, this claim is now refuted. Males with Jacob's syndrome are usually taller than average, suffer from persistent acne and tend to have speech and reading problems.

Many genetic disorders, especially those due to nondisjunction, can be detected during pregnancy. Chorionic villi sampling testing, amniocentesis and karyotyping are prenatal testing methods. *Karyotyping* (visual examination of chromosomes) may be used to determine the gender of a fetus and look for chromosomal abnormalities.

Karyotype of a normal male patient

The structure of the sex chromosomes can deduce the gender since Y chromosomes are markedly smaller than X chromosomes. Missing or extra chromosomes can visualize nondisjunction. If there are two of each chromosome, the 23 chromosomes pairs should result in 46 chromosomes in total. Deviations from this, such as three copies of chromosome 21, signifies a nondisjunction.

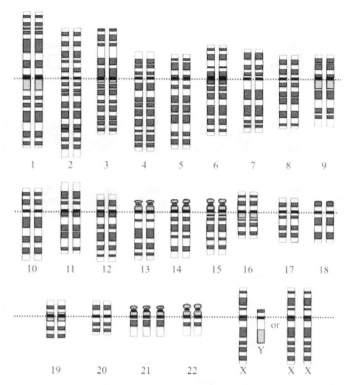

Karyotype of a male patient with Down syndrome (three chromosomes, 21) and an extra set of X chromosomes as Klinefelter syndrome (XXY) or as a variant (XXXY) as shown.

Inborn errors of metabolism

Inborn errors of metabolism are genetic disorders which cause mild to severe metabolic issues. These diseases are caused by a mutant gene that results in abnormal enzyme production, which may affect the gastrointestinal system, the circulatory system, the nervous system or any area of the body. They are typically rare and have severe health implications. However, there are more benign inborn errors of metabolism, such as lactose intolerance, which arises from an inability to produce the digestive enzyme lactase. Unlike many genetic disorders, inborn errors of metabolism are caused by the mutation of a single gene.

Autosomal recessive disorders can be discerned from pedigrees by establishing the presence of certain patterns of inheritance. The first observation is that affected children usually have unaffected carrier parents since recessive alleles are statistically rare in the general population. Two homozygous dominant parents produce all unaffected children. However, if one parent is affected, the children are unaffected carriers. If one parent is affected and the other is a carrier, they have a 50% chance of producing a carrier child or affected child. This is in the pedigree chart below. Note the many carriers (half-filled circles or squares), due to their affected parents.

It must be noted that individuals 15 and 16 (third generation) may be homozygous dominant or carriers. Only genetic testing reveals if they received two dominant alleles from each carrier parent or a dominant allele from one and a recessive allele from the other parent.

Tay-Sachs disease is an autosomal recessive disorder that is rare in the general population but afflicts approximately 1 in 3,600 Ashkenazi Jews at birth. Tay-Sachs results in death by about age three due to progressive neurological degeneration. A genetic mutation prevents the production of the enzyme hexosaminidase A (Hex A), leading to accumulations of its substrate, glycosphingolipid, in lysosomes of brain cells. Tay-Sachs is one of many *lysosomal storage disorders,* caused by abnormal lysosomal function.

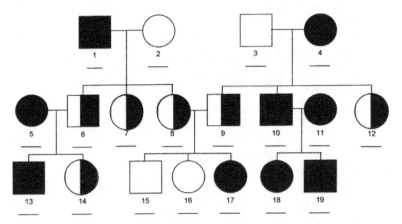

Pedigree for autosomal recessive: squares denote males, circles denote females;
completely shaded figures are afflicted, while half-filled figures are carriers.

Cystic fibrosis is among the common lethal genetic diseases in Northern European ancestry. About 1 in 20 Caucasians in the U.S. is a carrier for cystic fibrosis, and about 1 in 3,000 is afflicted. The disease is caused by a mutation of chromosome 7 that prevents chloride ions from passing into some cells. Since water normally follows Cl⁻, lack of water in lung cells causes the production of viscous mucus and subsequent respiratory issues. This disease has gastrointestinal, kidney and fertility effects.

Phenylketonuria (PKU) is the common inherited disease of the nervous system, occurring once in about 5,000 births. A mutant gene on chromosome 21 results in a lack of the enzyme that metabolizes the amino acid phenylalanine. The absence of the enzyme causes accumulation of phenylalanine in nerve cells and impairs the CNS. From neonatal diagnosis, children are placed on low-phenylalanine diets that prevent severe neural degeneration.

Sex-linked recessive disorders, like autosomal recessive disorders, results in all children affected if the parents are both affected. Furthermore, two unaffected parents can bear affected offspring (male only), if the mother is a carrier. She has a 50% chance of donating a recessive allele to a son, afflicting him with the disease. If the mother is homozygous recessive, this results in 100% of male offspring as affected. Female offspring are all unaffected because the father donates a dominant X-linked allele; however, all are carriers.

If an affected male mates with a homozygous dominant female, all offspring are unaffected. However, if the father is affected and the mother is a carrier, 50% of their children, regardless of sex, are affected.

Color blindness can be an X-linked recessive disorder involving mutations of genes coding for green-sensitive pigment or red-sensitive pigment; the gene for blue-sensitive pigment is autosomal. About 8% of Caucasian men have red-green color blindness.

Duchenne muscular dystrophy is the common form of muscular dystrophy and is characterized by the wasting (atrophy) of muscles, eventually leading to death. It affects 1 in 3,600 male births. This X-linked recessive disease involves a mutant gene that fails to produce the protein dystrophin. The lack of dystrophin promotes the action of an enzyme that dissolves muscle fibers. Affected males rarely live to be fathers; the allele survives in the population due to transmission by carrier females.

About 1 in 10,000 males is a hemophiliac with an impaired ability of blood clotting. This is a classic example of an X-linked recessive disorder, famously seen in the royal families of Europe throughout the 19th and 20th century. Queen Victoria was a carrier of the disease and passed it on to many of her descendants. Due to diplomatic marriages within a small subpopulation, it was transmitted to royal families in Russia, Germany, and Spain. The issue was exacerbated by incest, not uncommon at the time to keep power and assets within the family.

Autosomal dominant disorders can be discerned from pedigrees by establishing the presence of certain patterns. The first is that all affected children must have an affected parent. Two affected parents can have a child that is unaffected if both parents are heterozygous. However, it is impossible for two unaffected parents to have a child that is affected. As with all autosomal disorders, both males and females are affected with equal frequency.

Neurofibromatosis is an autosomal dominant disorder found in about 1 in 3,500 people. An altered gene causes it on chromosome 17 that controls the production of the neurofibromin protein, which normally inhibits cell division. When this gene is mutated, neurofibromin is nonfunctional and affected individuals develop neurofibromas, benign skin tumors. In most cases, symptoms are mild, and patients live healthy lives but can be severe. Since the severity of symptoms varies, this is an example of *variable expressivity*.

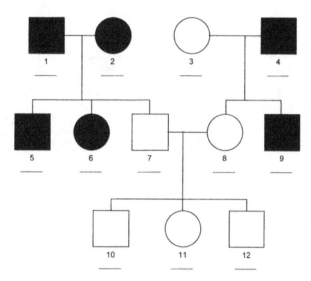

Pedigree for autosomal dominant: circles denote females, squares denote males;
filled shapes are affected individuals, while unfilled shapes are not carriers of the disorder.

Huntington's disease is an autosomal dominant disorder that, while fatal, usually does not onset until middle age, after an afflicted individual may already have children. Therefore, the disease continues to pass through the generations. The gene for Huntington's disease is on chromosome 4. This gene encodes for the *huntingtin protein* as extra glutamine in the amino acid sequence, which causes the mutant huntingtin protein to form clumps inside neurons.

Achondroplasia is a form of dwarfism caused by a defective bone growth that occurs in about 1 in 25,000 people. Individuals with achondroplasia have short limbs, a deformed spine and a normal torso and head. Like many genetic disorders, being homozygous dominant for achondroplasia is lethal; afflicted individuals are heterozygotes.

Sex-linked dominant disorders have certain characteristics distinguished from other forms of inherited genetic disorders, which can be discerned by analyzing a pedigree. If a male is affected, then all of his female offspring are affected because the male donates his affected X chromosome to his female offspring, and since the allele is dominant, all offspring are affected. By contrast, male offspring can be affected if the mother has the disease because the father donates a Y chromosome (does not carry the gene) to all of his male offspring. Unlike autosomal genetic disorders, sex-linked genetic disorders affect the sexes disproportionately, as in the pedigree below. Note that there are no carriers, since having one dominant allele guarantees affliction. Like autosomal dominant disorders, dominant sex-linked disorders are not common in the population, since they lead to health problems which reduce the reproduction frequency. This makes the alleles rarer in the gene pool, a self-fulfilling cycle that keeps them at a low frequency.

The *fragile X syndrome* is an X-linked dominant disorder in which the *FMR1* gene is mutated. This causes a deficiency of the protein FMRP protein, affecting neural and physical development. The mutation is found among both sexes, though it is more prevalent in females. Affected children often have hyperactive behaviors, intellectual disabilities and autism spectrum disorders. These symptoms are more severe in males, although about one-fifth are unaffected due to incomplete penetrance as compared to females.

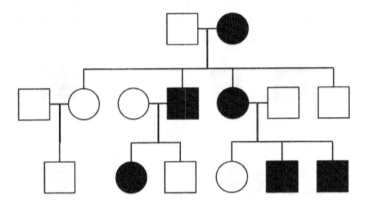

Pedigree for dominant sex-linked disorder: squares denote males, circles denote females; filled shapes are afflicted individuals, while unfilled are healthy individuals

Pedigrees must determine sex-linked traits in humans since it is not ethical to orchestrate human mating, while other organisms can be bred to determine patterns of inheritance. In non-humans, *reciprocal cross* involves two sets of parents, in which the male and female of each set have opposite traits. For example, in one set a female pea plant has white flowers, and the male has purple flowers, and in another, the female has purple flowers, and the male has white flowers. This determines the inheritance of sex-linked traits. If the trait is autosomal, both crosses produce the same results, but if not, they produce different results.

Test cross uses the homozygous recessive to mate with an organism of known phenotype but unknown genotype. If all progeny resemble the known phenotype parent, the parent is homozygous dominant. A 50:50 ratio means that the parent is heterozygous for the phenotypic trait. For example, AA × aa = Aa and Aa × aa = Aa and aa.

Relationship of mutagens to carcinogens

The genetic component of cancers is the leading cause of death in developed nations and the second leading cause of death in developing nations. Most cancers are caused by both a genetic predisposition and by carcinogens. *Carcinogens* are any physical, chemical or biological agents that cause cancer. The majority are *mutagens,* harmful agents which cause DNA mutations. Toxic chemicals, radiation, free radicals, viruses, and bacteria are all possible mutagens. *Exogenous mutagens* come from an external event, like smoking a cigarette or exposing one's skin to UV radiation. *Endogenous mutagens* arise internally as byproducts from metabolic processes. *Reactive oxygen species* (ROS) are a class of endogenous mutagens that contain oxygen and are highly reactive (e.g., H_2O_2 and O^{-2}).

Mitogens are another class of carcinogens that trigger an increase in the rate of mitosis. While all carcinogens are either mutagens or mitogens, there are mutagens and mitogens that do not lead to cancer.

Genetic drift, gene flow, and balanced polymorphisms

Genetic drift refers to random changes in allele frequencies of a gene pool over time. This occurs in both large and small populations, but the effect is magnified in small populations. Isolated gene pools can quickly diverge from the parent population. Over time, large populations may speciate (organisms are unable to reproduce to produce viable and fertile offspring). Genetic drift causes some alleles to be lost and others to become *fixed*, meaning they are the only allele for a particular gene in the population. Variation among populations can often be attributed to the random effects of genetic drift.

The *founder effect* is an example of genetic drift, whereby a handful of founders leave a source population and establish a colony. The new population contains a fraction of the total genetic diversity of the original population. Over time, the founders' alleles may occur at high frequencies in the new population, even if they are rare in the original population. For example, cases of dwarfism are much higher in the Pennsylvania Amish community because a few German founders were dwarfs.

The *bottleneck effect* may occur after excessive predation, habitat destruction or a natural disaster, rather than a founding event. After the catastrophe, there is a major decrease in the total genetic diversity of the original gene pool. Purely by chance, some alleles may be lost, and this affects the future genetic makeup of the population. Today, relative infertility is found in cheetahs due to a bottleneck in earlier times. Small populations suffer low genetic variation due to the high rates of inbreeding.

Genetic drift is a random process, greatly enhanced when other agents of genetic diversity are random. Random mating, in which individuals pair by chance and not by any selection, is one example. However, the majority of populations practice some nonrandom mating which inhibits genetic diversity. *Inbreeding*, where relatives mate, can occur as a form of nonrandom mating because these individuals are near others. *Assortative mating* occurs when individuals mate with those that have similar phenotypes. This may divide a population into two phenotypic classes with reduced gene exchange. Phenotypes can be selected due to *sexual selection* when males compete for the right to reproduce, and (often) the females select males of a particular phenotype.

Gene flow is the introduction (or removal) of alleles from populations when individuals leave (emigration) or enter the population (immigration). Gene flow increases variation within a population by introducing novel alleles from another population. Continued gene flow decreases variation between populations, causing their gene pools to become similar. Because of this, gene flow can be a powerful opposing force in speciation.

Balanced polymorphisms add to genetic variability by maintaining two different alleles in the population rather than encouraging homozygosity. Balanced polymorphisms are maintained by heterozygote advantage, hybrid vigor, and frequency-dependent selection.

Frequency-dependent selection is when the frequency of one phenotype affects the frequency of another. For example, a prey animal population may have several coloring phenotypes in the population (i.e., gray, brown and black fur). When the gray phenotype becomes the most frequent in the population, predators become familiar with this phenotype and can identify prey by their gray fur. Natural selection makes it so that the rarer phenotypes (brown and black fur) have an advantage. More prey evolves these phenotypes until one becomes common, at which point frequency-dependent selection changes. This is *minority advantage,* in which the rarest phenotype has the highest fitness (i.e., chance of survival).

Phenotypes can have a positive frequency dependent relationship from safety in numbers. For example, some individuals of a poisonous species may evolve coloring that signals their toxicity. Predators learn this signal and avoid individuals with this phenotype. In this example, it is a disadvantage to have a unique phenotype that is not identifiable as poisonous, because these individuals have an increased probability of being eaten by predators.

Synapsis (crossing-over) for increasing genetic diversity

It is hypothesized that meiosis evolved from either the bacterial analog of sexual reproduction (transformation) or from mitosis. It is ubiquitous in eukaryotes and is the source of genetic variation in sexual reproduction. Recombination creates recombinant chromosomes, and then meiosis independently sorts chromosomes into different gametes.

Suppose a woman inherited the alleles A and b from her mother and a and B from her father. She has genotype AaBb. Her alleles are not necessarily arranged in a *cis* configuration:

$$\frac{\text{A B}}{\text{a b}}$$

The top alleles (AB) represent one chromosome, and the bottom (ab) represent its homolog inherited from the other parent.

She could have inherited the alleles on the chromosomes as a *trans* configuration:

$$\frac{\text{A b}}{\text{a B}}$$

It is not possible to know from her phenotype alone what configuration (*cis* or *trans*) she has, since both results in the same phenotype. One must know her parents' genotypes or perform statistical analysis of her children's phenotypes. However, the sample size in the hundreds would be required to make the latter strategy accurate, which is improbable. Her configuration is determined by her parents' gametes and influences how she produces gametes.

Suppose she is *cis* (AB / ab), and the genes are linked. When she produces gametes, the crossover is unlikely because the genes are close together. Each somatic cell divides into the four gametes: AB, AB, ab, and ab. She has produced all parental chromosomes since they are identical to herself (parental). However, if the alleles are farther apart, there is the increased probability of crossover.

Crossover allows a *cis* configuration to become a *trans* configuration or vice versa. A *single crossover* is a crossing-over between two adjacent non-sister chromatids of a tetrad, at a single chiasma. The two chromatids which crossed over are recombinant, while the other two remain parental (nonrecombinant). The following image illustrates a tetrad that has undergone recombination to produce some recombinant chromatids.

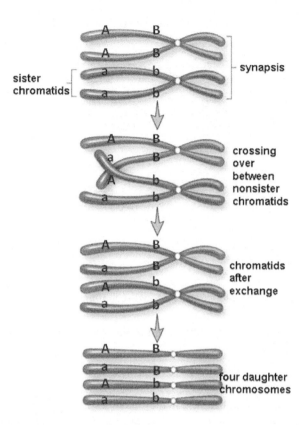

Crossing over with exchange at tetrad with A for a is shown.
From AB and ab, the four gametes produced are AB, aB, Ab and ab.

A *double crossover* is more complicated and can have a few different outcomes. A *two-stranded* double crossover involves two chromatids that overlap each other at two points. They exchange alleles at first, but then exchange them back, resulting in no net recombination. When a crossover occurs between alleles, the following summaries are accurate. Although each chromatid ends up with a region of the other, these are noncoding regions between the loci, so the crossing-over has no observable difference. This results in four parental chromatids.

Double crossover results from two exchanges and preserves the parental genotype chromosomes

A *three-stranded* double crossover involves three chromatids of two chromosomes. Like a single crossover, this results in two recombinants and two parentals.

A *four-stranded* double crossover involves all four chromatids in the tetrad. It results in four recombinants and no parentals.

If the crossover event flanks an allele on each side, the following is observed:

Double-crossover gametes

Noncrossover gametes

The result is two noncrossover chromosomes and two recombinant chromosomes.

The random orientation of homologous chromosomes during metaphase I and their independent assortment into separate daughter cells is another important mechanism of recombination. The number of possible orientations at the metaphase plate is equal to 2^n, where n is the haploid number of chromosomes.

Since humans have a haploid number of 23, they have 2^{23} possible outcomes, yielding over 8,388,000 possible combinations of gametes from the division of a single cell. Compounded with the effects of exchange of genetic material on a chromosome during crossing over, the number of combinations increases even further to virtually infinite genetic variety.

Summary of important terms in genetics

Carrier - an individual that has one copy of a recessive allele that causes a genetic disease in individuals that are homozygous for this allele.

Codominant alleles - pairs of alleles that both affect the phenotype when present in a heterozygote.

Dominant allele - an allele that has the same effect on the phenotype, whether it is present in the homozygous or heterozygous state.

Genotype - the alleles of an organism.

Heterozygous - having two different alleles of a gene.

Homozygous - having two identical alleles of a gene.

Locus - the particular position of a gene on a chromosome.

Phenotype - the characteristics of an organism.

Recessive allele - an allele that only has an effect on the phenotype when present in the homozygous state.

Notes for active learning

Notes for active learning

Analytic Methods

Hardy-Weinberg principle

In the 1930s, scientists were able to apply genetics to populations and observe the small-scale evolution of a gene pool.

A population in stasis has constant gene frequencies and is in *Hardy-Weinberg equilibrium*. This provides a baseline by which to judge whether evolution has occurred. Populations can only be in Hardy-Weinberg equilibrium if they meet the requirements of the *Hardy-Weinberg principle*. These assumptions describe a population without changes in allelic and genotypic frequencies, due to the absence of evolutionary pressures. The conditions are as follows:

1) Mutation does not occur at any significant rate.

2) Gene flow is absent as individuals do not migrate among populations.

3) Nonrandom mating does not occur; individuals pair by chance and do not engage in mate selection.

4) Genetic drift is minimal; the population is large, so changes in allele frequencies due to chance are insignificant.

5) Natural selection does not occur; the population does not experience competition, and no traits have a selective advantage.

In the natural world, the conditions of the Hardy-Weinberg principle are rarely, if ever, met, so allelic and genotypic frequencies change, and thus evolution occurs.

The Hardy-Weinberg principle includes mathematical models to predict frequencies.

1) Allele frequencies: $p + q = 1$, represented by p and q, sum to 100% in the gene pool.

2) Genotype frequencies: $p^2 + 2pq + q^2 = 1$, which arise from the two alleles, sum to 100% in the gene pool. The homozygous dominant genotype (pp) equals the product of $p \times p$ (or p^2). The homozygous recessive genotype (qq) equals the product of $q \times q$ (or q^2). The heterozygous genotype is represented by two possibilities, pq, and qp, and therefore is the sum of both their products (or $2pq$).

Example: A plant population has two phenotypes for flower color: the wild-type red and the white mutant phenotype. The wild-type red flowers are inherited from at least one dominant allele (R), and the mutant white flowers are inherited from two recessive alleles (r). In this gene pool, 84% of the flowers have the red phenotype, and 16% have the white phenotype. What are the frequencies of the alleles? What are the frequencies of the genotypes?

Solution:

Assume that the red allele (R) is "p" and the white allele (r) is "q."

Since the frequency of the white phenotype is 16%, then $q^2 = 0.16$. This is the frequency of the homozygous recessive genotype.

Since the frequency of the red phenotype is 84%, then $p^2 + 2pq = 0.84$. Remember that p^2 and $2pq$ are the homozygous dominant and heterozygous genotypes, respectively. Together, they represent the wild-type (red) phenotype.

Solving for the white allele, q:

$$q = \sqrt{q^2} = \sqrt{0.16} = 0.4$$

Therefore, the frequency of the white allele in the population is 0.4 (or 40%).

Solving for the red allele, p:

$$p + q = 1$$

$$p = 1 - q$$

$$p = 1 - 0.4 = 0.6$$

Therefore, the frequency of the red allele in the population is 0.6 (or 60%).

Solving for p^2:

$$p^2 = 0.6^2 = 0.36.$$

The frequency of the homozygous dominant genotype is 36%.

Solving for $2pq$:

$$2pq = 0.84 - p^2$$

$$2pq = 0.84 - 0.36$$

$$2pq = 0.48.$$

The frequency of the heterozygous genotype is 48%.

Testcross for parental, F1, and F2 generations

A *test cross* is mating of an individual of unknown genotype against an individual with a homozygous recessive genotype. This may be done for one or more traits. Mendel used this to ensure his plants were true breeding. For example, he may have had a plant with white flowers (a recessive trait), so he knew it was homozygous recessive for white flowers; genotype pp. Another plant may have had purple flowers, but since this is the dominant phenotype, he could not be sure whether it was Pp or PP. He would cross the purple (unknown genotype) plant with the white plant. The phenotypic results of a test cross indicate the presence of the different genotypes even though the genotypes (PP or Pp) could not be observed only phenotype can be observed.

Example:

A white-flowered pea plant (genotype pp) and an unknown purple-flowered pea plant (genotype P_) are test-crossed to determine the genotype (PP or Pp) of the purple parent.

Solution:

To analyze a test cross between a white plant and an unknown purple plant, first, establish the possible gametes.

Since the white parent is a homozygote (pp), there is a 100% chance it contributes a p allele and a 0% chance it contributes a P allele; every gamete contains a p allele.

If the purple parent is a homozygote (PP), there is a 100% chance it contributes a P allele to its offspring and a 0% chance that it contributes a p allele. Therefore, by the laws of probability, the chance that their offspring are genotype Pp is $1.0 \times 1.0 = 1.0$ (or 100%). The chance of genotype PP is 0%, and the chance of genotype pp is 0%; all offspring are Pp to exhibit the phenotype of a purple flower.

However, if the purple parent is a heterozygote (Pp), there is a 50% chance it contributes a p allele and a 50% chance it contributes a P allele. Therefore, by the laws of probability, the chance that they have an offspring with genotype Pp is $1.0 \times 0.5 = 50\%$. The chance of genotype pp is $1.0 \times 0.5 = 50\%$. The chance of genotype PP is 0%. Half of their offspring will be Pp and exhibit a purple flower phenotype, and half will be pp and exhibit a white flower phenotype.

Its offspring with the white plant can determine the purple plant genotype. If the offspring are all purple, the unknown parent must be genotype PP. If the offspring are half purple, half white, the unknown parent must be genotype Pp.

This test cross (homozygous recessive with unknown genotype) is summarized:

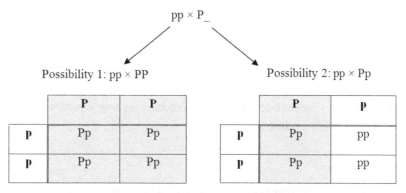

100% purple offspring indicated a purple
a parent that is homozygous

50% purple offspring and 50% white offspring
indicates a purple parent that is heterozygous

For a two-trait test cross (e.g., seed color and seed shape) the results are an extension of the single trait test cross. If a double homozygous recessive parent (rryy) is crossed with a round-seeded yellow parent of unknown genotype, the unknown parent has four possible genotypes: RRYY, RrYY, RRYy, RrYy.

After creating hybrid F1 individuals from a parental generation, a *backcross* can be performed by breeding the offspring with the parents (or an individual with the same genotype as the parents). This is used to conserve desirable traits in the F2 plants and animals or to "knock out" (remove) a certain gene from an organism. Backcrossing occurs naturally in small populations, especially among plants. Artificial backcrossing is done in genetic research to study the function of certain genes by eliminating them and then observing the effect when absent.

Known parent genotype	Possible parent genotype	Possible parent gametes	Offspring phenotype ratio
rryy	RRYY	RY, RY, RY, RY	1 round yellow
rryy	RrYY	RY, RY, rY, rY	1 round yellow : 1 wrinkled yellow
rryy	RRYy	RY, RY, Ry, Ry	1 round yellow : 1 round green
rryy	RrYy	RY, rY, Ry, ry	1 round yellow : 1 wrinkled yellow : 1 round green : 1 wrinkled green

Gene mapping from crossover frequencies

The rate of "unlinking" of genes is used to map the physical distances between two genes on the same chromosome. The further apart two genes are, the more likely they become unlinked during crossing over. The frequency of recombination is an estimate of linkage because it indicates the distance between loci. The maximum frequency of recombination is 50%. For example, genes undergoing recombination 50% of the time are completely unlinked. Genes undergoing recombination 10% of the time must be close together since it is difficult for them to be separated.

Frequencies are found by dividing the number of recombinant offspring by the number of total offspring. Recombinants are identified by their rarity amongst the offspring since parental type offspring are always more frequent. If more than two genes are studied, different types of crossing over can occur, and the recombinants can be further divided into two-, three-, or four-stranded crossovers. Two-stranded crossovers occur more frequently than three-stranded crossovers; four-stranded crossovers are rarest. 1% recombination frequency equals 1 map unit, measured in *centimorgans* (cM) as an arbitrary, relative unit and not physical distances. If crosses are performed for three genes, and their recombination frequencies are calculated, the genes can be ordered (arrange by their relative distance) since a one map relationship explains the distances between them. Biochemical methods are used to map the physical distances between loci by the number of DNA nucleotide bases. Human chromosomes must be mapped this way since it is not possible to measure recombination frequency among a person's offspring due to the small sample size and lack of control over reproduction.

Biometry and statistical methods

Mendel's knowledge of statistics, a new branch of mathematics at the time, greatly aided his work. Today, statistics is an integral field of life sciences. *Biometry,* or *biostatistics,* is the application of mathematical models and statistics to a vast array of biological fields. Biometry is used for biological experiments, the collection, summarization, and analysis of data, and interpretation of and inferences from the data. Problem-solving in genetics usually relies on statistics. Allelic, genotypic and phenotypic frequencies are calculated using statistics to determine the characteristics of a family (or population). Models can be applied that describe genetic inheritance, even for complex non-Mendelian patterns.

Notes for active learning

Notes for active learning

Chapter 8

DNA,
Protein Synthesis,
Gene Expression

- **DNA Structure and Function**

- **DNA Replication**

- **Genetic Code**

- **Transcription**

- **Translation**

- **Eukaryotic Chromosome Organization**

- **Control of Gene Expression in Eukaryotes**

- **Recombinant DNA and Biotechnology**

DNA Structure and Function

Description

Deoxyribonucleic acid (DNA) is the sequence of paired nucleotides that stores the genetic code, necessary for its replication and determining the sequence of amino acids in proteins. The process of transcription uses DNA as a template to form a *ribonucleic acid* (RNA), which serves as a temporary transcript of the hereditary genetic information. *Ribosomes* translate the information from mRNA into a sequence of amino acids to form polypeptides, which fold into proteins.

DNA contains four different nucleotides (adenine, cytosine, guanine, and thymine). *Nucleotides* consist of 1) at least one phosphate group, 2) a pentose sugar, and 3) a one or two-ringed structure containing carbon and nitrogen (i.e., nitrogenous base). The term "base" relates to its ability to accept hydrogen ions (protons). First, glycosidic bonds link the sugar to the nitrogenous base, creating a *nucleoside* (sugar and base only), as shown below.

Nucleoside formation by a condensation reaction that joins the ribose to the adenine to form adenosine (lacking the phosphate group of a nucleotide)

(Nucleoside)   (Nucleotide)

Phosphate   Adenosine   Adenosine monophosphate (AMP)

Phosphodiester bonds link nucleotides between
the phosphate of one nucleotide and the sugar of another

The phosphate group then links to the nucleoside similarly through a condensation reaction,
forming a nucleotide (sugar, base, phosphate)

These nucleotides form a long strand and the chain of phosphodiester bonds in the sugar-phosphate backbone for DNA. A polymer of nucleotides comprise a *nucleic acid*, and its acidity is due to the abundant phosphate groups. Nucleic acids (i.e., RNA and DNA) store, transmit and express hereditary, genetic information in cells.

DNA has two nucleic acid strands combined to form the double-stranded DNA molecule. Strands are joined when the bases of each strand (e.g., A = T and C ≡ G) form *base pairs*. The DNA in a single human cell contains about 3 billion base pairs. Because DNA has a helical twist, further coiling of the DNA strand makes the DNA more compact. The 3 billion base pairs in one human cell would stretch to about 6 feet in length. The sequence of base pairs encodes the genetic information of the cell. This genetic code, in the form of nucleic acids, determines the sequence of amino acids in the proteins synthesized by the cell.

DNA composition (purine and pyrimidine bases, deoxyribose and phosphate)

Early researchers knew that the genetic material must have a few necessary characteristics. It must store information used to control both the development and the metabolic activities of cells, it must be stable to be accurately replicated during cell division and be transmitted for many cell cycles and between generations of offspring (i.e., progeny), and it must be able to undergo mutations, providing the genetic variability required for evolution.

In 1869, Swiss chemist Friedrich Miescher removed nuclei from pus cells and isolated "nuclein." It was rich in phosphorus and lacked sulfur. Nuclein was analyzed by other scientists who found that it contained an acid—specifically, nucleic acid. The two types of nucleic acids were soon discovered: deoxyribonucleic acid (DNA) and ribonucleic acid (RNA). In the early twentieth century, researchers discovered that nucleic acids contain four types of nucleotides, the repeating units that make up the long DNA molecule.

Purines or *pyrimidines* are the two types of nucleotides within DNA.

Purine   *Pyrimidine*

There are four different bases in DNA nucleotides. *Adenine* (A) and *guanine* (G) are purine bases and consist of two nitrogen-containing rings, while *thymine* (T) and *cytosine* (C) are pyrimidine bases and consist of one nitrogen-containing ring.

Adenine (A)   Guanine (G)
(DNA and RNA)   (DNA and RNA)

Purines with a double ring structure

Cytosine (C)   Thymine (T)   Uracil (U)
(DNA and RNA)   (DNA only)   (RNA only)

Pyrimidines with a single ring structure

325

Deoxyribose is a pentose (5-carbon) sugar in DNA. By convention, the carbons of the sugar are numbered. The phosphate group of DNA is attached to the 5' carbon. Deoxyribose has a hydroxyl group (OH) at the 3' carbon (as does the ribose sugar in RNA).

Comparison of the pentose sugars in RNA (left) and DNA (right).
Ribose has a 2' hydroxyl, while DNA has no oxygen (deoxy) at the 2' position

RNA has a similar but not identical structure to DNA. The pentose sugar in RNA is *ribose*, which has the same structure as deoxyribose, except RNA has a hydroxyl group instead of hydrogen at the 2' position. Because deoxyribose is missing this hydroxyl group, it is *deoxy* (without oxygen). RNA contains the *uracil* pyrimidine instead of thymine (uracil replaces thymine in RNA). These two pyrimidine bases have similar structures, except for a methyl group (CH$_3$) present in thymine, but not in uracil.

Chain elongation of DNA with the nucleophilic attack of the 5' carbon phosphate
by the 3' OH of the sugar. Elongation always proceeds 3'→5'.

Although the primary structures of DNA and RNA are similar, their structures in three-dimensional space (tertiary structure) are particularly distinct. RNA molecules are single-stranded, so base pairs can form between different parts of the same molecule, resulting in shapes such as stem-loops. Double-stranded DNA is a double helix with two strands bonded in an anti-parallel orientation and held together by hydrogen bonds between the bases (C≡G and A=T).

By convention, the 5' phosphate end of a nucleic acid strand is written on the left, and the 3' hydroxyl end is written on the right

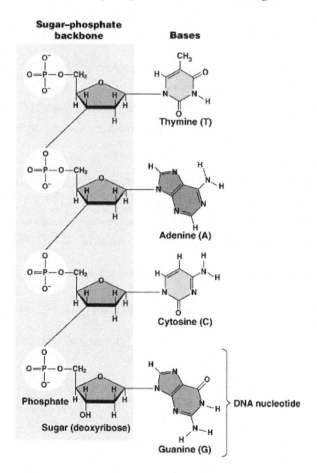

Single-stranded DNA with negatively-charged sugar-phosphate backbone and bases projecting inwards when the second strand of DNA hydrogen bonds with it to form a double helix

Base pairing specificity: A with T, G with C

In the 1940s, biochemist Erwin Chargaff analyzed the base content of DNA using chemical techniques. Chargaff discovered that for a species, DNA has the *constancy* required of genetic material. This constancy is *Chargaff's rule*, which states that the number of pyrimidine bases (T and C) equals the number of purine bases (A and G). Additionally, the bases always make hydrogen bond base pairs in the same way: the purine A uses a double bond with the pyrimidine T, and the purine G uses a triple bond with the pyrimidine C. This is a *complementary base pairing*. Therefore, Chargaff's rule states that the number of adenine in a DNA molecule equals the number of its base pair, thymidine, and the number of guanine equals the number of its base pair, cytosine. Hence, A = T and G = C.

Adenine has 2 hydrogen bonds to Thymine   *Guanine has 3 hydrogen bonds to Cytosine*

Despite the restriction of base pair bonding, the G/C content relative to A/T content differs among species while still adhering to Chargaff's rules. Furthermore, because G/C pairs have three hydrogen bonds as opposed to the two hydrogen bonds in A/T pairs, the strands in DNA molecules with higher G/C content are more tightly bound than those with higher A/T content. Therefore, G/C base pairs have a higher T_m (melting temperature when ½ bonds are broken) than A/T base pairs.

Although there are four bases (A, C, G, T) and two types of base pairs (A/T, C/G) in DNA, the variability in the base sequence is enormous. A human chromosome contains about 140 million base pairs on average, and since any of the four possible nucleotides can be present at each nucleotide position, the total number of possible nucleotide sequences in a human chromosome is $4^{140,000,000}$, or 4 raised to 140,000,000.

Use this mnemonic to remember which bases are purines or pyrimidines:

CUT the PIE (Cytosine, Uracil, and Thymine are pyrimidines)

PURe As Gold (purines are Adenine and Guanine)

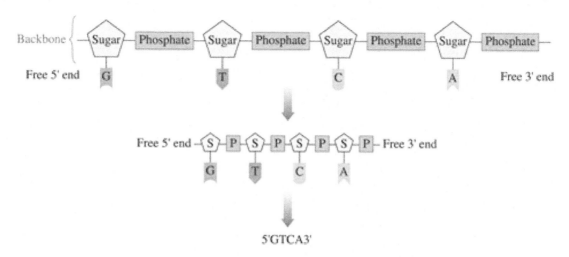

5'GTCA3'

Chargaff's rule identifies the amount of all bases when one purine (A or G) and one pyrimidine (C or T) are hydrogen bonded in a complementary-paired double-stranded DNA molecule

DNA: double helix, Watson–Crick model of DNA structure; RNA Structure

During the 1950s, English chemist Rosalind Franklin produced X-ray diffraction photographs of DNA molecules. Franklin's work provided evidence that DNA has a helical conformation, or more specifically, that the two strands of DNA wind together in a double helix. A double helix can be envisioned as a twisted ladder.

An American, James Watson, and an Englishman, Francis H. C. Crick, received the Nobel Prize in 1962 for their model of DNA. Using information gathered by Chargaff and Franklin, Watson and Crick built a model of DNA in a double helix secondary structure. Sugar-phosphate molecules form a backbone on the outside of the helix, while bases point toward the middle and form base pairs with the complementary strand. Their model was consistent with both Chargaff's rules and the dimensions of the DNA polymer provided by Franklin's x-ray diffraction photographs of DNA.

Each strand in DNA has a direction relative to the numbering on the pentose ring. In a free nucleotide, the phosphate is attached to the 5'−phosphate of deoxyribose, while the 3'−OH of deoxyribose is exposed. When phosphodiester bonds form, a 3' hydroxyl of one deoxyribose sugar attaches to a 5' phosphate of an incoming sugar. Thus, DNA strands have a distinct polarity, with a 5' end and a 3' end. Two strands bound in a double helix orient in opposite directions and the two strands are *antiparallel*.

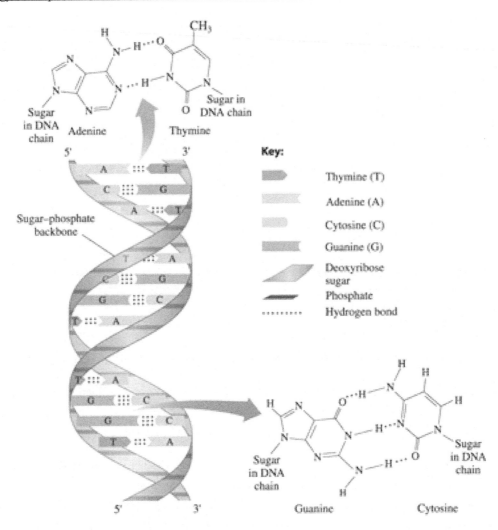

Key:

- Thymine (T)
- Adenine (A)
- Cytosine (C)
- Guanine (G)
- Deoxyribose sugar
- Phosphate
- ·········· Hydrogen bond

Antiparallel strands of DNA with phosphodiester bonds between the sugar-phosphate backbone. Hydrogen bonds hold the complementary base pairs together

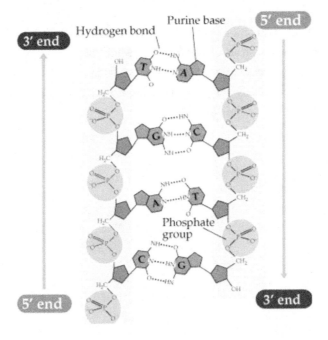

DNA as two antiparallel strands with hydrogen bonds between complementary base pairs

Function in the transmission of genetic information

In 1931, bacteriologist Frederick Griffith experimented with *Streptococcus pneumonia,* a pneumococcus bacterium that causes pneumonia in mammals. He first injected two sets of mice with different strains of pneumococcus: a virulent strain with a mucous capsule (S strain) due to the colonies' smooth appearance, and a non-virulent strain without a capsule (R strain) due to the colonies' rough appearance. Mice injected with the S strain died, while mice injected with the R strain survived.

To determine if the capsule alone was responsible for the virulence of the S strain, Griffith performed two more sets of injections. In one set of mice, he injected S strain bacteria that had been first subjected to heat ("heat-killed bacteria"). These mice survived. In another set of mice, he injected a mixture of the heat-killed S strain and the live R strain. These mice died, and Griffith was even able to recover living S strain pneumococcus from the mice's bodies, despite only heat-killed S strain being injected into the live mice.

Griffith concluded that the R strain had been "transformed" by the heat-killed S strain bacteria, allowing the R strain to synthesize a capsule and become virulent. The phenotype (virulent capsule) of the R strain bacteria must have been due to a change in their genotype (genetic material), which suggested that the transforming substance must have passed from the heat-killed S strain to the R strain. This passing of this unknown substance is *transformation.*

In 1944, molecular biologists Oswald Avery, Colin MacLeod, and Maclyn McCarty reported that the transforming substance in the heat-killed S strain was DNA. This conclusion was supported with several pieces of evidence that showed that purified DNA is capable of bringing about the transformation. In one experiment, they showed that enzymes that degrade proteins (proteases) and RNA (RNase) do not prevent a transformation. However, using enzymes that digest DNA (DNase) does prevent transformation. Additionally, the molecular weight of the transforming substance appeared great enough for some genetic variability. These results supported that DNA is the genetic material and controls the biosynthetic properties of a cell.

In 1952, researchers Alfred Hershey and Martha Chase performed experiments with bacteriophages (the virus that infects bacteria) to confirm that DNA was the genetic material. A *bacteriophage* (phage) is a virus that infects bacteria and consists only of a protein coat surrounding a nucleic acid core. They used the T2 bacteriophage to infect the bacterium *Escherichia coli*, a species of intensely studied bacteria that lives within the human gut.

The purpose of their experiments was to observe which of the bacteriophage components—the protein coat or the DNA—entered the bacterial cells and directed reproduction of the virus. In two separate experiments, they radiolabeled the bacteriophage protein coat with ^{35}S and then the DNA with ^{32}P and allowed each aliquot of phages to infect bacterial cells. The separate populations of bacterial progeny were then lysed (blender experiment) and analyzed for the presence of isotope-labeled sulfur or phosphorous. The progeny became labeled with ^{32}P, while the sulfur of the progeny was unlabeled, confirming that DNA (contains P), not protein (contains S), is the transmissible genetic material.

Genes are sequences of DNA nucleotides that contain and transmit the information specifying amino acid sequences for protein synthesis. Each DNA molecule contains many genes. The *genome* refers collectively to the total genetic information encoded in a cell. Except for reproductive cells and red blood cells, human cells contain 23 pairs of bundled DNA as *chromosomes* in each cell nucleus, totaling 46 chromosomes per cell.

RNA molecules transfer information from DNA in the nucleus to the site of protein synthesis in the cytoplasm. RNA molecules are synthesized during transcription according to template information encoded in the hereditary molecule of DNA. These RNA molecules are then processed, and mRNA is translated by ribosomes to synthesize proteins.

DNA→ replication during S phase → DNA chromosome with sister chromatids

DNA → transcription → mRNA → translation → protein

Notes for active learning

Notes for active learning

DNA Replication

Mechanism of replication: separation of strands, the specific coupling of free nucleic acids, DNA polymerase and primer required

DNA replication is the copying of a DNA molecule. During the S (synthesis) phase of the cell cycle, DNA replicates when the strands of the double helix separate, and each exposed strand acts as a template for DNA synthesis. Free deoxyribonucleoside triphosphates (dNTPs) are base-paired to form new, complementary strands. Errors in the base sequence during replication may be corrected by a mechanism of *proofreading* or DNA repair.

DNA Replication in Prokaryotes and Eukaryotes	
Prokaryotes	Eukaryotes
Five polymerases (I, II, III, IV, V)	Five polymerases ($\alpha, \beta, \gamma, \delta, \varepsilon$)
Functions of polymerase:	Functions of polymerase:
I is involved in synthesis, proofreading, repair, and removal of RNA primers	α: a polymerizing enzyme
II is also a repair enzyme	β: a repair enzyme
III is main polymerizing enzyme	γ: mitochondrial DNA synthesis
IV, V are repair enzymes under unusual conditions	δ: main polymerizing enzyme
	ε: function unknown
Polymerase are also exonucleases	Not all polymerases are exonucleases
One origin of replication	Several origins of replication
Okazaki fragments 1000-2000 residues long	Okazaki fragments 150-200 residues long
No proteins complexed to DNA	Histones complexed to DNA

This text references polymerase III and I;
substitute the corresponding polymerases when considering eukaryotic cells.
The exact polymerase for eukaryote's function is still actively investigated by researchers

Replication of linear DNA in eukaryotes starts at multiple points of origin (circular DNA in prokaryotes have a single origin). Once replication is initiated, the DNA strands separate at each of these points of origin as *replication bubbles*. The two V-shaped separating ends of the replication bubble are the sites of DNA replication or *replication forks*. Once a strand of DNA is exposed, the enzyme *DNA polymerase III* for prokaryotes (pol γ for eukaryotes) incorporates free deoxyribonucleoside triphosphates (dNTPs), which are nucleotides with three phosphate groups, into the complementary strand by catalyzing the exergonic loss of phosphate. The two phosphate groups cleaved in the process become nucleotides and release energy ($-\Delta G$), making the overall polymerization reaction thermodynamically favorable, thus driving the reaction forward.

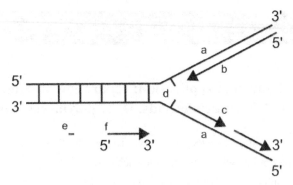

DNA replication: a: template strands, b: leading strand, c: lagging strand,
d: replication fork, e: RNA primer, f: Okazaki fragment

Polymerization occurs on both strands and both ends of the replication bubbles until the entire DNA is replicated, a process that results in two complementary DNA molecules. Eukaryotes replicate their DNA at a relatively slow pace of 500 to 5,000 base pairs per minute, taking hours to complete replication, while prokaryotes can replicate their DNA at a much faster rate of 500 base pairs per second.

The time sequence of DNA replication process with 'bubbles' joining to form complementary DNA

The process of DNA replication can be divided into three steps:

1. Unwinding—the enzyme *DNA helicase* unwinds the double helix, pulling the DNA strands apart and breaking hydrogen bonds between base pairs. Each separated strand is now a template for the synthesis of a new (daughter) strand of DNA.

2. Complementary base pairing—free dNTPs form hydrogen bonds with their complementary base pair. Adenine pairs with thymine, and guanine pairs with cytosine.

3. Joining—DNA polymerase (III or γ) catalyzes the incorporation of nucleotides into the new strand. Incoming dNTPs cleave two phosphate groups, becoming nucleotides (only one phosphate group remains) as they are incorporated in a 5' to 3' direction, and the deoxyribose

sugar and phosphate are covalently added to the new backbone.

Semiconservative nature of replication

Meselson-Stahl experiment during replication with heavy nitrogen as the original growth medium

In 1958, Matthew Meselson and Franklin Stahl provided evidence for the model of DNA replication. They first grew bacteria in a medium with heavy nitrogen (^{15}N) and then switched the bacteria to light nitrogen (^{14}N) for further divisions. When they measured the density of the replicated DNA using centrifugation, they observed that the density of the replicated DNA was intermediate—less dense than a molecule made entirely with ^{15}N, but denser than a molecule made entirely with ^{14}N.

After one division, only these hybrid DNA molecules (1 light and 1 heavy strand) were present in the cells. After two divisions, half the DNA molecules were light, and half were hybrid. These results support the *semiconservative model,* one of three main theoretical models originally proposed in DNA replication.

DNA replication is semiconservative because each daughter double helix consists of one parental strand and one new strand, meaning that half of the double helix is conserved from material in the parent generation.

In a *conservative model*, one entire double strand acts as the template, while the new double strand is composed entirely from scratch. If this model were true, Meselson and Stahl's experiment would produce only heavy and light DNA molecules in the daughter cells, with no hybrid strands of intermediate density.

In a *dispersive model*, the parent double-strand is made into two new strands, with each daughter containing a mixture of old and newly-incorporated nucleotides. The two different densities in the DNA of the cells in the second generation of the Meselson and Stahl experiment were inconsistent with the dispersive model because that model would have resulted in DNA of a single density.

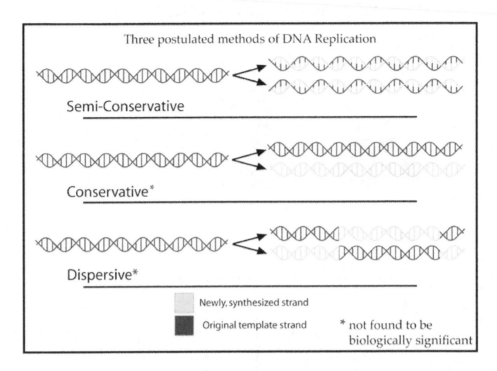

Three models of DNA replication with semi-conservative replication supported by experimentation

Specific enzymes involved in replication

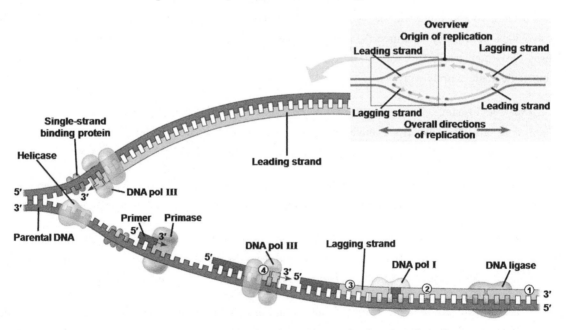

DNA replication with the associated protein involved in strand synthesis.
Pol III is used by prokaryotes and is functionally equivalent to γ in eukaryotes

DNA replication involves a complex of many proteins. The enzyme DNA *helicase* unwinds DNA to expose each template strand for DNA synthesis, forming two Y-shaped replication forks on the two sides of each replication bubble. ATP hydrolysis is required for helicase to break the hydrogen bonds between the complementary strands of DNA. *Single-stranded binding proteins* (SSBP) attach to exposed single strands to keep them from reforming base pair hydrogen bonds, as well as to prevent degradation by DNase. *Topoisomerase* relieves tension in the DNA supercoiling and prevents knots by breaking and rejoining strands. This is essential in allowing helicase to unwind the DNA without causing tension elsewhere along the DNA strand.

DNA polymerase III in prokaryotes (γ in eukaryotes), the primary polymerase responsible for replication, cannot attach directly to an exposed single strand of DNA; it can only start polymerizing from an existing strand, or more specifically from an existing nucleotide 3′−OH. The enzyme *primase* first creates a small sequence of complementary *RNA primer* of approximately 18−22 ribose bases. DNA polymerase begins synthesis after binding to this RNA primer. Primase can begin synthesis *de novo*, unlike DNA polymerase.

DNA polymerase III moves from 3′ to 5′ along the template strand, synthesizing a new antiparallel strand; thus, the new strand is formed from 5′ to 3′. Since the original double strand is antiparallel, polymerization occurs in opposite directions on each strand at a replication fork. Nucleotides are incorporated as they form hydrogen bonds with their complementary base pairs and covalent phosphodiester bonds with their adjacent nucleotides.

The strand synthesized in the same direction as the movement of the replication fork is the *leading strand*, and the strand synthesized in a direction opposite the movement of the replication fork is the *lagging strand*. DNA polymerase (III or γ) can continuously polymerize DNA as the template unzips without detaching from the template, hence the continuous nature of the leading strand. However, DNA polymerase must repeatedly detach and reattach to remain in the proximity of the moving replication fork on the lagging strand. This action produces distinct fragments of new DNA on the lagging strand each time the polymerase detaches and reattaches, known as *Okazaki fragments*. In prokaryotes, Okazaki fragments are 1,000−2,000 nucleotides, while there are 150−200 nucleotides in eukaryotes.

Okazaki fragments each have an RNA primer, which is later replaced with DNA by *DNA polymerase I*. This polymerase can remove the ribonucleotides ahead of it while it synthesizes DNA to replace them. Since polymerases cannot connect separate fragments, *DNA ligase* connects the DNA sugar-phosphate backbones of adjacent Okazaki fragments. This enzyme is necessary because other polymerases can add a free dNTP to a 3′−OH end but cannot connect the ends of nucleotides that have already been incorporated. Ligase seals the DNA backbone between Okazaki fragments or when a repair mechanism replaces any nucleotides.

In summary:

1. Helicase uncoils and separates the DNA strands.

2. Primase adds RNA primers to which DNA polymerase III can bind.

3. DNA polymerase III begins polymerizing new DNA strands 5′ to 3′.

4. Deoxyribonucleoside triphosphates lose two phosphate groups during incorporation, becoming typical nucleotides (sugar + base + phosphate).

5. The leading DNA strand is synthesized continuously.

6. The lagging DNA strand is synthesized in fragments (Okazaki fragments).

7. DNA polymerase I replaces the RNA primers with DNA.

8. DNA ligase joins Okazaki fragments together into a continuous DNA strand.

Origins of replication, multiple origins in eukaryotes

The average human chromosome contains 140 million nucleotide pairs, and each replication fork moves at a rate of about 50 base pairs per second. At this rate, the replication process would take about a month, but since there are many replication origins on the eukaryotic chromosome, the process takes hours. Replication begins at some origins earlier than others, but as replication nears completion, the replication bubbles meet and fuse to form two new DNA molecules. DNA replication occurs in S phase of interphase and must be completed before a cell can divide (e.g., mitosis or meiosis). Drugs with molecules similar to the four nucleotides (i.e., nucleotide analogs) can be used by patients to inhibit cell division of rapidly dividing cancer cells.

There are many origins of replication in linear DNA of eukaryotes, and several replication forks are formed simultaneously, forming several replication bubbles. In prokaryotes, there is just one origin of replication in each circular DNA molecule and replication occurs at one point. Accordingly, the Okazaki fragments in eukaryotes are shorter (100 – 200 nucleotides), while Okazaki fragments in prokaryotes are longer (1,000 – 2,000 nucleotides). Replication occurs about twenty times faster in prokaryotes than it does in eukaryotes, which undergoes more proofreading during DNA replication.

Replicating the ends of DNA molecules

DNA polymerase adds nucleotides to a 3' –OH end of a preexisting polynucleotide, i.e., it cannot synthesize *de novo*. This is not an issue for circular DNA in prokaryotes, but it is a problem for the synthesis of the lagging strand at the ends of linear DNA in eukaryotes. Although primase can add an RNA primer to the end of the DNA molecule on the lagging strand, DNA polymerase I cannot replace DNA without RNA primers, since it cannot perform *de novo* synthesis. Without any special process, the RNA segment, as well as its complementary DNA on the opposite strand, would be degraded, since chromosomes are regulated to consist of complementary DNA. This would lead to degradation of the RNA nucleotides of about 8-12 nucleotides at the ends of DNA strands after each round of replication, eventually encroaching on important genes on chromosomes and leading to cell death.

Telomeres are the end pieces of each chromosome. There are two telomeres on each of the 46 human chromosomes, which adds up to 92 telomeres in total. Their repetitive sequences and associated proteins protect the ends from degradation and provide a way for DNA ends to be replicated without loss of important sequence when the RNA primer initiates replication along the leading strand. In the 1980's, telomeres were proposed for the creation of special segments of DNA that are synthesized by the telomerase enzyme. This enzyme essentially lengthens the ends of DNA with repeating sequences, usually TTAGGG in humans and other vertebrates. The problem with terminal degradation of DNA still occurs, but since extra sequences have been added during embryogenesis and in stem cells, no essential information is lost. In healthy adult cells, telomerase is off.

The telomerase enzyme carries an internal RNA template. It attaches to the end of the DNA molecule and extends the 3' end with additional DNA. The new DNA that is added is complementary to the internal RNA template located on the enzyme. This new DNA is added during embryogenesis, leading and lagging strand synthesis takes place as normal, and a portion of the telomere is lost with each replication cycle during the organism's lifetime.

Since a double-stranded break is often indicative of DNA damage, telomeres have developed associated proteins that inhibit the cell's ability to recognize DNA damage, thereby preventing the unwanted activation of repair mechanisms, cell-cycle arrest or apoptosis.

*Telomerase has an internal RNA template to which
complementary DNA is synthesized to extend the ends of the chromosomes*

Repair during replication

The accuracy of DNA replication cannot be attributed solely to the specificity of base pairing, which has an error rate of 1 out of 10^5 base pairs. This rate is not consistent with the observed total error rate of 1 in 10^9 base pairs. To arrive at this fidelity, errors during replication must be repaired, the first of which is proofreading and performed by DNA polymerases.

DNA polymerase is an aggregate of subunits that combine to form an active *holoenzyme* complex. These aggregates often catalyze more than one type of reaction. When polymerases inevitably make errors in polymerization, DNA polymerase I and III use proofreading to make corrections.

Both DNA polymerase I and III have 3' to 5' exonuclease activity. When these polymerases incorporate an incorrect nucleotide into the strand (does not base pair correctly with the complementary strand), the exonuclease subunit breaks the phosphodiester bond at the 5' end, excises the nucleotide, and the polymerase subunit inserts the proper nucleotide. Since polymerases synthesize in the 5' to 3' direction, this excision is named for the complementary strand's 3' to 5' direction.

In addition to 3' to 5' exonuclease activity, DNA polymerase I (but not III) has a 5' to 3' exonuclease. This enzymatic activity allows DNA polymerase I to remove nucleotides ahead of it while synthesizing a new strand at the same time (5' to 3' polymerization). This is the basis by which DNA polymerase I excise ribonucleotides in the RNA primers and replaces them with DNA. This coupling of 5' to 3' exonuclease activity with 5' to 3' polymerization is *nick translation* since a single-stranded cut (nick) essentially translates along the strand as the sequence is replaced with new nucleotides. Ligase must seal the nicks with phosphodiester bonds in the backbone when repairs are made.

Repair of mutations

In addition to proofreading, *mismatch repair* and *excision repair* are two common systems that correct errors in DNA. In mismatch repair, a different group of enzymes detects a mismatched base pair in a double-stranded DNA molecule that has been missed by the DNA polymerase proofreading mechanism. The repair enzyme decides which DNA strand is the template (parent) strand of the new (daughter) DNA molecule by recognizing methylation sites. Newly synthesized DNA is unmethylated; therefore, the base located on the unmethylated strand must be the mismatched base. *Hemimethylation* is the temporary pattern where one strand is methylated. Since full methylation is eventually reached after a period, mismatch repair is most accurate immediately after DNA synthesis.

Two types of excision repair, *base-excision repair* (BER) and *nucleotide-excision repair* (NER), act on bases with a mutated structure, rather than merely mismatched base pairs. BER generally works on small mutations such as deamination, alkylation or oxidation of the base that does not distort the helical structure. The excision of the damaged base occurs through breakage of the phosphodiester backbone at the resulting abasic site, and gap filling by DNA polymerase replaces the base while ligase seals the backbone. BER is accomplished through the concerted effort of a collection of many enzymes (DNA glycosylases, apurinic/apyrimidinic endonucleases, phosphatases, phosphodiesterases, kinases, polymerases, and ligases).

NER is a similar process, but it is used for mutations that more seriously affect the helical structure. For example, DNA exposure to UV light may cause the dimerization of adjacent thymines and sometimes the dimerization of adjacent cytosines (pyrimidine dimers). These dimers distort the DNA structure, potentially causing problems during replication, resulting in a pre-cancerous state (which is why UV exposure is linked to higher occurrences of skin cancer). NER recognizes the damage, removes the offending stretch of single-stranded DNA, and polymerizes new DNA using the remaining sequence as a template. NER usually replaces a larger region of DNA, rather than a single nucleotide or a small patch as in BER.

Sometimes during replication in bacteria, damage can accumulate so extensively that the NER system cannot keep up, and the *SOS repair system* is activated. SOS repair involves the induction of low-fidelity polymerases to prevent the normal high-fidelity polymerases from getting stuck along the DNA strand during synthesis.

Notes for active learning

Notes for active learning

Genetic Code

Central Dogma: DNA → RNA → protein

The *central dogma* of molecular biology describes the flow of genetic information in living systems. It states that information flows from DNA to mRNA to protein. DNA is *transcribed* by RNA polymerase to create mRNA molecules, and mRNA is *translated* by ribosomes to produce the polypeptide chains comprising proteins. The central dogma identifies DNA and RNA as information intermediates; information can flow back and forth between DNA and RNA (exemplified by retroviruses, where reverse transcriptase catalyzes the formation of DNA from RNA), but identifies the protein as an information sink. A protein sequence does not act as a template for the synthesis of DNA or RNA.

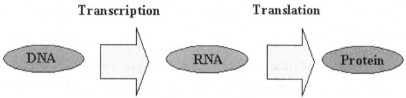

The central dogma of the flow of genetic information

Classical geneticists classify a gene as any of the particles of inheritance on a chromosome, while molecular biologists describe a gene as a sequence of DNA nucleotide bases that encodes for a protein. DNA is responsible for the genotype, or genetic makeup of an organism. Protein is responsible for the phenotype, or the observable characteristics (i.e., physical, physiological, developmental or behavioral traits) of the organism. Phenotypes result from the actions of enzymes, which are biological catalysts (mostly proteins) that regulate biological functions. Any alteration of the processes in the central dogma of molecular biology may affect the formation of proteins and thus affect the phenotype.

In the early 1900s, English physician Sir Archibald Garrod introduced the phrase *inborn error of metabolism*, in which inherited defects could be caused by the lack of an enzyme in a metabolic pathway. Knowing that enzymes are proteins, Garrod suggested a link between genes and proteins.

In 1940, George Beadle and Edward Tatum x-rayed spores of red bread mold *Neurospora crassa*. They discovered that some cultures lacked a particular enzyme for growth on the medium, and soon after they found that a single gene was mutated, which resulted in the lack of this single enzyme. From their experiments, they proposed the *one gene-one enzyme hypothesis*, which states that one gene specifies the synthesis of one enzyme.

Later experiments built on this hypothesis. In 1949, biochemists Linus Pauling and Harvey Itano compared hemoglobin in red blood cells of persons with sickle-cell anemia with those of unafflicted individuals. By using electrophoresis to separate molecules by weight and charge, they discovered that the chemical properties of the chain of sickle-cell hemoglobin protein differed from the normal hemoglobin. Years later, biologist Vernon Ingram showed that the biochemical change to the sickle-cell hemoglobin chain was due to the substitution of a nonpolar valine amino acid for the negatively charged glutamate amino acid. Pauling and Itano proposed the *one gene-one polypeptide hypothesis*, which states that each gene specifies one polypeptide of a protein (proteins may contain multiple polypeptide chains). This hypothesis clarified the earlier one gene-one enzyme hypothesis.

The two strands of DNA are named by their relationship to the RNA and protein. The *template strand* is used as the template for RNA synthesis and has a complementary sequence to the coding strand. The *coding strand* has an identical sequence to the transcribed RNA but substitutes thymine for uracil. The template strand is the *antisense strand* or *anticoding strand*, and the coding strand is the *sense strand*.

Messenger RNA (mRNA)

RNA (ribonucleic acid) is a nucleic acid that carries a complementary copy of the genetic code of DNA and is translated into the amino acid sequence of proteins. Unlike DNA, RNA a 2'−OH sugar on the ribose instead of deoxyribose (2'−H) and the pyrimidine base uracil replacing thymine. RNA generally does not form helices. *Messenger RNA* (mRNA) is a single-stranded piece of RNA containing the bases complementary to the original DNA strand. The mRNA transcript is synthesized in the nucleus, but after *processing* it is transported into the cytoplasm where ribosomes are located. The ribosomes *translate* the mRNA sequence into amino acids and synthesize the polypeptide chains of proteins.

RNA, like DNA, can be replicated in special cases. However, a single-stranded RNA template must be used to synthesize a complementary strand, and then the new strand must serve as a template for another round of synthesis to create an additional RNA molecule identical to the first template.

Codon-anticodon relationship and degenerate code

Ribosomes read the RNA containing information for the synthesis of protein as a series of base triplets as *codons*. The three bases that make up each codon determine the amino acid that is incorporated into the growing polypeptide as the ribosome moves along the mRNA transcript. Each amino acid is added to the polypeptide chain, linked by peptide bonds between the amino acids. After the completed polypeptide dissociates from the ribosome, special modifications and three-dimensional folding take place (in the ribosome for eukaryotic cells) to form the final protein.

From the four types of ribonucleotide bases (adenine, cytosine, guanine, uracil), there are $4^3 = 64$ different codons possible from a series of three ribonucleotides. However, with few exceptions, there are 20 naturally-occurring amino acids that make up an organism's proteins. In this way, the code is *degenerate*, meaning that more than one codon may specify the same amino acid.

In 1961, Marshall Nirenberg and J. Heinrich Matthaei assembled the initial relationships between naturally occurring amino acids and the codons that specify them. They found that an enzyme can be used to construct synthetic RNA in a cell-free system. By translating just three ribonucleotides at a time and observing the amino acid incorporated, they began to decipher the triplet code. This demonstrated the role of nucleotides in protein synthesis. Three nucleotides (codon) specify a single amino acid.

Initiation and termination codons (function, codon sequences)

The 64 codons also include 4 special codons. AUG (start codon) codes for methionine and signals the start of translation on an RNA transcript, forming the first amino acid in the nascent polypeptide. Three other codons, UAG, UGA, and UAA, do not encode for any amino acid but signal a ribosome to terminate translation. Although the code is degenerate (a single amino acid is specified by more than one codon), it is *unambiguous*: each nucleotide triplet encodes a single amino acid.

From the genetic code, the amino acid sequence of a peptide encoded for by a specific nucleotide sequence can be determined. For example, AUG–CAU–UAC–UAA encodes for: Met–His–Tyr–Stop. Additionally, the degeneracy of the genetic code can be observed in the table. For example, CCC, CCU, CCA, and CCG all encode for the amino acid proline.

Second letter

		U	C	A	G	
First letter	**U**	UUU UUC } Phe UUA UUG } Leu	UCU UCC UCA UCG } Ser	UAU UAC } Tyr **UAA Stop** **UAG Stop**	UGU UGC } Cys **UGA Stop** UGG Trp	U C A G
	C	CUU CUC CUA CUG } Leu	CCU CCC CCA CCG } Pro	CAU CAC } His CAA CAG } Gln	CGU CGC CGA CGG } Arg	U C A G
	A	AUU AUC AUA } Ile AUG Met	ACU ACC ACA ACG } Thr	AAU AAC } Asn AAA AAG } Lys	AGU AGC } Ser AGA AGG } Arg	U C A G
	G	GUU GUC GUA GUG } Val	GCU GCC GCA GCG } Ala	GAU GAC } Asp GAA GAG } Glu	GGU GGC GGA GGG } Gly	U C A G

(**Third letter** label at right)

Genetic code with 3 nucleotides specifying an amino acid

Mutations

A genetic mutation is a permanent change in the sequence of DNA nucleotide bases, evading proofreading and repair mechanisms. Major types of mutations include *point mutations*, in which a single base is replaced; *additions*, in which sections of DNA are added; and *deletions*, in which sections of DNA are deleted. The result is the potential for a misread in the DNA nucleotide code or the loss of a gene. Their effect can categorize mutation; these categories include *nonsense* mutations, *missense* mutations, *silent* mutations, *neutral* mutations, and *frameshift* mutations. Mutations have consequences that range from no effect to total inactivation of a protein's function.

At some point mutations, the corresponding change in the RNA may cause a change in the resulting polypeptide. For example, a DNA sequence C̲CA mutated to T̲CA would cause the RNA codon G̲GU for glycine to be changed to the A̲GU codon for serine. In this case, a single nucleotide change has caused a single amino acid change. *Missense mutations* cause codons to specify different amino acids. *Nonsense mutations* cause a codon that specifies for an amino acid to change to a stop codon, which results in a truncated (often nonfunctional) protein.

Not all mutations in DNA lead to changes in the resulting protein. For example, a DNA sequence G̲AT mutated to G̲AA would cause the RNA codon C̲UA to change to C̲UU; both codons translate the same amino acid, leucine. This is a *silent mutation* because it cannot be observed in the phenotype (i.e., protein sequence) of the organism.

A *neutral mutation* neither benefits nor inhibits the function of an organism. For example, a mutation leading to an amino acid change from aspartic acid to glutamic acid, both of which have negatively-charged side chains, may not cause a major structural or functional change in a protein. In this example, the organism may be unaffected by the amino acid change. Silent mutations are essentially neutral mutations unless there is some mechanism affected that depends specifically on the DNA or corresponding amino acid sequence.

There are several ways in which a mutation may not have a negative effect. For example, mutations within introns (segments excised when mRNA is processed), may not affect the final protein. Proteins may be unaffected by a particular amino acid change, especially if the new amino acid has similar properties. If a gene is damaged, there may be no negative effect on the organism if there is an intact homologous gene on the paired chromosome able to produce an intact protein. Damage to genes that synthesize amino acids may not affect if that amino acid can be obtained from an external source, such as the medium a bacterium is growing on.

Mutations can result in nonfunctional proteins, and even a single nonfunctioning protein can have dramatic effects. For example, phenylketonuria is a disease that results when the enzyme that breaks down phenylalanine is nonfunctional, causing phenylalanine to build up in the system. Albinism is caused by a faulty enzyme elsewhere in the same pathway. Cystic fibrosis results from the inheritance of a change in a chloride transport protein in the plasma membrane. A faulty receptor for male sex hormones causes androgen insensitivity in men, where the body's cells cannot respond to testosterone and instead develop like a female, even though all the cells have XY sex chromosomes.

Sickle cell anemia is the result of a single base change in the DNA: in the hemoglobin polypeptide chain, a glutamate amino acid is changed to valine at the sixth residue of the β-chain, distorting the structure of red blood cells into a sickle shape. The malformed red blood cells break down at a faster rate, causing anemia (low red blood cell count), and can become lodged within small vessels (capillaries), causing ischemia (restriction in blood supply).

A *frameshift mutation* alters the normal triplet reading frame so that codons downstream from the mutation are out of register and not read properly. They occur when one or more nucleotides are inserted or deleted, resulting in a new sequence of codons and nonfunctional proteins; it may affect the position of the stop codon. For example, if there is a mRNA sequence GAC CCG UAU corresponding to aspartic acid, proline, and tyrosine, a deletion of the first amino acid would cause a frameshift mutation. The mutated mRNA sequence would be ACC CGU AU, and it now encodes for threonine and arginine. The human transposon *Alu* causes hemophilia when a frameshift mutation leads to a premature stop codon in the gene for clotting factor IX.

Spontaneous mutations occur randomly in the cell, but they are rare and due largely to imperfections in the replication machinery. *Mutagens* are environmental agents that produce changes in DNA. Proofreading and other repair mechanisms lower the likelihood of mutation to one out of every billion base pairs replicated, but high exposure to mutagens may increase this rate. Many mutagens are also *carcinogens* or cancer-causing agents.

If a mutation occurs in a somatic cell (cell other than an egg or sperm), it affects only the individual organism and can cause conditions like cancer. Future generations can inherit mutations that occur in germ cells (sperm or egg cells) and cause genetic diseases; more than 4,000 genetic diseases have been identified.

Radiation is a common mutagen. X-rays and gamma rays are forms of ionizing radiation that create dangerous free radicals (atoms with unpaired electrons), and ultraviolet (UV) radiation can cause pyrimidines (thymine or cytosine) to form covalent linkages as pyrimidine dimers, cellular repair enzymes must remove these dimers. A lack of repair enzymes can cause xeroderma pigmentosum, a condition leading to a higher incidence of skin cancer.

Organic chemicals can act directly on DNA. The mutagen 5-bromouracil pairs with thymine, so the A–T base pair becomes a G–C base pair. Other chemicals may add hydrocarbon groups or remove amino groups from DNA bases. Tobacco smoke contains some chemical carcinogens. One common chemical mutagen is sodium nitrite ($NaNO_2$), used as a preservative in processed meats. In the presence of amines, sodium nitrite forms nitrosamines, which assist in the conversion of the base cytosine into uracil.

Transposons are DNA sequences that can move within and between chromosomes and can cause mutations when they change the DNA sequence. These "jumping genes" were proposed by Barbara McClintock and first detected in maize (corn). Now transposons have been observed in bacteria, fruit flies and other organisms. Charcot-Marie-Tooth disease is a rare human disorder where muscles and nerves of legs and feet wither away. It is believed to be the result of a transposon that caused the partial duplication of a chromosome, giving the patient three copies of a series of genes, leading to the breakdown of myelin (insulating sheath around neurons) and thus affects nerve transmission. Viruses can cause mutations when they integrate their DNA into the host genome.

Notes for active learning

Transcription

mRNA composition and structure:
RNA nucleotides, 5' cap, 3' poly-A tail

Messenger RNA (mRNA) is the single-stranded RNA transcript comprising the nucleotide sequence information for the synthesis of polypeptides. It is different from tRNA or rRNA because it has modified guanine (7-methylguanosine) base 5' cap at the 5' end and a series of adenine nucleotides as a 3' poly-A tail. 5' capping occurs early, often even before the RNA polymerase is finished transcribing RNA. The cap is used by a ribosome for attachment to begin translation; it provides some stability for the mRNA molecule. The polyadenylation at the 3' end of the transcript creates the poly-A tail of approximately 150-200 adenine (A), nucleotides. This is *template-independent* because it does not require a template strand for the polymerization to occur. This tail inhibits degradation of mRNA in the cytoplasm by hydrolytic enzymes. Delay of degradation allows the mRNA to remain in the cell cytoplasm for longer, leading to more polypeptides translated from the same transcript. Polyadenylation can occur in prokaryotes, but it instead promotes degradation.

The region between the 5' cap and the mRNA start codon is the 5' untranslated region (5'−UTR). Similarly, the region between the mRNA stop codon and the poly-A tail is the 3'−UTR. Although UTRs are not translated, they function for stability and localization of the pre-processed mRNA (pre-mRNA, heterogeneous nuclear RNA or hnRNA).

mRNA structure including the untranslated regions (UTRs)

mRNA processing in eukaryotes, introns, and exons

In eukaryotes, the newly-formed RNA (*primary transcript RNA* or *pre-RNA*) are processed before leaving the nucleus to yield a *mature RNA product*. Processing involves capping and polyadenylation (described above). Additional processing that must occur during the formation of the mature RNA molecule is the splicing of the *introns*, the non-coding RNA regions that must be excised. The *exons* are the coding regions that remain in the final transcript. After the introns are excised, the exons are joined in the process of *RNA splicing*. The mRNA exons are eventually translated into polypeptides after leaving the nucleus. The organization of genes into introns and exons is of particular evolutionary importance. Exons generally represent functional protein domains, so splicing and changes in exon composition allow the easy shuffling of protein domains to create new proteins. Splicing differs between developmental stages (i.e., fetus or adult) or tissue-specific differences (e.g., lung or heart).

mRNA with introns removed and exons ligated together

An exception for RNA processing involves mitochondria, which have the complete set of machinery needed to produce their proteins, and their circular DNA molecules (like prokaryotes) lack introns.

DNA is not always transcribed into mRNA; it produces other types of RNA such as *transfer RNA* (tRNA) or *ribosomal RNA* (rRNA). tRNA molecules travel out of the nucleus after transcription, where they are "activated" when a tRNA synthetase enzyme attaches the corresponding amino acid. rRNA (synthesized in the nucleolus within the nucleus), along with a variety of proteins, form the subunits of ribosomes before the subunits migrate out of the nucleus into the cytoplasm.

Mechanism of transcription:
RNA polymerase, promoters, primer not required

Transcription (DNA → RNA) transforms the information in stable DNA into dynamic mRNA, a necessary component for the production of protein.

A segment of DNA with upstream promoter region where RNA polymerase binds to initiate transcription

Transcription takes place in the nucleus, where DNA to be transcribed into an "open" conformation, uncoiling and thus exposing the template strand. DNA is usually tightly bound to histones, but the binding of histone deacetylases causes a conformational change in the DNA-histone complex, allowing the association to become loose and open. In an open conformation, exposed DNA promoter regions are likely to be recognized by transcription factors. The *promoter* is regions on DNA where the RNA polymerase binds to begin transcription of mRNA. Promoters are often found at 30, 75, and 90 nucleotide base pairs upstream (towards the 5' end) from the *transcription start site* (TSS) where transcription begins.

RNA transcription is influenced by transcription factors that increase the affinity of the RNA polymerase and the rate of mRNA synthesis as enhancers or decrease the rate as inhibitors

RNA polymerase uncoils DNA to expose the template strand and processes from 3' to 5' along the DNA, incorporating free ribonucleotide triphosphates (NTPs) into the growing mRNA strand, where these NTPs (ATP, CTP, GTP or UTP) become ribonucleotides. Since RNA polymerase moves from the 3' to the 5' end of a particular DNA template sequence, the RNA transcript is synthesized in a 5' to 3' direction (same as in DNA synthesis), which require a free 3'–OH end.

The direction of transcription with bases added to the 3' end of mRNA

The mRNA strand is complementary to the DNA template and the same as the DNA coding strand (except uracil replaces thymine). Phosphodiester bonds link ribonucleotides as is DNA, but with ribose sugars instead of deoxyribose as for DNA.

RNA polymerization creates transcripts that must dissociate from the template DNA. A short portion of the RNA is base paired with the DNA for the correct sequence to be polymerized, but otherwise, the 5' end of the RNA transcript is not hydrogen bonded to the template strand of the DNA double strand. The strands of DNA then reform their double helix once the newly synthesized RNA dissociates from the DNA.

Unlike DNA polymerase III, RNA polymerase does not require a primer to initiate synthesis; the stretch of DNA template strand that encodes for a single RNA transcript is the *transcription unit* (i.e., promoter, RNA-coding sequence, and terminator).

In addition to the promoter and TSS, eukaryotes can contain a *TATA box* (or *Hogness box*) in their promoter, which is a specialized sequence of thymine and adenine nucleotides. Eukaryotic transcription requires special proteins, or *transcription factors*, to control and enable transcription. Many of these transcription factors bind at the TATA box to regulate transcription. Not all genes have a TATA box. The *transcription initiation complex* is the complete assembly of transcription factors and RNA polymerase bound to the DNA.

Prokaryotes do not require transcription factors; the RNA polymerase recognizes the promoter and begins transcription. *Pribnow box* is a sequence in their promoter similar to the TATA box.

Termination of transcription occurs when RNA polymerization ends, and the RNA transcript is released from the DNA coding strand. Termination in prokaryotes occurs when the RNA polymerase transcribes the *terminator* sequence. Termination is not well understood in eukaryotes, but it includes various protein factors that interact with the DNA strand and the RNA polymerase. Transcription in eukaryotes usually proceeds at least 30 base pairs after the RNA stop codon, and termination usually occurs in one of two ways. *Intrinsic termination* is where specific sequences, *termination sites*, create a stem-loop in the RNA that causes the RNA to dissociate from the DNA template strand. The second mechanism is *rho (ρ) dependent termination*, where the ρ protein factor travels along the synthesized RNA and dislodges the RNA polymerase off the DNA template strand.

Cells produce thousands of copies of the same RNA transcripts. Since there are so many transcripts available for translation, protein synthesis occurs more quickly than if translation were to occur along a single mRNA. In both prokaryotes and eukaryotes, multiple RNA polymerases can transcribe the same template simultaneously.

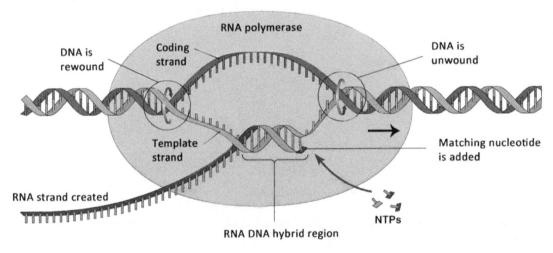

RNA polymerase synthesizes a single strand of RNA complementary to DNA template strand

Summary of transcription:

1. RNA polymerase binds to the promoter region on the DNA, initiating transcription.

2. RNA polymerase uncoils and separates the DNA strands as it synthesizes the RNA strand in a 5' to 3' direction.

3. One DNA strand is used as a template (antisense strand). The other strand (coding strand) is not used but has the same sequence as the RNA transcript (sense strand), except with thymine (in DNA) instead of uracil (in RNA).

4. Free nucleoside triphosphates (NTP) are incorporated, losing two of their phosphates. The new RNA nucleotides temporarily form base pairs with the template DNA.

5. The terminator sequence causes the RNA polymerase to stop transcription and separate from the DNA, and the DNA rewinds.

6. RNA destined for protein translation is messenger RNA (mRNA).

7. mRNA processes in the nucleus with splicing (remove introns and join exons), adding 5' G–cap and 3' poly–A tail.

8. Processed mRNA migrates through nuclear pores to enter the nucleus for translation into protein.

Ribozymes, spliceosomes, small nuclear ribonucleoproteins (snRNP), small nuclear RNA (snRNA)

RNA splicing is necessary for the production of processed mRNA. Originally it was thought that eukaryotic genomes are completely continuous (as bacterial genomes), but in the late 1970s, sequencing technology became sophisticated enough to allow the comparison of vertebrate mRNA and DNA sequences. The results replaced the hypothesis that mRNA is a direct copy of DNA and marked the first real conception of differential gene expression. A remarkable facet of eukaryotic biology is that every cell has the same genetic information but is capable of making completely different proteins. For example, a duct cell in the kidney makes certain proteins that allow the passage of ions across a membrane to direct the flow of water, but a neuron (using the same genome) synthesizes completely different proteins to maintain and harness a membrane potential.

Splicing does not often decide cell fate, but it does allow for the synthesis of different proteins from the same DNA template by ligating (joining) exons and removing introns. *Small nuclear RNA* (snRNA) are special types of RNA that combine with proteins to form *small nuclear ribonucleoproteins* (snRNPs), which make up *spliceosomes*, the complexes that perform RNA splicing. The spliceosome recognizes splice sites (exon and intron boundaries) and enzymatically forms stretches of RNA as *lariats* from the intron sequences. The lariat is then cleaved from the transcript, and the remaining exons are ligated together. Splicing, like all mRNA processing, occurs in the nucleus, separate from the ribosomes. After the RNA is fully processed, it is exported from the nucleus via nuclear pores into the cytoplasm to be translated. Splicing does not occur in bacteria since they do not have introns; instead, translation often occurs immediately after transcription since both processes are in the nucleus.

Alternative splicing allows an array of unique mRNAs to be generated from the same primary RNA transcript. A change in the splice recognition site can cause a putative exon in a different transcript to become an intron in another transcript (i.e., cell type or stage of development). In this way, different proteins can be constructed by shuffling exons. This is done by selectively removing parts of a primary RNA transcript and arranging different combinations; as a result, each mRNA encodes for a different protein.

DNA alternative splicing allows the same genome to transcribe tissue or developmentally-specific proteins for specific functions

In 1989, American scientists Sidney Altman and Thomas Cech were awarded the Nobel Prize for their discovery that some RNA molecules have an enzymatic function. *Ribozymes* are RNA molecules that include the snRNA involved in RNA splicing and the RNA molecules in the protozoan *Tetrahymena*, which catalyze condensation and hydrolysis of phosphodiester bonds. It is postulated that RNA has served as both the genetic material and as enzymes in early life forms. The ribozyme suggests that RNA is the answer to the persistent uncertainty about whether DNA or RNA came first in evolutionary history.

Functional and evolutionary importance of introns

The role of RNA non-coding (intronic) regions of the genome is still contested. Molecular biology is moving toward understanding that these regions are important in the regulation of gene products. Intron sequences often contain short stretches of RNA, small interfering RNA (siRNA), which have important effects in regulating gene expression. The evolutionary importance of the noncontinuity of the genome is controversial. Some researchers assert that because spliceosome-splicing is not conserved in prokaryotes, it can have limited importance to the origin of species. However, others hypothesize that the ability to shuffle genes is important to the evolution of unique phenotypes within a population.

Introns can provide important evolutionary advantages, particularly because they can enable alternative splicing. For example, the thyroid and pituitary glands use the same primary mRNA transcript, but via alternative splicing produce different proteins. Investigators have found that the simpler the eukaryote, the less likely is the presence of introns. Though introns are mostly restricted to eukaryotes, an intron has been discovered in the gene for a tRNA molecule in the cyanobacterium *Anabaena*; this particular intron is *self-splicing* (similar to a ribozyme) and capable of splicing itself out of an RNA transcript.

Notes for active learning

Notes for active learning

Translation

Roles of mRNA, tRNA, and rRNA; RNA base-pairing specificity

Messenger RNA (mRNA) molecules containing information transcribed from DNA are transported into the cytosol from the nucleus after processing (e.g., 5' cap, 3' poly-A tail and splicing – removal of introns and ligation of exons). The mRNA contains the information necessary for ribosomes to assemble amino acids into polypeptides, the building blocks of proteins.

Translational control occurs in the cytoplasm after mRNA leaves the nucleus, but before there is a protein product. The life expectancy of mRNA molecules and their ability to bind ribosomes can vary. The longer an active mRNA molecule remains in the cytoplasm; the more proteins are synthesized. Some mRNAs may need additional changes before they are translated.

Ribonucleases are enzymes that degrade RNA (e.g., mRNA). Mature mRNA molecules contain a 5'–cap and 3'– poly-A tail, non-coding segments that influence how long the mRNA can avoid being degraded by ribonucleases. An example of translational control is mature mammalian red blood cells that eject their nucleus, but synthesize hemoglobin protein for several months, so the mRNAs in red blood cells must persist during this time since no additional RNA is transcribed. Another example of translational control involves frog eggs that contain mRNA as "masked messengers" that are not translated until fertilization occurs. When fertilization of the frog egg occurs, the mRNA is "unmasked" ,and there is a rapid synthesis of proteins.

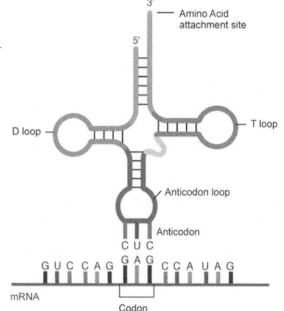

Transfer RNA (tRNA) is the interpreter of the codons contained in a mRNA. tRNA associate each three-nucleotide anticodon with a particular amino acid and transfer the corresponding amino acids to growing polypeptides. tRNA carries a single amino acid on its 3' end and have an anticodon segment. An *anticodon* (contained within the *anticodon loop*) is a special three-nucleotide sequence on the tRNA molecule that base-pairs with a complementary three-nucleotide codon on the mRNA. After a tRNA activated with an amino acid base pairs (via hydrogen bonds) with a codon, the ribosome incorporates the amino acid into the growing polypeptide. The tRNA, now free from the amino acid which is part of the growing polypeptide, dissociates and returns to the cytoplasm, ready to become charged by binding another specific amino acid at its 3'– end.

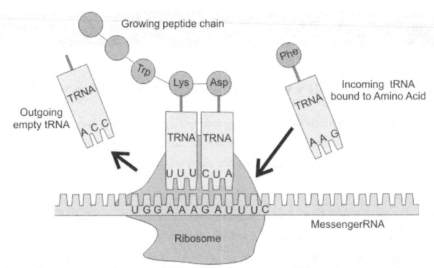

Peptide synthesis using codons on mRNA and anticodons on tRNA with associated amino acids

There are many tRNA with specific anticodons which are complementary to codons. A tRNA-activating enzyme (aminoacyl tRNA synthetase) charges the 3'−end of a tRNA with the correct amino acid, a process of *aminoacylation*. There are twenty tRNA-activating enzymes, corresponding to each of the 20 unique amino acids. The different chemical properties and three-dimensional structures of each type of tRNA allow the tRNA-activating enzymes to recognize their specific tRNA. When the amino acid is attached to the tRNA molecule, a high-energy bond is created using ATP. The energy stored from this high energy bond is used to transfer and bind the amino acids to the growing polypeptide chain during translation.

A recent analysis of entire genomes revealed that some organisms do not have genes for all twenty aminoacyl-tRNA synthetases. They do, however, use all twenty amino acids to construct their proteins. The solution, as is often the case in living cells, is that more complex mechanisms are used. For instance, some bacteria do not have an enzyme for charging glutamine onto its tRNA. Instead, a single enzyme adds glutamic acid to the glutamic acid tRNA molecules and the glutamine tRNA molecules. A second enzyme then converts the glutamic acid into glutamine on the latter tRNA molecules, forming the proper pairing of the tRNA with the amino acid.

The third base of a mRNA codon is the *wobble position* because there is some "flexibility" in the third position of codon-anticodon (hydrogen bonding) base pairing. For example, the base U of a tRNA anticodon in the third position can base pair with either A or G. However, the most versatile tRNA have the modified base inosine (I) in the wobble position, because inosine can form hydrogen bonds with U, C or A. Wobble explains why degenerate (synonymous) codons for a given amino acid differ by the third position. It allows a tRNA holding a particular amino acid to potentially bind to multiple codons with a different third base, that each encodes for the same amino acid specific to that tRNA.

Ribosomal RNA (rRNA) is synthesized from a DNA template in the nucleolus (organelle within the nucleus). Many proteins are transported from their site of synthesis in the cytoplasm into the nucleus, where rRNA and proteins form the small subunit (the 30S for prokaryotes and 40S for eukaryotes) and the large subunit (50S for prokaryotes and 60S for eukaryotes) of the complete ribosome. These two subunits travel out to the cytoplasm through the nuclear pores, where they join to form the complete ribosome (the 70S for prokaryotes and 80S for eukaryotes) when translation occurs. Each ribosome is composed of dozens of associated proteins. The "S" stands for Svedberg units, which measures density and corresponds to the sedimentation value during configuration of particles.

tRNA and rRNA composition and structure (e.g., RNA nucleotides)

Each tRNA molecule is a single strand containing 75 to 95 nucleotides, and particular sequences on this single strand form base pairs with other parts of the molecule, forming a tightly-compacted T-shaped structure. Most of the ribonucleotides in tRNA are the normally-occurring RNA bases (A, C, G, and U), but there are some variant bases, such as pseudouridine, that result from modifications (alkylation, methylation, and glycosylation) to the typical bases that occur after RNA transcription. These modified bases, which usually occur in restricted sites of the tRNA molecule, allow for the formation of unusual base pairs.

tRNA with amino acid joined at the 3'−OH end, creating a phosphodiester bond

The secondary (two-dimensional) structure of a tRNA molecule resembles a cloverleaf while the tertiary (three-dimensional) structure is L-shaped. Five regions in tRNA are not base-paired: the CCA acceptor stem, the D-loop, the TΨC loop, the anticodon loop, and the extra arm.

The nucleotide sequence CCA is at the 3'−OH end of the tRNA and allows for the attachment of an amino acid by a phosphodiester bond, creating a charged tRNA. Which amino acid is attached depends on the anticodon, the three-base sequence binding to a complementary triplet codon on the mRNA according to the base-pairing rules. Each tRNA has a slightly different chemical property and three-dimensional structure, which allows the tRNA-activating enzyme to attach the correct amino acid to the 3'−OH end of the tRNA. The cell's cytoplasm contains all twenty amino acids either by synthesizing them or importing them into the cell.

Ribosomal RNAs, which are structural components of the ribosome, perform critical functions for protein synthesis. rRNAs are synthesized in the nucleolus, while ribosomal proteins are synthesized in the cytoplasm and are brought to the nucleolus to be joined with the rRNAs for the assembly of the two ribosomal subunits: the *large subunit* and the *small subunit*. The rRNA in the large subunit has ribozyme activity and catalyzes the formation of peptide bonds between adjacent amino acids. The secondary structure of rRNA is extensive, and it plays an important role in recognizing tRNA and mRNA that bind to the ribosome. Secondary rRNA structure has been conserved throughout evolution. Prokaryotes contain 16S (in small subunit), 23S and 5S (both in the large subunit) rRNA, while eukaryotes contain 18S (in small subunit) and 5S, 5.8S, 28S (in large subunit).

Role and structure of ribosomes

The ribosome is composed of a few rRNA molecules and many proteins. Each ribosome consists of a small subunit and a large subunit. Prokaryotic ribosomes are the 70S (30S small subunit + 50S large subunit), while eukaryotic ribosomes are 80S (40S small subunit + 60S large subunit). Note that the Svedberg units for the subunits do not add up to the total sedimentation coefficient for the whole ribosome due to differences in density of the complete structure compared to the individual subunits.

In ribosomes, the ribonucleotide sequence of mRNA is interpreted and synthesized into an amino acid sequence. The mRNA strand fits into a groove on the small subunit with the bases pointing toward the large subunit. The ribosome acts as a "reader," and when it reaches a termination sequence in the mRNA, the link between the synthesized polypeptide chain and tRNA is broken. Then, the completed polypeptide is released from the ribosome.

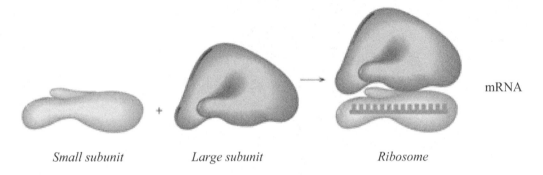

Small subunit   *Large subunit*   *Ribosome*

Ribosomes can float freely in the cytosol or attach to the endoplasmic reticulum (ER); the *rough ER* is due to its appearance caused by the ribosomes studding its surface. Prokaryotic cells contain about 10,000 ribosomes, and eukaryotic cells contain many times more. Ribosomes have binding sites for mRNA and tRNA molecules.

Free ribosomes synthesize proteins that are primarily used within the cytosol of the cell. As small proteins emerge from the ribosome, they undergo folding. Larger proteins fold within the recess of small, hollow chambers in proteins as *chaperones*. *Bound ribosomes* on the rough endoplasmic reticulum usually synthesize proteins used for the secretory pathway (e.g., secreted from the cell, embedded into membranes or targeted for organelles). Multiple ribosomes can simultaneously translate the same mRNA with elongating polypeptides of different lengths about the ribosomes' progress. A group of ribosomes on a single RNA is a *polyribosome* (polysome). However, mRNA molecules cannot be translated indefinitely and are eventually degraded into ribonucleotides by cytoplasmic enzymes.

A ribosome has three sites that can each hold a tRNA: the *E* (exit) *site*, *P* (peptidyl) *site* and *A* (aminoacyl) *site*. The sites are in the order of the E site on the 5' of the mRNA held by the ribosome and the A site on the 3'– side. The E site holds a discharged tRNA that is ready for dissociation, the P site tRNA holds the growing polypeptide, and the A site tRNA holds the next amino acid to be added to the polypeptide chain.

Initiation and termination co-factors

Translation, the process by which a mRNA nucleotide sequence is read as triplet codons to assemble a polypeptide chain, involves three steps: chain initiation, elongation, and termination. The mRNA codons base pair with the tRNA anticodons, which represent specific amino acids based on the nucleotide sequence. Enzymes are required for all three steps, and energy is needed for the first two steps. Once the polypeptide is fully formed and translation has terminated, the ribosome then dissociates into its two subunits.

Chain initiation is the first step in translation. Before translation begins, the two subunits of the ribosome are not yet combined. They are assembled separately in the nucleus and travel through the pores of the nuclear envelope and combine in the cytoplasm to form a functional ribosome when translation starts. Since translation moves 5' to 3' along the mRNA strand, the small subunit first binds the 5' end of the mRNA. The subunit moves along the transcript until it finds the start codon, AUG. The tRNA for AUG (attached amino acid is methionine) hybridizes to the start codon using its anticodon, and the large subunit binds the small subunit, forming the complete ribosome. This first tRNA is the *initiator tRNA*.

Initiation factor proteins drive this initial binding. The activity of these factors regulates the rate of protein synthesis. The initiation phase is the slowest of the three phases of the assembly process.

Chain elongation is the process of adding new amino acids to the growing polypeptide chain. After initiation, the tRNA holding the first amino acid (methionine) is bound to the P site.

The A site is now empty and has an exposed codon for the next amino acid. The tRNA with the appropriate anticodon then binds the A site, which requires hydrolysis of a GTP. *Elongation factor* proteins facilitate this base pairing. With the two amino acids on the tRNAs now nearby, the methionine forms a peptide bond with the amino acid held in the A site, dissociating from the tRNA in the P site at the same time. A ribozyme catalyzes this transfer in the large subunit. The tRNA in the A site now holds two amino acids, with the methionine at the N-terminus (the end with the free amino group) of the growing polypeptide and the newest amino acid attached to the tRNA.

The mRNA transcript now slides through the ribosome, 3 ribonucleotides forward. The tRNA anticodons are still associated with their matching codons, so this movement causes the tRNA to move sites, a process of *translocation*. The discharged tRNA in the P site moves to the E site, and the tRNA holding the growing polypeptide moves to the P site. The A site is now empty and ready for a charged tRNA to recognize the next codon. As the tRNA holding the next amino acid binds the A site, the discharged tRNA in the E site dissociates away from the ribosome, where it is free to associate to a new amino acid in the cytoplasm.

A peptide bond attaches the newly-arrived amino acid. After translocation, the tRNA attached to the recent amino acid moves into the P site, and the tRNA formerly attached to A site moves to the E site and is released. An amino acid–tRNA complex is in the P site.

This process of elongation continues as more codons on the mRNA move through the ribosome. The growing polypeptide chain elongates and is passed from tRNA to incoming tRNA, and the N-terminus of the polypeptide emerges. This elongation step is rapid and occurs about 15 times per second in *E. coli*.

The elongation repeats until the ribosome eventually reaches one of three stop codons on the mRNA, which leads to *chain termination*. No tRNA anticodons recognize the stop codons; instead, *release factors* bind to the stop codon, causing translation to stop. This binding causes the addition of a water molecule instead of an amino acid to the polypeptide chain. The polypeptide chain is released, the uncharged tRNA dissociates from the ribosome, and the ribosomal subunits dissociate.

Summary of translation:

1. mRNA attaches to a small subunit of the ribosome and binds to a charged tRNA molecule (with an attached amino acid) based on its specific codon sequence.

2. The large subunit of ribosome joins the complex.

3. Initiator tRNA resides in P site of the ribosome, and a new tRNA recognizes the next codon sequence on mRNA and attaches to the A site of the ribosome.

4. A peptide bond is formed between the amino acid attached to the tRNA in the P site and the amino acid attached to the tRNA in the A site.

5. The uncharged tRNA in the P site moves to the E site, where it is then released, and the tRNA in the A site moves to the P site.

6. Another tRNA binds to the A site, and the pattern continues, creating a growing polypeptide chain until a termination codon is reached.

Post-translational modification of protein

Post-translational control regulates the activity of the protein in the cell after translation. For a polypeptide product of translation to become a functional protein, post-translational modifications are made. These modifications include bending and twisting the chain into the correct three-dimensional shape (protein folding), sometimes facilitated by chaperone molecules. The growing polypeptide folds into its tertiary structure, forming disulfide links, salt bridges, or other interactions that make the polypeptide a biologically-active protein. Other changes include additions to the polypeptide chain, such as carbohydrate or lipid derivatives that may be covalently attached when the functional protein is folded. The initial amino acid methionine is often removed from the beginning of the polypeptide. Some molecules are composed of multiple polypeptide chains that must be joined to achieve the final protein (quaternary structure).

Post-translational control may involve degradation to "activate" a protein. For example, the bovine protein proinsulin is inactive when first translated, but after a sequence of 30 amino acids is removed from the middle of the chain and disulfide bonds join the two pieces, the protein becomes active. In other cases, proteins are degraded to cause deactivation. *Proteasomes* (enzymes that target proteins) are large protein complexes that carry out this task. For example, cyclins that control the cell cycle are present temporarily and must be degraded.

Proteins to be secreted from a cell have a signal sequence that binds to a specific membrane protein on the surface of the rough endoplasmic reticulum. Early during translation, the protein is fed into the lumen of the rough ER;

the signal sequence is removed. Once the protein is properly folded in the rough endoplasmic reticulum, portions of the endoplasmic reticulum bud off, forming vesicles that contain the properly folded protein. The vesicles migrate to the Golgi apparatus and fuse with the Golgi membrane. Within the Golgi, carbohydrates and other groups may be added or removed according to final destinations of the proteins (almost all secreted proteins are glycoproteins). The proteins are then again packaged into vesicles that bud off the surface of the Golgi membrane and may travel to the plasma membrane (secretory pathway), where they fuse and release their contents in the extracellular fluid through *exocytosis.*

Notes for active learning

Eukaryotic Chromosome Organization

Chromosomal proteins and supercoiling

Histones are positively-charged chromosomal proteins responsible for the compact packing and winding of chromosomal negatively-charged DNA. A histone protein octamer and a histone H1 protein (nucleosome) form a protein core around which DNA winds to achieve a compact state. Nonhistone chromosomal proteins are associated with the chromosomes. They have various functions, such as regulatory and enzymatic roles. An active area of research is chromatin remodeling via histones to regulate gene expression within cells.

A chromosome consists of a single DNA molecule wound tightly around thousands of *histone* proteins. The basic unit of compact DNA is a *nucleosome*, which consists of negatively-charged DNA wound around a positively-charged histone octamer core and held in place by an additional histone H1. A nucleosome consists of two H2A, two H2B, two H3, two H4 and one H1 histone.

The nucleosome consists of an octamer and a histone H1 between the linked regions of the chromosome

Chromatin is a strand of nucleic acid and associated protein. A nucleosome is a bead-like unit made of DNA wound around a complex of histone proteins. When DNA is wrapped around several of these nucleosomes in sequence, the resulting structure looks like beads on a string.

Nucleosomes form the basic unit of coiling in DNA. In turn, these nucleosomes then form higher-order coils, as *supercoils*. The level of supercoiling influences transcription, with a decreasing level of transcription for more compacted DNA. Human DNA is separated into 46 compact, supercoiled pieces (organized into 23 pairs) with the help of nucleosomes and other proteins. These separate pieces of nucleic acid comprise the chromosomes.

Single copy vs. repetitive DNA

Highly repetitive base sequences in DNA are between 5 and 300 nucleotide bases long and may be repeated up to 10,000 times. They are not translated into proteins. Highly repetitive base sequences constitute 5–45% of eukaryotic DNA. Single-copy genes (unique genes) are transcribed and translated to constitute a small proportion of eukaryotic DNA.

Centromeres

A *centromere* is a region of heterochromatin on the chromosome that can be at the center (metacentric) or close to one of the ends (telocentric). After replication, sister chromatids are attached at the centromere. During mitosis, spindle fibers (comprised of tubulin) are attached to the centromere (via the kinetochore) and pull the sister chromatids apart during anaphase. During anaphase of mitosis, the centromere splits and the sister chromatids become chromosomes in the daughter cell during cell division.

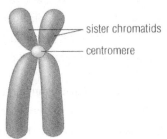

One chromosome with two sister chromatids attached at the centromere

Notes for active learning

Notes for active learning

Control of Gene Expression in Eukaryotes

Transcription regulation

Transcriptional control in the nucleus determines which structural genes are transcribed as well as the rate of their transcription. It includes the organization of chromatin and the protein transcription factors initiating transcription. Regulatory proteins include repressors and activators, and they influence the attachment of RNA polymerase to the promoter region on the DNA.

RNA transcription is influenced by transcription factor proteins that increase the affinity of the RNA polymerase and the rate of mRNA synthesis as enhancers or inhibitors

DNA binding proteins and transcription factors

Transcription factors are positively charged proteins that have DNA-binding domains that allow them to bind to the promoter, enhancer and silencer regions of DNA to regulate transcription. *Enhancers* increase transcription when bound, while *silencers* decrease it.

Transcription factors can be influenced by intracellular or extracellular signals, accounting for the wide variation in gene expression in different cell types. Many pathways and types of signals exist to influence the activity of transcription factors, including the allosteric regulation of proteins as well as covalent modifications by kinases, phosphatases, and other enzymes. The DNA-binding domains themselves are varied in the way they interact with the DNA double helix. Some common domains include the helix-turn-helix (HTH), the zinc finger, and the basic-region leucine zipper (bZIP).

Pre-initiation complex forms when transcription factors gather at the promoter region (segment of DNA where RNA polymerase binds) adjacent to a structural gene. The transcription factor complex leads to activation (or repression) of the gene. The complex may attract and bind RNA polymerase, or even promote the separation of DNA strands, but transcription may or may not begin at this point, depending on which transcription factors (activators or repressors) are bound.

While promoters are generally close to the affected gene in both prokaryotes and eukaryotes, eukaryotic regulatory elements (i.e., enhancers and silencers) can be far from the promoter – even thousands of nucleotides away along the DNA strand that bends to stabilize the structure. This is not true for prokaryotic regulatory elements. Since the enhancers and silencers must interact with the promoter to influence transcription, eukaryotic DNA can loop back on itself so that the transcription factor bound to the enhancer or silencer can make contact with the promoter or RNA polymerase. Intermediate proteins between the transcription factors and RNA polymerase are often involved in the process.

Eukaryotes differ in that they lack certain special transcription regulation mechanisms in bacteria, such as the operon (except in rare cases) and attenuation. The *operon* (e.g., *lac* or *trp* operon) is a cluster of tandem genes in bacterial DNA under the control of a single promoter. Transcription of the operon results in several genes being transcribed simultaneously. *Attenuation* is a process where transcription and mRNA structure can influence ribosome translation. It is possible in prokaryotes because transcription and translation can occur simultaneously. In eukaryotes, the two processes are separate; transcription occurs in the nucleus and translation occurs in the cytoplasm.

Gene amplification and duplication

Gene duplication (gene amplification or chromosomal duplication) is a mechanism by which genetic material is duplicated and can serve as a source for molecular evolution. There are many ways in which gene duplication can occur. *Ectopic recombination* occurs during unequal crossing over between homologous chromosomes (during meiosis) due to the DNA sequence similarity at duplication breakpoints.

Replication slippage arises from an error in DNA replication; the DNA polymerase dissociates and then reattaches to the DNA at an incorrect position and mistakenly duplicates a section. *Aneuploidy* (an abnormal number of chromosomes, often harmful) is another example of gene duplication, as is *polyploidy* (whole genome duplications), which are both due to *nondisjunction*, the failure of sister chromatids (i.e., mitosis) or homologous chromosomes (i.e., meiosis) to separate properly during cell division.

Gene duplication may be evolutionarily advantageous because it creates genetic redundancy, and a mutation in the second copy of a gene may not have harmful effects on the organism because the original gene can still function to encode functional protein products. Since mutations of the second copy of a gene are not directly harmful, mutations accumulate more rapidly (in the duplicated region) than usual, and the second copy of the gene can even develop a new function. Therefore, gene duplication is believed to have played an important role in evolution.

Point mutations are common in duplicated regions and may accelerate the evolution of new proteins

Post-transcriptional control, the basic concept of splicing (introns, exons)

Post-transcriptional control occurs in the nucleus after DNA has been transcribed and mRNA has formed. In this regulation, the RNA strands are processed before they leave the nucleus with certain variations for a particular effect in the cell.

Timing is one form of control. The speed at which mRNAs leave the nucleus affects the ultimate amount of gene product available per unit of time. Various mRNA molecules may differ in the rate they travel through the nuclear pores. Additionally, mRNA must eventually be degraded, and the rate and timing of mRNA degradation, controlled by the cell, affect how much protein is translated. Some modifications, such as the addition of a 5' cap and a 3' poly-A tail, affect control by protecting the mRNA from ribonuclease degradation.

Post-transcriptional control affects the sequences present in the final RNA products. Alternative splicing is the process by which introns are removed (cut from the transcript), and exons are ligated (rejoined) in different ways, forming different mRNA products from the same initial hnRNA transcript. Both the hypothalamus and the thyroid gland contain the gene that encodes for the peptide hormone calcitonin, but the mRNA that leaves the nucleus, and therefore the translated protein, are not the same in both types of cells.

Alternative splicing of the calcitonin gene occurs in the hypothalamus, leading to the production of a distantly-related peptide, calcitonin-gene-related peptide (CGRP), while the thyroid gland produces regular calcitonin. Radioactive labeling experiments show different splicing in these strands. Evidence of alternative splicing has been found in cells that produce neurotransmitters, muscle regulatory proteins, and antibodies. Additionally, experiments indicate that alternative splicing occurs at different stages of development (i.e., embryogenic vs. adult cells).

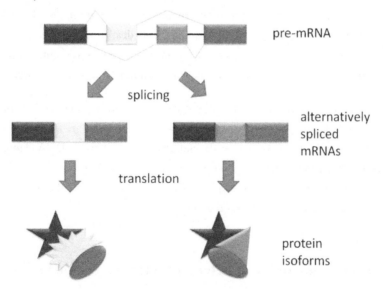

Different types of RNA are subject to post-transcriptional control. For example, special modifications to nucleotides are made to control the structure of tRNA and rRNA.

Cancer as a failure of normal cellular controls, oncogenes and tumor suppressor genes

Cancer is a disorder that arises from mutations in the somatic cells and results from the failure of the control system that regulates cell division, which leads to uncontrolled growth. Cancer may develop in different tissues and has special terminology depending on the location and the way it develops. *Carcinomas* are cancers in epithelial cells, *sarcomas* are cancers in muscle cells, and *lymphomas* are cancers involving white blood cells. The lungs, colon, and breasts are the organs most commonly affected by cancer. The incidence of cancer increases with age due to the accumulation of defective mutations (i.e., mutagen exposure or errors during DNA replication).

Oncogenes are dominant cancer-producing genes that encode for abnormal forms of cell surface receptors that bind growth factors, producing a continuous growth signal. Oncogenes cause cancer when they are activated. The products of many oncogenes are involved in increasing cell division. Before an oncogene is activated, it may be a harmless *proto-oncogene*. Researchers have identified many proto-oncogenes whose mutation to an oncogene cause increased growth and leads to tumor formation. The *ras* (lowercase for a gene and capitalized for reference to the corresponding protein) family of genes is the most common group of oncogenes implicated in human cancers. The alteration of one nucleotide pair converts a normal functioning *ras* proto-oncogene to an oncogene.

Tumor suppressor genes are recessive cancer-producing genes with mutated forms. Tumor suppressor genes protect cells from becoming cancerous by inhibiting tumor formation through the control of cell division. Mutations in tumor suppressor genes alter the protective proteins encoded by these genes and disrupt their function and thus can lead to cancer. A *tumor* is an abnormal replication of cells that form a mass of tissue. If the cells remain localized, the tumor is *benign* (i.e., remains localized), but if the tumor invades the surrounding tissue because it undergoes metastasis, it is *malignant*.

A major tumor-suppressor gene, *p53*, is more frequently mutated in human cancers than any other known gene. The p53 protein acts as a transcription factor to turn on the expression of genes whose products are cell cycle inhibitors. The p53 can stimulate *apoptosis* (i.e., programmed cell death), the ability of cells to self-destruct by autodigestion with endogenous enzymes. In apoptosis, the plasma membrane is kept intact, and the digested contents are not released; instead, phagocytic cells engulf the whole cell to eliminate these undesirable cells.

Cancer cells continue to grow and divide in situations where normal cells would not (lack contact inhibition); they fail to respond to cellular controls and signals that would halt growth in normal cells. Cancer cells avoid the apoptosis (self-destruction) that normal cells undergo when extensive DNA damage is present. Cancer cells stimulate angiogenesis (the formation of new blood vessels) to nourish the cancer cell, and they are immortal (continue to divide for more generations than a normal cell), while normal cells die after some divisions. Cancer cells can *metastasize* (relocate) and then grow in another location.

Chromatin structure: heterochromatin vs. euchromatin

DNA exists as euchromatin and heterochromatin within the cell. *Euchromatin* is a looser conformation of DNA and histones, compared to the tightly-condensed *heterochromatin*. Euchromatin appears lighter than the darker heterochromatin when viewed under an electron microscope. DNA sequences in heterochromatin are generally repressed, while those in euchromatin are available and actively transcribed when the RNA polymerase binds to the single-stranded DNA. Much of the satellite DNA (large, tandem repeats of noncoding DNA) appears in heterochromatin.

Euchromatin is transcribed while heterochromatin is not transcribed

When DNA is transcribed, activators as remodeling proteins can push aside the histone portion of the chromatin, allowing transcription to begin. During interphase (G_1, S and G_2 phase), chromatin exists as either of the two types, but during mitosis, it condenses to supercoiled heterochromatin.

The form of compactness that the DNA adopts depends on the cellular needs of the cell and can be regulated by covalent *histone modifications* by specific enzymes. Examples of modifications are *histone methylation*, which causes tighter packing that prevents transcription, and *histone acetylation*, which involves uncoiling of the DNA and promotes transcription. There are many other types of histone modifications, such as ubiquitination and phosphorylation. As an active area of investigation, the *histone code hypothesis* states that DNA transcription is partly regulated by these histone modifications, especially on the unstructured ends of histones.

Chromatin remodeling complexes is another mechanism for regulating chromatin structure. These protein complexes are ATP-dependent and thus have a common ATPase domain. ATP hydrolysis gives these domains the energy to reposition nucleosomes and move histones, which creates uncoiled DNA regions available for transcription.

DNA methylation

DNA methylation, which reduces the rate of transcription, is another method that the cell uses to regulate gene expression. DNA methyltransferase enzymes add a methyl ($-CH_3$) group to the cytosine bases of DNA, converting these bases to 5-methylcytosine. The methylated cytosine residues are usually adjacent to guanine, which results in methylated cytosines that are diagonal from each other. The patterns of DNA methylation are heritable to daughter cells, as it is passed on during cell division. *Epigenetics* is the study of changes in transcriptional potential (such as DNA methylation and histone modification) that do not involve changes in DNA sequence.

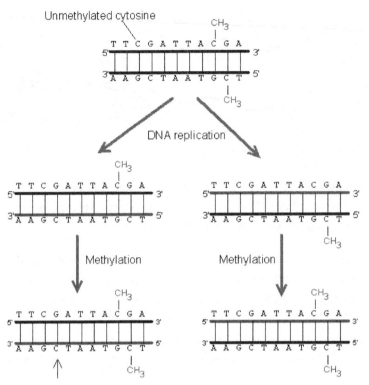

Modifications such as methylation facilitate proper DNA repair

Role of non-coding RNAs

Non-coding RNAs (ncRNA) are functional RNA that is not translated into proteins. They have an important role in many cellular processes, including RNA splicing, DNA replication, and the regulation of gene expression. ncRNA can participate in histone modification, DNA methylation, and heterochromatin formation. The majority of ncRNA are *long ncRNA* (over 200 nucleotides) that form a complex with chromatin-modifying proteins, and function in chromatin remodeling.

There are three classes of *short ncRNA* (less than 30 nucleotides), including microRNA (miRNA), short interfering RNAs and piwi-interacting RNA. *MicroRNAs* (miRNA) are folded RNA molecules with hairpin loops that bind to target mRNA sequences through complementary base pairing. miRNA can induce degradation of the mRNA by shortening its poly-A tail, which destabilizes the mRNA, or they can cleave the mRNA into pieces. This silences the mRNA and prevents translation from occurring. A single miRNA molecule can target and repress several different mRNAs.

Short interfering RNAs (siRNAs) are double-stranded RNA molecules that are often created through catalysis by the Dicer enzyme, which produces siRNAs from longer double-stranded RNAs. siRNAs function similarly to miRNAs, as they interfere with the expression of genes that have complementary sequences. siRNA can degrade mRNA, blocking translation, and can induce heterochromatin formation, blocking transcription.

Piwi-interacting RNAs (piRNA) form RNA-protein complexes with the piwi family of proteins, and they are the largest class of short ncRNA in animal cells. They suppress transposon activity in germline cells through the formation of an *RNA-induced silencing complex*. piRNAs do not have any known secondary structure motifs.

Notes for active learning

Notes for active learning

Recombinant DNA and Biotechnology

Recombinant DNA refers to a genetic material that has been artificially "recombined" from disparate sources. The recombination of these DNA segments can occur by viral transduction, bacterial conjugation, transposons or through artificial recombinant DNA technology. Crossing over during meiosis prophase I produce recombinant chromosomes.

Recombinant DNA plays a significant role in contemporary society. For example, genetically modified crops and many meat sources rely on recombinant DNA technologies. Additionally, several important pharmaceuticals are assembled using recombination technologies. As the techniques available to manipulate genetic material become more sophisticated, recombinant technologies become a larger part of everyday life.

Gene Cloning

A *clone* is a genetically identical organism (or a group of genetically identical cells) derived from a single parent cell. *Gene cloning* refers to the production of identical copies of the same gene. When a gene is cloned, the first step is to extract and purify the DNA from the organism of interest. Then, the gene of interest is introduced into the nucleotide sequence of another organism.

Restriction enzymes (i.e., extracted from bacterial cells) cut double-stranded DNA at specific nucleotide sequences to generate DNA fragments (some with sticky ends). Then, these fragments are incorporated into commercially available bacterial vector plasmids (circular pieces of DNA) that may be cut by the same restriction enzymes, so that the sticky ends hybridize. The plasmid is the vector. The foreign gene is sealed into the vector DNA by the enzyme DNA ligase, and the plasmids are then introduced into bacteria by transformation. Before this, the bacteria must be "made competent" to take up the plasmid; this is done through *electroporation*, where an electric field is used to increase the cell membrane's permeability, or *heat shock*, which increases the fluidity of the membrane, allowing plasmids to travel through the membrane more easily.

After transformation (i.e., an update of DNA by bacterial cell), a screening method, such as the incorporation of an antibiotic-resistant gene on the plasmid and cultivation on an antibiotic-containing medium, is used to identify the colonies that do not have the recombinant DNA. The transformed bacteria are then allowed to grow at optimum conditions, thus creating more copies (i.e., cloning) of the gene of interest.

If a eukaryotic gene is to be expressed in a bacterium, the gene must be accompanied by the regulatory regions unique to bacteria. The eukaryotic gene cannot contain introns, because bacteria do not have the mechanisms necessary to remove introns. If a prokaryotic gene is to be cloned into a mammalian cell, a poly-A tail must be added for the mRNA to survive.

Subcloning is used to move a gene of interest from a parent vector (i.e., source vector) to a destination vector (i.e., target vector). This allows the protein to be expressed within the recombinant cells for the gene's functionality to be further studied.

Restriction enzymes

A *restriction enzyme* (restriction endonuclease) is an enzyme that can recognize and cut double-stranded DNA at specific nucleotide sequences. They are naturally produced by bacteria and archaea to defend the cell (analogous to a primitive immune system) against viruses by destroying viral DNA and restricting the growth of the viruses: "restriction" enzymes. The restriction enzymes synthesized by a strain of bacteria do not recognize "self" and therefore do not cut the endogenous DNA. Therefore, a bacterium is unaffected by its restriction enzymes. Restriction enzymes are usually named for the species from which they were isolated; for example, *Bam*HI was isolated from *Bacillus amyloliquefaciens* strain H, and *Eco*RI was isolated from *E. coli* strain RY13.

Recombinant DNA technology uses restriction enzymes as molecular scissors, cleaving DNA pieces at specific nucleotide palindrome sequences. *Palindrome sequences* read the same from 5' → 3' of one strand and 5' → 3' of the other strand.

The restriction enzyme cuts DNA along the sequence shown by the arrow

Restriction fragments are the resulting fragments of DNA after cleavage by the restriction enzymes. Some restriction enzymes cut to make *blunt ends*, which cannot hybridize. Other restriction enzymes cut at staggered locations to make short single-stranded segments with *sticky ends*, which can hybridize (i.e., anneal by forming hydrogen bonds between the plasmid DNA and the restriction fragment DNA). The "sticky ends" allow for directional insertion of foreign DNA into vector DNA (catalyzed by DNA ligase, which creates phosphodiester bonds between the pieces of DNA).

An example of a blunt end, where N represents one of the four unspecified nucleotides:

```
5'    NNNNNNNATT        AATNNNNNNNNNN 3'
3'    NNNNNNNTAA        TTANNNNNNNNNN5'
```

An example of a sticky end:

```
5'    NNNNNNNNNNNNNNNG        AATTCNNNNNNNNNN 3'
3'    NNNNNNNTTAA        CNNNNNNNNNNNNNNNNNNNN5'
```

The nucleotides at the location of the cut must be the nucleotides specified as the target sequence recognized and cut by a restriction enzyme.

DNA libraries

After DNA is extracted from an organism, a *DNA library* (gene library) can be constructed to organize the DNA of an organism. A DNA library represents, stores and propagates a collection of genes by using live populations of microorganisms; each population contains a different restriction fragment inserted into a cloning vector.

There are different types of DNA libraries. A *genomic library* contains a set of nucleotide clones that represent the full genome of an organism. The number of clones in a genomic library can vary, depending on the size of the genome of that particular organism and the size of the DNA fragment that can be inserted into the particular cloning vector used in the library. Genomic libraries are useful for studying the function of regulatory sequences, introns, untranscribed regions of DNA and for studying genetic mutations that may occur in disease or cancer tissues.

A *cDNA library* represents the genes from a particular organism that are actively being expressed. The cDNA (complementary DNA) is reverse transcribed from expressed mRNA isolated from the cell. This is usually less than 1% of the genome in an organism. cDNA libraries are useful for studying the mRNAs expressed in different cells or tissues, and for detecting alternative splicing of genes.

A *randomized mutant library* is created by the *de novo* synthesis of a gene. While the DNA is being synthesized in the laboratory, alternative nucleotides are added into the sequence at various positions, resulting in a mix of DNA molecules that are variants of the original gene. These different variants are then cloned into vectors, creating the library. Randomized mutant libraries can be used to screen for proteins that have favorable properties, such as improved binding affinity, enzyme activity or stability.

Generation of cDNA

cDNA can be synthesized by the enzyme reverse transcriptase, which synthesizes a DNA copy of processed mRNA. Reverse transcriptase is generally associated with *retroviruses*, which use this enzyme to reverse-transcribe their RNA genome into DNA when infecting a host (e.g., HIV). Reverse transcriptase can naturally be found in viruses, prokaryotes, and eukaryotes. This enzyme is utilized for the mRNA-template synthesis of cDNA, which is necessary for biotechnology for several recombinant techniques.

cDNA does not contain introns. Bacteria can be transfected with cDNA of human genes to produce large quantities of human proteins. For example, mRNA that encodes for insulin is extracted from a human pancreatic cell which produces insulin. cDNA copies are then made from this mRNA by using reverse transcriptase.

Meanwhile, a selected plasmid is cut using the same restriction enzymes. Once the plasmid and the gene are ready, they are combined, and the DNA (gene and plasmid) fragments hybridize. Bacterial host cells are then transformed with recombinant plasmids with the integrated human insulin gene. The bacteria cell then translates the insulin protein, which can then be collected and purified. cDNA, rather than genomic DNA, must be used for this process because bacterial DNA does not have the cellular proteins to undergo splicing (i.e., a mechanism to excise introns and ligate exons).

DNA denaturation, reannealing, hybridization

Double-stranded DNA is reversibly *denatured* into single-stranded DNA when the molecule is subjected to heat or extreme pH, causing the hydrogen bonds linking A−T and C−G complementary nitrogenous bases to disassociate. *Annealing* is the opposite process, where subsequent cooling, or return to physiological pH in the presence of salt, causes the hydrogen bonds to re-associate, forming double-stranded DNA from single-stranded DNA. During *hybridization*, which is an important part of many biotechnology techniques, complementary base pairs anneal by hydrogen bonding.

Expressing cloned genes

Genes are cloned into an expression vector (plasmid or a virus) and are inserted into a host (usually bacteria, but may be yeast, fungi or other eukaryotes). *Expression* of that gene is when the host cells with the donor DNA produce protein from the gene of interest (recombinant) as they undergo normal protein synthesis. When cloned genes are expressed in industrial settings, the goal is to make a large quantity of the protein, so the expression is at an extremely high level as *overexpression*. *The recombinant protein* is the targeted protein that can be subsequently isolated and purified.

Eukaryotic host cell lines (host cells) are used for the production of proteins that require significant post-translational modifications or RNA splicing because prokaryotic cells lack the necessary machinery for these processes. However, using bacteria for protein expression has a distinct advantage because bacterial cells allow for the large-scale production of protein (due to short replication times for bacterial cell growth). Because of the ease of growth, low cost to maintain the cells and short replication cycles, *E. coli* is among the most frequently used hosts for expressing cloned genes.

Polymerase chain reaction (PCR)

Polymerase chain reaction (PCR) was developed in 1983 by Kary Mullis. It can exponentially generate millions of copies of a specific piece of DNA in a test tube. PCR is specific, so the targeted DNA sequence can be less than one part in a million of the total DNA sample. Even a single gene can be amplified. There are several components necessary for PCR. One component is the DNA template that contains the DNA region to be amplified. Additionally, two primers (short strands of DNA, usually between 14 and 20 nucleotides) that are complementary to the 3' ends of the coding and template strand of the DNA target are needed ("forward" and "reverse" primer, respectively). The enzyme DNA polymerase replicates the DNA during PCR, and DNA polymerase requires primers to initiate synthesis.

PCR involves high temperatures, so the DNA polymerase enzyme must be able to withstand heat without being denatured. *Taq* polymerase from *Thermus aquaticus* (the bacterium that lives in hot thermal springs) is frequently used. Other important components of PCR are the deoxynucleoside triphosphates (dNTP – dATP, dGTP, dCTP and dTTP); these are the four "building blocks" used by DNA polymerase while synthesizing a complementary strand of

DNA. These dNTPs lose two phosphate groups when they are incorporated into the growing strand, and become adenine, guanine, cytosine, and thymine. PCR uses a buffer solution that contains cations (often Mg^{2+}), which are required to stabilize the DNA polymerase as it binds to the complementary strand of the negatively-charged DNA sample to be amplified.

PCR involves three steps. First is denaturation, where heat is applied (about 94 °C) to separate the double-stranded DNA template. Annealing is where the mixture is cooled (about 54 °C) for primers to hybridize (anneal) to the now single-stranded DNA template. Excessive primers are added so that they outcompete in re-annealing of the parent DNA strands that were separated during the initial heating. The last step is elongation (about 72 °C), where heat-stable DNA polymerase extends the primers along the respective target DNA strands. Several rounds of PCR (usually 20 to 30) are performed to create large quantities of the amplified DNA fragment.

Polymerase Chain Reaction: temperatures depend on DNA sample and primers

PCR amplification and subsequent DNA analysis are often used to detect viral infections, genetic disorders, and cancer. It is used to determine the nucleotide sequence of human genes (e.g., Human Genome Project) and in the study of heredity. PCR can use DNA from any source, including blood, semen, and various tissues, so it is useful in forensics when only a small amount of DNA is available, but a large amount is required to undergo testing. If only two copies of a DNA fragment undergo 30 rounds of PCR, the result is $2^{30} = 1,073,741,824$ copies of the DNA fragment. A limitation of PCR amplification is in the fidelity (i.e., mistakes involving mismatching between the new and parent strand) because the heat-resistant bacterial DNA polymerases for PCR amplification lack the proofreading ability of the eukaryotic polymerases.

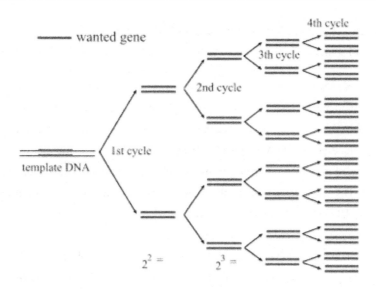

Gel electrophoresis; Southern, Northern and Western blotting

In *gel electrophoresis*, macromolecules such as DNA, RNA, and proteins are separated (resolved) by size or charge. The macromolecules move through an agarose or polyacrylamide gel due to an applied electric field consisting of a negative charge on one end and a positive charge at the other end. DNA is negatively charged, so it moves away from a negative cathode toward a positive anode. Electrophoresis uses an electrolytic cell so the charge of the cathode is negative and the anode is positive. Based on function, shorter fragments of DNA move further than larger DNA fragments, and during gel electrophoresis, the DNA molecules are resolved according to size, resulting in a visible pattern of bands. The same separation based upon size is observed for RNA, proteins or macromolecules.

A *molecular weight ruler*, or *DNA ladder*, that contains a mixture of DNA fragments of known sizes is run on the gel along with the DNA fragments so that the unknown sizes of the resolved fragments can be measured by comparing them to the known sizes of the ladder once electrophoresis is complete.

Proteins are separated by polyacrylamide gel electrophoresis (PAGE), and before electrophoresis, they are denatured (linearized) with sodium dodecyl sulfate (SDS), which imparts an even distribution of negative charge per unit mass on the proteins. The procedure is referred to as SDS-PAGE. The rate of the migration of proteins in SDS-PAGE (similar to DNA) is inversely proportional to the macromolecules' molecular weight.

Southern blotting identifies target DNA fragments (or known DNA sequences) in a large sample of DNA. The DNA is cut into fragments by restriction enzymes, and the fragments are separated by gel electrophoresis. Then, the double-stranded DNA is denatured in an alkaline environment, separating the DNA into single strands for later hybridization. The single-stranded DNA is transferred to a nitrocellulose membrane by the application of pressure, and capillary action is used to transfer the DNA from the gel to the membrane. The membrane is then baked at a high temperature so that the DNA becomes permanently attached. Finally, the hybridization probe (a single radioactively-labeled or fluorescently-labeled DNA fragment) with the predetermined sequence is added to the solution containing the nitrocellulose membrane. This labeled probe hybridizes to the nitrocellulose membrane to identify the location of the specific sequence of DNA (resolved by gel electrophoresis). After hybridization, the excess probe is washed away, and autoradiography (or fluorescence) is used to visualize the hybridization pattern on the radioactively-labeled (via x-ray film) or fluorescent sample (via spectroscopy).

Southern blot method where DNA is resolved by gel electrophoresis and the specific fragment is located by hybridization of the labeled probe with a complementary sequence to the target gene

Northern blotting is similar to Southern blotting but uses RNA instead of DNA. *Western blotting* is the equivalent technique used for proteins, where antibodies bind to the protein of interest and mark it for visualization.

Use the mnemonic SNoW DRoP and match the letters.

S - Southern - DNA - D

N - Northern - RNA - R

o -   - o

W - Western - Protein - P

DNA sequencing

DNA sequencing is the determination of the precise nucleotide sequence in a DNA molecule. The most popular method is the *dideoxy method*, known as the *chain termination method* or "Sanger sequencing." It was created by Fredrick Sanger, who was awarded the 1980 Nobel Prize in chemistry for this discovery.

In nature, DNA is synthesized from four different deoxynucleotide triphosphates (dNTPs), each of which contains a 3' OH group. The Sanger sequencing method uses fluorescently-tagged synthetic dideoxynucleotides (ddNTP) that lack the 3'–OH group. When a dideoxynucleotide is randomly added to a growing DNA strand, the strand cannot be further elongated because there is no 3'–OH for the next nucleotide to attach. The ddNTPs are present only in limited quantities, so depending on probability, a dNTP may get added, allowing the growing DNA strand to continue elongation, or a ddNTP may get added, terminating the strand. This results in a variety of DNA strands of different lengths, which are then separated by gel electrophoresis. An instrument identifies the fluorescent ddNTPs, and since each of the four ddNTPs is labeled with a different color, the DNA sequence can be read by an automatic scanner.

Sanger sequencing works well for DNA fragments of up to 900 nucleotides. For longer pieces of DNA, even entire genomes, the *shotgun sequencing* can be used. In shotgun sequencing, a long piece of DNA is randomly cut into smaller fragments which are cloned into vectors and then sequenced individually by the dideoxy method. The sequences are analyzed by a computer to search for overlapping sequences and then reassembled into the proper order. This yields the full sequence of the original piece of DNA. *Pairwise-end sequencing* is a variety of shotgun sequencing that analyzes both ends of the DNA fragments for overlap and is an ideal method for longer genomes.

Several high-throughput sequencing methods do not use Sanger sequencing; these methods are *next-generation sequencing* and have been developed to meet the high demand for low-cost sequencing. These sequencing techniques utilize parallel processing and can generate millions of sequences concurrently.

Analyzing gene expression

Different cells in the body express various combinations of genes that encode for distinct products. In addition to quantifying gene expression, analyzing the location of expression (cell type or stages of development) can be useful. There are methods to quantify the level at which particular genes are expressed, and the information obtained from these gene expression analysis methods can be useful. For example, the expression levels of an oncogene (growth factor promoting gene) can determine a person's susceptibility to cancer.

Genes are first transcribed into mRNA and then translated into proteins, so both mRNA and protein are considered gene products. Depending on the intent of the study, expression levels of either mRNA or proteins can be quantified. One approach for measuring mRNA levels is the Northern blot, mentioned earlier. Another approach is using *reverse transcriptase PCR* (RT-PCR). In RT-PCR, a primer is used to anneal to a specific mRNA strand, and the enzyme reverse transcriptase is used to synthesize a cDNA copy of the mRNA.

RT-PCR identifies expressed genes from mRNA containing a poly-A tail as the original template

Standard PCR protocol then replicates this cDNA, followed by gel electrophoresis to separate the resulting DNA fragments. If the DNA fragment with the suspected molecular weight appears on the gel, then the mRNA sequence of interest is present in the sample, and it may be concluded that the gene of interest is being expressed. Gel electrophoresis of the RT-PCR product is performed along with standardized samples of known mRNA amounts, so by comparison, the expression level can be calculated from how much mRNA is being produced by the gene.

DNA microarrays evaluate gene expression by using small glass chips that contain a large number of DNA fragments to probe for certain genes. DNA microarrays allow for the simultaneous analysis of thousands of gene products. To use a DNA microarray, mRNA must be extracted from the cells being studied and reverse transcribed (RT-PCR) into cDNA labeled with a fluorescent probe. Then, the cDNA is combined with the microarray so that it can base pair with the attached DNA fragments. An automated microscope scans the DNA microarray to determine which DNA fragments have bound. This analysis provides a complete and precise profile of gene expression.

For protein quantification, a Western blot can be performed, which gives information about the protein's size (its location on the gel) as well as its identity (antibody bound). Although modifications to the protein (e.g., ubiquitination) can easily be identified because this method is sensitive to changes in protein size, the quantification of the level of protein expression is not accurate. *Quantitative mass spectrometry* (MS) is a more reliable method to determine the amount of protein expressed. In quantitative MS, isotopic tags distinguish the proteins. When viewing the mass spectrum, the peak intensities of isotope pairs indicate the abundance of corresponding proteins.

Determining gene function

One of the most direct methods to determine the function of a gene is to study mutant organisms that have changes in their nucleotide sequence that disrupt the gene. Spontaneous mutants may be found in populations, but it is much more efficient to generate mutations with DNA-damaging mutagens. Aside from exposing the organism to mutagens, *insertional mutagenesis* is another method to create interruptions in the genetic code by inserting exogenous DNA into the genome. Although humans are not used in either of these processes for ethical reasons, model organisms such as Drosophila flies, zebrafish and yeast are used. After a collection of mutants has been created, a *genetic screen* is performed to determine the altered phenotypes.

If the phenotype of interest is a metabolic deficiency (e.g., organism that cannot grow without a certain nutrient), the genetic screen is simple to perform, but screening for more subtle phenotypes can be more complex. The next step is to identify the gene that caused the altered phenotype. If insertional mutagenesis was used, the DNA fragments that contain the insertion could be amplified via PCR, sequenced (e.g., Sanger sequencing), and searched in a DNA database to find homologous genes. However, if mutagens were used, the process of locating and identifying the gene is more laborious. One way to determine the chromosomal location of the gene is by estimating the distance between genetic loci through calculation of the recombination frequency, a technique of *linkage analysis*. Then once the gene has been located, it can be searched on a database to find homologous genes and thus ascertain its function.

It is possible to create a *knockout organism*, where the gene of interest is specifically "knocked out" (i.e., inactivated) in the organism. Knockout organisms are often made by inserting DNA with the altered gene into target vectors, which are then transformed into embryonic stem cells and inserted into early embryos of the organism. By studying the phenotype of the resulting organism and comparing it to the wild type (i.e., the most common phenotype in nature), the function of the knocked out gene can be determined.

Mutant libraries can be created as collections of organisms of a specific species that have every gene systematically deleted. These are extremely valuable tools for studying the roles of various genes. In addition to knockouts, mutants can be generated that overexpress a gene or express it at the wrong time or in the wrong tissue. These studies provide important information about a gene's function.

DNA microarrays determine changes in the level of gene expression. This can lead to an evaluation of the genes' functions. For example, DNA microarrays with probes for all 6,000 yeast genes have been used to monitor gene expression as the yeast is made to shift from growing on glucose to growing on ethanol. About 1,000 genes increase in activity during this change, while about 1,000 other genes decrease in activity. Thus, about 2,000 genes are involved in the reprogramming, when yeast switches from metabolizing glucose to metabolizing ethanol.

Stem cells

Stem cells are not fully differentiated (i.e., morphologically or biochemically distinct), yet can renew themselves through cell division, and divide and differentiate into specialized cell types. For example, a single stem cell may differentiate into a blood cell, liver cell or kidney cell. In many tissues, *somatic stem cells* (adult stem cells) function as an internal repair system and can replace damaged cells or tissues by differentiating into the type of cell-specific to that tissue. Since different types of cells in the adult organism originate from a single zygote, *embryonic stem cells* are necessary for embryonic development.

Stem cell therapy uses stem cells to treat diseases. A bone marrow transplant is the most common therapeutic use of stem cells. Stem cells in the bone marrow give rise to red blood cells, white blood cells, and platelets. When a patient has cancer and is given high doses of chemotherapy, the chemotherapy targets the intended cancer cells but destroys noncancerous cells in the bone marrow, which prevents the patient from producing blood cells. To avoid this, before the patient is treated with chemotherapy, she can undergo a bone marrow harvest where stem cells are removed from the bone marrow by using a needle inserted into the pelvis (hip bone).

Alternatively, if the patient's stem cells cannot be used, they can be harvested from a matching donor. After the chemotherapy treatment, the patient undergoes a bone marrow transplant in which the stem cells are transplanted back into the patient through a drip, usually via a vein in the chest or the arm. These transplanted stem cells then migrate to the bone marrow and start to produce healthy blood cells. Therefore, the therapeutic use of stem cells in bone marrow transplants allows cancer patients to undergo high-dose chemotherapy treatment. Without this therapeutic use of stem cells, patients would only be able to take low doses of chemotherapy to avoid destroying their bone marrow cells needed for replenishing blood cells, and their chances of recovering from cancer would be reduced.

Several ongoing studies are testing the use of stem cells for the regeneration of brain tissue, heart tissue, and other tissue, to treat diseases such as Alzheimer's, diabetes, heart disease, and Crohn's disease. Different types of stem cells are being studied, including adult stem cells, amniotic stem cells (from the fluid of the amniotic sac where the fetus develops), induced pluripotent stem cells (created by reprogramming adult cells) and embryonic stem cells. Embryonic stem cells are taken from the inner cell mass of a blastocyst, a structure formed in the early stages of embryo development.

There are some disadvantages to stem cell therapy. If stem cells are harvested from a donor with a different major histocompatibility complex (MHC), the patient's immune system may target the stem cells, (i.e., antibodies mount an immune response) and reject them. Additionally, the stem cells' ability to differentiate into a specific type of cell may pose a problem if they do not differentiate into the specific cell type that is needed for treatment. Some stem cells pose the risk of forming tumors (uncontrolled cell growth).

Practical applications of DNA technology: medical applications, human gene therapy, pharmaceuticals, forensic evidence, environmental cleanup, and agriculture

Recombinant DNA technologies have many practical applications, especially in medicine and in the development of pharmaceuticals. For example, some medical products (e.g., insulin) are expressed in *E. coli* cells, so that large quantities of the protein can be cultured and used for the treatment of diseases (e.g., diabetes, cancer and viral infections). Recombinant DNA is utilized in the creation of vaccines, where the outside protein shell of an infectious virus is combined with a harmless host so that the surface proteins activate the patient's immune system but not infected with the virus.

Gene therapy involves techniques used to give healthy patient genes to compensate for defective ones, helping to treat genetic diseases and other illnesses. Gene therapy can be classified into two types: *ex vivo* (cells are modified outside the body) and *in vivo* (cells are modified inside the body). Gene therapy is still being developed for use in the clinic.

Treatment of adenosine deaminase (ADA) deficiency may involve manipulation of stem cells in the form of *ex vivo* gene therapy. ADA deficiency is a severe combined immunodeficiency (SCID), in which the lack of functional ADA enzyme causes inhibition of DNA synthesis as well as toxicity to immune cells, leading to immunodeficiency. In this treatment, bone marrow stem cells are removed, infected with a retrovirus that carries a normal gene for the ADA enzyme, and then returned to the patient. Because the genes are replaced in the stem cells, the genes are spread into many cells during cell division, leading to greater production of the functional enzyme. Patients have shown significant improvement.

In one type of *ex vivo* gene therapy, familial hypercholesterolemia, a condition where liver cells lack a receptor for removing cholesterol from the blood, is treated. High cholesterol leads to fatal heart attacks at a young age. In the treatment, a small portion of the liver is surgically removed and infected with a retrovirus with a normal gene for the receptor. The cells infected with the gene are then reintroduced into the patient, leading to lowered cholesterol levels in the patients receiving this treatment.

A potential *in vivo* gene therapy treatment for cancer involves making cancer cells more vulnerable to chemotherapy and making normal cells more resistant. Injecting a retrovirus containing a normal *TP53* gene that promotes apoptosis of cells into tumors may inhibit their growth. In another *in vivo* gene therapy, a gene for vascular endothelial growth factor (VEGF) can be injected alone (or within a virus) into the heart to stimulate branching of coronary blood vessels (i.e., angiogenesis), helping to treat heart disease.

To properly utilize gene therapy treatments, it is important to understand the genetic basis of disease fully. The Human Genome Project, launched in the 1980s by the National Institutes of Health (NIH) and assisted by other research teams, was a major help with these efforts. The Human Genome Project aimed to map the nucleotide base pair sequences along the 23 human chromosomes. It took 15 years to learn the sequence of the three billion base pairs along the length of human chromosomes. Through advances in technology, the cost to sequence a genome of the human (or a person) has decreased from $2.3 billion to less than $5,000, making sequencing for medical applications more affordable.

The Human Genome Project found that there are few differences between the sequence of bases within humans and many other organisms with known DNA sequences. Since more complex organisms (e.g., humans) share such a large number of genes with simpler organisms, the uniqueness of a complex organism may be due to the regulation of these genes. For example, about 97% of human DNA does not encode for protein product and includes noncoding DNA, regulatory sequences, introns, and untranscribed repetitive sequences. *Tandem repeats* (*satellite DNA*) are abnormally long stretches of contiguous repetitive sequences within an affected gene, and they can even cause disease in certain cases (e.g., Huntington's disease). The Human Genome Project helped to elucidate the identity and relative amounts of these different types of DNA sequences. Additionally, the Human Genome Project studied mitochondrial DNA sequences, which provided more information on the origins, evolution, and migration of ancestral humans.

With the sequencing of the complete human genome, it is now easier to study how genes influence human development and to identify many genetic diseases. Sequencing of the human genome allows for the production of new pharmaceuticals based on DNA sequences of genes or the structure of proteins encoded for by these genes.

Information about the human genome is useful in *forensic science*, which is a method of analyzing physical evidence by crime investigators and presented in court during a trial. The genome of humans differs roughly one every 1,000 nucleotides; these differences are known as *single nucleotide polymorphisms* (SNPs). Short tandem repeats (STR) are repeats of 2 to 5 nucleotides, and these differ among all individuals except identical twins.

Restriction fragment length polymorphisms (RFLPs) are the differences in fragment lengths after restriction enzymes cut the DNA sequences from different samples. The genetic sequences that give rise to RFLPs are inherited in a Mendelian fashion. Forensic scientists use RFLP analysis to compare the DNA found at the crime scene (e.g., in traces of blood or semen) with the DNA of the suspect. For a paternity test, the child's DNA is compared with that of the putative father. These are examples of *DNA fingerprinting*, the technique of using DNA to identify individuals since no two individuals share identical genomes. DNA fingerprinting, along with PCR, can identify deceased individuals from skeletal remains.

Genetic engineering is the manipulation of the genome of an organism. An important aspect of genetic engineering is the ability to move a gene from one organism to another. This process first involves splicing out a gene of interest by a restriction enzyme. This gene is then placed into another organism by cutting the target chromosome and sealing the new sequence in with DNA ligase. The target organism now has a gene sequence for production of the polypeptide.

Transgenic organisms, or organisms with a foreign gene that has been inserted, can be genetically engineered to produce specific protein products. Some products include enzymes that can be used in chemical synthesis for substances which may otherwise be expensive to produce. For example, phenylalanine, used in aspartame sweetener, can be produced by transgenic bacteria.

Transgenic bacteria have been used to protect the health of plants from environmental issues. Ice-minus bacteria have been created by removing the gene that encodes for a certain protein on the outer cell wall of *Pseudomonas syringae* that facilitates ice formation. The introduction of this genetically modified bacteria protects the vegetative parts of plants from frost damage. Root-colonizing bacteria with inserted insect toxin genes can be used to protect the roots of corn from damage by insects.

Cleanup of various substances can utilize genetic engineering. For example, transgenic bacteria can be optimized for oil degradation or can be formed into a bio-filter to reduce the number of chemical pollutants flowing into the air. Some bacteria can remove sulfur from coal before it is burned to clean up toxic dumps. Furthermore, these bacteria can be given "suicide genes" that cause them to die after they have done their job.

Bacteria can be engineered to process minerals. Genetically engineered "bio-leaching" bacteria extract copper, uranium, and gold from low-grade ore. Many major mining companies already use bacteria to obtain various metals.

In addition to bacteria, transgenic plants and animals can be engineered. *Protoplasts* are plant cells that have had their cell wall removed. An electric current makes tiny holes in the plasma membrane through which genetic material enters the cell. The protoplasts then develop into mature plants. Foreign genes now give cotton, corn and potato strains the ability to produce an insect toxin, and crops can be made resistant to certain herbicides so that the crop plants can be sprayed with the herbicide and not be affected by it.

Plants are being engineered to produce human proteins (e.g., hormones, clotting factors and antibodies) in their seeds. Antibodies made by corn can deliver radioisotopes to tumor cells, and a soybean-engineered antibody can treat genital herpes. Mouse-eared cress has been engineered to produce a biodegradable plastic in cell granules.

The creation of transgenic animals requires methods to insert genes into the eggs of animals. Foreign genes can be manually micro-injected into the eggs, or a vortex mixing can be used. Vortex (mixing) involves placing the eggs in an agitator with DNA as well as silicon-carbide needles that make tiny holes through which the DNA can enter the egg. Using this technique, many types of animal eggs have been injected with bovine growth hormone (bGH) to produce larger fish, cows, pigs, rabbits, and sheep. It may even be possible to use genetically engineered pigs to serve as a source of organs for human transplant. *Gene pharming* uses transgenic farm animals to produce pharmaceuticals; the product is obtainable from the milk of females. One example is the transfer of the gene for factor IX, a blood clotting factor, from humans into sheep, so that this factor is produced in the sheep's milk.

Earlier in the chapter, gene cloning was described. Clones are cells identical to the parent and arise in nature by organisms that reproduce asexually. An underground stem or root sends up new shoots that are clones of the parent plant. Members of a bacterial colony on a petri dish are clones because they all came from the division of the same cell.

For many years, it was believed that adult vertebrate animals could not be cloned. Then, in 1996, the first cloned mammal, Dolly, the sheep, was born. Since then, some other animals have been cloned. Dolly was cloned by taking udder cells (i.e., somatic – not germline cells) from a donor sheep. These cells were then cultured in a low-nutrient medium to switch the genes off and make the cell dormant (i.e., not undergoing cellular activities as in the adult cell). Then, an unfertilized egg was taken from another sheep, and its nucleus was removed using a micropipette. The egg cell was then fused with the udder cells using a pulse of electricity. The fused cells developed like normal zygotes and became an embryo, which was then implanted into a "surrogate mother" sheep. One lamb was born and named Dolly. This lamb was genetically identical to the sheep from which the udder cells were taken. Dolly survived for almost seven years, but due to the use of somatic cells—not germline cells—she survived for about half the normal life expectancy of a sheep.

Safety and ethics of DNA technology

Genetic engineering is likely to become more common due to the numerous applications involved. The advances in DNA technology have allowed for the detection of people, plants or animals that are genetically prone to disease, i.e., *hereditary diseases*. Preparation for the effects of the disease, or for the passing of the disease to offspring, is valuable to minimize the risks of some diseases. Within the realm of bioethics, if an abnormality is detected while a fetus is in the womb, it can sometimes be treated. However, abortion is an option in these circumstances, which adds ethical aspects to this issue.

Beyond simple detection, animals and plants can be engineered to exhibit desirable characteristics (e.g., bacteria that produce human insulin). Infectious diseases can be treated by introducing genes that encode for antiviral proteins specific to a particular antigen. However, there are ethical considerations. Nature is an extremely complex, interrelated chain consisting of many species linked in the food chain. Some scientists believe that creating genetically modified organisms may have irreversible effects with unknown and potentially undesirable consequences.

Genetic engineering is on the border of many ethical issues that question whether humans have the right to manipulate the course of nature. Therefore, governments have produced legislation to control what experiments can be performed and therapies developed that involve genetic engineering. In some countries, strict laws are prohibiting any experiments involving the manipulation of genetic content or cloning of humans. Some feel that it is unethical to create transgenic animals with an increased potential for suffering (e.g., a pig with no legs).

Despite the ethical issues and legal restrictions, several experimental breakthroughs have been made possible by genetic engineering. For example, scientists successfully manipulated the genetic sequence of a rat to grow a human ear on its back. This was unusual but was done to reproduce human organs for medical purposes. Therapeutic cloning of human cells (i.e., production of human embryos) could be useful for harvesting pluripotent embryonic stem cells for the treatment of diseases, but there are many unresolved ethical issues involved.

A summary of some arguments for and against therapeutic cloning in humans.

Arguments for	*Arguments against*
Embryonic stem cells can be used for therapies that save lives and reduce pain for patients. Since a stem cell can divide and differentiate into any cell type, they can be used to replace tissues or organs required by patients.	Every human embryo is a potential human being and should be given a chance to develop.
Cells can be taken from embryos that have stopped developing, so these embryos would have died anyway.	More embryos are generally produced than are needed, so many are needlessly destroyed.
Cells are taken at a stage when the embryos have no nerve cells and cannot feel pain.	There is a risk of embryonic stem cells developing into tumor cells.

It is common for genetic modifications in crop plants. For example, the transfer of a gene that encodes for a Bt toxin protein from the bacterium *Bacillus thuringiensis* (Bt) to maize crops. This is done because insects that eat the corn often destroys maize crops; adding the Bt toxin gene kills the insects. However, this is controversial. The table below summarizes some of the benefits and possible harmful effects of genetically modifying the maize crops.

Benefits

Since there is less damage to the maize crops, there is a higher crop yield which can lessen food shortages for populations.

Since there is a higher crop yield, less land is needed to grow more crops. Instead, the land can become an area for wildlife conservation.

There is a reduction in the use of pesticides, which are expensive and harmful to the environment, wildlife and farm workers.

Harmful Effects

The consequences of humans and animals consumption of modified crops are still unclear, though concerns have been raised among consumer advocates. The bacterial DNA or the Bt toxin gene could be harmful to human or animal health.

Other insects which are not harmful to the crops could be destroyed. The maize pollen contains the toxin, and so if it is blown onto nearby plants, it can kill the insects feeding on these plants.

Cross-pollination can occur, which results in some wild plants being genetically modified, as they contain the Bt gene. These plants have an advantage over others as they are resistant to certain insects, causing some wild plants to become endangered.

As these technologies develop, ethical issues become more important to society.

Notes for active learning

Notes for active learning

Notes for active learning

Chapter 9

Development

- **Embryogenesis**

- **Mechanisms of Development**

Embryogenesis

Development describes the changes in the life cycle of an organism. *Embryogenesis* begins the process of growth and development of an embryo.

Fertilization

In sexually reproducing organisms, *fertilization* is the first step of embryogenesis. It marks the combination of sperm and egg to form a zygote. Reproduction may be sexual or asexual. *Asexual reproduction* does not involve fertilization, as one parent is required. Asexual reproduction is the primary form of reproduction for single-celled organisms (e.g., bacteria, many protists, and fungi). Rarely are animals exclusively asexual, but most animals that can reproduce asexually use a combination of sexual and asexual reproduction. In *sexual reproduction, ovum* (egg) of one parent is fertilized by the sperm of the other. The ovum and sperm are *gametes* and are produced by sexually mature organisms in *gametogenesis*. Sexually-reproducing animals use various strategies to ensure that their gametes find each other. Fertilization of the ovum by the sperm may occur externally (e.g., in water) or internally (i.e., within the organism).

Animals that use external fertilization (e.g., fish and amphibians) must release thousands (or even millions) of gametes (egg or sperm) since the chance of fertilization is low. However, the advantages of external fertilization are a greater degree of genetic variation and a low chance of disease transmission. Most externally fertilizing animals synchronize the release of their gametes using environmental signals. Tides, which fluctuate with the lunar cycle, are one such trigger.

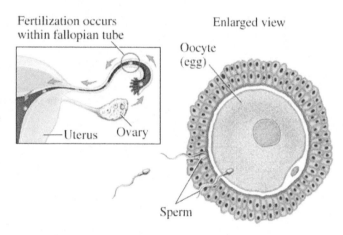

Animals that use internal fertilization, including all terrestrial vertebrates, require one (or a few) ova and have the advantage of being more selective about reproductive partners. The disadvantage of this reproductive strategy is that it reduces genetic variation and requires direct contact between male and female, which promotes the transmission of disease. Most mammals, including humans, use internal fertilization, and their young develop within the mother's uterus until birth. Reptiles, birds and a class of mammals called monotremes fertilize internally, but subsequently, lay eggs in which their young develop.

To preserve the existence of the species and pass on their genetic material, it is essential that mature adults are capable of producing fertile offspring. Many animals are fertile during certain periods. In human females, the ovum is available for fertilization by sperm once per cycle, during *ovulation*. During ovulation, an ovary releases an ovum, which is then swept by ciliary cells into the *uterine tube* (the oviduct or Fallopian tube). During intercourse, millions of sperm are ejaculated and then move through the vagina, uterus and uterine tube towards the ovum using their *flagella*, whip-like tails. Temperature and chemical signals direct the sperm towards the ovum. They are aided in their journey by rhythmic propulsions of the vagina and uterus. However, most sperms die before reaching the ovum due to their depleted energy supply (ATP) and the acidic vaginal environment.

A sperm secretes proteins that bind to receptors on the glycoprotein layer surrounding the plasma membrane of a same-species ovum, preventing cross-species fertilization. This glycoprotein layer is the *vitelline layer* or *zona pellucida* in mammals. Upon binding, the *acrosome* in the sperm head digests a path through the zona pellucida with the release of hydrolytic enzymes. The sperm body follows into the ovum.

Most of the sperm cells that reach the ovum are viable and have the potential to fertilize it. Many sperm cells attach to the ovum, but only one should succeed in penetrating the ovum. *Polyspermy* occurs when more than one sperm penetrates the ovum. Usually, a fertilized ovum has 2 copies of each chromosome, but an ovum affected with polyspermy has 3 or more copies, which usually leads to the formation of a non-viable zygote.

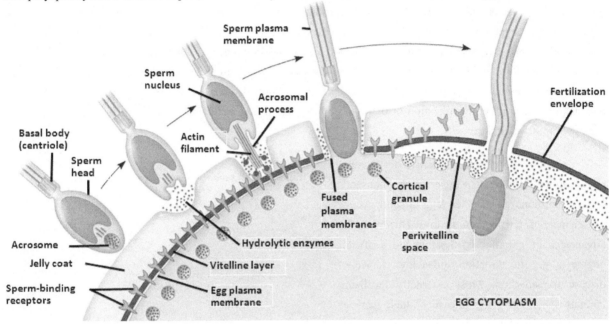

Fertilization of the egg by sperm

Prevention of polyspermy depends on certain changes that occur when a sperm cell first binds and fuses to an ovum. During this time, the ovum is vulnerable to other sperm attempting to fertilize it, so immediate action must be taken to avoid this scenario by two mechanisms: fast block and slow block to polyspermy.

In marine invertebrates (e.g., sea urchins), fertilization triggers an influx of sodium ions into the ovum, which causes its membrane potential to depolarize rapidly. Sperm cells are immediately unable to bind to the positively charged ovum, so this is the *fast block* because it quickly prevents polyspermy.

The *slow block* is a slower and more long-term process. Many species other than mammals utilize *both* a fast block and slow block because although the fast block is effective, it is transient and another countermeasure to polyspermy is often needed. The slow block is initiated upon fertilization, as the ovum secretes various hormones to prevent it from being overwhelmed by the hundreds of sperm attempting fertilization. In most species that use this technique, the slow block is the *cortical reaction*.

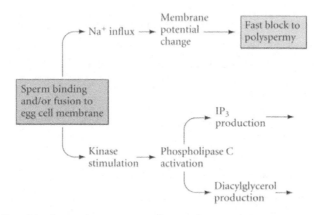

Fast block to polyspermy involves a change to the membrane potential that inhibits additional sperm from penetrating the fertilized egg

Slow block to polyspermy uses cortical granule to create a physical barrier around the zygote

The cortical reaction involves calcium release from the ovum, which causes *cortical granules* in the ovum to secrete calcium, which modifies the *zona pellucida*. Proteases lift the vitelline layer as hyaluronic acid pushes the vitelline layer away from the surface of the ovum, forming a barrier that prevents entrance of other sperm. Hyalin and peroxidases harden the fertilization envelope and inactivate the sperm-binding sites to prevent additional sperm cells from fusing. The vitelline layer is the *fertilization envelope*.

In mammals, the vitelline layer is the zona pellucida, so the cortical reaction is the *zona reaction*. The zona pellucida hardens, and its binding sites become inactivated. The zona reaction of mammals is less effective than the cortical reaction found in other species. Research shows that in the zona reaction, contents of the cortical granules inactivate ZP2 and ZP3 sperm receptors on the zona pellucida. Note that mammals use only a slow block to polyspermy, and not a combination fast block and slow block as found in other species (e.g., sea urchins).

Even after the sperm binds to and fuses with the ovum, fertilization is not complete until the gametes fuse their two haploid nuclei, as *pronuclei*. The pronuclei form a single diploid nucleus, which contains the unique genome of the zygote.

In most animals, including humans, the sperm contributes more than just its pronucleus to the zygote. The sperm centriole enters the ovum along with the pronucleus and flagellum. Recent evidence suggests that sperm mitochondria also enter but are destroyed by the ovum. The centriole replicates and is assembled into a centrosome, which then replicates to organize the assembly of the first mitotic spindle in the zygote. This explains why extra mitotic spindles form in cases of polyspermy since several sperm cells contribute their centrioles to the ovum.

Cleavage

As the zygote is being swept by ciliary movement through the uterine tube into the uterus, it begins a series of cell divisions as *cleavage*. Once the zygote begins mitotic division, it is now an *embryo*. Cleavage involves rapid cell divisions without cell growth; therefore, with each division, *blastomeres* (cells) become smaller.

Cleavage may be either *indeterminate* or *determinate*. When cleavage is indeterminate, blastomeres can individually complete normal development if separated. Blastomeres formed by determinate cleavage do not develop if separated; each is a necessary part of the embryo. This is typical of *protostomes*, a superphylum of animals (e.g., arthropods, nematodes, platyhelminths, rotifers, mollusks and annelids). They are the counterpart to the *deuterostomes*, the most well-known of which are the chordates and the echinoderms.

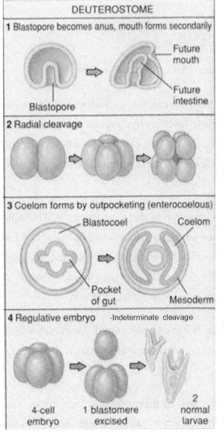

Deuterostomes typically display indeterminate cleavage, which gives rise to identical twins. Identical twins are *monozygotic* twins because they originate from a single zygote that divided into two completely separate organisms. Fraternal twins result from two separately fertilized ova which both implant and develop in the uterus independently.

In many species, the ovum has an animal pole (upper) and a vegetal pole (lower hemisphere), known as embryo polarity. The *vegetal pole* contains larger cells filled with *yolk*, a nutritious substance that feeds the embryo. The yolk is denser than the cytoplasm, which causes it to settle at the bottom. In mammals, it later differentiates into *extraembryonic membranes* that protect and nourish the embryo. The *animal pole* is made of smaller, more rapidly dividing cells, and forms the embryo itself.

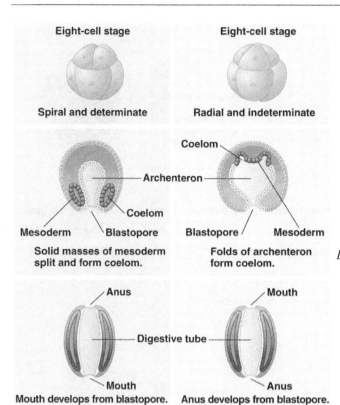

Determinative vs. intermediate cleavage

The *archenteron* is the center cavity formed by gastrulation, and its opening is the *blastopore.* The fate of the blastopore defines deuterostomes and protostomes. The term protostomes ("first mouth") has the blastopore first form the mouth. The term deuterostome ("second mouth") has the blastopore first form the anus, and the mouth develops second.

Animal pole is on the upper portion while vegetal pole is the lower portion of the egg; pronucleus is at the boundary above marginal zone

For the zygote, the first cleavage is *polar* and divides the ovum into two segments along the vegetal-animal axis. It is followed by cleavages perpendicular to the vegetal-animal axis, which is *equatorial. Radial cleavage* is the alternation of polar and equatorial cleavage and is a hallmark of deuterostome development. In contrast, protostomes typically display *spiral cleavage.*

The amount of yolk in the zygote influences the manner of cleavage. Species that lay external eggs (e.g., birds, some fish, reptiles and most insects) have a large amount of yolk. This leads to *meroblastic* (incomplete cleavage). Mammals, worms, insects, and some other fish have eggs with much less yolk. This leads to *holoblastic* (complete cleavage).

Blastula formation

In humans, a few days after fertilization, cleavage creates a *morula*, a solid ball of cells. By the fifth day, the morula is transformed into a hollow *blastula* (*blastocyst* in humans). The blastocyst is formed as blastomeres migrate to the outside of the morula, leaving behind the *blastocoel*, a fluid-filled cavity. A blastocyst consists of two parts: an outer ring of cells as a *trophoblast* and an inner cell mass, the *embryoblast*.

The trophoblast accomplishes implantation of the blastocyst by embedding into the nourishing epithelium of the uterus, the *endometrium*. Upon implantation, the trophoblast releases *human chorionic gonadotropin* (HCG) to maintain estrogen and progesterone production from the *corpus luteum* of the ovary, which maintains the endometrium.

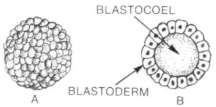

Blastula with the surface (A) and a cross-sectional view (B)

The amount of yolk affects the first three stages of development (cleavage, blastulation, and gastrulation). The lancelet and frog develop quickly in water and travel into the larvae to feed themselves. The chick provides a significant amount of yolk inside a hard shell, and its development continues until the chick can exist on its own. The early stages of human development resemble the chick due to our common evolutionary history. Frog embryo cells at the animal pole have little yolk while the vegetal pole contains more yolk.

The presence of yolk causes cells to cleave more slowly. Thus, cells at the animal (less yolk) pole are smaller due to rapid cell division compared to the vegetal (more yolk) pole. Chick cell cleavage is incomplete; only those cells lying on top of the yolk cleave and spread out over the yolk surface, in contrast to the ball-like morula of the lancelet. The frog blastocoel is formed at the animal pole.

The cells containing yolk do not participate in gastrulation and do not invaginate; instead, when the animal pole cells begin to evaginate from above, a slit-like *blastopore* is formed. Other pole cells move down over the yolk; the blastopore then becomes rounded. These yolk cells temporarily left in the region form a *yolk plug*. Cells from the *dorsal lip* of the blastopore migrate between the ectoderm and endoderm, forming the *mesoderm*. Later, the *coelom* is created by splitting off from the mesoderm.

For example, in a chick, a blastocoel is created when cells lift up from the yolk and leave a space between the cells and the yolk. There is so much yolk that endoderm formation does not occur by invagination. Instead, the upper layer of the cells differentiates into the ectoderm, and the lower layer differentiates into the endoderm. The mesoderm arises by an invagination of cells along the edges of the longitudinal furrow in the embryo midline, named the primitive streak. Later, the newly formed mesoderm splits to form the coelomic cavity.

Gastrulation

After fertilization (3 weeks in humans), *gastrulation* occurs with an invagination of some cells into the blastocoel to form the *primary germ layers*. These are the initial cell layers from which all the body tissues develop.

Vertebrates and other higher animals are *triploblastic* with three primary germ layers. The most primitive animals (cnidarians and sponges) are *diploblastic*, with only two germ layers.

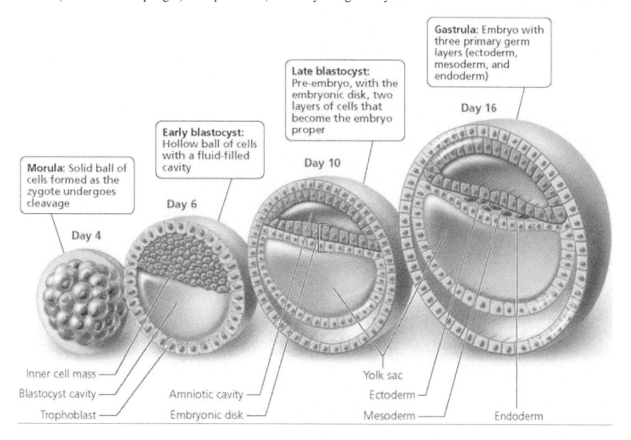

First cell movements

Gastrulation involves a series of orchestrated cell movements, modulated by complex cell-signaling pathways.

The exact manner of gastrulation varies by species. In humans (and other mammals), before gastrulation, the inner cell mass flattens into the *embryonic disc*, which is divided into two layers: the *epiblast* and the *hypoblast*. The beginning of gastrulation is marked by the appearance of the *primitive streak,* a line of cells along the midline of the embryo. The epiblast then ingresses along the primitive streak, pushing the hypoblast along with it. This first ingression is the blastopore. As invagination continues, the blastopore deepens to form the *archenteron*, the primitive gut. The *hypoblast* becomes the amnion, one of the extraembryonic membranes.

Formation of primary germ layers: endoderm, mesoderm, and ectoderm

The first epiblast cells that migrate inwards differentiate into the *mesoderm* (middle germ layer). Diploblastic animals like sponges and cnidarian develop *mesoglea*, a non-cellular layer, instead of a mesoderm. Epiblastic cells that continue to invaginate the blastocyst become the *endoderm* (inner germ layer), while those that remain outside are the *ectoderm* (outer germ layer). After gastrulation, the germ layers begin to develop into the entire array of structures and organs in the body.

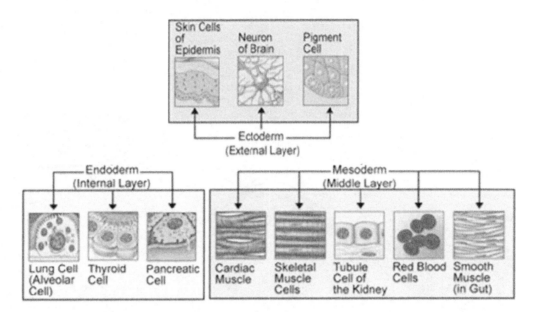

Primary germ layers and some representative tissue types formed from each layer

Neurulation

The newly formed mesoderm cells of the gastrula coalesce along the main axis to form a dorsal *notochord* as a stiff rod that provides support in lower chordates and is replaced in amphibians, birds, and mammals by the vertebral column. The portion of the ectoderm located just above the notochord develops into the nervous system in *neurulation*.

At first, the ectoderm cells on the dorsal surface of the embryo thicken, forming the *neural plate*. A *neural groove* develops down the midline of the neural plate; on either side of the neural groove, *neural folds* begin to fold upward and fuse together. This forms the *neural tube*, which eventually becomes the central nervous system. At this point, the embryo is a *neurula*.

Neurulation with the formation of the neural tube

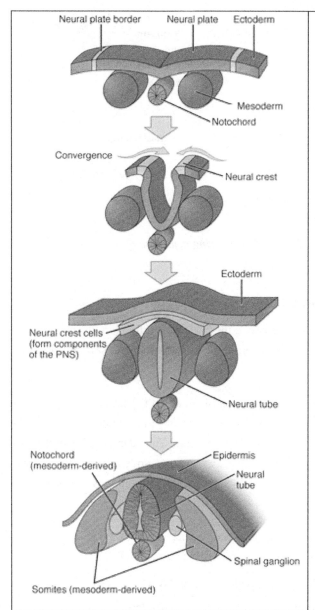

1 – Neuroectodermal tissues differentiate from the ectoderm and thicken into their neural plate. The neural plate border separates the ectoderm from the neural plate.

2 - The neural plate bends dorsally, with the two ends eventually joining at the neural plate borders, which are now referred to as the neural crest.

3 – The closure of the neural tube disconnects the neural crest from the epidermis. Neural crest cells differentiate to form most of the peripheral nervous system.

4 – The notochord degenerates and persists as the nucleus pulposus of the intervertebral discs. Other mesoderm cells differentiate into the somites, the precursors of the axial skeleton and skeletal muscle.

Neural crest

The *neural crest* is the ectoderm at which the two neural folds close together to form the neural tube. Neural crest cells migrate and differentiate into a variety of cell types (e.g., neurons and glial cells of the peripheral nervous system, melanocytes of the epidermis, epinephrine-producing cells of the adrenal gland, portions of the heart and the connective tissue of the head).

Although derived from ectoderm, the neural crest is referred to as the fourth germ layer because of its importance.

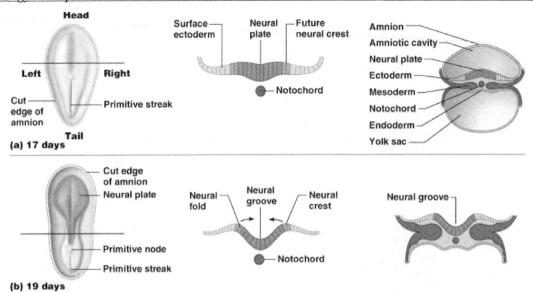

The neural crest is ectoderm that forms during neurulation

Major structures arising from primary germ layers

Aside from the nervous system, the ectoderm gives rise to the epidermis of the skin, the epithelial lining of the mouth and rectum, and several glands. The ectoderm is the origin of the nails, hair and skin glands, as these are all epidermal derivatives.

During neurulation, midline mesoderm cells that did not contribute to the formation of the notochord now become two longitudinal masses of tissue as *somites*, a process of *somitogenesis*. In vertebrates, the somites give rise to the dermis, skeletal muscle, tendons, cartilage and bone of the axial skeleton. The other portions of the mesoderm develop into the other connective, muscular and skeletal portions of the body. Mesoderm forms the excretory and reproductive system, along with the heart, blood vessels and blood cells, and the linings of all body cavities (coeloms).

The endoderm gives rise to the epithelial linings of the digestive tract, respiratory tract and excretory tract, along with associated organs and glands of the digestive and respiratory systems.

Structures forming from primary germ layers		
Ectoderm	Mesoderm	Endoderm
Epidermis Nervous system Epithelial linings: mouth and rectum Glands: adrenal medulla, pineal, pituitary	Dermis Skeletal system Muscular system Excretory system Reproductive system Circulatory system Lymphatic system Epithelial linings: coelom Glands: adrenal cortex	Epithelial linings: respiratory, digestive and excretory system Glands: pancreas, thymus, thyroid, parathyroid Liver

Notes for active learning

Notes for active learning

Mechanisms of Development

Development is the changes in the life cycle of an organism due to growth, differentiation, and morphogenesis. Most animals go through the same embryonic stages: zygote, morula, blastula, and gastrula. Gastrulation is succeeded by neurulation, which is the first event of *organogenesis* when body organs begin to develop. Neurulation marks the point at which the embryo leaves the embryonic stage and becomes a *fetus*. Organogenesis is related to *morphogenesis,* the development of an organism's body plan and shape.

Cell specialization

Cells are specialized when they have a specific function. For example, epidermal cells produce keratin to protect the skin against abrasion, myocytes produce actin and myosin to make muscles contract, and neurons produce neurotransmitters that transmit electrochemical impulses. *Stem cells* are undifferentiated cells which have yet to specialize. As an embryo develops, its stem cells differentiate to give rise to the different tissues of the body.

Cell specialization is achieved in two stages: *determination* and *differentiation.* Determination of a cell is the period when the cell begins to commit to a certain cell type, and it can be divided into two states: a cell is *specified,* and then it is *determined.* If a specified cell is placed into different body tissue, the cell alters its differentiation pathway to match that tissue. In this regard, the specification is reversible. However, once the cell is determined, the cell is irreversibly committed to its differentiation pathway and does not adapt to a different environment by altering its differentiation.

Determination

Determination begins with the specification (reversible) and ends with an irreversible commitment to a certain cell type. A cell is determined if influences from the cytoplasm cannot change its final form. These cytoplasmic influences are narrowed with successive cell divisions; complete determination usually occurs late in the cell specialization process.

Differentiation

Cellular differentiation is when cells become specialized in their structure and function. Although the two terms are sometimes used interchangeably, differentiation is the process by which cells commit to a certain cell type, while specialization refers to what that particular cell type is. Differentiation is an action, while specialization is a state of being.

Differentiation is an important component of *morphogenesis* when the overall form of the organism and its body parts are shaped; this includes both early cell movement and later *pattern formation,* the process by which cells assume different functions in different parts of the body. As cells differentiate, their functions change, and they interact with one another, eventually organizing into body tissues. Cells can be traced during differentiation to build a lineage map of their development by *fate mapping.*

Each body cell contains a full set of chromosomes and therefore all the genetic information required to perform the functions of any cell. Cells do not differentiate because they receive different genes, or because certain genes are lost as cells divide. Rather, cell specialization is accomplished via *differential gene expression*. All cell types have the same genome but differ in which genes they express and to what degree. There are two important mechanisms of differential gene expression: cytoplasmic segregation and induction.

The foundation of cell specialization in an embryo is laid even before fertilization. Ova contain mRNA and proteins as *maternal determinants* that influence the course of development. One method of differential gene expression, *cytoplasmic segregation,* parcels out the maternal determinants as cleavage occurs. Different blastomeres receive different concentrations of maternal determinants, which lead to differential gene expression. Experimentally, the cytoplasm of a frog zygote is not uniform in content. After the first division of the frog zygote, only a daughter cell that receives a portion of the *gray crescent* develops into a complete embryo.

Induction is a common mechanism of differential gene expression, in which one group of cells influences development by changing the behavior of an adjacent group of cells. Hans Spemann, who received the Nobel Prize in 1935 for his work on embryonic induction, found that particular chemical signals within the gray crescent activate the genes that regulate development.

Tissue types

The tissues of animals can be divided into four types: epithelial tissue, connective tissue, nervous tissue, and muscle tissue. Each tissue type contains specialized cells and extracellular matrix that the cells secrete.

Connective tissue   Epithelial tissue

Muscle tissue   Nervous tissue

*Epithelial tissue*s may be multilayered, or one cell thick, and usually function in secretion, absorption or protection. Epithelial tissues are in the linings of glands, organs, body cavities, and blood vessels, and in the skin and mucous membranes. Various epithelia are originally derived from all three germ layers.

*Connective tissue*s often connect tissues and organs to one another but can have structural and support functions. These are the most versatile and widespread of the body tissues. Cartilage, bone, blood and adipose tissue (fat) are special connective tissues. Proper connective tissues are divided into *loose* and *dense connective tissues*, which are divided into subtypes. These tissue types are originally derived from the *mesenchyme,* a portion of the mesoderm.

Nervous tissue includes the neurons and glial cells of the nervous system. Neurons (nerve cells) transmit electrical signals, while glial cells protect and support the neurons. All nervous tissue, both central and peripheral, arises from the ectoderm during neurulation.

Muscle tissue is a contractile tissue that can be divided into skeletal muscle, smooth muscle, and cardiac muscle. *Skeletal muscle* tissue makes up all of the muscles of the body under voluntary control and is attached to the skeletal system by tendons. *Smooth muscle* is under involuntary control and is found in the walls of hollow organs (e.g., the uterus, stomach and blood vessels). Cardiac muscle is under involuntary control but is found only in the heart, where it creates the powerful contractions which move blood throughout the body. All three muscle types are originally derived from the mesoderm.

Embryonic and fetal development during gestation

Human gestation is 9 months, calculated by adding 280 days to the start of the last menstrual cycle. About 5% of infants arrive on their forecasted birth date, due to some complicating variables. Embryonic development occurs during months 1 and 2 of pregnancy and involves early cleavage of the zygote and initial organ development (organogenesis). Fetal development occurs during months 3 through 9 when organ systems grow, mature and increase in size and weight by a factor of nearly 600.

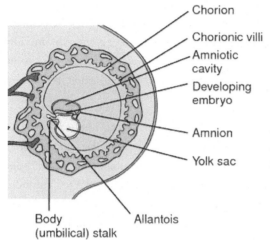

Chorion
Chorionic villi
Amniotic cavity
Developing embryo
Amnion
Yolk sac
Body (umbilical) stalk
Allantois

After fertilization, implantation of the blastocyst in the endometrium occurs about 1 week into pregnancy. Upon implantation, the trophoblast begins to secrete human chorionic gonadotropin (HCG) to stimulate the corpus luteum to maintain the endometrial lining. As the week progresses, the inner cell mass detaches from the trophoblast to become the *embryonic disc*, while the yolk sac forms below. The *yolk sac* is a membranous sac attached to the embryo. It is one of several *extraembryonic membranes* which lie outside of the embryo and protect and nourish the embryo and later the fetus.

The evolution of extraembryonic membranes in reptiles made development on land possible. An embryo that develops in water receives oxygen from the water and wastes float away. The surrounding water prevents desiccation and provides a protective cushion. However, for an embryo on land, these functions must be performed by extraembryonic membranes. These membranes are modified depending on whether the organism undergoes internal or external development.

In birds and reptiles, the yolk sac contains yolk which nourishes the developing embryo. In placental mammals, the umbilical cord and placenta are responsible for nourishing the embryo, so the "yolk sac" is, in fact, empty of yolk and rather functions as an early blood supply for the embryo before becoming part of the primitive gut later in gestation. Therefore, it is an *umbilical vesicle* to distinguish it from the yolk sacs of egg-laying animals.

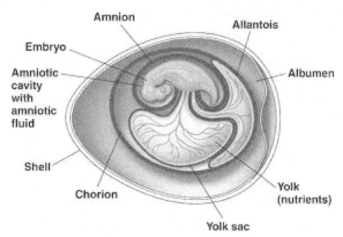

Amnion
Allantois
Embryo
Amniotic cavity with amniotic fluid
Albumen
Shell
Chorion
Yolk (nutrients)
Yolk sac

Egg-laying animals have large yolk sac with nutrients needed during embryogenesis

As the yolk sac forms, a second extraembryonic membrane of the *amnion* encloses the embryo. The amnion surrounds the amniotic cavity, which contains protective amniotic fluid that bathes the developing embryo.

Amniotic fluid is a buffer to mechanical and chemical disturbances, and for thermal regulation. Some genetic disorders can be diagnosed by sampling this amniotic fluid in a prenatal test, like *amniocentesis*. Whether externally or internally, chordate animals develop in water, either in bodies of water or within the amniotic fluid.

The *chorion* is another extraembryonic membrane which, in birds and reptiles, lies next to the shell of an egg and carries on gas exchange. In placental mammals, the chorion implants into the endometrium and projects treelike extensions called *chorionic villi* into the maternal tissues. The maternal blood circulates these villi so that exchange of molecules between the fetal and maternal blood may take place. CO_2 and wastes move across from the fetus, and O_2 and nutrients flow from the maternal side. As the embryo develops, the interface of the chorionic villi and the uterine tissue becomes an organ the *placenta*. Placental formation begins at about week 1 after the embryo is fully implanted in the endometrium. The placenta is the life support structure of the developing embryo, providing oxygen and nutrients while removing wastes (e.g., CO_2). In humans, maternal blood directly contacts the chorion, but gas, nutrients and wastes across the chorion without the maternal and fetal blood mixing. Thus, the placenta facilitates gas and nutrient exchange, but not fluid exchange.

The *umbilical cord* stretches between the placenta and the fetus and contains 2 fetal arteries and 1 fetal vein. The umbilical cord allows fetal blood to reach the placenta and exchange molecules with the maternal blood. Umbilical arteries transport CO_2 and other waste molecules to the placenta for disposal; the umbilical vein transports O_2 and nutrient molecules from the placenta to the rest of the fetal circulatory system. Although the fetal umbilical artery transports deoxygenated blood, it is an artery because it carries blood away from the fetus's heart. Likewise, the fetal umbilical vein carries oxygenated blood and is a vein because it brings blood to the fetus's heart.

The *allantois* is an extraembryonic membrane that evaginates from the archenteron of the gastrula. In birds and reptiles, the allantois initially stores waste products such as uric acid. It later fuses with the chorion. In mammals, the allantois initially transports waste products to the placenta but regresses in later stages of gestation. After birth, it may remain as a vestigial structure or disappear altogether. In birds and reptiles, the allantois and chorion form a double membrane that lies next to the shell and functions in gas exchange.

During week 3 of gestation, gastrulation occurs, followed by neurulation that initiates the development of the nervous system. The neural tube is visible as a thickening along the entire dorsal length of the embryo as the ectoderm develops into neural folds forming the neural tube. Towards the end of the first month, the heart starts to form, while designated cells begin to form the basic structure of the limbs, spine, nervous and circulatory systems. *Limb buds* appear for arms and legs. As a result, the head enlarges, the sense organs become more prominent, and the rudiments of the eyes, ears, and nose are evident.

During week 3, the development of the heart begins and continues into week 4. During this period, the right and left heart tubes fuse and the heart begins pumping blood, although the chambers are not fully formed. The veins enter this largely tubular heart posteriorly, and the arteries exit anteriorly. Later the heart twists so that all of the major vessels are located anteriorly.

During week 4 and 5, a bridge of mesoderm called the *body stalk* connects to the caudal (tail) end of the embryo via the chorionic villi. The head and tail then lift, and the body stalk moves anteriorly by constriction. Once this process is complete, the allantois, found in the body stalk, has extended into the blood vessels of the umbilical cord. Throughout, organs such as the heart, lungs, and liver are continuing to develop.

Through weeks 6 through 8, the developing embryo becomes more human-like in appearance. As the brain develops, the head achieves its normal relationship with the body as the neck region develops. At this point, the nervous system is developed well enough to permit reflex actions such as the startle response to touch. By week 8, the embryo is about 38 millimeters long and weighs no more than an aspirin tablet; however, all organs have been established.

During week 7, the fetus, regardless of sex, initially exhibits the same external and internal genital structures. Externally, the fetus exhibits a *genital tubercle,* a pair of *urogenital folds,* and a pair of *labioscrotal folds.* By week 12 of prenatal development, the genital tubercle differentiates into the glans (head) of the penis or clitoris, the urogenital folds enclose the urethra of a male or become the labia minora of a female, and the labioscrotal folds become the scrotum of a male or labia majora of a female. Now, the gender of the fetus can be identified anatomically.

Internally, the fetus has a pair of *gonadal ridges*, *mesonephric,* or *Wolffian ducts*, and *paramesonephric,* or *Müllerian ducts.* In an XY (male) fetus, the *SRY gene* encodes for the protein *testis-determining factor,* which initiates the development of male genitalia. The gonadal ridges become a pair of testes, which secrete testosterone and *Müllerian-inhibiting factor* (anti-Müllerian hormone).

By week 8, these hormones cause the Müllerian duct to degenerate at week 8 and induce the Wolffian duct to develop into the male reproductive tract. In a female fetus, where there is no Y chromosome, the gonads become ovaries. Around week 10, the absence of anti-Müllerian hormone, the Wolffian ducts degenerate, and the Müllerian ducts develop into the female reproductive tract.

By week 10, the placenta is fully formed and begun to produce progesterone and estrogen. Due to negative feedback control by the hypothalamus and anterior pituitary, no new ovarian follicles mature. Rather, ovarian follicles maintain the lining of the uterus and ensure that there is no menstruation during pregnancy. Facial characteristics of the fetus become recognizable at this time.

By week 14, all the major characteristics of the fetus have mostly developed. A fetus at first is only able to flex its limbs; later, it can move its limbs so vigorously that the mother can feel movements beginning in the fourth month. A fetus soon acquires hair, eyebrows, eyelashes, and nails. Fine, downy hair *lanugo* covers the limbs and trunk of the fetus but sheds shortly before or after birth. The skin grows so fast that it wrinkles. *Vernix caseosa* is a waxy substance that protects the skin from the watery amniotic fluid.

After 16 weeks, a fetal heartbeat can be heard by a stethoscope.

At 24 weeks, a fetus born prematurely may survive, however, the lungs are still immature and often cannot capture O_2 adequately.

From this time onwards, the fetus continues to grow in size rather than in complexity. At 38 weeks after fertilization, the fetus is mature enough to enter the world.

Fetal growth from week 8 to week 40. The gestational period in humans is 38 weeks; however, in obstetrics, the term is counted from the first day of the last menstruation (which is usually 2 weeks earlier), making the length of pregnancy to be 40 weeks.

Cell-to-cell communication in development

Development of the embryo is mediated by communication between cells. Induction is an important mechanism of differentiation that involves cell-to-cell signaling. The inducer is the cell that sends the signal for others to change, while the responder (or target) is the cell that receives the signal and changes accordingly. For example, *optic vesicles* are embryonic brain structures that induce the ectoderm to develop into the lenses of the eye.

Induction may result from juxtacrine mechanisms or paracrine mechanisms. *Juxtacrine* signaling involves communication between two cells that directly touch. *Paracrine* signaling occurs when an inducer cell releases a chemical signal which diffuses through space and is received by a target cell a short distance away.

In the early 20th century, amphibian embryologists Hans Spemann and Hilde Mangold experimented on the dorsal side of the embryo, where the notochord and the nervous system develop. They found that notochord tissue induces the formation of the nervous system, even when placed in a separate tissue environment such as beneath the belly ectoderm. Spemann showed that the dorsal lip of the blastopore, as the *primary organizer*, is necessary for development. The primary organizer directs the formation of germ layers during gastrulation. Those cells which invaginate first are closest to the primary organizer, so they become endoderm. The next cells at an intermediate distance from the primary organizer become mesoderm. Finally, the cells farthest away from the primary organizer become ectoderm.

Cell migration

For development, it is not enough for cells to differentiate; they must also move. This movement of cells to predetermined areas in a controlled, organized manner as *cell migration*. Migrating cells have polarity and a distinguishable front and back (posterior). Without polarity, cells would be unable to maintain controlled movement; all sides of the cell would attempt to move at once in various directions. Researchers hypothesize that no matter the exact model behind cell migration, cytoskeletal filaments help establish and maintain a cell's polarity. The mechanisms of cell migration are not fully understood, but the foremost models are the cytoskeletal model and the membrane flow model.

The *cytoskeletal model theory* is based on the action of cytoskeletal elements. These elements interact to support and alter a cell's plasma membrane. Experimentation has shown that rapid actin polymerization of the cytoskeleton occurs at a migrating cell's front edge. Some researchers propose that the formation of actin filaments (microfilaments) at the front edge of a cell is the driving force behind cell movement. Furthermore, microtubules may act to contract the trailing edge of the cell. Thus, this model relies on a collaboration of the cytoskeletal filaments: microfilaments which push the front edge of the cell forward, and microtubules which retract the trailing edge.

The *membrane flow theory* is based on changes in the plasma membrane, rather than the cytoskeleton. Cells undergo membrane recycling by continually returning membrane sections that are brought into the cell during endocytosis back to the plasma membrane. This process is the basis for the membrane flow theory, which posits that cell migration occurs by the addition of plasma membrane to the front of a cell. Under this hypothesis, the microfilaments found at the front edge of the cell are stabilizing agents. The membrane flow model states that integrin proteins attached to the plasma membrane "walk" the cell along its migratory path. Integrins are continually recycled by endocytosis to the rear of the cell as fresh integrins are brought to the front of the cell by exocytosis.

The two models are not mutually exclusive, so a hybrid of the two may explain cell migration.

Stem cells and pluripotency

Stem cells in the early stages of an embryo are *totipotent* and capable of becoming any type of cell in the organism. A single totipotent stem cell can give rise to an entire organism, provided the organism displays indeterminate cleavage. Only the zygote and subsequent cells of the morula are totipotent.

After just a few cell divisions, the embryonic stem cells become *pluripotent*, as each cannot individually divide into an entire organism but may differentiate into any embryonic cell. As the pluripotent embryonic cells continue to divide, they gradually become committed to a specific path. These cells, which have become committed to a single cell type, are *unipotent* and represent the majority of cells in an adult human.

However, adults do have stem cells. Their pluripotency is debated, and most adult stem cells are considered *multipotent*. Multipotent stem cells are between pluripotent and unipotent; they have a narrow range of possible cell types, but they still greatly benefit the organism for regeneration and repair of damaged tissue. Adult stem cells are in body tissues that must be frequently replaced (e.g., skin, as well as in places such as the bone marrow and the liver). Stem cells, both adult and embryonic, are the subject of intense research into their medical applications for tissue repair and treatment of degenerative diseases.

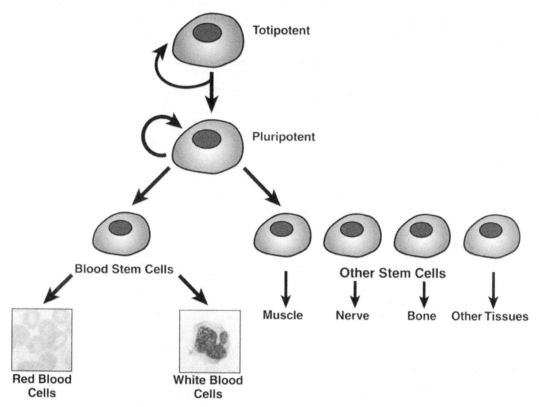

Stem cells undergo determination before differentiation where they exhibit the morphology and biochemistry of the specialized cell

Gene regulation in development

Gene regulation of embryonic cells is the basis for cellular migration and differentiation during development. Knowledge of developmental gene regulation has been primarily based on research on *Caenorhabditis elegans* (roundworm) and *Drosophila melanogaster* (fruit fly), along with other animal models.

Maternal determinants are usually homogenously distributed throughout the ooblast of the ovum. However, *Drosophila melanogaster* exhibits cytoplasmic segregation of maternal determinants. The developing *Drosophila* ovum (oocyte) asymmetrically distributes *maternal effect genes*. These genes then produce mRNA and proteins (maternal determinants) in the mature ovum, which remain asymmetrically distributed. Maternal determinants directly influence the expression of certain zygotic genes. In this way, the genotype of the mother directly influences the phenotype of the zygote.

Gap genes are the first class of zygotic genes regulated by maternal effect genes. The proteins produced by gap genes regulate the transcription of *pair-rule genes*, which then influence the transcription of *segment polarity genes*.

The proteins produced by gap genes, pair-rule genes and segment polarity genes interact to influence *homeotic genes*. Together, gap genes, pair-rule genes, segment polarity genes, and homeotic genes partition the developing *Drosophila* embryo into body segments (i.e., pattern formation). Their function has been studied extensively by mutating these genes and observing the ensuing malfunctions in the body plan.

Gene regulation in development follows the proposed sequence of
gene expression and production of protein products

The initial gradients of maternal determinants are not the only method of gene regulation in a developing embryo. As in the cells of adult organisms, gene regulation is a highly complex process due to the multitude of ways in which genes may be regulated. At any step along the path from DNA to protein, and even after protein synthesis, gene expression can be regulated. At the highest level is transcriptional regulation, which includes histone modifications that make chromatin accessible (or inaccessible) to RNA polymerase, along with modulation of transcription factors that facilitate (inhibit) the binding of RNA polymerase during transcription.

Post-transcriptional regulation occurs after transcription and before translation, targeting the mRNA transcript as it moves from the nucleus to the cytoplasm. This may be accomplished by modulation of nuclear export, RNA splicing, RNA editing and modifications such as capping and polyadenylation, which protect the RNA from degradation while in the cytoplasm.

Once mRNA is processed (splicing of exons and removal of introns, the addition of a 5' G cap and 3' poly–A tail) and exported from the nucleus, the cell may continue to alter gene regulation at the translational level. This is accomplished by promoting (or inhibiting) ribosome recruitment to the mRNA.

Gene regulation does not cease once a protein is translated. Post-translational gene regulation acts upon proteins that have been synthesized. For example, proteins may be sequestered to certain parts of the cell or assembled with other proteins to form a working unit. Additionally, *zymogens* are enzymes that must be cleaved (or modified) to become active.

Post-translational modifications to histones, such as phosphorylation and acetylation, are responsible for the rearrangement of chromatin and is an active area of research.

Regulation of gene expression: transcriptional control (DNA → RNA), post-transcriptional control (e.g., splicing), post-translational control (e.g., glycosylation).
These examples of regulation are only a limited number of all mechanisms used by the cell during development.

Environment-gene interaction in development

Both genetic and environmental factors contribute to the complex etiology of congenital disabilities (birth defects) by disrupting the highly regulated embryonic developmental processes. The intrauterine environment of the developing embryo and fetus is easily altered by maternal factors such as health and disease status, lifestyle, medications, and maternal genotype, as well as exposure to environmental teratogens.

Teratogens are agents which cause congenital abnormalities. They may cause mild to severe congenital disabilities or terminate the pregnancy altogether. Radiation, harmful chemicals, certain drugs, and pathogens may be classified as teratogens. Congenital disabilities (1 in 33 babies in the US) continue to be the leading cause of infant death (about 5,500 per year) in the U.S., and therefore is a field of intense biomedical and clinical research. The field of teratology has focused on the causes and underlying mechanisms of congenital disabilities for decades, yet our understanding of these critical issues remains relatively vague.

Unfortunately, while the placenta is an effective mediator between the fetus and the mother, it is highly susceptible to penetration by chemicals. This is of particular concern during the embryonic period (fertilization through the 10th week of gestation or 8th week of embryonic age), when crucial structures are in the vulnerable first stages of development. Each organ has a sensitive period when toxic substances can alter normal development. For example, between 1958 and 1961 it was common for a pregnant woman in England and other countries to take the tranquilizer thalidomide between days 27 and 40 of pregnancy, which likely resulted with an infant born with deformed limbs, but after this period, the fetus is resistant to the effects of thalidomide and the child would be born healthy.

Studies conducted over the last few decades have suggested that the relationship between genes and environmental factors plays a major role in the propagation of these congenital disabilities. It is now widely believed that the study of gene-environment interactions leads to a better understanding of the biological mechanisms and pathological processes that contribute to the development of complex congenital disabilities.

Programmed cell death

Apoptosis is programmed cell death and is a part of normal cell development. Apoptosis is a central player in gametogenesis, embryogenesis, removal of damaged cells and aging.

During apoptosis, internal *caspases* (proteases) and nucleases digest the cell. These enzymes are inactive in a normal cell and are activated by a complex signal transduction pathway, which may be initiated by external commands or by internal recognition of cell malfunction, infection or DNA damage. The basis for apoptosis in embryogenesis and fetal development has been extensively studied in animal models. Fate maps of *C. elegans* show that 131 cells must undergo apoptosis for normal worm development. The cell-death protein in these cells is normally inhibited, but when the cells are signaled via induction, the cell-death cascade becomes active and produces proteases and nucleases to slice proteins and DNA.

Regardless of the reason for apoptosis, all apoptotic cells undergo characteristic changes: protrusion of the plasma membrane (blebbing), shrinkage, nuclear fragmentation, chromatin condensation, and chromosomal DNA fragmentation. An apoptotic cell attracts nearby cells, which consume the dying cell to avoid harmful cell contents from spilling out into the extracellular fluid and infecting other cells or causing inflammation.

During embryonic development, apoptosis removes harmful, abnormal or unneeded cells. Dysregulation of apoptosis during gestation can lead to severe congenital disabilities. Apoptosis is present from the beginning of development, as when cells in the blastula die off to form the gastrula. Morphogenesis is accomplished through apoptosis; organs overproduce cells and then "prune" the excess cells to sculpt the intricate shape of the organ. This is most readily visible in the fingers and toes, which are webbed early in gestation but later lose their webbing and become recognizable digits. Another example of apoptosis-assisted morphogenesis occurs in the center of ducts and tubes to hollow them out.

Many fetal structures must be shed via apoptosis before birth. For example, female fetuses must degrade the Wolffian duct, while males must degrade the Mullerian duct.

Apoptosis continues its function after birth as a method of tissue remodeling and immune system maintenance in the adult organism. Cancer, autoimmune diseases and neurodegenerative diseases are all the result of dysregulated apoptosis. The absence of proper apoptosis allows dangerous cells to divide and invade other tissues, possibly leading to malignant tumors. However, excessive apoptosis leads to tissue degeneration. Both malfunctions are implicated in aging and disease.

The existence of regenerative capacity in various species

Regeneration is the reactivation of development to regrow a missing (or damaged) body structure. While regenerative abilities are limited in humans, many species of animals retain the capacity to regrow entire limbs after embryonic development.

For example, most echinoderms have robust regenerative powers. Some sea stars can regrow an entirely new organism from a single arm, while others can only replace lost limbs. Regrowth is not always guaranteed; it takes months or years, and sea stars are vulnerable to infection during the regrowth period. Separated limbs must survive off nutrient stores until they regenerate the rest of the sea star and begin to feed.

Newts and salamanders (particularly the axolotl) are noted for their regeneration. Newt and salamander regeneration proceeds in two stages. First, adult cells at the site of the limb's separation de-differentiate into *progenitor cells*. Second, the progenitor cells proliferate and differentiate until they replace the missing tissue.

Humans exhibit regeneration via progenitor cells, although regrowth of entire limbs is impossible. The most remarkable regeneration is found in the liver. Through the use of several complicated signaling cascades, the liver manages to restore any lost mass and adjust its size to that of the organism, all while fulfilling its duties. Human embryos do have the ability to regenerate complete organs and limbs. Like many other vertebrates, however, this ability is lost during embryogenesis, leaving adult humans with a limited capacity to restore tissue damage.

Senescence and aging

Senescence is the gradual deterioration of function in an organism, eventually leading to death. All organisms, except for a few with remarkable properties of immortality, undergo senescence. One of the most puzzling questions humans currently face is *why* they age at all. Some have suggested that senescence avoids cancer, while others blame environmental factors such as radiation and oxidative agents, which cause DNA damage and cellular damage. The reasons for senescence are likely a combination of these and other factors.

At the cellular level, senescence refers to a cell which is no longer able to divide. Generally, cells are limited to 50 to 70 divisions, a threshold of the *Hayflick limit*. A senescent cell is not dead; rather, it actively continues its metabolic functions. The condition may be initiated by activation of oncogenes or by the cell's recognition of its DNA damage. *Oncogenes* signal abnormal cells to avoid senescence or undergo apoptosis to avoid the development of tumors.

Causes of DNA damage include radiation, oxidation (free radical damage) and shortening of telomeres. *Telomeres* are nonsensical DNA sequence repeats that are added to the 3' ends of DNA strands by the enzyme *telomerase*. Replication inevitably incurs shortening of the DNA, which eventually leads to DNA damage so severe that the cell is unable to continue dividing. Telomeres act as fodder for the inevitable losses from DNA replication to protect the encoding regions from destruction. Telomerase allows cells to proliferate for incredibly long periods of time because they are not affected by the loss of DNA incurred by replication. Most cells are subject to the Hayflick limit, but embryonic cells and certain adult cells contain high levels of telomerase so that they may divide continually.

The shortening of telomeres is associated with a wide variety of diseases involving premature aging, such as pulmonary fibrosis (scarring of the lungs). Shortened telomeres prevent the cells from properly dividing without losing genes, leading to cellular senescence. The lack of sufficient telomeres may cause chromosomes to fuse together, which corrupts the genetic blueprint of a cell, making the chromosomes appear broken. The cell eventually recognizes what appears to be DNA damage, and thus enters apoptosis.

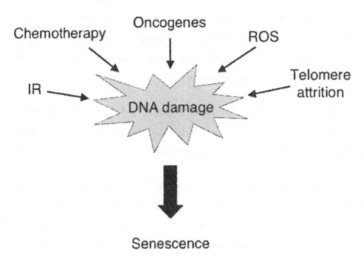

Environmental and biochemical factors contributing to senescence

Certain hydra, jellyfish, and flatworms are *biologically immortal*, so they exhibit negligible senescence and thus do not age. However, these organisms cannot truly escape death, because they are still subject to disease, injury, and predators. There is intense research into modeling therapies based on these organisms and their "immortal" cells, in the hope that aging and mortality can be slowed. For the present, however, they are inevitable parts of human development.

Notes for active learning

Notes for active learning

Chapter 10

Evolution

- **Background**
- **Natural Selection**
- **Speciation**
- **Evolutionary Time Measured by Changes in Genome**
- **Origin of Life**

Background

The pre-Darwinian worldview was defined by deep-seated beliefs held to be intra̸ each species was specially designed and has not changed since Earth's creation. Variations among o̸ᵣᵦ· same species were explained as circumstantial imperfections in a perfectly-adapted creation. However, Cha̸ᵣ̸ᵤ̸ Darwin (1809-1882) lived during a time of great change in the scientific and social realms. His ideas were part of a larger change in thought and perspective already underway among scientists.

Georges Louis Leclerc (1707–1788), known by his title Count Buffon, was a French naturalist who wrote the 44-volume *Natural History of All Known Plants and Animals*. Buffon provided evidence of descent with modification and speculated on how environment, migration, geographical isolation and competition influence the traits of organisms. His work was essential to the development of the theory of evolution and natural selection, as he was among the first to assert that traits are inherited from earlier descendants. Paradoxically, Buffon's beliefs often directly contradicted his work, as he believed in a young Earth and the fixity of species.

Erasmus Darwin (1731–1802), the grandfather of Charles Darwin, was a physician and a naturalist whose writings on both botany and zoology suggested the possibility of *common descent*, the theory that organisms descended from common ancestors. He based his conclusions on observations of embryonic development and the changes incurred in domestic plants and animals due to selective breeding by people. However, Erasmus Darwin offered no mechanism by which descent with modification might occur.

Jean-Baptiste Lamarck (1744–1829) was the first credited with definitively stating that descent with modification occurs and that organisms adapt to their environments. Lamarck was an invertebrate zoologist who went against the thinking of many of his contemporaries by embracing evolution. His assertion that organisms change over time would prove to be correct, but his proposed mechanism for this phenomenon was flawed. *Inheritance of acquired characteristics* was the Lamarckian belief that organisms become adapted to their environment during their lifetime and pass on these adaptations to their offspring. Lamarck suggested that body parts are enhanced by increased usage, while unused parts are weakened. Under this theory, a giraffe's neck would lengthen over its lifetime as it continually stretched to reach leaves, and the slightly-lengthened neck would be passed onto the giraffe's offspring. Over time, these adaptations would accumulate in the long-necked giraffes of modern times. Today, Lamarck's theory of inheritance of acquired characteristics has been dismissed in favor of Darwin's theory of natural selection, along with modern additions to the Darwinian theory of evolution.

At the time, however, Lamarck's ideas were fervently held by some scientists, while others, including the naturalist Georges Cuvier, adamantly opposed his theory. The term "evolution" was not used; Lamarck referred to the changes of species as *transmutation.*

In 1831, at the age of 22, an English naturalist named Charles Darwin (1809-1882) accepted a position aboard the ship *HMS Beagle*; this worldwide voyage would provide Darwin with a wealth of observations that shaped his theories. He spent several weeks of his journey on the Galapagos Islands, volcanic islands off the South American coast. He was astonished by the wide variety of island species, which often varied drastically from the mainland species and from island to island. The finches of the Galapagos are one such example. Darwin noted that they resembled the mainland finch, but varied in their nesting sites, beak size and eating habits. These variations led Darwin to ruminate about the descent of these finches from the mainland species, and how isolation on the islands may have contributed to their different traits.

After the *HMS Beagle* returned to England in 1836, Darwin waited over 20 years to publish his findings, as he knew the publication would be controversial. He used the time to publish other works and to gather further evidence on his grand theory of how life forms arise by descent from a common ancestor and change over time. In 1859, Darwin was compelled to publish *On the Origin of Species*, when the English naturalist Alfred Russel Wallace (1823-1913) published a similar theory.

At the same time that Darwin was developing his theories in the mid-1800s, Gregor Mendel was quietly studying genetics. It is unclear whether Darwin ever read Mendel's work, but he did not include any mention of genetics in *On the Origin of Species*. Mendel's research went largely unnoticed until after his death when early 20th century scientists realized the profound implications of his work. Working from the foundations he had laid, they gradually came to understand that organisms have a genetic code, the *genotype*. The observable expression of the code, the *phenotype*, depends on gene variants as *alleles*. The newly emerging wealth of knowledge about genetics provided an explanation and elaboration on natural selection that Darwin had not been able to describe.

On the Origin of the Species popularized the term *evolution*, as the cumulative change in the heritable characteristics of a population, species or group over time. It occurs when the *Hardy-Weinberg Law,* a central tenet of population genetics, is violated. This law states that phenotypic (allelic) and genotypic frequencies do not change from generation to generation, provided the following: genes are unaffected by evolutionary forces (no mutation), the population is infinitely large and is not affected by migration, and sexual selection does not occur (i.e., mating is random). In nature, these assumptions are often violated, resulting in evolution. Darwin described one mechanism of evolution, natural selection, but genetic drift, gene flow, and mutation are violations of the Hardy-Weinberg law.

Genetic drift is random changes in an allele's frequency in a population and occurs by chance. Some organisms, even if they are not the fittest of the population, may pass on more of their genes by the probability of chance.

Gene flow is the transfer of genes between two populations. This may occur by migration when one population moves into a new habitat and encounters another population. Gene flow may be within a species or between two different species for hybridization. *Hybrids* are offspring from two genetically dissimilar parents. Parents may be different from the same species or different species altogether. When two species hybridize, genes flow between the groups, introducing genetic diversity.

Mutations are changes in an organism's DNA genetic code from damage or replication errors. Mutations can be harmless, beneficial or fatal. When mutations introduce new traits that allow an organism to be more successful, that organism may survive and pass on its mutated code. Mutations are powerful agents of evolution.

Evolution can be regarded from two perspectives. *Microevolution* describes a change in allele frequency within a population. The population (i.e., gene pool or deme), is the arena of microevolution. Microevolution can be observed over short periods of time, especially in organisms such as bacteria.

Macroevolution is a pattern of change in groups of related species over long periods of geologic time. In a sense, macroevolution is the sum of all microevolution. The patterns of macroevolution determine *phylogeny*, the evolutionary relationships among species and groups of species. There are two models of macroevolution: phyletic gradualism and punctuated equilibrium.

Phyletic gradualism describes the constant, uniform accumulation of small changes, resulting in the gradual transformation of one species into a new species. Phyletic gradualism is generally disregarded as a model of macroevolution due to fossil evidence which indicates sudden, drastic speciation. *Punctuated equilibrium,* which describes geologically long periods of stasis with little to no evolution, is the model supported by the fossil record where geologically short periods show rapid evolution.

Notes for active learning

Notes for active learning

Natural Selection

Both Wallace and Darwin proposed *natural selection* as a driving mechanism of evolution. They theorized that environmental pressures select for organisms adapted in ways that make them most fit to reproduce. There are three pre-conditions for natural selection. The first condition is that the members of a population have random but heritable variations. Individuals in a population differ due to mutations and chromosomal recombination; new adaptations arise.

The second condition is that in the population more individuals are being produced in each generation than the environment can support. This creates selective pressure to adapt to survive in the face of scarce resources.

The third condition relies on both the first and second; it states that some individuals have adaptive characteristics that enable them to survive and reproduce.

Natural selection results in the better-adapted individuals passing on their adaptations to their offspring, while the less-adapted individuals have their alleles eliminated from the gene pool, as they are more likely to die before they can reproduce. An increasing proportion of individuals in succeeding generations have these adaptive characteristics. With time, the population may become a new species altogether. Since the environment is always changing, there is no perfectly-adapted organism. Over time, the fittest organisms may be poorly adapted to their changing environment. Extinction occurs when the fitness of a population (or species) has declined to the point that in each generation more individuals die than are born. This leads to a dwindling population and eventually to the complete elimination of the group.

Fitness

Fitness is the ability of an organism to pass genetic information onto future generations. Fitness is a measure of an organism's reproductive success. Evolutionary fitness differs from the colloquial term used to refer to a strong, healthy individual. Even the healthiest organism is considered to be "unfit" if it fails to reproduce. *Relative fitness* compares the fitness of one phenotype to another.

Organisms whose traits enable them to reproduce to a greater degree have greater fitness. For example, black western diamondback rattlesnakes are more likely to survive on lava flows, while lighter-colored rattlesnakes are more likely to survive on desert soil. Therefore, each species has adapted to maximize their fitness to survive in their habitat. *Survival of the fittest* is a component of the theory of natural selection that describes the process by which fitter individuals survive and pass on their traits, while fewer fit individuals die out.

Selection by differential reproduction

The term "survival of the fittest" is a bit misleading as it implies that mere survival of the organism is the driving force behind natural selection. However, organisms may be well-suited for survival but still fail to reproduce for some reasons. Evolutionary success relies on reproduction so that adaptations may be passed to subsequent generations. Because of this consideration, survival of the fittest may be more accurately termed reproduction of the fittest or *differential reproduction*. Differential reproduction is linked to the survival of the fittest and describes the way some individuals have a reproductive advantage over others.

Differential reproduction occurs naturally in the wild, but humans have manipulated natural selection for thousands of years. *Artificial selection* refers to the selection of certain traits in plants and animals that humans deem desirable, otherwise breeding. For example, humans have bred dogs from wolves by selecting for wolves with friendlier, more domestic traits. Over time, this artificial selection compounded, eventually producing the domestic dog; further selection for specific traits resulted in the wide variety of breeds seen today. Other domesticated animals have been produced by artificial selection, as well as many crop plants. Breeders of plants and animals are trying to produce organisms that possess desirable characteristics, such as high crop yields, resistance to disease, high growth rate and many other phenotypical characteristics that benefit people who consume or make use of these organisms.

Selective breeding is often performed with the goal of producing a hybrid from two parents that have different traits which are both desirable. Usually, the hybrid offspring possess the desirable traits of both parents. For example, one parent may possess dominant alleles for long life, while the other parent possesses dominant alleles for fast growth. When *crossed*, or bred*, the hybrid offspring ought to be both long-lived and fast-growing. The high fitness characteristic of hybrids is *hybrid vigor.* Hybridization often occurs in nature when two groups with overlapping habitats mate at a geographic boundary in the *hybrid zone.*

Concepts of natural and group selection

Natural selection can only utilize variations that are randomly provided; therefore, there is no directedness or anticipation of future needs. The organism is incapable of consciously picking and choosing the genome which it desires.

Only alleles that cause phenotypic differences are subject to natural selection. In diploid organisms, recessive alleles may only be expressed when there are two copies (i.e., homozygosity). Heterozygosity is responsible for the preservation of recessive alleles over time, as heterozygotes carry rare recessive alleles that may otherwise be selected against.

An example of this preservation is two alleles that encode for hemoglobin: a dominant, normal allele and a recessive, defective allele. Heterozygous expression of one abnormal hemoglobin allele results in the sickle cell trait, while homozygous expression of both recessive alleles results in full-blown anemia. Homozygotes with both dominant alleles have normal hemoglobin production.

There is a high frequency of the sickle cell allele in Africa, where there is a high incidence of malaria. A substantiated link has been made between those with the sickle cell trait and immunity to the effects of malaria. The sickle cell trait proves to be advantageous in areas where malaria is a greater threat to survival. Therefore, the higher the frequency of the sickle cell allele in Africa is evidence of natural selection. There is, of course, a tradeoff, as a higher frequency of the allele results in a higher frequency of regressive heterozygosity, causing sickle cell anemia. Theoretically, anemia is an excellent defense against malaria, but this is offset by the severe health issues which it can inflict.

Natural selection can be described in a variety of ways. *Directional selection* occurs when a trait at one extreme of a spectrum is favored, while traits on the opposite end of the spectrum are selected against. Over time, directional selection results in a shift of the distribution curve of allele frequency towards the favored allele. Natural selection leading to drug resistance in bacteria represents this type of selection. Another example is in trees in the rainforest, where trees compete for sunlight and selection favors the taller spectrum for trees.

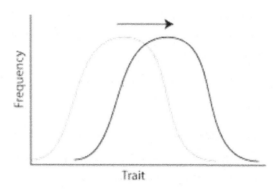

Directional selection shifts the distribution toward favored traits

Artificial selection is mostly directional selection as humans progressively select one trait over another. It has allowed humans to increase the efficiency of livestock animals and crop plants, such as increasing milk yield from cows by continuously breeding cows with high milk production.

Stabilizing selection occurs when both extreme phenotypes are eliminated, and the intermediate phenotype is favored. For example, the optimum number of eggs laid by Swiss starlings is four or five. If the female lays more or less than this number, fewer survive. Stabilizing selection results in the selection of those alleles that produce intermediate clutch sizes.

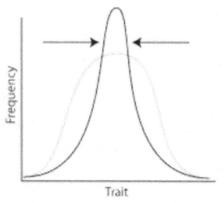

Stabilizing selection favors a narrow range of phenotypes

Disruptive selection occurs when the phenotypes at both extremes are favored. Birds occupying an area with two distinct niches, such as eating berries and eating seeds, may exhibit disruptive selection. Small beaks are selected for eating berries, while large beaks are selected for cracking seeds. The intermediate phenotype (medium beaks) is selected against because a medium beak is not useful for either berries or seeds.

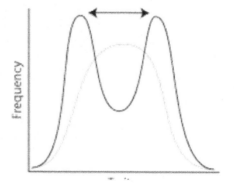

Disruptive selection favors traits at the extreme

Group selection is a natural selection which acts upon the group and not the individual. Group selection is often provided as an explanation for the existence of altruism. Altruism is when the fitness of an individual is sacrificed to benefit the group, usually the family, as the family shares similar genes. If altruism enables another family member to survive so that the genes can be passed on, the individual may exhibit altruism even if it means sacrificing his survival.

Sexual selection is the differential mating of males (or females) in a population. In most species, the females select for superior males, which increases the fitness of their offspring. Females invest more energy in reproduction and thus attempt to maximize the quality of their mates. Males primarily attempt to maximize the number of their mates. Male competition for mates leads to fights, with mating opportunities awarded to the strongest male. The genetically superior males exhibit traits which aid them in this competition and prove their strength (e.g., musculature, large stature or bigger horns). Sexual selection by females may lead to traits or behaviors in males that are not practical and do not increase the male's ability to survive. An example is colorful bird plumages, which may make certain species more easily identifiable by predators. The pressure for males to attract females usually leads to *sexual dimorphism*, in which males and females are observably different.

Adaptive radiation is the rapid development and evolution of many new species from a single ancestral species. It occurs when the ancestral species is introduced into an area where diverse geographic or ecological conditions are available for colonization. The observations by Darwin of finches illustrates the adaptive radiation of several species from one founder species of mainland finch.

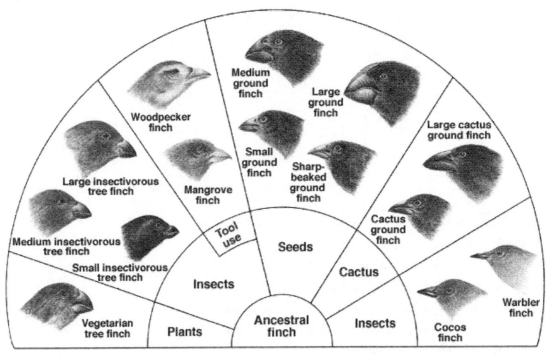

Darwin's theory of finches on the Galapagos Islands
illustrates adaptive radiation from differences in their environments

Evolutionary success as an increase in percent representation in the gene pool of the next generation

An increase in allele frequency represents evolutionary success for that allele. An increase in an individual's allele frequency is an evolutionary success for that individual.

The peppered moth in European cities can illustrate the changes in allele frequency over time. Pre-industrialization, these moths were light-colored. However, as pollution increased in the 1800s, soot collected on the sides of buildings, making the light-colored peppered moth more visible to predators. Mutations resulted in a new phenotype, darker than that of the white peppered moth. These new, darker peppered moths were favored over the lighter moths by natural selection, specifically directional selection. Over time, the frequency of the dark allele increased in the population, reaching 95% in most industrial European cities. However, in more recent years, soot has been reduced, and most buildings are lighter than in the late 1900s. Therefore, the allelic frequency of dark-peppered moths has decreased since then, demonstrating directional selection back towards the light phenotype.

Notes for active learning

Speciation

At a certain stage of evolution, one population may become so genetically different from the other that it becomes a new species, the process of *speciation*. After enough changes in gene pool phenotypic and genotypic frequencies have amassed, speciation is an inevitable result. The definition of a species is controversial and inexact, but a good rule of thumb is that members of different species are unable to reproduce with another and produce viable and fertile offspring.

Biogeography is the study of the geographic distribution of life forms on earth. Comparison of the animals of South America and the Galápagos Islands led Darwin to conclude that adaptation to the environment can cause diversification, including the origination of new species. His conclusions were greatly influenced by Charles Lyell (1797-1875), a geologist who first presented the idea that geological variations were formed over time by slow, continuous processes such as erosion. This notion was in direct contrast to the beliefs of the time, which stated that the contours of the Earth had been shaped by divine intervention and had only changed due to sudden, violent catastrophes. Lyell's theory of *uniformitarianism* supported what Darwin had observed in his study of geology and fossils.

Lyell and Darwin's conclusions were the precursors to tectonic plate theory, which describes the movement of Earth's crust. In 1920, German meteorologist Alfred Wegener presented data from across disciplines supporting continental drift. By the 1960s, the theory of continental drift was widely confirmed due to overwhelming geologic and evolutionary evidence. For example, many of the same fossils have been found on different continents, indicating there was a time when the continents were united.

Continental drift explains why the coastlines of several continents are mirror images of each other, as in the outlines of the west coast of Africa and the east coast of South America. The same geological features are found throughout the world in regions where the continents separated or collided.

The single, ancestral supercontinent of Pangea has separated over millions of years into the land masses seen today. As the continents drifted apart, organisms were separated, and this resulted in great speciation. One example is the marsupials of Australia, who were isolated from other mammals, and therefore are different from mammals on other continents.

Allopatric speciation is when a new species results from populations being separated by a geographic barrier. While geographically isolated, variations accumulate via natural selection, mutation, gene flow, and genetic drift until the two populations are reproductively isolated.

Sympatric speciation occurs when members of a single population develop genetic variations that prevent them from reproducing with the original population without geographic isolation. An example of sympatric speciation is polyploidy in plants. *Polyploidy* is the possession of more than two sets (2N) of chromosomes (e.g., 3N, 4N). The failure to reduce the chromosome number produces polyploid plants that reproduce successfully only with other polyploid plants. Backcrosses with diploid plants are sterile. Polyploidy leads to new species of plants.

Aside from the special case of polyploidy, evidence for sympatric speciation is sparse. Many researchers contend that sympatric speciation is, in fact, a poorly understood subtype of allopatric speciation. They assert that without a geographic barrier, interbreeding makes true sympatric speciation impossible. This issue is under intense research and debate in evolution.

Taxonomy

Taxonomy is the science of classifying organisms, an undertaking which humans have attempted for thousands of years. Carl Linnaeus (1707–1778), a Swedish naturalist, revolutionized the field of taxonomy when he introduced a streamlined, standardized taxonomic system which soon replaced the hundreds of disorganized systems previously used. Linnaeus' system featured binomial nomenclature, in which a two-part name is given for each species (e.g., *Homo sapiens*). Like other taxonomists of his time, Linnaeus believed that each species had an "ideal" structure and held a fixed place in the *scala naturae*, the divine hierarchy of life. Linnaeus thought that classification should describe the fixed features of species and reveal God's plan, and believed that the ideal form of each organism could be deduced and arranged according to the scala naturae. However, his later work with hybridization suggested species might change with time. He was the first prominent scientist to propose that humans were closely related to other primates. This was a bold declaration which clashed with the predominant belief that humans were fundamentally distinct from animals.

Classification establishes categories to assign species by their relationship to other species. A *taxon* is a group of organisms in a classification category; *Homo* or *Felis* are taxa at a genus level, describing the genera of hominids and cats, respectively. The term *species* is used for a taxonomic category below the rank of *genus*. When a species has a wide geographic range, variant types may interbreed where they overlap; these populations may be named as subspecies. For example, the wolf species *Canis lupus* contains around 40 subspecies, including *Canis lupus lupus* (Eurasian wolf) and *Canis lupus familiaris* (domestic dog). Addition of the subspecies makes for a trinomial, or three-part name.

Previous taxonomic classifications separated organisms into two categories, Animalia and Plantae. This proves to be incorrect, as many new organisms were discovered that appeared to fit in both or neither category. Currently, at least seven categories of classification are used. From broadest to narrowest, these taxa are a kingdom, phylum, class, order, family, genus, and species. Additional classification can be added to all taxonomic levels by adding the prefixes super-, sub-, or infra-.

The *domain* is a taxon above the level of the kingdom and is used to classify all organisms into Eukarya, Bacteria, and Archaea. These domains, as well as all the subsequent taxa, are under revision, controversy, and debate.

Definition of species

Most of the contention in taxonomy comes from trying to define a species. The controversy of what makes a species has sparked entire books and movements, and the discussion has been ongoing since the earliest days of taxonomy. Many of the arguments come down to philosophy, which makes consensus incredibly difficult.

One of the common definitions in use is that a species is a group of organisms that could interbreed and produce fertile, viable offspring without outside intervention. This is the *biological definition of a species*.

Gene flow, via sexual reproduction, cannot occur between species which are reproductively isolated. A *reproductive isolating mechanism* is any structural, functional or behavioral characteristic that prevents successful reproduction. *Prezygotic isolating mechanisms* are barriers that prevent two species from successfully mating or undergoing fertilization. These barriers include habitat and temporal, behavioral and mechanical isolation.

Habitat isolation occurs when two species occupy different habitats so that they are less likely to meet and attempt to reproduce. *Temporal isolation* is another prezygotic barrier, where two species occupy the same habitat but mate at different cycles (i.e., times of the year).

The species may have certain behaviors which preclude them from mating, as *behavioral isolation*. Flowers exhibit behavioral isolation when one is bee-pollinated, and the other is bird-pollinated so that the two do not exchange gametes. Another example is two species with different mating rituals so that the females of one species do not recognize the males of the other species as a mating partner. Even if a male and female manage to mate, *mechanical isolation* can prevent successful mating due to incompatible reproductive structures or another anatomy.

Gamete isolation is prezygotic reproductive isolation involving incompatibility of the gametes from two different species so they cannot fuse to form a zygote (i.e., fertilized egg). For example, the egg may have receptors for the sperm of its species.

Postzygotic isolating mechanisms prevent the development of a hybrid after fertilization. These barriers include sterility or inviability of the hybrid. Hybrids may be fertile in the first generation, but the second generation is infertile, as a *hybrid breakdown*. Sometimes populations are reunited before reproductive isolation is complete. In this scenario, they may still be able to reproduce fertile hybrids with increased genetic diversity, which is a benefit to the population.

Defining species based on reproductive isolation has limitations. Some groups are considered separate species based on other differences, even if they can hybridize where their ranges overlap. Furthermore, many species do not reproduce sexually and thus cannot be characterized by their sexual reproduction abilities. Finally, it is difficult to test and observe reproductive isolation.

Polymorphism

Early taxonomists such as Linnaeus classified organisms based on morphology, but this method has several limitations. This becomes apparent for variations among members of the same species, like sexual dimorphism. Sexual dimorphism is an example of morphological variations within a species or *polymorphism*.

Phenotypic polymorphism is the existence of two or more distinct phenotypic variations within a species. Sexual dimorphism falls under phenotypic polymorphism, as does blood type.

Polymorphism may be a result of sexual selection (e.g., sexual dimorphism) or due to different ecological niches. The two different forms of the peppered moth discussed earlier, are an example of polymorphism. As might be expected, it is sometimes difficult to determine whether two groups are polymorphs within the same species or different subspecies.

Genetic polymorphism applies the concept of polymorphism to the genotype. In the age of genomics, genetic polymorphism refers to the unique differences between the genomes of two individuals. In this regard, a species has a virtually infinite number of possible genetic polymorphs.

Balanced polymorphism is a form of natural selection which favors the balance of different polymorphs in the population, meaning the frequencies for each allele are equal. The *heterozygote advantage,* in which the heterozygous expression of two alleles is favorable, is one mechanism of balanced polymorphism. For example, the conservation of the recessive sickle cell allele in populations afflicted by malaria illustrates this mechanism, as heterozygotes have an advantage over homozygous individuals.

Balanced polymorphism may be a consequence of *frequency-dependent selection*. In this mechanism, the fitness of one phenotype is dependent on the frequency of another phenotype, so that an increase in the frequency of either phenotype is eventually balanced by the other.

In some cases, polymorphism may be controlled by environmental effects. In contrast to genetic polymorphism, this is a *polyphyletic system* (i.e., phyletic polymorphism), in which the phenome of the individual, rather than the genome, is altered to produce a morph. For example, many organisms have polyphyletic sex determination, in which the sex of an individual is regulated by factors such as temperature, predator density or current male-to-female ratio in the population. When polyphenic forms are in balance, they can be hard to distinguish from genetic polymorphs.

Adaptation and specialization

An *adaptation* is any change that an organism evolves to become more suited to its environment. Because of natural selection, adaptive traits accumulate in each succeeding generation. *Specialization* occurs as these adaptations allow the species to adopt a niche.

Most environments change, and so organisms must adapt or become extinct. Organisms might adapt to an environmental change in their habitat (e.g., change in soil acidity or precipitation). They may adapt to a new habitat due to migration or an invasion from outside species. Organisms must adapt in response to the evolution of other species in their habitat. When two species evolve in response to one another, they exhibit *co-adaptation*. For example, pollinating insects and flowers continually co-adapt with one another to maximize their mutualistic relationship. Co-adaptation may be more threatening, as when a host species evolves a more hostile gut environment, and the parasitic species must then adjust to maintain its survival in the host species' gut.

Exaptation is when, over time, many traits are readapted for a new purpose. *Maladaptation* is when traits are selected against because they became a distinct disadvantage.

Concepts of ecological niche and competition

Organisms occupy an *ecological niche,* the environment in which it lives and the role which it performs. The ecological niche is the organism's habitat as well as its behavior and relationship with the habitat. Organisms attempt to fill their niche by maximizing resources. This is accomplished by the specialization of the organism, as it adapts for its unique niche.

Resources can be best used when organisms occupy distinct niches, as they do not have to compete with one another. When niches overlap, resources become scarce, and the organisms threaten each other's survival. This results in competition, which can be both interspecific and intraspecific. Since members of the same species tend to occupy similar niches, *intraspecific competition* is common. Competition is a powerful selection pressure that drives organisms to evolve so that they can adapt to a different niche or better compete for resources in their current niche.

The concept of population growth through competition

Population growth is balanced by competition. At a low population density, competition is minimal, and population growth can occur rapidly. However, as the population grows, the number of available resources dwindle. *Carrying capacity* describes the maximum population that can be supported by the environment. As a population approaches its carrying capacity, intraspecific competition increases and slows population growth. Competition within a species can force members within the species to occupy different niches, which drives speciation.

Individuals may directly fight for mates, food, water, space or other such advantages. They may compete indirectly by depleting a resource which other organisms utilize. The *competitive exclusion principle* says that when two species use the same resource in the same place at the same time, the species diverge into different niches. This process is *niche differentiation*. If this divergence does not occur quickly enough, one species outcompetes the other by pushing the species from the shared overlap of their niches.

Exponential population growth is rare due to the pressures of competition. However, humans exhibit exponential population growth due to our ability to constantly find and exploit new resources.

Evolutionary ecology places species on a spectrum that relates to their population growth strategy. *r-selected* species mature rapidly, reproduce early and produce many offspring. A classic example of an r-selected organism is the mouse. Mice populations can grow exponentially due to their early onset of reproductive capacity and large brood sizes. They reserve the energy that would otherwise be spent on caring for their young by minimizing parental investment. Of course, this results in a high offspring mortality rate. The mice population often quickly grows above the carrying capacity of the environment, exhausting their resources. This results in sudden and intense competition (along with disease, overcrowding, and other threats), and the population dwindles. This fluctuation in population growth and subsequent decline is characteristic of r-selected organisms.

K-selected organisms, such as primates, tend to mature slowly. Once at reproductive age, they produce a few offspring at a time but reproduce throughout their lifetimes. These organisms live longer and have a higher offspring survival rate, but at the expense of great energy investment. They usually maintain a steady population near their carrying capacity.

Most organisms lie somewhere between r-selection and K-selection and may even be able to shift strategy depending on the environment and population density. Furthermore, organisms frequently exhibit r-selected traits in some areas and K-selected traits in others.

Inbreeding

Inbreeding is mating between individuals that are closely related. It increases the frequency of homozygotes, decreases the frequency of heterozygotes and decreases genetic diversity. Some organisms avoid inbreeding because it results in increased rates of disease and other undesirable traits. However, inbreeding occurs in the wild often, being unavoidable in small populations.

Inbreeding is a common result of artificial selection by humans. Continuous inbreeding for selection of particular genes results in the loss of certain genes decreased genetic diversity and can cause the accumulation of genetic defects. *Inbreeding depression* is the loss of fitness that results from these effects. In the long term, it is generally more advantageous for organisms to promote genetic diversity, and most present-day breeders strive to avoid inbreeding.

Genetic diversity serves as a way for populations to adapt to changing environments. More variation in the gene pool may help a species be prepared for a wide range of scenarios such as food shortage or an epidemic of disease. For example, an extremely contagious disease may threaten 99% of a species, but the remaining 1% possess an allele that provides them with resistance to the disease. With this allele, the population has a chance of surviving the disease that would otherwise force their extinction.

Outbreeding

Outbreeding (opposite of inbreeding) is when genetically dissimilar individuals are mated to increase genetic diversity. Generally, outbreeding increases the fitness of a population. However, crossing individuals from different populations rarely result in offspring that are less fit than those from within the same population. This is *outbreeding depression*.

Outbreeding depression may be the result of disruptive selection when the heterozygous genotype is selected against in favor of the homozygous genotypes. Then, the outbred progeny displays an intermediate phenotype that is not useful in either of the populations from which its parents originated.

Bottlenecks and genetic drift

A bottleneck is a severe reduction in population size. This can be caused, for example, by a natural disaster that eliminates a majority of the population. Bottlenecks can be deleterious to the population because the population is less able to adapt to environmental changes with a smaller, less diverse gene pool.

Bottlenecks increase the effect of genetic drift, because certain traits may be represented disproportionately when a population drastically decreases, especially if the decrease is random. For example, in a population of white and brown rabbits in equal numbers, a natural disaster may kill mostly brown rabbits by random chance. The bottlenecked population then displays a disproportionate representation of the white rabbits' alleles. In subsequent generations, the population may grow to its former size but still be made of mostly white rabbits.

The effects of genetic drift are amplified when a small group migrates out of a large population. As with a bottleneck, the small population has a small gene pool which may not accurately represent the original population. This is the *founder effect*. Founders can have a profound effect on the gene pool of the population after many generations. Genetic drift, along with mutations, gene flow, and natural selection, may cause the two populations to diverge over time greatly.

Divergent, parallel and convergent evolution

Divergent evolution occurs when species that originate from the same lineage or common ancestor evolve to become increasingly different over time. An example can be seen in bats and horses. Both bats and horses share the same mammalian lineage, but the ancestral mammalian forelimbs became wings in bats, hooves in horses. *Homologous structures* are different structures that arose from the same common ancestor (e.g., bat's wings and horse's hooves).

Divergent evolution giving rise to homologous structures

Parallel evolution involves two related species that are of the same lineage and evolve similarly. An example of this is the feeding structure in different species of crustaceans. The feeding structure of these crustaceans came from a mutation of their ancestors' legs, evolving them into mouthparts. This is a prime example of parallel evolution: the same lineage, similar traits, evolving from similar mechanisms or mutations.

Parallel evolution for two related species undergoing a similar evolution

Convergent evolution is a phenomenon in which two unrelated species of different lineage, by different mechanisms, evolve closer together to become more similar. An example can be seen in bats and butterflies. Both have wings, but they came from totally different lineages and evolved through different mechanisms or mutations. These similar structures which arose by convergent evolution are *analogous structures.* Analogous structures can be deceptive, as they often seem to suggest common lineage when in fact the structures are similar merely by chance.

Convergent evolution from unrelated species that become more similar

Coevolution occurs when two species evolve in response to one another. It is essentially the accumulation of co-adaptations. For example, a predator may develop a new trait that aids in better hunting prey. In response to this newly developed trait in the predator, the prey may develop a trait that allows it to evade the predator more successfully.

Coevolution with an evolutionary relationship due to another species

Symbiotic relationships: parasitism, commensalism, and mutualism

Symbiosis is a relationship between two species involving three types: parasitism, commensalism, and mutualism.

Parasitism is a relationship in which one organism, the parasite, benefits at the expense of the other organism, the host. An example of this is in tapeworms that live in the intestines of animals, causing illness. All pathogenic bacteria and viruses are parasites.

Commensalism occurs when one organism benefits while the other is not affected. Plants exhibit commensalism when they disperse their seeds by sticking them to an animal's fur. The animal is neither harmed nor benefited, but the plant has the advantage of wider seed distribution.

Mutualism is when both species benefit. A classic mutualistic relationship is that between fungi and algae. The fungus provides anchorage and absorption for the alga, while the alga provides photosynthesis; together they form a *lichen.*

Notes for active learning

Notes for active learning

Evolutionary Time as Measured by Gradual Random Changes in Genome

Random genetic mutations that are not acted on by natural selection occur at a constant rate. By measuring the amount of these neutral mutations, the amount of elapsed time can be determined. The genome differences between two species can be compared to determine how long ago they may have diverged. This concept of dating is the *molecular clock*.

Molecular clock to estimate time-based on genomic differences

Genetic differences may be measured in the *phenome* (i.e., the sum total of phenotypic traits), or in the genome, by DNA nucleotide sequences.

The simple molecular clock may indicate relative periods of time between two organisms but cannot be used to assign a numerical date. Calibration of the clock, via comparison against known fossil dates or other evidence, allows for this precision.

Notes for active learning

Origin of Life

About 13.8 billion years ago (b.y.a.), all material in the universe was created in a massive expansion of matter as the Big Bang. From a singularity of infinite density, all matter and space were suddenly expelled. The sudden cooling of the superheated ejecta facilitated the combination of atomic components into atoms and molecules. These clouds of gasses eventually cooled and formed the principal components of galaxies, including stars and planets.

The Earth came into being about 4.6 b.y.a. when dust and gasses leftover from the formation of the sun coalesced. Heat and gravity stratified the Earth into several layers: a molten core of iron and nickel, a semi-liquid mantle of silicate minerals and a solid crust created by the upwelling of lava from the mantle. The early Earth was so hot that water existed as a vapor in dense, thick clouds. As the Earth cooled over the first billion years, water vapor condensed into rain, which formed the primordial oceans.

The Earth's size provides a gravitational field strong enough to hold an atmosphere. Earth's primitive atmosphere differed from its current atmosphere, which consists of water vapor (H_2O), nitrogen (N_2), carbon dioxide (CO_2), small amounts of hydrogen (H_2), and carbon monoxide (CO). The primitive atmosphere was likely formed by gases from volcanoes and celestial bodies which bombarded the earth.

The primitive atmosphere contained little free oxygen and was probably a reducing atmosphere, as opposed to the oxidizing atmosphere of today. An *oxidizing atmosphere* contains free O_2 and inhibits the formation of complex organic molecules. A *reducing atmosphere* lacks free O_2 and allows the formation of complex organic molecules (i.e., carbon-based compounds). Scientists believe that this characteristic of the primitive atmosphere was crucial to allow simple elements to form organic molecules that are the basis of life. Another important contribution may have come from the comets and meteorites which pelted the Earth, as they may have carried organic chemicals. Abiotic (non-living) factors are the physical and chemical components of a system (e.g., light, temperature, soil, pH, etc.)

Some evidence suggests that the primitive atmosphere was less reducing than previously thought, containing less ammonia. In this case, abiotic synthesis may have been carried out in the oceans at hydrothermal vents, which expelled large amounts of ammonia. It is possible that chemical evolution occurred both at these vents and in the atmosphere.

Monomers evolve

Chemical evolution is the increase in complexity of chemicals that led to the first cells. Chemical evolution gave way to biological evolution when the first self-replicating molecules arose and began to undergo natural selection. Like living organisms, biotic molecules are subject to variations and natural selection, enabling evolution.

In the early 1900s, a biochemist named Alexander Oparin suggested that organic molecules could be formed from the elements of the reducing atmosphere: methane (CH_4), ammonia (NH_3), hydrogen (H_2) and water (H_2O). In Oparin's vision, lack of oxidation and decay allowed organic molecules to form a thick, warm organic soup from which life arose.

His theory motivated chemists, such as Stanley Miller, to perform experiments that imitated the conditions of the early Earth. In 1953, Miller published the results of his experiment on the chemical origin of life, called the Miller Spark-Discharge Experiment, or the Urey-Miller Experiment. His experiment assumed a reducing atmosphere that had been bombarded by kinetic energy from lightning. A sealed flask of water vapor simulated this early Earth. The methane, ammonia, and hydrogen being continually subjected to electrical sparks. Within a week, a deep red solution formed that contained hydrogen cyanide (HCN), formaldehyde (CH_2O) and other related compounds. These simple organic molecules then assembled into many different amino acids, the monomers of proteins.

Miller concluded that preliminary organic molecules could have been originated in a reducing atmosphere. Amino acids formed readily in Miller's spark-discharge experiment so that they could have formed in the conditions of early Earth. More recent evidence suggests that amino acids could have been seeded from comets and meteorites. Interstellar dust that constantly falls on Earth contains hydrogen cyanide and aldehydes, key reactants for forming amino acids.

Other evidence since Miller's experiment has indicated that Earth had a more oxidizing atmosphere than previously thought. Experiments based on this assumption have yielded more diverse molecules than those from the Urey-Miller experiment, including amino acids, nitrogenous bases, sugars, and hydroxy acids – all crucial for the existence of life. Current scientific thought assumes an atmosphere that is 60% hydrogen, 20% water vapor, 10% carbon dioxide and 5% hydrogen sulfide.

One puzzle that persists is that chemical evolution experiments have yielded a mixture of left-handed and right-handed enantiomers (non-superimposable mirror images). Although both forms of every amino acid exist in nature, only the left-handed forms are found in living organisms. Scientists have not yet been able to answer the question of how the left-handed forms were utilized in living organisms.

Polymers evolve

As the Earth's primordial oceans began to collect the organic monomers formed in the atmosphere, amino acids and nucleotides polymerized to form proteins and nucleic acids, respectively. Polymerization occurred by condensation, the removal of a molecule of water from two monomers to form a bond between them. The opposite process, hydrolysis, depolymerizes macromolecules by the addition of water to break bonds.

There are a few challenges that come with the formation of polymers. The first is that hydrolysis dominates in the chemical equilibrium over condensation because hydrolysis increases entropy (randomness) while condensation decreases it. This means that the breaking of polymers by hydrolysis is a more thermodynamically (energetically) favorable reaction. Polymerization requires energy input, which is accomplished in living organisms by coupling the reaction with an energy-producing reaction (e.g., hydrolysis of ATP). However, scientists still do not know exactly how this was done in the pre-biotic era. It can be challenging to model polymerization reactions based on the presumed conditions of ancient Earth.

More recently, scientists showed that macromolecules could have polymerized in the muddy tide pools and beaches of ancient Earth. They mixed nucleotides and minerals from mud and collected the resulting polymers, finding nucleic acids up to 40 nucleotides long. The experiment was repeated with amino acids, and once again they found that the monomers had managed to polymerize into proteins up to 55 amino acids long.

Sidney Fox, who demonstrated that amino acids form peptides abiotically if exposed to dry heat, described the *Protein World Hypothesis*, or *Protein-first Hypothesis*. This hypothesis states that amino acids collected in shallow puddles along the rocky shore and the heat of the sun caused them to form *proteinoids,* small polypeptides that have some catalytic properties. Proteinoids form small *microspheres* in water due to their hydrophobic amino acids. These proteinoid microspheres have some similarity to lipid cell membranes, so the Protein World Hypothesis contends that polypeptides were the first precursors to living entities.

This hypothesis has been largely refuted since it was found that proteinoids are not proteins. Furthermore, the first living macromolecules would need to be able to self-replicate, something that neither proteinoids nor proteins are capable of accomplishing.

The *RNA World Hypothesis* states that RNA was the precursor of the first cell. It has been proven that special RNA called *ribozymes* can act as enzymes. It is known that some viruses contain RNA genes with a protein enzyme called reverse transcriptase that uses RNA as a template to form DNA. This evidence shows that RNA could have possibly assumed the roles of both DNA and protein enzymes on early Earth, and eventually have led to the rise of both. Supporters of this hypothesis label this an "RNA world."

RNA is an excellent model for chemical evolution. When replicating, many inexact copies (mutations) are made randomly, which produces diversity in the population of self-replicating RNA.

Mutants that are more efficient self-replicators produce more copies of themselves, dominating the population. UV radiation or a chemical reaction may destroy less efficient self-replicators before they can copy themselves. Thus, chemical evolution results, changing the composition of the population over time. This is essentially natural selection, just directed toward abiotic systems rather than living organisms.

Most researchers subscribe to the idea of an RNA world, but this is not a definitive theory.

The Clay Hypothesis, first suggested by Graham Cairns-Smith in the 1960s, proposes that amino acids polymerized in clay, with radioactivity providing energy. Clay attracts small organic molecules and contains iron and zinc atoms, which serve as inorganic catalysts for polypeptide formation. In this hypothesis, clay would have collected energy from radioactive decay and discharged it whenever there were temperature or humidity changes. Nucleotides and amino acids may have polymerized in this environment and began to associate with one another, meaning they evolved simultaneously. An advantage of this theory is that it addresses the chicken-and-egg paradox, with both RNA and proteins arising at the same time.

DNA is not considered a possible candidate for the first living entity because it has low reactivity and therefore would not be an effective catalyst. Unlike RNA, DNA has never been shown to have catalytic properties in a living organism.

Evolution of a protocell

Before the first true cell arose, there would have been a *protocell* with a lipid-protein membrane and the ability to perform metabolic reactions. Although the concept of the proteinoid has questioned, Fox's experiments proved that lipids and proteins could form complex membranes under the right conditions.

Oparin believed that the protocell could have developed from *coacervate droplets*. Coacervate droplets are spheres of lipids that spontaneously form under the right temperature, ionic environment, and pH. Coacervate droplets selectively absorb and incorporate various substances from the surrounding solution, similar to the semipermeable membranes of cells. Oparin's hypothesis still has relevance today, but some of his concepts have been superseded. Modern scientists cannot decide on a model for the protocell. Some scientists postulate that fatty acids organized into *micelles*, another form of a lipid sphere, in a mineral-rich clay environment. The clay would have allowed for the development of nucleotides that would spontaneously assemble into RNA.

There is evidence that abiotic amino acid synthesis and peptide polymerization could have occurred at hydrothermal vents. The first protocells may have used pre-formed ATP to drive reactions, but as supplies dwindled, natural selection would favor protocells that could synthesize ATP.

Several hypotheses now operate under the assumption that life began at hydrothermal vents. *Chemosynthetic* models claim that energy for peptide synthesis came from the electrochemical gradients within the microcompartments of the vents, while *thermosynthetic* models suggest thermal cycling as the primary energy source.

In 1998, Gunter Wachtershauser and Claudia Huber published a paper describing how they created peptides using iron-nickel sulfides under vent-like conditions. These minerals have a charged surface that attracts amino acids and provides electrons to polymerize them. Supporters of the *Iron-Sulfur World Hypothesis* (a chemosynthetic model) suggest that life arose in these hydrothermal vents, aided by the high pH, high temperature and the richness of iron and sulfur. Under this theory, lipids would be synthesized and anchor to the walls of the vent, before forming into a lipid membrane sphere and associating with proteins to form a protocell. Another hydrothermal vent hypothesis focuses on zinc rather than iron and sulfur (the *Zinc World Hypothesis*). Both hypotheses assume that early energy production was accomplished by fermentation, which generates ATP in the absence of oxygen. This would make glycolysis a crucial adaptation for the first protocells. The glycolysis pathway is prevalent in living organisms, indicating that it must have evolved early in the history of life.

Thermosynthetic models posit chemiosmosis rather than glycolysis as a method of ATP production. Chemiosmosis is an important part of cellular respiration and photosynthesis, describing the movement of hydrogen atoms across a membrane to drive the enzyme ATP synthase. Thus, thermosynthesis assumes ATP synthase was the first protein enzyme to evolve.

A *heterotroph* is an organism that cannot synthesize organic compounds from inorganic substances and therefore must take in preformed organic compounds. An *autotroph* is an organism that makes organic molecules from inorganic nutrients. If a protocell were a heterotrophic fermenter living on the organic molecules in the prebiotic soup, this would indicate heterotrophs preceded autotrophs. However, if the protocell evolved at hydrothermal vents in the oceans, then chemosynthetic autotrophs would have preceded heterotrophs.

A self-replication system evolves

The chemical evolution theory rests on the idea that the precursor to life was a self-replicating molecule, which many agree would have to be RNA. Supporters of the Protein-first Hypothesis argue that proteins could have self-replicating abilities that have not yet been discovered.

In most biological systems, genetic information flows from DNA to RNA to protein. It is possible that this path developed in stages. Once the protocell was capable of reproduction, it became a true cell and began the age of biological evolution.

After DNA formed, the genetic code still had to evolve to store information. Because the current code is subject to fewer errors than other possible codes, and because it minimizes mutations, it is likely to have undergone a natural selection process.

In summary, most biologists suspect life evolved in basic steps. Abiotic synthesis of organic molecules such as amino acids occurred in the atmosphere or at hydrothermal vents. Monomers then joined together to form polymers, perhaps in tidal pools, clay or hydrothermal vents. The first polymers were likely RNA, followed by proteins. A self-replicating RNA molecule appeared in the prebiotic soup due to chemical evolution and made copies of itself using free ribonucleotides in its environment. Lipids aggregated to form a protocell that had limited ability to grow; if it developed in the primordial soup, it was a heterotroph, but if it developed at a hydrothermal vent, it was a chemoautotroph. Once the protocell was able to replicate its genetic code, it became a true cell.

Development of species from protocell

The history of Earth is divided into *eons,* which are further subdivided into *eras,* then *periods*. Life first arose in the eons before the *Phanerozoic Eon,* the current eon. Collectively, these eons are the *Precambrian Supereon,* because they occurred before the first period of the Phanerozoic, the *Cambrian*. The Precambrian encompasses more than 80% of the geologic time scale. This time is when the chemical and biological evolution of life, the early development of prokaryotes, eukaryotes and even the first multicellular life.

After the development of the protocell, it would evolve for millions of years until it developed into a true unicellular organism as far back as 4 b.y.a. In all likelihood, these organisms were chemoautotrophs that resemble today's archaea as prokaryotic, lacking any membrane-bound organelles.

The unicellular chemoautotrophs found around 3.5 b.y.a. were the *last universal common ancestor* (LUCA) of all living organisms. LUCA diverged into two major domains: *Bacteria* and *Archaea*. Photosynthesis arose with the emergence of cyanobacteria around 3.4 b.y.a. These bacteria use water as a reducing agent during photosynthesis, producing oxygen as a by-product. *Stromatolites*, fossilized remains of the sediments excreted by cyanobacteria, provide fossil evidence of their age. From cyanobacteria, oxygen levels in the primitive oceans rose so high over the next billion years that it converted the reducing atmosphere into an oxidizing atmosphere. This *Great Oxygenation Event* resulted in the extinction of many obligate anaerobes, which could only survive in areas of low or nonexistent oxygen. Since that time, aerobic organisms have dominated the Earth.

Eukaryotic cells appeared later in the Precambrian, around 1.6 to 2.1 b.y.a. Their exact origin is unclear. Some scientists propose that membrane-bound organelles arose from invaginations of a prokaryote's cell membrane. Others propose that two prokaryotes fused together, or one engulfed the other by phagocytosis. These may have been two bacteria, or perhaps a bacterium and an archaeon. They would have developed a symbiotic relationship, with the host cell becoming the eukaryote and the other evolving into an organelle. This is the *symbiogenesis* or *endosymbiotic theory*. Under this theory, the anaerobic host cell would have taken in an aerobic bacterium which would share its genome with the host cell and eventually develop into a mitochondrion. Some host cells would take in a cyanobacterium that would develop into a chloroplast. Endosymbiosis can still be observed in modern unicellular organisms, lending credence to the theory. Mitochondria are present in all eukaryotic cells, while chloroplasts exist only in plants and algae. This observation suggests that mitochondria arose before chloroplasts in the evolutionary timeline since they are universal.

At this time, some eukaryotes were developing cilia and flagella to facilitate movement. Motility was a huge advantage in the Precambrian Eon, allowing species to explore new niches. Organisms were continually diversifying to occupy and adapt to these previously sterile environments. Early prokaryotes and eukaryotes were exclusively asexual, but around 1.2 b.y.a. Some of them evolved meiosis and sexual reproduction. It is not known exactly when multicellular organisms appeared, but they would have been microscopic. The variety of eukaryotic microorganisms that emerged around this time are *protists* (e.g., algae, plankton and amoebas). They took the form of large unicellular organisms or multicellular colonies. Their size must have been an advantage at the time, allowing them to out-compete other organisms.

At the time, all organisms existed in the sea, because on land the harsh UV radiation made life improbable. The oxygen content of the air continued to increase until 600 million years ago (m.y.a.) when it allowed for the formation of an ozone layer in the upper atmosphere. This ozone layer shielded most UV radiation from reaching the earth's surface, allowing organisms to live on land for the first time. Near the end of the Precambrian, complex multicellular life began to arise. Most data about this time comes from fossils of the Ediacaran Hills in South Australia, which date to 600 m.y.a. These organisms were soft-bodied primitive invertebrates, which likely inhabited the oceans and shallow mudflats.

Following the eons of the Precambrian came the Phanerozoic Eon. The first era of the Phanerozoic is the *Paleozoic Era* ("ancient life"), which includes the Cambrian Period along with five others: Ordovician, Silurian, Devonian, Carboniferous, and Permian. The Paleozoic Era lasted over 300 million years and was an active period with three major *mass extinctions*, events in which a large number of organisms went extinct in a small window of time. Tectonic, oceanic and climatic changes are often cited as possible triggers of mass extinction. These changes may be drastic (e.g., asteroid impact) or gradual (e.g., sea level change and global heating or cooling).

The *Cambrian Explosion*, about 542 m.y.a., marked the beginning of the Cambrian Period. This time included widespread evolution and diversification of existing prokaryotes and eukaryotes, along with the arrival of fungi and invertebrate animals. Nearly all modern phyla evolved at this time.

Animals are believed to have descended from flagellated colonial protists, making their closest relatives the modern choanoflagellates. Colonies of the choanoflagellate ancestor perhaps gave rise to the first animals: the sponges. Sponges could grow to one meter across, making them massive compared to existing species at the time. They have no nervous system and are asymmetrical.

Shortly after the sponges, the cnidarians (jellyfish, sea anemones, etc.) and the ctenophores (box jellies) evolved. These animals had symmetry in all planes, as *radial symmetry*, along with rudimentary sensory organs.

Animals higher than the sponges, cnidarians, and ctenophores are *bilaterians* for their bilateral symmetry. The first bilaterians were protostomes, which evolved throughout the Cambrian Period. *Protostomes* are defined by gastrulation during embryonic development. In protostomes, the first opening formed in the blastula, the blastopore, becomes the mouth. The earliest would have been small, primitive, parasitic organisms, such as flatworms and nematodes. Soon, mollusks overtook the Cambrian seas. At this time, marine arthropods (crustaceans) and early deuterostomes such as *echinoderms* (sea stars and kin) were evolving. *Deuterostomes* are characterized by a blastopore which first becomes an anus, with the mouth forming afterward.

In the early Cambrian Period, plants were simple, unicellular and aquatic. Throughout the Cambrian and the ensuing *Ordovician Period,* 490 m.y.a., marine algae expanded to freshwater. Fungi began symbiotic relationships with plant roots, allowing plants to colonize bare rocks. Back in the oceans, invertebrate fish diverged from the deuterostome ancestor, but protostomes such as mollusks and crustaceans still dominated.

At the end of the period, 450 m.y.a., the *Ordovician-Silurian extinction* eliminated 70% of all marine life, paving the way for fish to dominate in later periods. The marine invertebrates re-diversified, and crustaceans overtook mollusks as the rulers of the seas.

The *Silurian Period* 450 m.y.a. Includes the establishment of terrestrial plants. More advanced adaptations such as vascular structures, stems, leaves, roots, and seeds evolved over the next 100 million years. The Silurian witnessed the first terrestrial arthropods, the arachnids. Jawless fish emerged at this time, evolving into jawed fishes some 395 to 420 m.y.a. Some jawed fish became "armored" with heavy, bony plates; these armored fish are all but extinct. The armored fishes diverged into bony and cartilaginous fish at the end of the Silurian Period. As competition increased and available habitats decreased, most cartilaginous fish adapted to be large, aggressive, and predatory, leading to shark species. Other cartilaginous fish include skates and rays.

In the ensuing *Devonian Period,* 420 m.y.a., the bony fish diversified into ray-finned and lobe-finned fish. This period is the "Age of Fishes," as they dominated the seas. However, arthropods were undergoing significant diversification, and an explosion of plant life also occurred at this time, resulting in the first true trees and seeds. Near the end of the Devonian, as early as 395 m.y.a., lobe-finned fishes ventured onto land. These became amphibians, the first *tetrapods* (four-limbed vertebrates). The *Late Devonian extinction* 360 m.y.a. eliminated 70% of species worldwide.

The end of the Late Devonian extinction marked the beginning of the *Carboniferous Period,* which spawned the growth of forests and an abundance of seedless vascular plants such as horsetails and ferns. These ancient plants provided most of the carbon (in the form of coal) that is used today. Insects, which had by now ventured onto land, developed wings and exploded in diversity. Amphibians began to dominate land in the *Carboniferous Period,* marking this the "Age of Amphibians." Some amphibians became particularly well-adapted to land, evolving into reptiles at the end of the Carboniferous, around 300 m.y.a. Reptiles quickly colonized land and specialized even further to their terrestrial environment. At this time, terrestrial prey was scarce because not many animals were able to survive on land. As a result, many reptiles were herbivores so that they could take advantage of the plants available on land and shorelines. The first reptiles and amphibians to reach land and die would have broken down into simpler organic compounds. This enriched the nutrients in the soil, allowing plants to grow and microorganisms to exist on a larger scale. Organisms that relied on these microorganisms would migrate to land, followed by predators of these organisms. This continued ecological succession would eventually allow land to support life on a scale that approached that of the sea.

After the Carboniferous, came the final period of the Paleozoic Era: the *Permian Period.* At the border of the Carboniferous and Permian, reptiles had diverged into sauropsids and synapsids. The *sauropsids* were the ancestors of dinosaurs, modern reptiles, and birds, while the *synapsids* were proto-mammals that resembled reptiles more than the mammals of today. These organisms are also para mammals, proto-mammals or mammal-like reptiles. During the Permian, sauropsids and synapsids continued to flourish in a climate which was becoming increasingly dry; a massive desert developed in the interior of the supercontinent Pangea. Early conifers and seeded ferns largely replaced the swampy forests of the Carboniferous. The end of the Permian, 252 m.y.a., saw the greatest extinction in history, the *Permian-Triassic extinction.* This resulted in the decimation of over 95% of marine life and 70% of terrestrial vertebrates, as well as many insects. The cause of this event, like most other extinctions, is unknown, but it has been suggested that an excess of carbon dioxide due to a change in ocean circulation contributed to the extinction.

The Permian-Triassic extinction marks the beginning of the *Mesozoic Era.* Throughout the Mesozoic, gymnosperms flourished, but flowering plants had yet to evolve. Marine animals began to diversify to re-occupy all the niches that had been left empty by the extinction. Meanwhile, many of the surviving reptiles became larger and evolved into true dinosaurs and crocodilian species. The entire era is the "Age of Dinosaurs."

The first period of the Mesozoic, the *Triassic Period,* covered the evolution of dinosaurs into both avian (bird-like) and reptilian species. It included the splitting of *Pangea* (hypothetical supercontinent including all land masses) into separate continents. The mass *Triassic-Jurassic Extinction* at the end of the Triassic (around 200 m.y.a.) eliminated most synapsids and almost all large amphibians. This event allowed dinosaurs to dominate in the succeeding *Jurassic Period.* The diversification of dinosaurs was truly astonishing; they came to occupy a massive number of ecological niches. Dinosaurs ruled the land, sea, and air, and grew to mammoth proportions throughout the Jurassic. The surviving synapsids evolved into the first true mammals, but these were small and resembled rodents.

Dinosaurs were the most advanced tetrapods at the time, and some of them even moved towards bipedal motion. Many dinosaurs were huge compared to any previous organisms on Earth. Their sheer bulk and power had an obvious selective advantage. These herbivores were tall enough to graze on the top of trees, which other organisms were not able to reach. Many predators became bigger and stronger, such as the *Tyrannosaurus rex*, the largest carnivore on Earth at the time. The Jurassic Period witnessed the emergence of flying reptiles as *pterosaurs,* the most famous of which is the pterodactyl.

The Jurassic was succeeded by the *Cretaceous Period* some 145 m.y.a. This period was when avian dinosaurs evolved into true birds, some of which dominated the skies and began to outcompete flying dinosaurs. The first flowers emerged. Meanwhile, the continents from Pangea had come to resemble the continents of today. This geological change was a major factor that molded the evolution of species. For example, the collision of the supercontinent Eurasia with Africa allowed species from each region to interbreed, compete or predate on one another, greatly accelerating evolution.

From the Triassic Period until the dinosaurs' last moment of glory in the Cretaceous Period, a competitor was quietly emerging: the mammals. Throughout the Mesozoic Era, mammals gradually shed their reptilian features in favor of hair, live birth (viviparity) and other mammalian characteristics. By the Cretaceous Period, they had diverged into placentals and marsupials. Although the dinosaurs still dominated, the mammals became a competitor for land resources and even preyed on smaller dinosaurs.

No one knows exactly how the dinosaurs became extinct, but their disappearance at the end of the Cretaceous, 65 m.y.a., made many ecological niches available to other organisms. The consensus is that a major geological event of the *K-T* or *K-Pg extinction* extinguished nearly all the dinosaurs except for the avian dinosaurs, which would develop into birds. It spared many of the non-dinosaur reptiles and mammals. Many causes of this extinction have been proposed. One of the most popular theories is that an asteroid struck the Earth, resulting in catastrophic changes to Earth's climate. It has been suggested that mammals survived because they were smaller and required fewer resources to survive.

Furthermore, many lived underground and thus could have survived an event like an asteroid impact. Whatever the reason for their survival, the mammals flourished once relieved of competition and predation by dinosaurs. The K-T extinction 65 m.y.a. marks the end of the Mesozoic Era and the beginning of the *Cenozoic Era,* which extends to the present day. It is rife with the evolution and proliferation of mammals, as well as drastic climate changes. Although the entire era is the "Age of Mammals," birds dominated in the first period, the *Paleogene Period.* Many of these ancient birds were large and aggressive and posed a great threat to mammals in the early years of the Cenozoic.

In the Paleogene Period, mammals were small and inhabited overcrowded jungle environments. Flowering plants were diverse and plentiful by the Cenozoic era, and primates had adapted to living in flowering trees. The first primates were small squirrel-like animals, eventually evolving into monkeys and apes. Early whales were semi-terrestrial but fully returned to the oceans in later years as their limbs regressed.

Later in the Paleogene, global cooling resulted in the reduction of jungles and the proliferation of grasslands, allowing mammals to grow large. This trend continued throughout the *Neogene Period,* which began about 23 m.y.a. Many modern mammals evolved during this time, including the apes. At the end of the Neogene, it is believed that some of the great apes evolved into the *hominids,* the human-like ancestors of modern *Homo sapiens sapiens.* These apes would have moved from the jungles and ventured into the open savanna. They developed bipedal motion, an important advantage which allowed them to look across the tall grasses of the savanna for predators and prey alike. Bipedalism freed the hands and allowed for more efficient terrestrial travel in savannahs and scattered forests. They are *australopithecines,* which translates as "southern ape."

The previous scientific thought held Europe to be the birthplace of hominids, due to the Eurocentric outlook of the time and the discovery of some fossils in Europe. However, throughout the 20th century, archaeologists uncovered even older australopithecine remains in Africa, with Africa coming to be generally acknowledged as the origin of humans. The most famous of these discoveries was Lucy, found in Ethiopia in the 1980s. She represents the species *Australopithecus afarensis*, meaning "southern ape from afar," which roamed the earth 3 to 5 m.y.a. While *A. afaranesis* is generally cited as a direct ancestor to modern humans, that title may have belonged to other australopithecines of the time.

The paleoanthropologists who discovered Lucy and other fossilized remains used skeletal features to map the subtle evolutionary changes in hominids. The position of the pelvis and spine can be used to determine whether an organism was bipedal and upright or walked on all fours. Lucy would have been bipedal, with short, stout stature and a relatively small cranium. The skull is one of the most important skeletal features in hominid fossils. Development of a larger brain, and thus a larger skull, is one of the most prominent markers of human evolution.

Today, the advent of DNA sequencing, genomics, and molecular biology has helped researchers map evolutionary relationships between humans and the great apes. There is evidence to suggest that the species *Australopithecus africanus* would have eventually superseded *A. afarensis* some 2 to 3 m.y.a. due to some key adaptations. They would have been taller and slimmer, and their hands better adapted for tool use. Most notably, they had a larger cranium with more human-like facial features. *Africanus* developed into *Australopithecus robustus* and *Australopithecus boisei,* two species once thought to be direct ancestors of man. However, it is now believed that they became extinct and that other descendants of *A. africanus* fathered the first members of genus *Homo.*

Homo habilis, dated to 2.8 m.y.a. at the earliest, may mark the transition from genus *Australopithecus* to genus *Homo.* These hominids exhibited the first evidence of intelligence comparable to that of modern man, most notably in their use of basic stone tools.

The *Quaternary Period,* which continues today, began 2.6 m.y.a. Early in the Quaternary Period, global cooling resulted in extensive glaciation, the Ice Ages. The Ice Ages spurred the evolution of mammals with significant capacity to retain heat, such as giant ground sloths, beavers, wolves, bison, woolly rhinoceroses, mastodons and mammoths. Many of these species are now extinct, likely due to hunting by humans. While the other latitudes iced over, deserts developed at the tropics.

During the Quaternary Period, *H. habilis* diverged into some groups, the classification of which is still debated. The prevailing view is that *Homo erectus* evolved from *H. habilis* around 1.3 to 1.8 m.y.a. *and* began to migrate out of Africa into Asia and Europe.

The earliest evidence of true humans has been dated to around 1.6 m.y.a. These individuals, *archaic humans,* included numerous groups, such as *Homo neanderthalensis* and *Homo heidelbergensis*, which are extinct today. It is often debated whether these groups were subspecies of *Homo sapiens* or a different species. There is still little consensus on the issue, and it is nearly impossible to draw clear lines between the various *Homo* species and subspecies.

Archaic humans spread throughout Africa, Asia, and Europe over the next 1 million years. They began to develop wooden tools, like spears and exhibited cranial capacity comparable to modern humans. Their cognitive abilities allowed them to survive in hostile environments and begin to dominate Earth. Humans would eventually learn to control their environment and protect themselves against many of the pressures of natural selection. *Homo sapiens sapiens* is the subspecies which represents modern humans, originating as far back as 500,000 years ago and persisting down to the present day. Intentional duplication of sapiens distinguishes them from their direct ancestor *Homo sapiens idaltu.*

The *Neanderthals* are well known for their hypothesized common ancestry and co-existence with modern man. They became widespread across both Europe and Asia around 250,000 years ago. Once believed to be of a separate genus, it is now accepted that they were a species or subspecies of genus *Homo.* Neanderthals' robust and stocky nature made them well-suited to the cold, but *Homo sapiens* dominated the deserts. Eventually, *Homo sapiens* prevailed even in the tundra. Opinion is divided on whether modern man outcompeted the Neanderthals or incorporated them via interbreeding, or both. Whatever the reason, the Neanderthals vanished, and *Homo sapiens sapiens* became the sole humans on earth around 40,000 years ago. They eventually inhabited all continents except Antarctica.

The advent of *Homo sapiens* characterizes the Quaternary Period as the "Age of Man." Many argue that a sixth mass extinction event, driven by humans, is occurring at the present moment. This would signal the end of the Quaternary within the unknown future.

Present day	Eon	Era	Period	Events
2.6 m.y.a.	Phanerozoic	Cenozoic	Quaternary	▪ Homo sapiens appears ▪ Modern mammals continue to evolve ▪ Ice ages
23 m.y.a.			Neogene	▪ Continents drift to current positions ▪ First australopithecines ▪ Modern mammals evolve and dominate ▪ Grasslands proliferate
65 m.y.a.			Paleogene	▪ Mammals diversify and grow ▪ Birds dominate land and skies
145 m.y.a.		Mesozoic	Cretaceous	▪ First flowering plants ▪ First true birds ▪ Mammals evolve and diversify ▪ Dinosaurs continue to dominate
200 m.y.a.			Jurassic	▪ Dinosaurs grow, diversify and dominate the land ▪ Mammals evolve and diversify
252 m.y.a.			Triassic	▪ Pangea separates ▪ First true mammals ▪ First true dinosaurs ▪ Life recovers from Permian-Triassic extinction
300 m.y.a.		Paleozoic	Permian	▪ Pangea forms ▪ Sauropsids and synapsids proliferate
360 m.y.a.			Carboniferous	▪ Trees proliferate ▪ Reptiles diverge into sauropsids and synapsids ▪ First reptiles (evolution of amniotic eggs)
420 m.y.a.			Devonian	▪ First amphibians ▪ Global heating ▪ First trees and seeds ▪ Arthropods diversify ▪ Bony fish diversify into ray-finned and lobe-finned fish
445 m.y.a.			Silurian	▪ Vascular plants colonize land ▪ Arthropods colonize land ▪ Fish evolve into jawed fish, then cartilaginous and bony fish
490 m.y.a.			Ordovician	▪ Glaciation ▪ First fish ▪ Invertebrate marine life proliferates

Present day	Eon	Era	Period	Events
540 m.y.a.			Cambrian	▪ Cambrian explosion
2.5 b.y.a.	Proterozoic			▪ First fungi and invertebrates ▪ Ozone layer forms ▪ First protozoa ▪ First multicellular organisms ▪ First eukaryotes
4 b.y.a.	Archaean			▪ Cyanobacteria evolve and begin producing oxygen; Great Oxygenation Event ▪ LUCA diverges into Bacteria and Archaea ▪ First life
4.5 b.y.a.	Hadean			▪ Cooling of crust ▪ Water condenses into oceans ▪ Reducing atmosphere ▪ Volcanic activity ▪ Celestial bombardment ▪ Earth forms

Chapter 11

Classification and Diversity

- **Common Ancestry: Shared Conserved Features**

- **Phylogenetic Trees and Cladograms**

- **Comparative Anatomy**

Common Ancestry: Shared Conserved Features

Structural and functional evidence of the relatedness of all domains

The theory of *common descent* is a central tenet of evolutionary biology. This theory states that any given group of living organisms share a common ancestor from which they have descended. It naturally follows that there is a common ancestor to every single organism on Earth, called the *last universal common ancestor* (LUCA). Darwin and his contemporaries gathered much of the evidence that is the foundation of this theory, but modern advances in molecular biology have provided many new insights.

In contemporary biology, life is generally divided into the three domains of Archaea, Bacteria, and Eukarya. It is in relatively recent years that scientists have realized that Archaea constitutes a separate domain from Bacteria. Although both are unicellular prokaryotes, the archaea are too different from bacteria to be classified under the same domain. It is believed that the LUCA first diverged into bacteria and archaea, with eukaryotes later developing from one of these domains or a combination of both.

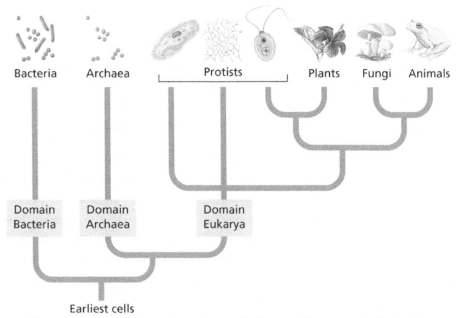

Three domains of archaea, bacteria, and eukarya with proposed relationships

Archaea live in a wide range of habitats, but the most well-known species are the extremophiles, which inhabit hostile environments such as hot springs, salt lakes, and anaerobic swamps. Bacteria and archaea exhibit common prokaryotic features, such as a cell wall, but they are different on a biochemical level.

Domain Eukarya comprises a diverse array of unicellular to multicellular organisms, the most well-studied on Earth. It includes the kingdoms Animalia, Plantae, Fungi, and Protista.

While all three domains have their unique differences, their underlying structure and function display undeniable similarity. Modern evidence comes from DNA and RNA sequencing, analysis of common enzymes and metabolic pathways, fundamental similarities in cell structure and observation of ongoing evolution. There is a large body of evidence gathered from fossils, comparative anatomy, and other investigations that have been underway since the 18th century.

Biochemical evidence is some of the most compelling. All living organisms essentially use the same fundamental building blocks, genetic code, and metabolic pathways. There are certain genes which are largely conserved across all domains of life, coding for proteins that can be remarkably similar or even identical. This all alludes to the fact that all three domains of life descend from a common ancestor. It is seen consistently in all forms of life that the same biomolecules are used in the same way, i.e., all organisms use DNA and RNA as carriers of genetic information, encoded in the same base nucleotides (A, T, G, C, and U). All organisms interpret these bases as triplet codes to produce proteins made of the same twenty amino acids. Furthermore, the code and, not just the method of interpretation, is widespread in its similarity. Many organisms even share the same introns (noncoding sequences of mRNA), which is notable because these units are inoperative and there is no functional reason why they need to be so similar.

Structural evidence of the relatedness of all eukaryotes

The eukaryotes are the most well-researched domain on the earth, as they are the most readily observable and of the most interest to humans. Consequently, there is a wide array of evidence for the relatedness of all eukaryotes.

Common structural features of eukaryotes include an extensive cytoskeleton and organelles such as the mitochondrion, chloroplast, and nucleus. These organelles are all a part of the endomembrane system, a collective term for the membranous sacs that divide a cell into its constituent parts. Eukaryotes, in contrast to bacteria and archaea, are the only organisms with this system of membrane-bound organelles. Other notable similarities among eukaryotes include DNA bound linear chromosomes and common metabolic pathways, such as glycolysis.

The earliest evidence for the structural relatedness of all eukaryotes comes from fossils. The fossil record is the history of life as recorded by remains from the past. Fossils may be skeletons, shells, seeds, imprints, and even soft tissues. Unfortunately, the fossil record is often incomplete, because most organisms decay before they become fossilized, and soft-bodied organisms generally do not fossilize. The great majority of fossils are found embedded in or recently eroded from sedimentary rock. Sedimentation has been going on since the earth was formed; it is an accumulation of particles forming a stratum, a recognizable layer in a sequence of other strata. Its place in the sequence indicates the age of a fossil; a stratum is older than the one above and younger than the one below. This is relative dating.

Relative dating does not establish the absolute age of fossils. For this, radioactive dating must be used. The technique is based on radioactive isotopes that have a quantifiable half-life, the time it takes for half of a radioactive isotope to decay into a stable element. Carbon-14 (^{14}C) is a radioactive isotope contained within the organic matter. Half of the carbon-14 decays to nitrogen-14 every 5,730 years. Therefore, comparing carbon-14 radioactivity of a fossil to modern organic matter allows for calculating the age of the fossil. However, after 50,000 years, carbon-14 radioactivity is so low it can no longer be used to measure age accurately. For this, paleontologists turn to potassium-40 and uranium-238, which have half-lives in billions of years.

Paleontologists use strata and fossils to study the history of life. It is an essential principle of fossil study (paleontology) that a living organism most resembles a fossil that is the most recent in the line of descent. Underlying similarities become fewer the farther back is the lineage. Similar fossils can be used to construct a timeline showing changes from a common ancestor millions of years ago to a modern species. For example, transitional forms such as the bird-like dinosaur Archeopteryx establish that birds descended from reptiles.

Fossils can reveal a wealth of information about an extinct animal, as in the case of the horse ancestor Hyracotherium, which was small with cusped, low-crowned molars, four toes on each front foot, and three on each hind foot. These were all adaptations for forest living and were gradually replaced by larger size, grinding teeth and reduction of toes into hooves as the forests gave way to grasslands. Intermediate forms show this transition between Hyracotherium and the modern horse, genus Equus.

However, it can be difficult to identify the true patterns in the fossil record and ignore misleading ones. Fossils are continually reclassified and reevaluated. For example, some paleontologists have taken a new look at turtle fossils and proposed that they are closer to crocodiles than previously thought.

Biogeographical evidence provides a valuable frame of reference for the fossil record. *Biogeography* examines the distribution of organisms across the earth, providing additional insight into evolutionary research. Physical factors, such as the location of continents, determine where a population can spread and greatly influence evolution. Related forms evolving in one locale and spreading to other accessible areas may explain the distribution of organisms. For example, in the 19th century, Darwin observed that the Galapagos Islands have a wide variety of finch species, but the mainland has one. He concluded that the Galapagos finches had originated on the mainland and diversified once they reached the islands. Biogeography, as applied to evolution, is sometimes known as *phylogeography*.

Notes for active learning

Phylogenetic Trees and Cladograms

Systematics (classification) is the study of the diversity of organisms using evidence from the molecular to the population level. It is often used synonymously with the term taxonomy, although *taxonomy* refers to nomenclature, a subset of the broader field of classification. Systematics may be applied only to modern species or extinct species, in which case it falls under the field of phylogeny. Studying the phylogeny of species reveals the evolutionary relationships between all organisms, past, and present.

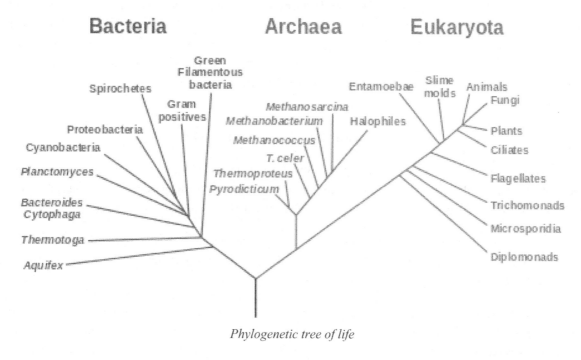

Phylogenetic tree of life

A phylogenetic tree visually indicates common ancestors and lines of descent. It is represented by a branching diagram that, naturally, resembles a tree. A common ancestor is found wherever two branches diverge at the node, while the tip of each branch is labeled with an individual taxon, usually a species. Often the tree includes an outgroup, which does not share the most recent common ancestor of other groups on the tree. The outgroup provides a frame of reference for the taxa of interest. Phylogenetic trees can be constructed as broadly or as narrowly as desired, from all of life to the subforms of a single species. A traditional phylogenetic tree has branches which correspond to the relative length of evolutionary time.

Traits derived or lost due to evolution

From the diversity of life, each of the species on a phylogenetic tree must have lost some traits seen in the common ancestor and adopted new ones. For the most part, by natural selection, these changes are influenced by the viability of certain traits in a given environment.

In systematics, *traits* (characters) are any structural, chromosomal or molecular features that distinguish taxa. Phylogenetic trees are constructed by comparing which characters are shared between organisms. For example, members of a kingdom share general characters, whereas members of a species share specific characters. These general characters, *plesiomorphies* (primitive character or ancestral states), are traits present in a common ancestor and the members of the descending group. For example, a vertebral column is a plesiomorphy of all vertebrates.

Apomorphy (derivate character) are characters which are found in one or a few descendants. Apomorphies are present in a specific line of descent. Different lineages that diverge from a common ancestor have different apomorphies but share plesiomorphies.

Although the terms "primitive character" and "derived character" are still in use, phylogeneticists prefer to use plesiomorphy or apomorphy. This is because "primitive" implies that the ancestral character was simpler and more rudimentary, which is not always the case. Furthermore, "derived" implies that the character is a trait not found in the ancestor but arose in the descendant. This is not necessarily true; a derived character can represent the absence of a trait. For example, the common reptilian ancestor had four limbs. Some reptiles became snakes as they gradually lost their limbs. The characteristic of four limbs was a plesiomorphy of reptiles (and indeed all tetrapods), while the characteristic of having lost them is an apomorphy shared amongst snakes.

Speciation and common ancestry

A speciation event occurs when two species diverge from a node of a tree. Defining speciation is a difficult process, but it can be aided by examining the genetic code of two species for changes in nucleic acid and amino acid sequences over time. Advances in this analysis have made abundant data available to researchers.

Comparing homologous (similar) DNA and RNA sequences elucidate the degree of difference between the two organisms. A high degree of homology indicates highly related organisms, while sequences which are drastically different indicate distantly related organisms.

Biomolecular studies may show that organisms that physically resemble each other are not as closely related as once thought. For example, the red panda and the Chinese giant panda both have false thumbs, but the former has raccoon-like teeth and bones, while the latter does not. Results of DNA analysis confirm that the two pandas are distantly related, the red panda having originated from the same lineage as raccoons and the giant panda from the same lineage as bears.

The rate of mutations in the DNA nucleotide sequence is fairly constant and provides a "molecular clock." Molecular dating compares the relative age of two organisms, quantifying the number of base pair changes between their genomes. By comparing trace DNA from two fossils thought to be of the same lineage, it can be determined which organism the ancestor was, and how long it took the other organism to evolve from the ancestor.

Mitochondrial DNA (mtDNA) is often used for molecular dating because it changes about ten times faster than nuclear DNA, which makes it useful for comparing related species. Mitochondrial DNA is passed directly from mother to offspring. This removes the effect of recombination as for chromosomal DNA and gives a clearer picture of the timeline. The fossil record can then be used to calibrate the clock and confirm the hypothesis drawn from molecular data. For example, a comparison of mitochondrial DNA sequences equated a 5.1% nucleic acid difference among a songbird common ancestor and descendant. In regards to the molecular clock, this means that the descendant diverged from its common ancestor 2.5 million years ago. However, mtDNA is less useful for distantly related organisms. For those applications, RNA or nuclear DNA is used.

Protein comparison is another method for determining speciation or common ancestry, albeit less robust. The amino acid sequences of homologous proteins can be compared, as with cytochrome c, to a protein found in all aerobic organisms. The 140 amino acid composition of cytochrome c differs between chickens and humans by twelve amino acids (8.6%), but by three (2.1%) between chickens and ducks. With this evidence, it can be reasonably assumed that humans, chickens, and ducks share a common ancestor, but that chickens and ducks are more related to each other than to humans. Protein analysis has limitations when it comes to distant relations since few proteins are found across all domains of life.

Biomolecular evidence has become one of the most invaluable tools of the modern phylogeneticist, but it is most useful in conjunction with other evidence.

Morphological similarities of living and extinct species

The evolutionary relationship between living and extinct species is observable in comparisons of the function and development of their morphology, the structures of external and internal anatomy. A living species appear morphologically similar to a recent ancestor, with perhaps a few modifications. By contrast, a distant ancestor may appear entirely alien compared to the modern organism. However, further analysis would reveal the evolutionary link between them.

George Cuvier, a distinguished French vertebrate zoologist, was the first to use comparative anatomy to classify animals. He recognized that organisms often have morphological similarities when they are related because of common descent. *Homologous structures* are similar anatomical traits which have been derived from the same ancestor but have been modified over time. For example, vertebrate forelimbs contain the same sets of bones organized in similar ways, despite their dissimilar functions. The flippers of a whale and the forelimbs of a human are homologous structures, providing evidence of divergent evolution from a common tetrapod ancestor. *Analogous structures* are inherited from unique ancestors but have come to resemble each other because they happen to serve a similar function. Fish and marine mammals have the same sleek, hydrodynamic body plan, but evolved this trait separately. Although the shape is present in their common ancestor, a primitive fish, it was lost in mammals, then later regained by a select few. Therefore, streamlined shape is an analogous structure that has evolved separately many times in response to an aquatic environment.

Using morphology to classify organisms can be misleading due to analogous structures. Organisms may appear to be closely related due to their similar morphologies, but genetic or fossil analysis may reveal that these traits evolved separately.

Many traits that do not provide a present-day advantage are still present in organisms because they do not negatively affect their fitness. *Vestigial structures* are traits which are regressive and nonfunctional in the modern organism but served a purpose in an ancestor. For example, whales have vestigial hind limbs that harken back to their tetrapod origins.

The process of losing vestigial structures is an ongoing process that has been well-studied in humans. Most humans no longer eat the plant roughage, which requires extra molars to break down. As a result, human jaws are becoming smaller and forcing out the wisdom teeth. In modern times, hundreds of millions of people lack wisdom teeth altogether. Another example of a vestigial structure in humans is the coccyx, a bone at the end of the spine (i.e., tailbone), essentially a regressed tail.

Dynamic changes of phylogenetic trees and cladograms

The first unified form of systematics arose in the 18th century when Carl Linnaeus devised a taxonomic system of classification. Because taxonomy assigns a hierarchy, this system required each taxon to have a rank about other taxa. This seemed logical to scientists at the time, who mostly subscribed to the idea that species have a fixed place in the divine hierarchy of God's plan. However, assigning ranks to groups can be confusing and prone to bias. Countless modifiers were added to the simple taxa of kingdom, phylum, class, order, family, genus and species, leading to variations such as infraclass, subspecies, superphylum, etc. Another weakness of Linnaeus' method was that it did not acknowledge evolution and allow for the inclusion of extinct species.

Linnaeus' original scheme divided life into kingdom Animalia, kingdom Plantae and the third kingdom for minerals (since abandoned). In much of the 20th century, a five-kingdom classification was popular, which included kingdom Animalia and kingdom Plantae, in addition to kingdom Monera (for prokaryotes), Protista (for protists) and Fungi. As discussed, the prokaryotes have more recently been divided into archaea and bacteria. To reflect this, Monera was eliminated, and the kingdom Bacteria and kingdom Archaea were established in its place. Because protists, animals, plants, and fungi are all eukaryotes, Eukarya was added to unify them under one domain. To represent bacteria and archaea as equal to eukaryotes, they were named as domains. This may seem pointless since each of their domains includes one kingdom of the same name. However, it would be misleading to say that life consists of domain Eukarya, kingdom Bacteria and kingdom Archaea because eukaryotes did not come any earlier than the other two and are not any more "overarching" of a group. This example reveals how taxonomy can become convoluted due to ranking.

Darwinian taxonomy, or *evolutionary taxonomy,* includes species past and present and relies heavily on the notion of common descent. At this time, taxonomy came to represent part of a larger whole: phylogeny. Darwinian taxonomy did not attempt to construct orderly lists, but to demonstrate phylogenetic relationships. However, it was still too constricted in the types of relationships that were allowed, and there was no consensus as to how these relationships should be constructed in the first place.

Phenetic systematics is a more quantitative notion of classification which arose in the 20th century. Phenetic systematics constructs phylogenetic trees based on mathematics and statistics, counting the number of shared characteristics between two species and running various analyses to construct the most likely tree. This method clusters species merely based on the number of shared characteristics, making no distinction between plesiomorphies and apomorphies. It does not take into account the nuanced forms of evolution, such as parallel, divergent, convergent and co-evolution. This form of classification is vulnerable to misleading similarities, such as analogous structures or those which have evolved alongside one another. Systematists of this school do not believe that a classification that reflects phylogeny can be constructed; it is better to rely strictly on a method that does away with nuance. Results of their analysis are depicted in a *phenogram*. Phenograms vary for similar groups of organisms, depending on how the data is collected and processed.

Phenetic systematics has been mostly superseded in modern times by *cladistic systematics*, or *cladistics*. Cladistics requires more complex mathematics and processing power to take into account how evolution may influence characteristics. Analysis of characteristics classifies organisms into *clades*. A clade is any taxon with a single common ancestor; it may be broad or narrow. Clades can be organized into trees called *cladograms*, which show the relationships between species based on their shared characteristics. A cladogram, unlike a traditional phylogenetic tree, does not infer how much species have changed over time, but merely that they diverged at one point. In a cladogram, all branches are placed equidistant from one another and do not correspond to relative evolutionary time since the common ancestor.

Clades are usually *monophyletic*, meaning they include a given common ancestor and every one of the ancestor's descendants. Even if one descendant is left out of the clade, it is no longer monophyletic, but *paraphyletic*. A paraphyletic clade has a common ancestor and many of its descendants, but not all. Monophyletic clades are the most useful in phylogeny, but paraphyletic clades have their place as well. However, there is seldom good cause to construct a *polyphyletic* clade. In this case, the group contains several descendants who do not share the same common ancestor. Polyphyletic clades are often accidentally created due to misleading evidence. With further investigation, researchers may be able to remedy them into monophyletic clades.

Cladistics is guided by the principle of *parsimony*, which states that the solution with the least amount of assumptions is the most logical. According to parsimony, the best cladogram is the one with a minimal number of assumptions made, generally the simplest one. This approach attempts to minimize bias but is still dependent on the knowledge and skill of the particular investigator, as well as the evidence available. Like earlier methodologies, cladistics is prone to ambiguity and confusion. It is no easy task to pinpoint a common ancestor or to articulate what exactly makes two organisms more evolutionarily related to one another. Cladistics cannot be improved until there is a consensus as to what exact characters should be used to distinguish different groups.

Notes for active learning

Comparative Anatomy

Although sequence analysis and molecular dating are integral to modern phylogenetics, morphology remains the simplest and most accessible way to describe the relationships between organisms. For this reason, this text uses comparative anatomy to present the diversity of the plant and animal kingdoms. Understand that underneath these anatomical traits is molecular evidence which strengthens the classifications presented.

The diversity of Kingdom Plantae

Kingdom Plantae is a clade of eukaryotes which are autotrophic by photosynthesis. This clade usually includes the multicellular green algae and terrestrial nonvascular plants ("lower plants") and terrestrial vascular plants ("higher plants"). However, many phylogeneticists would exclude multicellular green algae, since their inclusion arguably makes the clade paraphyletic; unicellular green algae can be found in kingdom Protista.

Algae and the *bryophytes* (terrestrial nonvascular plants) are green, low to the ground and generally found in moist environments. They do not have a vascular system or true stems, leaves, and roots, but are anchored to the ground by root-like *rhizoids*. Capsules at the end of stalks protrude from a bryophyte and release spores into the wind or water. Algae and bryophytes reproduce via these spores, rather than seeds.

The development of vascular tissues allowed the higher plants to reach unprecedented heights. Vascular plants can be divided into seed and seedless plants. The most well-known phylum of the vascular seedless plants are the ferns, also *Filicophyta* or *Polypodiophyta*. These plants have true roots, leaves, and stems, but reproduce using spores like the nonvascular plants. Spores are produced on the underside of long fronds divided into many leaflets. In the Paleozoic Era, ferns ruled the forests, becoming so large that they resembled trees. Today, most ferns are much smaller, with a maximum height of about 15 meters. Other seedless plants are the "fern allies" and are classified under phylum *Lycopodiophyta*. The lycopods include club mosses, spike mosses, and quillworts. These plants designated as "mosses" are not mosses. The lycopods are distinguished from the ferns by their *microphylls,* simple leaves with a single vein. Ferns have *megaphylls,* which have complex, branching veins.

The *spermatophytes* (seed plants) comprise a monophyletic clade of all plants reproducing with seeds. This group is the largest, most recent, and most successful taxon of plants on Earth. It can be divided into the *angiosperms* (flowering plants) and the *gymnosperms* (cone plants). Angiosperms have their seeds fully enclosed within the ovaries of flowers, while gymnosperms have their seeds partially exposed on the scale-like leaves of cones. Both groups include the tallest plants on Earth: angiosperms with Eucalyptus, which may reach 100 meters tall, and gymnosperms with the redwood, up to 115 meters.

General characteristics of angiosperms include vascular tissues, roots, stems, leaves, flowers, and fruit. Flowers contain ovaries that enclose *ovules.* When pollinated by a male flower, an ovule is fertilized and develops into the seed. The ovary ripens around the seed to form a fruit, which may be dispersed by wind, water, gravity or animals. Once dispersed, the seed germinates in the soil and begins to grow.

Gymnosperms have neither flowers nor fruit. They are typically woody; the most well-known gymnosperms are the conifers (e.g., pines and fir trees). Gymnosperms have their ovules on female cones, called *ovule cones* or *seed cones.* Pollen from male cones, called *pollen cones,* fertilizes an ovule cone and causes a seed to develop. The ovule cone then drops to the ground to allow the seed to germinate.

The diversity of Kingdom Animalia

Kingdom Animalia is a monophyletic clade of multicellular eukaryotes which are heterotrophic by ingestion, and generally motile. The most primitive animals are sponges (phylum Porifera, meaning "pore bearer"), which are asymmetrical and lack specialized tissues or organs. Sponges are diploblastic with two cell layers. The sponge intake water through pores lined with *choanocytes,* flagellated cells which filter food and then expel the remaining water through their mouth, the *osculum.* The choanocytes pass food to *amoebocytes* for digestion and distribution of the nutrients. Many sponges feature a calcium carbonate exoskeleton secreted by their cells. They may feature *spicules,* skeletal needles of silica or calcium carbonate that strengthen their body walls. Unlike other animals, sponges are sessile and lack even a rudimentary sensory system.

Phylum Cnidaria evolved shortly after the sponges. The cnidarians include jellyfish, hydra, sea anemones and corals. Like the sponges, they are diploblastic but exhibit more complex cell specialization. A gelatinous layer of *mesoglea* between their two cell layers develops into muscle-like tissue. Cnidarians may take either a sessile form, the *polyp,* or a swimming, bell-shaped form, the *medusa.* Polyps may live in colonies, as do coral, while medusae are free-living, as do jellyfish. Many cnidarians have a larval polyp stage and a medusa adult stage. Both forms have radial symmetry and exhibit symmetry in all planes. They have one opening, through which they ingest food, expel waste and carry out respiration. Cnidarians have a rudimentary nervous system and sensory organs, with nothing resembling a brain. They are noted for their *nematocysts,* stinging cells which they use to stun or kill prey.

Phylum Ctenophora, the comb jellies, are a group of diploblastic organisms with radial symmetry. They have traditionally been grouped with the cnidarians, but recent evidence suggests that they may be closer to the higher level *bilaterians.* Bilaterians are animals that are more complex than the sponges, ctenophores, and cnidarians. With a few exceptions, they exhibit bilateral symmetry and have two distinct, symmetrical sides. The bilaterians are triploblastic, having originated from three germ layers: ectoderm, mesoderm, and endoderm. Bilaterians exhibit *cephalization,* the concentration of nervous tissues at the anterior end of an organism.

Worms were some of the first bilaterians to evolve. "Worms" refer to a variety of phyla, including but not limited to the flatworms of phylum Platyhelminthes, the nematodes of phylum Nematoda and the segmented worms of phylum Annelida. Despite the umbrella term of the worm, these three phyla are more related to other organisms than to each other. The flatworms are the simplest because they have no body cavities (coeloms), making them *acoelomates.* They undergo respiration by simple diffusion and have one digestive opening. Flatworms may be free-living, as with the carnivorous *planarians,* or parasitic (e.g., flukes and tapeworms). Their closest relatives are the *rotifers* (phylum Rotifera), microscopic filter feeders. Rotifers are *pseudocoelomates;* they have a coelom, but it is not completely lined by mesoderm-derived tissue.

The nematodes are pseudocoelomates. These roundworms inhabit a wide range of habitats and have more complex respiratory and digestive systems. Often, they are free-living soil dwellers that help decompose and recycle nutrients.

Annelids, such as earthworms and leeches, are true *coelomates.* They have complex, segmented bodies; each segment contains a set of organs identical to those found in other segments. They move by muscle contraction, often aided by bristles called *setae* and limbs called *parapodia* that push them along the soil. Their closest relatives are the mollusks.

Mollusks, of phylum Mollusca, are the largest marine phylum today. They are triploblastic, true coelomates, and have a rudimentary nervous system with some cephalization. In general, mollusks have a mantle, a radula, and a foot. The *mantle* encloses a cavity used for respiration and excretion, while the *radula* is essentially a raspy tongue. The foot is used for motility, sensation and for anchoring to surfaces. The evolution of these features in the Cambrian seas would have given early mollusks advantages in motility, protection, and feeding. Many classes are found in phylum Mollusca, but three are widely known. The bivalves (class Bivalvia), such as clams and oysters, secrete a hinged shell from the mantle. They are generally filter feeders which can be found on the ocean floor, in tidal areas or even free swimming. The gastropods (class Gastropoda), the snails and slugs, have a single continuous shell and are noted for their large, developed feet. Most gastropods are herbivorous grazers. Finally, the cephalopods (class Cephalopoda) are the most advanced mollusks; these include octopus, squid, cuttlefish, and nautilus. They have well-developed cephalization and are primarily predatory, using their tentacles to attack prey.

Phylum Arthropoda includes the arthropods, an incredibly diverse phylum found on land, sea, and air. At a basic level, they can be characterized by their jointed limbs, segmented body plan, and an exoskeleton. The exoskeleton is made of *chitin,* a polysaccharide. It undergoes continuous molting and replacement. Their small coelom surrounds the reproductive and excretory system, with a special body cavity called a *hemocoel* facilitating their open circulatory system. Coelomic fluid and blood flow through the hemocoel, bathing surrounding tissues.

Arthropods have a relatively advanced nervous system, with rudimentary brains and sophisticated photo-, mechanoreceptors and chemoreceptors. They may exhibit one of two life cycles: the immature *nymph* gradually develops into an adult, or an immature *larva* enters a cocoon and undergoes *metamorphosis*, or sudden development, into an adult.

Phylum Arthropoda is divided into four extant subphyla. A fifth subphylum, Trilobita, now extinct, comprised the trilobites. These creatures were ubiquitous in the Cambrian and later periods.

Subphylum Crustacea, meaning "insects of the sea," includes the crustaceans: lobsters, crabs, shrimp, krill and barnacles, among others. Many crustaceans are herbivores and are of great importance to aquatic ecosystems. They feed on phytoplankton, making them a crucial link in the food chain. A few crustaceans have colonized land and freshwater environments, but the majority are marine, carrying on gas exchange with their gills.

By contrast, the species of subphylum Myriapoda are exclusively terrestrial. Myriapods include centipedes and millipedes, which use their many feet to their advantage. Centipedes have fewer legs and are fast, making them effective predators. They have venomous glands which assist in killing prey. Millipedes are slower, so they are mostly herbivores and detritivores. They have venomous glands, which they use as chemical defenses against predators.

Along with the myriapods, class, Arachnida (subphylum Chelicerata) were some of the first creatures to occupy the land. A few arachnids have returned to the water. The most famous arachnids are spiders, scorpions, ticks and mites. All arachnids have eight legs and advanced eyes, making them excellent predators. They exhibit unique "book lungs," stacks of alternating air pockets used for gas exchange.

Class Insecta (subphylum Hexapoda) is by far the most successful and diverse taxon on Earth. There are more species of insect than any other species combined. All insects are characterized by their three-part body plan, six legs, and antennae, but insect species has developed additional features.

The adaptation of wings allowed some insects to escape from predators and travel large distances. The more primitive insects (most likely the first insects) are wingless, which suggests that flying was an evolutionary adaptation over time. Most insects inhabit the land and air. Their respiratory systems have *spiracles* (openings), which allow air to enter their internal *tracheal tubes*. Insects are limited in their size because their anatomy cannot support a large body. Most insect species are relatively small, allowing them to occupy small areas and minimize their food requirements.

Collectively, the triploblasts (Platyhelminthes, nematodes, annelids, rotifers, mollusks, and arthropods, along with other smaller phyla and classes) are protostomes.

Taxa are continually debated, so only echinoderms and chordates have been definitively established as deuterostomes. For instance, scientists cannot decide whether the *bryozoans*, a phylum of marine invertebrates, are protostomes or deuterostomes. *Brachiopods*, bottom-dwelling animals which superficially resemble mollusks, are another such phylum which has come under question in recent years. Traditionally, the brachiopods have been classified as deuterostomes, but new evidence suggests that they may be protostomes.

Phylum	Common Names	Tissue Complexity	Germ Layers	Body Symmetry	Gut Openings	Coelom	Embryonic Development
Porifera	sponges	parazoa	-	none	0*	-	-
Cnidaria	jellyfish, corals	eumetazoa	2	radial	1	-	-
Platyhelminthes	flatworms	eumetazoa	3	bilateral	1	acoelomate	-
Nematoda	roundworms	eumetazoa	3	bilateral	2	pseudo-coelomate	-
Rotifera	rotifers	eumetazoa	3	bilateral	2	pseudo-coelomate	-
Mollusca	clams, snails, octopuses	eumetazoa	3	bilateral	2	coelomate	protosome
Annelida	segmented worms	eumetazoa	3	bilateral	2	coelomate	protosome
Arthropoda	insects, spiders, crustaceans	eumetazoa	3	bilateral	2	coelomate	protosome
Echinodermata	sea stars, sea urchins	eumetazoa	3	radial	2	coelomate	deuterostome
Chordata	vertebrates	eumetazoa	3	bilateral	2	coelomate	deuterostome

* *Amoebocytes carry out digestion*
- *Characteristic does not apply to this phylum.*

It is inconclusive which deuterostomes evolved first, but some of the evidence points to phylum *Echinodermata*. The echinoderms include sea stars, sea urchins, sea cucumbers, sand dollars, brittle stars, and sea lilies. Like all organisms higher than cnidarians and ctenophores, the echinoderms are classified as bilaterians. However, this is a misnomer, as echinoderms evolved radial symmetry after descending from their bilateral ancestor, making this an apomorphy. This legacy can be seen in their larvae, which are bilateral. Echinoderms had strong exoskeletons and accomplished camouflaging abilities. While they appear sessile, echinoderms do move. Some are herbivores, but many sea stars are carnivorous and can move surprisingly quickly. Echinoderms are noted for their robust powers of regeneration and their complex coelom, which includes a water vascular system for water pressure to extend *tube feet*, allowing the animal to move. It also functions in the respiratory, digestive and nervous systems.

The most advanced deuterostomes belong to phylum *Chordata* and are primarily defined by the development of a *notochord* in the early embryo. In most chordates, the notochord develops into a vertebral column; these organisms are classified under subphylum *Vertebrata*. Because nearly all chordates are vertebrates, the two taxa are often conflated. Non-vertebral chordates include tunicates and lancelets, both simple filter feeders. These species likely represent the earliest chordates.

Chordate features

Notochord

The notochord is a flexible rod that extends below the dorsal nerve cord along the length of all chordate embryos. It is derived from the mesoderm and develops during neurulation of the embryo. All chordates possess a notochord during the embryonic stage. In non-vertebral chordates, the notochord persists after birth; muscles work against it to help the animal move. It may be lost in sexual maturity or remain throughout adulthood. However, vertebral chordates have the notochord replaced by the vertebral column later in embryonic development.

Pharyngeal pouches and branchial arches

Another key distinguishing feature of chordates includes pharyngeal pouches, present in all chordate embryos. *Pharyngeal pouches* are openings between the pharynx (a portion of the throat) and the environment. They develop into various structures depending on the organism. In non-vertebrate chordates, the pouches develop into *pharyngeal slits,* used for filter feeding and gas exchange. In fish and some amphibians, the pouches are modified into the jaw, the hyoid bone, and the *branchial arches*. The branchial arches are *gill arches* because they support the gills. In all other vertebrates, the pouches form *pharyngeal arches,* which develop into the jaw, the hyoid bone, the thyroid, the larynx, the tonsils and other components of the neck and head.

Dorsal nerve cord

The *dorsal nerve cord*, derived from ectoderm, forms the central nervous system. Like the notochord, it develops during neurulation. This hollow chord extends the length of the embryo on top of the notochord. In vertebrates, most of the dorsal nerve cord develops into the spinal cord, and the anterior part enlarges into the brain. A *post-anal tail* extends at the posterior end and may be lost or retained in the adult organism.

Vertebrate phylogeny

Most scientists agree that the first vertebrates would have been jawless fishes similar to hagfish and lampreys. These primitive filter feeders diversified greatly in the periods after the Cambrian, some evolving into jawed fishes. Some of the jawed fish evolved a cartilaginous jaw and skeleton, today the cartilaginous fishes (class Chondrichthyes). In this class, which includes sharks, skates, and rays, the notochord is replaced by cartilage rather than bone. Cartilaginous fishes have tough skin and are typically predatory.

Shortly after the cartilaginous fish, the bony fishes (superclass Osteichthyes), would have split off from their common ancestor. They are the origin of nearly all other fish species. Bony fish have a bony jaw and skeleton and are divided into ray-finned fish (class Actinopterygii) and lobe-finned fish (class Sarcopterygii). Lobe-finned fish are primitive, and few survive today, while ray-finned fish represent the majority of fish species on Earth.

Nearly all fish are *ectothermic* ("cold-blooded"), as their body temperature is dependent on the environment and cannot be internally regulated. A typical fish has a streamlined shape to optimize swimming efficiency, although many fish diverge significantly from this morphology. Other typical characteristics of fish include scaly skin, fins, and reproduction with eggs. Most breathe with gills, pumping blood past the gills with their two-chambered heart, although a few fish have rudimentary lungs.

Those ancient lobe-finned fish that developed lungs were able to venture onto land with the help of their fleshy, lobed fins. These are the ancestors to lungfish as well as all terrestrial vertebrates, known as tetrapods (superclass Tetrapoda) for their four limbs. Within this group are class Amphibia, class Reptilia, class Aves, and class Mammalia. Many tetrapods lost most or all of their limbs over time, and some even returned to the water. Tetrapods were the origin of animals such as snakes and marine mammals.

The earliest tetrapods, the amphibians (class Amphibia), never fully left their aquatic origins. Most amphibians are adapted for both terrestrial and aquatic habitats, and many spend the entire first stage of their lives in water. Their larval form typically breathes with gills but undergoes metamorphosis into an adult form that breathes with lungs and through its skin. Their skin is moist and able to exchange gases and water with the environment. A two-chambered heart pumps blood throughout their closed circulatory system. Like fish, amphibians are ectotherms. The three main orders of amphibians are frogs and toads (order Anura), salamanders (order Caudata) and caecilians (order Gymnophiona). Caecilians are primitive, limbless amphibians which resemble a large worm.

As the ancient amphibians thrived, an important apomorphy was arising. The *amniotic egg*, a specialized egg with complex membranes that can sustain an embryo on land or, in the case of mammals, within the womb. Earlier organisms, such as the amphibians and fish, laid their eggs in water. These eggs are simple and gelatinous, and exchange materials with their aquatic environment. By contrast, amniotic eggs can be laid on land and carry on gas exchange with the air while protecting the embryo with their hard, leathery shells. The embryo fully develops within the egg before hatching, unlike fish and amphibian embryos, which are still in the larval stage when they exit the egg.

Those amphibians which evolved amniotic eggs, along with other adaptations such as scaly, waterproof skin, became the reptiles. Reptiles quickly colonized land and specialized even further to their terrestrial environment. Reptiles are widespread and diverse. Turtles, tortoises, and terrapins (order Testudines) inhabit the seas and land, protected by their large, tough shells. The lizards and snakes (order Squamata) are the most diverse reptile group, with nearly 10,000 known species. By contrast, the crocodilians (order Crocodilia) have 25 living species, and the tuatara (order Sphenodontia) is the only reptile of its kind. Many reptiles are capable of maintaining a remarkably stable body temperature despite being ectotherms. This is due to adaptations such as low resting metabolism, muscle contractions and sunning. A three-chambered heart pumps blood throughout their system. All reptiles have lungs and must breathe air, even the aquatic and semi-aquatic species.

When the dinosaurs ruled the earth millions of years ago, mammals began to evolve from a niche of reptiles deemed the synapsids. These organisms are para mammals, proto-mammals or mammal-like reptiles. They diverged from the true reptiles, the sauropsids, and became true mammals, gradually shedding their reptilian features for hair, internal amniotic eggs, and other mammalian characteristics. Although the dinosaurs still dominated for some time, the mammals became a competitor for land resources and even predated on some smaller dinosaurs.

Mammals (class Mammalia) are a diverse group of organisms, but they share common apomorphies. Some of these include hair, varied teeth (*heterodonty*), a warm-blooded metabolism (*endothermy*) and mammary glands which feed their young with milk. The majority of mammals are placental, with offspring developing in the uterus and are nourished by a placenta. The marsupials carry their offspring in an external womb, the pouch. Nearly all mammals give live birth, except for the monotremes, which lay eggs like their reptilian ancestors.

The other descendants of the reptiles were the birds (class Aves). They are a highly diverse class and represent thousands of species on Earth. Class Aves are divided into *paleognaths* (flightless and weak-flying birds) and *neognathae* (all other birds). Birds have many unique apomorphies which separate them from their reptilian kin. Unlike reptiles, most birds have bills rather than teeth. They are adapted for flight, having lightweight bones, forelimbs which have been modified into wings, large flight muscles, and feathers. To meet the high energy demands of flight, birds have a high metabolism and sophisticated respiratory and circulatory systems. A large amount of heat they generate makes them endotherms like the mammals. This is an analogous trait; endothermy was not present in their common ancestor but evolved separately in birds and mammals. A similar example is the ability of flight found in both birds and bats.

Birds have even more powerful lungs and massive four-chambered hearts than the mammals, allowing them to circulate oxygen efficiently. Respiration has the additional benefit of filling the spaces within their bones, contributing to their buoyancy. Many birds are such strong fliers that they can migrate thousands of miles each year.

Birds may be insectivorous, herbivorous, carnivorous, omnivorous or even eat carrion. The wide variation in bird morphology is a testament to their diversification into many different niches. However, their reptilian ancestry can be seen in their scales, feathers (scale derivatives) and their amniotic eggs.

The relationship between ontogeny and phylogeny

Ontogeny refers to the development of an organism throughout its lifetime, from the zygote to the adult form. *Phylogeny* is the development of a species over evolutionary time. Evolutionary biologists historically have subscribed to the idea that "ontogeny recapitulates phylogeny." This dogma, the *recapitulation theory*, states that the development seen in an organism (i.e., ontogeny) reflects the way in which the species evolved (i.e., phylogeny). Take for example the notochord. A vertebrate embryo has a notochord in early development, but vertebrae later replace it. Similarly, the chordate ancestor had a notochord which was replaced by vertebrae during the evolution of vertebrates. In this case, the theory holds. However, the notion that ontogeny recapitulates phylogeny is an exaggeration that has largely been refuted. If it were true, a human would appear as a mature invertebrate (e.g., fish, reptile) and then an ancestral mammal until it developed into a mature human. This does not occur. Rather, the human embryo diverges from more generalized forms as it matures. It is not that it looks like a fish at any point during development, but merely that an early embryo cannot be visually identified as either fish or human.

Embryology can be separated from the recapitulation theory to provide valuable insights into embryos of different species. It cannot be concluded that a human embryo must have evolved from a bird ancestor merely because a human embryo and bird embryo look the same until several weeks after fertilization. However, it *can* be reasonably inferred that since they look more similar, bird embryos are more related to human embryos than to fish embryos. Ontogeny can reveal evolutionary relatedness but not the order of evolution or the exact characteristics that were derived.

Notes for active learning

Chapter 12

Ecosystems, Biosphere and Conservation Biology

- **Ecosystems, Energy Flow and Nutrient Cycles**

- **The Biosphere and Biomes**

- **Conservation Biology**

Ecosystems, Energy Flow and Nutrient Cycles

The nature of ecosystems

An *ecosystem* includes a biotic community as well as its abiotic environment. The biotic community is organized by which organisms fuel their metabolic activities. *Autotrophs* are organisms which create their organic compounds using energy from the sun or inorganic compounds. They are divided into photoautotrophs and chemoautotrophs. *Photoautotrophs* (e.g., algae, plants, and cyanobacteria) use photosynthesis to convert solar energy into organic compounds. *Chemoautotrophs* are bacteria which oxidize inorganic compounds such as ammonia, nitrite, and sulfide to generate organic compounds. They are rare and are typically found in caves, hydrothermal ocean vents and other environments lacking light. Autotrophs are the basis of the ecosystem and feed heterotrophs.

Heterotrophs must obtain their nutrients by consuming other organisms. Herbivores feed on autotrophs and are typically prey animals for carnivores and omnivores. *Detritivores* are organisms which break down dead organic matter, recycle energy and nutrients throughout the ecosystem. The smallest detritivores, such as fungi and bacteria, are *decomposers*. Many decomposers are *saprotrophs,* which digest organic matter externally by secreting enzymes into the surrounding environment and then absorbing the broken-down products.

Energy flow

Ecosystems are characterized by nutrient production, movement, consumption, and recycling. Nutrients are forms of chemical energy which flow throughout the system in predictable ways, governed by the laws of thermodynamics. The first law of thermodynamics states that energy can neither be created nor destroyed, while the second law states that when energy is transformed into a different form, some energy is lost to the environment.

Energy flow is assembled into the *food chain* of a community. *Trophic levels* are the food chains organized into levels which describe how an organism feeds. Arrows in the food chain show the direction of energy flow. The greater the number of energy pathways in a food web, the more stable is the community. At the base of every food chain are the autotrophs as *primary producers.* They are responsible for *primary production*, the creation of organic compounds using energy from the sun or inorganic compounds. The chemical energy created by primary production nourishes both the producers and other organisms in the food chain. It can be quantified by *biomass* or the amount of organic material in a given area. Biomass may be either living or dead; the requirement is that it contains usable energy.

Herbivores that consume primary producers are *primary consumers.* Those organisms which consume the primary consumers are *secondary consumers,* and so on. Typically, food chains do not exceed the level of a tertiary consumer. At the top of the food chain are *apex predators,* organisms which have no natural predators.

As an example, a primary producer in a food chain may be a carrot plant. Its direct predator, the eastern cottontail rabbit, is a primary consumer. The red fox is a secondary consumer, and the golden eagle is the tertiary consumer and apex predator. However, golden eagles often prey on rabbits in addition to foxes. Here, the basic linear food chain fails to capture the complex interactions in an ecosystem. In reality, an ecosystem involves many food chains interconnected into a *food web.*

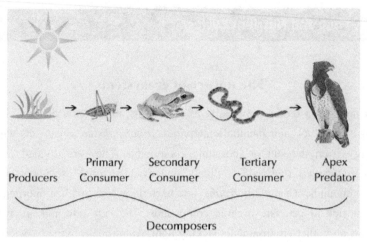

Example of a food chain from producers to apex predator

Detritivores are difficult to place on the food web and are often conceptualized as being separate. A food web which does not include detritivores is a *grazing food web;* it places primary producers at the basal level. A *detrital food web* places detritivores at the bottom.

The food web begins when producers receive energy from the sun through photosynthesis. *Gross primary productivity* is the total amount of energy they generate via photosynthesis. However, much of this energy must be used by the producers themselves to fuel their metabolism. The *net primary productivity* passed to heterotrophs is the unused energy.

Due to the second law of thermodynamics, energy is always lost at each trophic level, because all organisms lose heat through cellular respiration. Furthermore, some organic matter remains undigested at each trophic level and is lost as waste. Detritivores help recycle this energy.

Ecological efficiency describes the proportion of energy at each trophic level that is transferred to the next. On average, about 90% of an organism's energy is used for metabolism, and 10% is passed to the next trophic level. Therefore, 1,000 kilograms of plant biomass supports 100 kilograms of primary consumers, which converts to 10 kilograms of secondary consumers and finally 1 kilogram of tertiary consumers. Note that massive amounts of biomass are needed at the lower levels to support the apex predators at the top. This rapid loss of energy is why food chains rarely have more than four links. However, energy reclamation by decomposers greatly improves the efficiency of the overall ecosystem.

Energy and biomass are greatest at the primary producer level and lowest at the apex predator level. The result is that apex predator populations are the least stable and the most heavily impacted by population fluctuations at lower trophic levels. *Ecological pyramids* represent the trophic levels in a food web by their energy content, biomass or number of species. Naturally, the base of the pyramid is the producer trophic level, with consumer trophic levels rising upwards.

An *ecological pyramid of numbers* is based on the number of organisms at each trophic level, while a *pyramid of energy* is based on how much energy each level generates. A *pyramid of biomass* is based on the biomass at each trophic level.

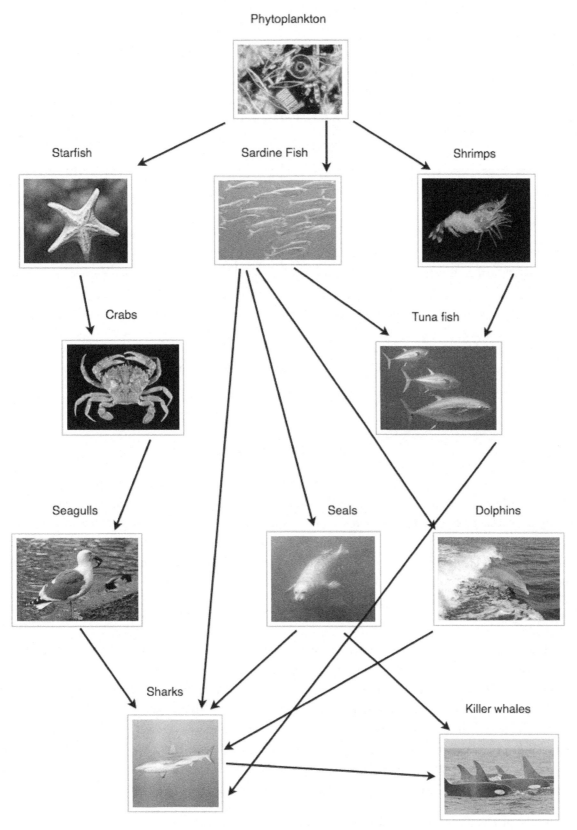

Food web from producer through consumers

	Fox ↑ Rabbit ↑ Nettle plant	Two-spot ladybird ↑ Small nettle aphid ↑ Nettle plant	Parasitic wasp ↑ Caterpillar of peacock butterfly ↑ Nettle plant
Pyramid of numbers compares the number of organisms at each trophic level			
Pyramid of biomass compares the mass of biological material at each trophic level			
Pyramid of energy compares the amount of energy passing through each trophic level over a period of time			

Ecological pyramids; the ecological pyramid of numbers, the pyramid of energy and pyramid of biomass

Most pyramids resemble a typical upright triangle. However, at particular points in time, the pyramid may have areas of inversion. For example, this occurs if an herbivore population feeds on a fast-growing producer, keeping its biomass low in comparison.

Biogeochemical cycles

Nutrients such as water, carbon, nitrogen and phosphorous are in limited supply in any ecosystem. They must be continually recycled through the biotic and abiotic components of an ecosystem via *biogeochemical cycles.* Reservoirs and exchange pools are abiotic portions of the biogeochemical cycle. A *reservoir* is an area that stores a particular nutrient for long periods of time, perhaps hundreds, thousands, or even millions of years. Some nutrients in the reservoir are made accessible to organisms by an *exchange pool,* which is temporary storage. Nutrients then flow through living organisms (i.e., the biotic community).

The water cycle

The *hydrologic cycle* describes the movement of water throughout Earth's crust, atmosphere, water bodies, and living organisms. At a basic level, the hydrologic cycle involves evaporation of water from freshwater and saltwater bodies, which eventually condenses and falls as precipitation. Some water flows below Earth's surface and becomes *groundwater,* contained in *aquifers.* The depth at which an aquifer is completely saturated with water is the *water table.* Some groundwater seeps back to the surface and forms freshwater bodies or runs off into the ocean. Groundwater is an example of a biogeochemical reservoir, which makes up about 20% of the world's freshwater. Freshwater makes up about 3% of the world's supply of water and is considered a renewable resource. Freshwater can, however, become locally unavailable when consumption exceeds supply or when it becomes polluted.

Freshwater bodies and the atmosphere are exchanged pools that store water temporarily and make it available to organisms. Ice in the polar regions and water in the deep oceans are reservoirs, like groundwater.

The carbon cycle

The *carbon cycle* involves the exchange of carbon between organisms and their environment. All terrestrial organisms and marine mammals exchange carbon dioxide (CO_2) directly with the atmosphere. Aquatic organisms that do not breathe air do this exchange indirectly by inhaling or exhaling dissolved carbon dioxide as bicarbonate (HCO_3^-).

Both terrestrial and aquatic autotrophs uptake of carbon and convert it into organic compounds, which then cycle through the food web. As heterotrophs respire, they return carbon dioxide to the air and water. Photosynthesis and respiration occur at relatively equal rates, keeping the cycle in balance.

Organisms return carbon as organic compounds, in the form of waste or ultimately from their decomposing bodies, which can be recycled by detritivores. Some organic compounds are not decomposed but rather become preserved as coal, oil and natural gas fossils. The global reservoirs of the carbon cycle are these fossil fuels, along with bicarbonate that remains deep in the oceans or becomes trapped as limestone.

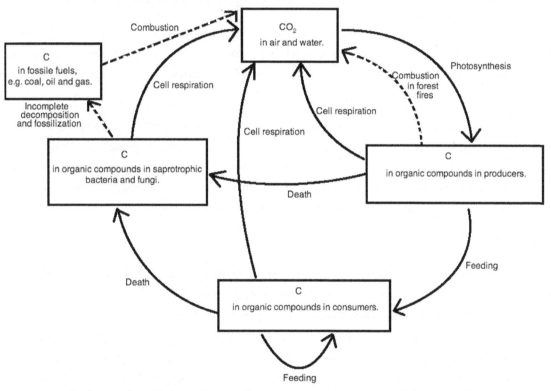

Carbon cycle with the exchange of carbon among organisms and the atmosphere

Carbon dioxide is one of three primary *greenhouse gases* that contribute to increasing the atmospheric temperature. The burning of fossil fuels and forests causes additional carbon dioxide to enter the atmosphere. Solar energy reaches the Earth and warms the planet, but a significant amount should be reflected back into space, primarily in the form of infrared radiation. Greenhouse gases absorb some of this reflected infrared radiation and trap it in the atmosphere, causing a rise in atmospheric temperatures. This additional CO_2 interferes with the normal exchange between photosynthesis and respiration and alters the carbon cycle. A source of carbon pollution is oil spills, which contribute millions of tons of oil to the ocean each year.

The Nitrogen Cycle

The cycle of nitrogen throughout its various forms is the *nitrogen cycle*. Nitrogen gas (N_2) makes up 78% of the atmosphere and is vital for plant and animal growth. Organisms use nitrogen compounds to assemble amino acids, nitrogenous bases and other nucleotides such as ATP and $NADP^+$.

Plants rely on relationships with certain bacteria to convert nitrogen into forms which they can use, a process of *nitrogen fixation*. Plants can absorb nitrogen as either ammonium (NH_4^+) or nitrate (NO_3^{-1}). Nitrogen-fixing bacteria may live within plant roots, or freely in the soil and water. They reduce nitrogen gas into ammonium which can be taken up by the plant. Ammonium can be created from the urea in animal wastes.

Bacteria can further convert ammonium into nitrate (NO_3^{-1}) by *nitrification*. This is a two-step process requiring certain bacteria to convert ammonium to nitrite (NO_2^-), and other bacteria to convert nitrite to nitrate. Nitrogen can be converted to nitrate when lightning or cosmic radiation provides energy for a reaction between atmospheric nitrogen and oxygen. *Denitrification* refers to the conversion of nitrate back to unusable nitrous oxide (N_2O) and nitrogen gas, thus completing the nitrogen cycle. This is performed by another class of bacteria.

The nitrogen cycle has been significantly altered by human production of fertilizer, which adds massive amounts of ammonium to the soil. Runoff from nitrogen-rich fields results in over-enrichment, or *eutrophication,* of lakes and oceans. Eutrophication causes large algal blooms which overtake the environment and kill off other organisms.

The burning of plants and fossil fuels adds nitrogen oxide to the atmosphere, contributing to air pollution. These emissions combine with atmospheric water vapor to form acids which precipitate and acidify the soil, *acid deposition*. Nitrogen oxides react with hydrocarbons in the atmosphere to form *photochemical smog,* which contains dangerous compounds that cause respiratory distress. These air pollutants can accumulate near the ground due to *thermal inversions*, in which warm air traps cold air just above the Earth's surface.

The Phosphorus Cycle

In the *phosphorus cycle,* plants take up phosphate ions (PO_4^{3-} and HPO_4^{2-}) made available in the soil, primarily from the weathering of rocks. However, while most phosphorus is found in sediments, some phosphorus which runs off into water bodies is incorporated into organic compounds by algae.

Animals eat these producers and incorporate some of the phosphates into phospholipids, ATP, and nucleotides. The decay of organisms and decomposition of animal wastes eventually makes phosphate ions available again. Phosphate incorporated into teeth, bones, and shells, however, does not decay for long periods of time. Phosphate is the limiting nutrient in most ecosystems, and any available phosphate is rapidly taken up by organisms.

Like the other biogeochemical cycles, humans have disrupted the phosphorus cycle. This is primarily due to mining of phosphate ores and runoff from livestock wastes and fertilized fields. Human and animal sewage is a contributor to phosphate buildup in water bodies. This pollutes the water, leading to eutrophication.

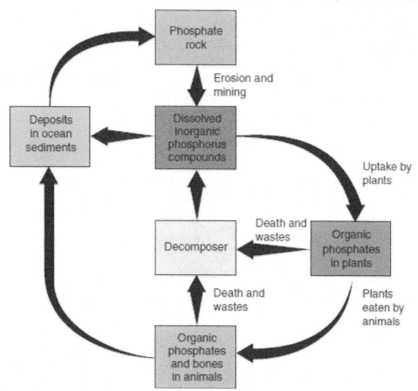

Phosphorus cycle is taken up by plants and primarily from soil

Climate

Climate refers to the prevailing weather conditions in a region over time. It is primarily dictated by temperature and rainfall and is the result of complex interactions between different elements, primarily solar radiation due to the tilt of the Earth, topography and the presence (or absence) of a nearby body of water. Water and air circulate through the oceans and atmosphere and create powerful climatic effects which drive weather conditions.

The tropics are the hottest region on Earth because the sun's rays strike the equator directly. Since the earth is a sphere, sunlight strikes the higher and lower latitudes at an angle, lessening the effect of the light. Earth is tilted on its axis, causing one pole to receive more sunlight than the other depending on Earth's position in its journey around the sun. These changes in sunlight through the year cause seasons.

Ocean water is warmest at the equator and coldest at the poles due to the distribution of the sun's rays. As air takes on the temperature of the water below, warm air moves from the equator toward colder latitudes, taking the heat with it. Moisture that evaporates into the air is carried with this heat energy. This movement of air, caused by the oceans, creates winds. The cooling and warming of air in the atmosphere drives *circulation cells,* closed circuits of wind circulation. The *Hadley cell* forms as warm, moist air rise at the equator and flows northward, high above Earth's surface. This causes hot, humid conditions in the tropics. At about 30° N, the air cools and sinks, absorbing moisture and causing desert conditions at this latitude. After it descends, the air circles back south to the equator, traveling close to the Earth's surface.

Meanwhile to the north, warm air rises at about 60° N. It flows northward as it cools and eventually descends at the pole (90° N), causing dry, frigid conditions. The air then moves back south to 60° N to continue this cycle, deemed the *Polar cell.*

The air of the Hadley cell sinking at 30° N and the air of the Polar cell rising at 60° N drives the circulation of an intermediate cell, the *Ferrel cell.* In the Ferrel cell, sinking air at 30° N flows north across the Earth's surface to about 60° N and then rises as it warms. It moves back south to 30° N and cools, restarting the cycle.

Hadley, Ferrel, and Polar cells are in the same sequence south of the equator.

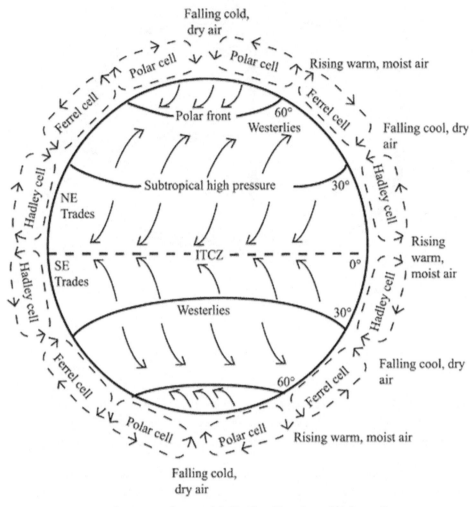

Atmospheric circulation with Hadley, Ferrel, and Polar cells

Due to the Earth's rotation, air does not move directly north to south but is deflected to the east or west. This is the *Coriolis Effect.* It influences both circulation cells and the *wind belts* which encircle the globe. Six wind belts are found on Earth: *trade winds* on either side of the equator, *westerlies* in the temperate regions between 30° and 60° N and S, and weak *polar easterlies* between 60° and 90° N and S.

Topography refers to the physical features of land, which can have a tremendous effect on the climate. Mountains, for example, can cause *rain shadows* in certain areas. Air blowing over a mountain is forced to rise, cooling the land. The windward side, therefore, receives moist air, producing more rainfall. By the time air descends on the leeward side of the mountain range, it is dry. As an example, rainfall on the windward side of the Hawaiian Islands measures over 750 cm but 50 cm in the rain shadow.

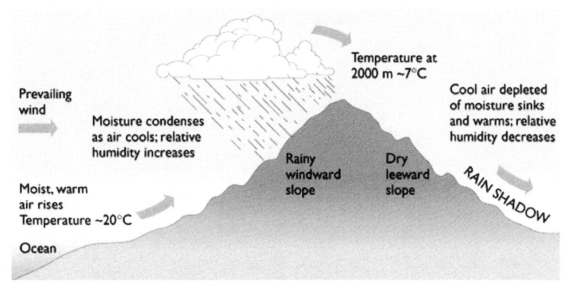

Mountains cause rain shadows with one side experiencing significant rainfall

Oceans help regulate land temperatures since they retain heat and remain cool longer than landmasses. During the day, land heats up, and warm air rises, allowing cool sea breezes to blow inland and replace the rising air. At night, the land cools and the cold air sinks, blowing out to sea. Water's excellent capacity for heat regulation (water has a high specific heat and can absorb energy) generally keeps coastal areas cooler than the inland and minimizes the temperature difference between day and night.

Notes for active learning

The Biosphere and Biomes

The Earth can be divided into layers, each with its distinct environmental conditions. The *geosphere* is the solid portion of Earth's surface that includes the cryosphere and lithosphere. The *cryosphere* contains all frozen water on Earth, most are found at the poles. The *lithosphere* is the rocky surface of the Earth that extends down about 100 kilometers. It comprises the crust as well as the upper mantle. The *hydrosphere* covers three-quarters of the lithosphere, the zone of liquid water primarily contained in oceans. The hydrosphere supports a vast diversity of life and helps regulate global temperatures by absorbing and slowly releasing large amounts of heat.

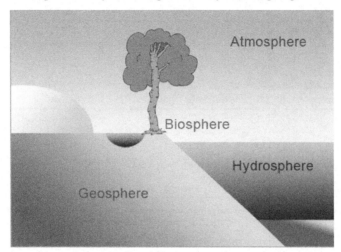

The intersection of geosphere, hydrosphere, atmosphere, and biosphere

The *atmosphere* is the gaseous layer wrapped around the Earth, which helps regulate temperatures by insulating the Earth from the frigid temperatures of outer space. It is held in place by the planet's gravity and is most concentrated near the Earth's surface. The major gases within the atmosphere are nitrogen and oxygen. Nitrogen makes up more than 75% of the atmosphere and is essential for the growth of plants and animals. Oxygen, about 20% of the atmosphere, is necessary for cellular respiration (ATP production) and makes up the protective ozone barrier which absorbs potentially damaging solar radiation. Other gases found in the atmosphere include carbon dioxide, water vapor and noble gases such as argon and neon.

Interacting with the geosphere, the atmosphere, and the hydrosphere is the *biosphere*, a thin layer that comprises all biomass on Earth. In a sense, the biosphere is the global ecosystem. It is further divided into large *biomes*, characterized by a certain climate which supports a unique community of plants and animals. Biomes change with latitude as well as elevation. For example, tundra yields to coniferous forests and then to deciduous forests as one moves from the poles towards the equator. This same sequence can be seen as one moves from a mountain peak to ground elevation.

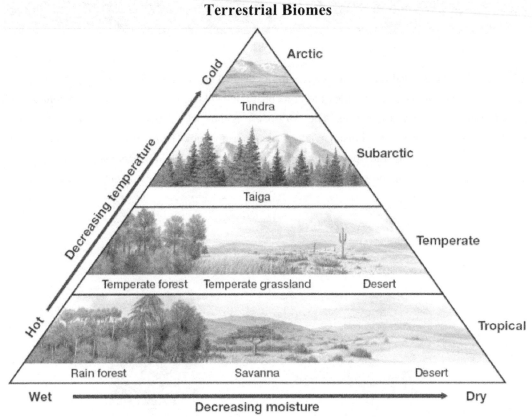

Biomes changes can be related to latitude and elevation

Tundra

The tundra is near the north and south poles, wherever there is no exposure to rock or ice-covered seas. It covers about 20% of the Earth's surface, including Greenland, Scandinavia, Siberia, northern Canada and the coasts of Antarctica and its surrounding islands. A form of tundra, *alpine tundra*, is at the tops of all high mountains, even at the equator.

Tundra is characterized by a cold, dry climate that receives less than 20 cm of annual rainfall. If not for the water provided by melting snow, the tundra would be defined as a desert. Except for alpine tundra, most tundra has a perpetually frozen layer of soil of *permafrost*. Tundra is a difficult environment for plants, due to high winds, a short growing season and hard permafrost. Trees cannot grow in the tundra, but short woody shrubs can survive, as they flower and seed quickly during the short period of available sunlight.

In the summer, the ground of the tundra is covered with bogs, marshes, and streams, with abundant grasses and mosses. Tundra has low biodiversity, and only a few animals are adapted to live in the tundra year-round. During the summer, the tundra supports a wider variety of insects and migratory birds and mammals, such as shorebirds, wolves and reindeer.

Coniferous forests

Coniferous forests have a milder climate than the tundra, as well as higher annual precipitation. They are primarily made of conifers such as spruce, fir, hemlock, and pine trees. These evergreens are well adapted to a snowy, dry climate and have thick, protective leaves or needles. Mountainous coniferous forests are *montane coniferous forests.*

Coniferous forests are divided into two or more biomes, depending on convention. The coniferous forest biome just below the tundra is a *taiga* or *boreal forest.* It extends across northern Europe, Asia, and North America, and makes up nearly 30% of the world's forest cover. It is the largest land biome on Earth and is exceeded in coldness and dryness only by the tundra. The soil does not contain permafrost but is relatively thin and nutrient-poor. It is acidic and covered by lichens, mosses, and fallen needles. The taiga supports greater animal diversity than the tundra, with hundreds of bird species and many year-round, large mammals such as bears, wolves, moose, elk, and bison. It supports many small mammals, such as beavers, hares, and squirrels. Unlike the tundra, cold-blooded reptiles and amphibians can survive in the taiga.

At the latitudes or elevations below the taiga are *temperate coniferous forests.* They have milder summers and winters than the taiga, along with higher precipitation. Temperate coniferous forests can be found throughout Europe, Asia, North America, and South America. They include the evergreens of the taiga as well as cedars, redwoods, juniper, and some deciduous trees. The understory is larger and more diverse, with a variety of shrubs and herbaceous plants.

Temperate deciduous forests

Temperate deciduous forests are at latitudes lower than the coniferous forests, primarily in eastern North America, eastern Asia and much of Europe. The climate in these areas is moderate with mild winters and appreciable rainfall, about 75 to 150 cm per year. They have four well-defined seasons, with a growing season that ranges between 140 and 300 days. Deciduous trees are characterized by their leaves, which they shed in the fall and regrow in the spring.

Deciduous forests support a wide variety of life, including countless birds, mammals, amphibians and reptiles. The forest is well-stratified, with large, mature trees shading saplings, shrubs, herbaceous plants, lichens, and mosses. This well-developed understory is possible because of the broad leaves of the deciduous trees, which allow sunlight to penetrate the canopy. Some major tree species found in a typical deciduous forest are maples, oaks, and elms.

Tropical forests

Tropical forests are at or near the equator and can be subdivided into several categories, depending on the biome classification system in use. *Tropical rainforests* are within 30° north and south of the equator, in South America, Central America, Africa, India, Southeast Asia, and Oceania. They are characterized by a warm climate and abundant rainfall, from 190 to 1,000 cm per year. Tropical rainforests are warm and humid year-round, with little change between the seasons. This climate sustains the highest diversity of any land biome with a staggering amount of insect life. Colorful birds and amphibians are abundant, as are snakes and lizards.

Many primates and other mammals can be found in the rainforest. The largest carnivores are big cats such as jaguars and leopards. The forest is highly stratified, with a tall canopy of evergreens and dense understory. The forest floor has rich soil but sustains few plants due to the heavy shade. A special type of tropical rainforest found in high mountains is a *montane rain forest* or *cloud forest* and has a remarkably cold climate compared to lowland tropical rain forests.

Other tropical forests are drier and may exhibit a mix of deciduous and evergreen trees. They are found north and south of the equatorial rain forest belt, in Africa, India, Southeast Asia, and South America. One of the largest of these biomes is the *tropical seasonal forest*, which is warm year-round but has long dry seasons. The tropical seasonal forest is less diverse than the tropical rainforest but still has a wide variety of fauna. This biome often gives way to grasslands.

Shrublands

Shrubland, also called *scrubland*, is dominated by short, woody shrubs with thick evergreen leaves. These shrubs must be highly resistant to forest fires and drought since shrubland is characterized by hot, dry summers and mild winters. The seeds of many plants in the shrubland even require heat from fires to induce germination. Shrublands found throughout California, and along the coasts of South America, Western Australia and the Mediterranean are *chaparral*. The chaparral is highly adapted to the climate, with extensive root systems and large leaves that retain water. In California, the chaparral is composed of oaks, manzanitas, sages and other short, thorny shrubs.

Drier shrubland found mixed with interior desert regions is *xeric shrubland*. The American West and other desert regions in Asia, South America and Africa have large expanses of xeric shrubland.

Grasslands

Grasslands are relatively arid but still receives greater than 25 cm of annual rainfall. Grasslands are found in areas too wet for desert and too dry for forests, and once covered 40% of Earth's surface. They are now significantly diminished since their rich soil is ideal for agriculture. Grasslands are highly adapted to droughts, flooding, fires and grazing from the many herbivores found in these regions.

The two types of grassland are temperate grasslands and tropical grasslands. *Temperate grasslands* are characterized by a mild climate and relatively low and predictable diversity. They are found throughout North America, South America, Eurasia, and South Africa, where they are *prairies, pampas, steppes,* and *veldts,* respectively. Many temperate grassland animals are large grazing mammals like bison and antelope. Other grassland prey animals are mostly birds and rodents. They are preyed on by coyotes, foxes, lynxes, wolves, snakes and predatory birds. Temperate grasslands can be further divided into the *tall-grass* and *short-grass* regions. Tall grasslands can support trees, are more humid and mild, and are found in the lowlands. Short grasslands are drier and cannot support trees, and may be found in cold highlands, (e.g., steppes of Russia and Ukraine). Many short grasslands are mixed with deserts and shrublands.

The tropical grasslands are *savannas*, which contain some trees but are mostly open. The most well-known savannas are in Africa, although they can be found in South America and Australia. They have a relatively cool dry season followed by a hot, rainy one. Savannas support higher biodiversity than temperate grasslands and have the largest variety of herbivores on Earth. Antelopes, zebras, wildebeests, water buffalo, elephants and giraffes make their homes in savannas along with large carnivores like lions, cheetahs, hyenas, and leopards. Insect life in savannas is plentiful and varied.

Deserts

Deserts are found at latitudes about 30° north and south of the equator, where dry air descends from the Hadley cell. They have an annual rainfall of less than 25 cm and subsequently a lack of cloud cover. The absence of clouds makes the days hot and the nights cold. Due to their inhospitable conditions, deserts have some of the lowest biodiversity on Earth. Their plants are highly adapted to heat and drought, but some deserts such as the Sahara are nearly devoid of vegetation. Most desert animals are small insects, reptiles, birds, and rodents since a large size poses a problem for heat regulation. However, large birds, camels, kangaroos, and coyotes can be found in various deserts.

The most well-known deserts are in low, interior regions, but a desert can be along the coast or at high altitudes, where they are *cold deserts.* Some scientists classify the tundra as a *polar desert* since it supports little life and is dry.

Aquatic Biomes

Aquatic biomes make up the majority of Earth's biosphere. They can be roughly classified as either freshwater or saltwater (i.e., marine).

Marshes, swamps, and bogs are all aquatic biomes called *wetlands* that can be found on coastlands across the globe. Wetlands may be freshwater, marine or a mix, called *brackish.* They have incredibly high diversity, with countless amphibians, reptiles, and birds. *Hydrophytes,* plants which are adapted to live in water, are in abundance.

Estuaries are where a freshwater river merges with the ocean. This may be a bay, a lagoon, an inlet, a sound or other partially enclosed aquatic body. They are intertwined with wetlands. Estuaries are brackish, but they are still considered to be marine biomes because of their importance to the seas. Over half of all marine fish are believed to have been born or raised in estuaries. Estuaries are provided with nutrients from rivers, ocean tides, and decayed vegetation, making them rich environments that can support a wide variety of aquatic flora and fauna. They are a unique biome that has been greatly threatened by habitat destruction and pollution, leading to the collapse of many important ecosystems.

The oceans comprise the other marine biome. The movement of water in the oceans is largely influenced by temperature, the friction of surface winds, salinity differences and the Coriolis effect. These factors all combine to create ocean currents. Since ocean currents are bounded by land, they move in a circular path, counterclockwise in the Northern Hemisphere and clockwise in the Southern Hemisphere. These currents are vital to regulating ocean temperatures and the global climate. Currents induce *upwelling,* the circulation of cold nutrient-rich waters to the surface. Ocean regions which experience upwelling are typically the most diverse and productive because they fuel the activities of *plankton,* a large group of free-swimming microorganisms. *Phytoplankton* is microscopic photosynthetic algae, while *zooplankton* is animals that feed on other plankton. Plankton is the basis of aquatic food chains because they are a food source for many other organisms. More importantly, phytoplankton generates the majority of primary productivity in oceans; other contributors include macroalgae, cyanobacteria, and hydrophytes.

Plankton can be found in the freshwater biomes, which include lakes, ponds, rivers, and streams. They contain salt in less than 1% concentration. Streams and rivers are connected to other ecosystems and can exhibit remarkable spatial heterogeneity. The *headwaters* of the river are cool, clear and well oxygenated. As the river travels towards the sea or a lake, nutrient content and species diversity increase. The waters at the mouth of the river are murkiest due to sediment accumulation, which affects light penetrance. There may be lower diversity, lower oxygen, and lower productivity as a result. Plant life in rivers and streams must be able to anchor tightly to the riverbed. In calmer waters, bottom-dwellers can be found that stay in place. In fast-moving waters, nearly all animals are fish that traverse great distances.

Ponds and lakes lack currents and have a more stable, permanent life. Aquatic plants, algae, insects, mollusks, crustaceans, amphibians, and fishes may be found in lakes. Birds and reptiles such as turtles, snakes or crocodiles may prey on these organisms. Many lakes and ponds have limited diversity due to their isolation from other regions.

Lakes

Lakes can be divided into four zones defined by their depth and distance from the shore. The *littoral zone* includes the shallow areas closest to shore, where the water is warmest and completely penetrated by light. Plants root themselves to the lakebed in this region and support animals such as mollusks, crustaceans, insects, amphibians and small fishes. Many larval organisms are reared in nurseries in the littoral zone.

The *limnetic zone* is the sunlit area in the open waters of the lake and is home to many plankton and fish. Most photosynthesis occurs here.

The *profundal zone* is below the limnetic zone in deeper waters, home to larger fish, turtles, and snakes. Many birds dive to the profundal zone to capture prey. There is little photosynthesis because sunlight cannot sufficiently penetrate the deeper waters.

The *benthic zone* is at the bottom of a pond or lake and is made of soft sediment that receives little if any, sunlight. It is inhabited by organisms that can tolerate low oxygen levels, including worms, mollusks, and crustaceans. These filter feeders thrive on the debris which falls from the higher zones.

In the temperate latitudes, deep lakes are stratified depending on the season. In summer, the surface waters are warm due to the heat of the sun, while the depths are cold. These layers are separated by the *thermocline,* a layer of abrupt temperature change. In winter, this is reversed, with the depths remaining temperate due to insulation by surface ice and the surface being cold since it is closest to the frigid outside temperatures. In fall and spring, changing temperatures cause mixing that returns the lake to a uniform temperature without a significant thermocline. Lake animals are adapted to these seasonal changes and may migrate to different depths for more favorable conditions

Lakes can be classified along a continuum from *oligotrophic* (nutrient poor) to *eutrophic* (nutrient rich). Oligotrophic lakes are not able to sustain much plant life and have low levels of primary productivity; consequently, they are dominated by fish. They have clear waters and are often found in cold, alpine regions. By contrast, eutrophic lakes have high productivity and can support an abundance of plants that outcompete fish. Excessive eutrophication results in massive algal blooms which deplete oxygen as they decompose. This creates hypoxic conditions that kill off animals. An influx of nutrients can change an oligotrophic lake into a eutrophic lake. Lakes which are *mesotrophic* have moderate nutrient levels and can sustain both plant and animal life.

Oceans

Oceans are bordered by continents, each of which is situated on a *continental shelf,* the continental crust which extends under the water for some distance from the coast. After several hundred meters it begins to drop off rapidly, forming a steep, downward *continental slope.* A *continental rise* follows the slope; contrary to the name, this region is still sloping downward, albeit less steeply than the slope. Finally, the rise levels off into the vast *abyssal plain,* which is the bottom of the majority of the world's oceans. Large ridges and deep trenches mark it.

Ocean zones are much larger and more complex than lake zones. Rather than the entire littoral zone, scientists typically refer to the *intertidal zone,* the area of the littoral zone that is periodically covered and uncovered by water. The changing of sea levels due to tides presents a challenge to intertidal organisms. Organisms must anchor themselves to rocks, hide in crevices or burrow in the sediment to avoid desiccation and being swept away.

Oceans are characterized by the continental shelf, slope, and rise

Past the intertidal zone, the waters begin to deepen, but the continental shelf continues below; this region is the *neritic zone*. The neritic zone is highly productive because sunlight and nutrients are relatively abundant. It is well-oxygenated and has stable conditions which make it suitable for the majority of ocean life. Organisms from microscopic plankton to large fish are in the neritic zone, as well as vast coral reefs. It is the *coastal zone* because it marks the boundary between the shore and the open ocean.

Once the continental shelf drops off into a slope, this marks the open seas of the *oceanic zone*. It is vast and sustains a variety of sea life, though relatively little compared to the neritic zone. The largest sea animals, such as whales, sharks, and giant fishes, are in the oceanic zone. Smaller animals and plankton can be found in the surface waters.

All waters of the ocean that are neither close to the bottom nor the shore are the *pelagic zone*. Pelagic waters are found throughout the neritic and oceanic zones and are vertically stratified based on light level. The *photic zone* extends from the surface to about 1000 meters deep and is where photosynthesis occurs due to phytoplankton activity. Fish, jellies, dolphins, and seaweed live in the photic zone. Apex predators in the upper waters of the photic zone include sharks, mackerels and tunas. The bottom of this zone is poorly lit or *disphotic*; consequently, it is dominated by predators with excellent photoreceptors and other adaptations to the low light. Prey organisms often have translucent or red coloring, which is both well-disguised in dark waters.

Below the photic zone is the *aphotic zone,* where no photosynthesis takes place because it is mostly, if not entirely, dark. It extends to the abyssal plain 6,000 meters below and often even deeper into massive ocean trenches. Familiar squids and sperm whales can be found in this zone, but most inhabitants are strange and poorly understood. Many animals at these depths let out occasional flashes of light to communicate with others or attract prey. Animals in this area are carnivores, filter feeders or scavengers which feed on dead organisms falling from above.

The *benthic zone* is the seabed, which may be completely exposed to the air in the intertidal zone or thousands of meters below the surface at the abyssal plain of the oceanic zone. Benthic organisms are adapted to living on or in the sediment, often anchoring themselves to the underlying substrate. The sediment may be sandy, rocky, muddy or silty. In many areas, the seabed is covered in coral. Benthic organisms rely on organic and inorganic nutrients falling from the water column above, as *marine snow.*

In the intertidal, littoral and neritic zones, the benthic zone receives sunlight and can support a varied food web with seaweed and filter feeders at the first trophic level. Starfish, crustaceans, mollusks and some bottom-dwelling fish occupy the upper trophic levels. In the oceanic zone, the benthic zone receives little to no sunlight, and therefore no photosynthetic organisms can be found. Rather, filter feeders and scavengers feed on marine snow. Starfish, crustaceans, mollusks and bottom-dwelling fish are common on the continental slope and rise. On the pitch black abyssal plain, there is a huge diversity of microbes but little macrofauna. Only a few select filter feeders and scavengers are found. These include sponges, worms, sea lilies, and other invertebrates. This is a region of extreme cold and intense pressure, except where hydrothermal vents expel superheated, sulfurous water. These vents support chemosynthetic bacteria, tube worms, and clams.

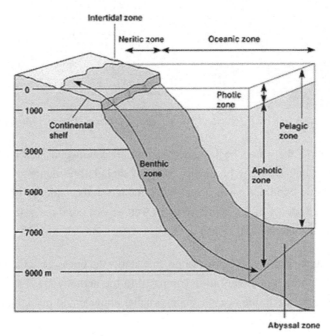

Ocean with zones at respective depths

Notes for active learning

Notes for active learning

Conservation Biology

Conservation biology applies ecology and social sciences to the study of preserving Earth's biodiversity. It stresses that biodiversity is vitally important for the health of humans and all other organisms, and strives to prevent extinction due to habitat destruction, pollution, invasive species, and overexploitation. Most conservation biology emphasizes practical applications, but there is still appreciable effort focused on the intrinsic value of nature to human cultures.

Biodiversity

The term *biodiversity* describes some concepts. *Species diversity* is the variety of species living in a given area. It is believed that there could be anywhere from 5 to 100 million species on Earth, and a fraction of this possible diversity has been cataloged. *Genetic diversity* describes the variety of alleles within the gene pool. It is the ultimate measure of biodiversity but is challenging to assess. Genetic diversity maintains the fitness and adaptability of a population; threats to genetic variation pose the risk of extinction. *Landscape diversity* refers to the variety of interacting ecosystems in a region. Homogenous landscapes can support a limited diversity of species, similar to isolated landscapes.

Biodiversity is not evenly distributed, but rather is highest at the tropics and lowest at the poles. It forms pockets of *biodiversity hotspots*, regions with unusually high concentrations of species. Biodiversity hotspots are characterized by their *endemic species,* organisms which are unique to that area alone. These regions make up a fraction of Earth's area but are estimated to contain 60% of all species; examples include the Mediterranean, the Amazon rainforest and Madagascar. Biodiversity frontiers such as the deep sea likely have more species than was formerly suspected.

Value of biodiversity

The benefits of biodiversity to humans are *ecological services,* which may be economic, scientific, aesthetic or ethical. Diversity strengthens an ecosystem and makes it healthier, increasing the efficiency of these services. For example, a greater diversity of crop plants increases their yield, while the greater diversity of fish keeps fisheries more stable and productive.

Economic benefits of diversity include goods such as food, oxygen, clothing, medicine, fuel, consumer products, and habitats. The rainforest contains up to $150 billion of possible prescription drugs, in addition to the many already discovered. The importance of natural products in the manufacturing of material goods cannot be overstated. Plastics, rubber, and lumber are just a small fraction of the materials derived from the environment. Fossil fuels, such as coal, oil and natural gas, are all provided by dead organisms.

Nature provides economically advantageous services, such as pest control, pollination, soil maintenance, and biogeochemical cycles. Unless these cycles can be someday approximated by technology, humans are reliant on the environment to purify water, break down pollutants, trap carbon dioxide, provide oxygen and recycle organic compounds into edible food.

Some ecosystem services are lifesaving. River and wetland ecosystems are natural buffers against flooding, storm surges, and other extreme weather events. Trees and other plants hold the soil and prevent erosion that clogs reservoirs, creates landslides, chokes coastal ecosystems and ruins fisheries. Trees are important because they are the largest providers of oxygen and removers of atmospheric carbon dioxide. Deforestation worsens the issue of global warming by diminishing the carbon dioxide sink.

Tourism of natural environments, or "ecotourism," is a multibillion-dollar industry; many cities and even countries base an entire economy on ecotourism. If these natural resources are threatened, it will cause debilitating economic collapses.

Even if the technology were able to replace the economic services of the environment, humans would be deeply impacted by the aesthetic loss and ethical conflict. Erosion and extinctions threaten relationships with plants, animals and natural habitats, and thus human culture as a whole.

Causes of extinction

The greatest threats to biodiversity are those that cause species extinctions. Research shows that the most powerful catalysts of extinction are habitat loss, introduced or invasive species, overexploitation of flora and fauna, and pollution.

Habitat loss may be caused by destruction, fragmentation or degradation. The most common form is direct human destruction. Examples include clearing forests for agriculture, draining wetlands, diverting rivers and building dams, mining, trawling the ocean floor with fishing nets and urbanization. Unfortunately, biodiversity hotspots are often the most threatened by habitat loss. A classic example is the tropical rainforests, which are being cleared at an astonishing rate. Other biomes that are particularly threatened are grasslands, deciduous forests, wetlands, estuaries, and the oceans. Habitat fragmentation is usually the result of urban sprawl and infrastructure, which can divide an area into fragments that are too small to support a species. Fragmentation hinders migration, which is crucial for the maintenance of diversity. Habitat degradation is an indirect form of habitat loss that is caused by pollution, climate change, and exotic species. For example, an invasive herbivore may weaken a grass population that is used as a habitat by native species.

Exotic species are often introduced accidentally or deliberately into new ecosystems. Human circumvention of natural barriers has resulted in the transport of many alien species to new environments. Ecosystems evolve with their native organisms in balance, and the introduction of a new species often disrupts the food chain and leads to extinction.

Overexploitation occurs when harvesting from a wild population becomes unsustainable. Animals may be overexploited for food, hides, furs, ivory, pets or sport. Nearly a third of fisheries have been dramatically overexploited, and tigers and elephants have been hunted nearly to extinction. Plants are typically overexploited for food, building materials, medicine, and agriculture. Often, overexploitation hinders an ecosystem's ability to recover even decades after it ceases.

The introduction of any harmful element to an ecosystem is pollution. For example, air pollution is mostly caused by exhaust from factories and motor vehicles. It results in the accumulation of greenhouse gases, acid deposition, disease, and other ill effects. Soil and water pollution are typically the result of agricultural, industrial and sewage runoff, which may contain pesticides, heavy metals, oil, fertilizers, animal wastes, and other toxic chemicals. The littering of trash is a form of physical pollution that affects the land and water.

However, pollution may take a more abstract form of light and noise pollution. Over-illumination from cities disorients animals and impacts their circadian rhythms, migration patterns, and reproduction. Noise pollution interferes with natural communication between animals, particularly those who use sonar. *Genetic pollution* is a recent phenomenon which is caused by human interference with the genetic diversity of a population. For example, breeding or engineering hybrids, homogenizing the gene pool or introducing new species— all affect the natural population. It can destabilize the population, cripple its fitness and even decimate it.

The causes of extinction are worsened by climate change. Global warming melts ice caps, increasing sea level and destroying coastal habitats. It warms the seas and increases pH, threatening many aquatic species which are adapted to certain conditions. The coral reefs, in particular, are already suffering from temperature and acidity shock. Global warming promotes the growth of pests and pathogens, increasing rates of disease. Climate change alters global weather patterns, causing extreme weather events which destroy habitats and kill wild populations. Regions with a suitable climate for species shift rapidly, probably faster than organisms can migrate or adapt, allowing exotic species to outcompete native species in the changing environment.

Conservation techniques

Rather than attempt to conserve every ecosystem on Earth, conservation biologists focus their efforts on biodiversity hotspots to maximize effectiveness. Hotspots may be detected in a variety of ways. Widespread field studies provide accurate counts of species diversity but are labor-intensive. An easier but sometimes misleading method is to look for *indicator species,* which highlight certain conditions of an ecosystem that may otherwise go undetected. For example, the presence of the spotted owl indicates a stable, old growth forest, while bleaching of corals indicates acidic waters. Indicator species are often keystone species, which can be useful targets for conservation since they prevent the extinction of several other species.

Endemic, rare and endangered species merit the primary attention of conservation efforts. Many of these organisms become *flagship species,* adored by humans for their looks or symbolism. Flagship species are almost always mammals, such as polar bears and giant pandas, and can be a powerful tool for mobilizing conservation. Unfortunately, many vitally important invertebrate and plant species are disregarded in favor of flagship species.

Umbrella species are spread over a range of habitats; they are often a flagship, keystone or indicator species. Because the umbrella species has a wide range and is easily observable, targeting conservation of the umbrella species undoubtedly assures conservation of other species. For example, protecting the spotted owl requires the protection of its habitat, old-growth forests in North America. These forests are home to hundreds of other species which benefit from the spotted owl's conservation.

Conservation efforts require cost-benefit analysis, statistical models and detailed proposals to achieve success. For example, *population viability analysis* helps determine how much habitat a species needs to survive. This can guide conservationists to balance the costs of habitat preservation with the benefits for the species. Governments take on conservation efforts if they are efficient and effective. One of the best ways to compel governments is to describe the practical, monetary advantages of taking action. It is helpful to provide clear guidelines for what actions should take place. For example, the *IUCN Red List* describes the conservation status of thousands of organisms, with categories such as "least concern," "vulnerable," "endangered," and "extinct." Hunting and fishing laws, the creation of nature preserves, sustainable building practices and restriction of development are conservation efforts which governments can enforce.

Hunting, poaching, and fishing may be banned outright for certain species, or somewhat restricted. Sustainable hunting and fishing practices aim to prevent the overexploitation of biodiversity.

Conservation aimed at invasive or introduced species often attempts to cull the populations of the problem species. This can be costly, difficult and often requires an ongoing effort. Introducing a *new* exotic species which preys on the problematic one can be effective if it is done carefully and scientists can be confident it will not backfire.

As habitat loss is the main cause of extinctions, habitat preservation is the foremost aim of conservation biology. One of the most difficult but important ways to protect biodiversity is to restore a degraded habitat to its former health. Habitat restoration falls under the category of *restoration ecology*, which studies strategies to restore ecosystems.

Planting vegetation may reduce erosion, for example, or controlled burns can clear species which are outcompeting all others. The ultimate goal of habitat restoration is to return the habitat to its natural state and ensure it can maintain this state without human intervention. This often takes the form of nature preserves, where species and their environment are protected from human interference. Wildlife corridors are a more recent technique used to connect habitats which have been fragmented by land development. Preserves and corridors are often selected using *gap analysis,* which involves overlaying land-use maps with species maps to highlight areas where biodiversity is high but unprotected or fragmented. Of course, it is always better to be proactive rather than reactive. Low impact development, reduction of logging and mining and pollution control are ways habitat loss can be prevented.

Pollution control is a facet of conservation that has received great attention and even international agreement in the *Kyoto Protocol.* This treaty was drafted to target climate change, the most important frontier of conservation at this time, primarily in the reduction of greenhouse gases and other pollutants. Pollution can be prevented or reversed by enacting an eco-friendly industry, better waste management, cleanup, recycling and new technologies which reduce the need for old, harmful substances.

The most effective conservation is *in situ,* efforts occurring in the ecosystem in question. *Ex situ* conservation occurs outside the original ecosystem and may include relocating species to a new environment or breeding them in zoos and then re-releasing them into the wild. *Gene banks* are a new focus of ex situ conservation, where scientists maintain samples of plant seeds, cuttings, and animal gametes. The idea is that these organisms may later be reintroduced in case the species become endangered or extinct.

Notes for active learning

Notes for active learning

Chapter 13

Population and Community Ecology

- **Ecology of Populations**

- **Community Ecology**

Ecology of Populations

Scope of ecology

Ecology is the study of the distribution and abundance of organisms and their interactions with one another and the environment. Humans have been studying the natural world for hundreds of years, but the term ecology was not coined until the 19th century by the German zoologist Ernst Haeckel. The field was greatly advanced by widespread acceptance of the theory of evolution. Evolution allowed scientists to fully understand how ecological pressures such as natural selection to shape the environment. Since then, ecology has become modernized, with rigorous, comprehensive studies and sophisticated statistical models. Modern ecology has applications to a wide range of fields, including conservation, agriculture, social science, and many others.

Ecology is hierarchical, as it can be studied at many levels, from cellular to the *biosphere,* the entire region of Earth in which all living organisms reside. Most ecologists begin their study at the organismal level. An organism's *habitat* includes both its physical and biological surroundings, including nearby organisms. Organisms of the same species often live in groups *populations,* which occupy roughly the same region. The *community* includes the populations of all species in a given locale. For example, a freshwater lake is a community that may include algae, plants, fish and microorganism populations. All living organisms and their interactions are *biotic factors.*

An *ecosystem* includes all biotic factors as well as the physical environment. In the lake example, the ecosystem would include the populations described above as well as water salinity, temperature, pH, density, light level, soil composition, and other factors. These are *abiotic factors.* Together, all ecosystems with similar abiotic factors make a *biome,* which is usually defined by its climate. For example, the tropical rainforest is a biome that includes all hot, humid ecosystems supporting a high diversity of life. Collectively, biomes comprise the biosphere.

Characteristics of populations

Population size and growth models

Population ecology is the study of the growth, abundance, and distribution of populations. The size of the population is denoted as N, the total number of individuals. Population size about living space is *population density* or the number of individuals per given unit of area. The way in which density is patterned over the population's range is *population dispersal.* Populations may be spread uniformly, randomly or be clumped. Ecologists often study the changes in population distribution across space or over time.

Generally, a population is densest near the center of its range and sparsest at the edge. This edge is the *zone of physiological stress* because it has suboptimal conditions for the species in question. Physiological stressors may include extreme temperatures, inadequate water or pollution. Beyond this is the *zone of intolerance,* where no individuals of the species can survive. The species' theoretical range is determined by the range of physiological stressors which it can tolerate. However, this range may be restricted by other species due to *biological stressors,* such as competition and predation.

Stressors are *limiting factors*, conditions which act to limit growth or abundance of a population. Limiting factors may be *density-independent,* which are independent of population density (e.g., light availability and precipitation). Limiting factors can be *density-dependent,* whereby the effect becomes more severe as population density increases. Density-dependent factors include competition, disease, parasites, and food scarcity. They typically fluctuate and drive a *population cycle,* a cyclic change in the population size.

The population size (N) over time can be predicted by *natality* (birth rate) and *mortality* (death rate). Together, natality and mortality can be used to calculate the *intrinsic rate of natural increase* (r).

$$r = \frac{(\text{birth rate} - \text{death rate})}{N}$$

However, population increase is usually subject to many factors. For example, population ecologists must consider the *immigration* of individuals out or the *emigration* of other individuals into the population.

Population growth typically exhibits one of two patterns. The first is *discrete growth* (discrete breeding or discrete reproduction), in which organisms breed all at once at a particular time of year. They may breed once in their lifetime, as *semelparous,* or they may reproduce year after year, as *iteroparous.* The former strategy produces *discrete generations,* in which the adult generation reproduces and soon dies, leaving behind the next generation. This results in a population that has one generation at any given time. Iteroparity produces *overlapping generations*, in which an elderly generation is living at the same time as a reproductive generation and a sexually immature generation. At any time, at least two generations can be observed in the population.

Continuous growth is the other pattern of population growth, which occurs when organisms reproduce continuously without regard for a certain breeding season. Populations which exhibit continuous growth are always iteroparous and have overlapping generations. Most organisms do not fit neatly into one of these two patterns and instead exhibit a combination of the two. For example, plants may reproduce sexually at a certain time each year but reproduce asexually at any time.

Exponential growth often occurs in populations which are iteroparous and have overlapping generations. It is represented by a J-shaped, *exponential growth curve*. The first phase of the curve is the *lag phase*. At this time, growth is slow because the population is small. At a certain critical size, the population enters the *exponential growth phase* when growth accelerates rapidly.

A population is undergoing the maximum population growth possible, with no hindrance from limiting factors, is fulfilling its *biotic potential.* Biotic potential is calculated by taking into account the number of offspring produced by each reproductive event (*clutch size*), the frequency and a total number of reproductive events, offspring survival rate and the age at which an individual reaches sexual maturity. Populations can reach their biotic potential when they have ample space, resources, and absence of predation.

However, these factors are often in limited supply, and the environment can only support so many organisms, the *carrying capacity* (K). When populations approach carrying capacity and deplete resources, they encounter *environmental resistance* and growth begins to slow. An S-shaped *logistic growth curve* represents growth under environmental resistance. The first portion of the curve is exponential, with the lag phase and exponential phase described earlier. However, the population eventually reaches a *transitional phase* or *deceleration phase*, when the birth rate begins to fall below the death rate due to resource competition, predation, disease, and other density-dependent factors. At this point, growth begins to slow. At carrying capacity, the population enters a *stable equilibrium phase* with minimal growth. During stable equilibrium, natality and mortality are roughly equal.

The logistic growth curve: $\frac{\Delta N}{\Delta t} = rN\left(\frac{K-N}{K}\right)$

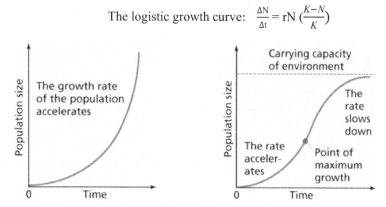

Exponential (unrestricted) growth (left) and logistic (restricted) growth (right)

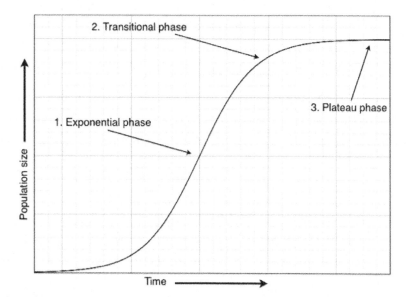

S-shaped logistic growth curve of population growth with environmental resistance

Age distribution

A population with overlapping generations typically exhibits *pre-reproductive*, *reproductive* and *post-reproductive* generations. The abundance of individuals of each gender and in each age group of a population is represented in an *age structure diagram*. Horizontal bars represent the number of individuals in each age group.

A pyramid shape indicates an expanding population with high birth rate and exponential growth. The pre-reproductive generation is largest because offspring are rapidly reproduced, while the reproductive generation is intermediate. The post-reproductive generation is smallest as the elderly die. A bell shape represents a relatively stable population, in which the pre-reproductive and reproductive generations are roughly equal, and the post-reproductive generation is smaller by a narrow margin. Finally, an urn-shaped diagram is indicative of a declining population. The post-reproductive generation is largest because of few new individuals. Individuals from the reproductive generation enter the post-reproductive generation and continually die, while the pre-reproductive generation is too small to sustain growth.

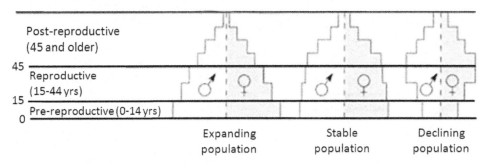

Age structure diagrams: pyramid (left), bell-shaped (center), urn-shaped (right).

Carrying capacity

Carrying capacity is determined by the available water, space, food, light, and other factors. It is density-dependent, becoming more restricted as growth increases. Stable populations do not attempt to maximize biotic potential but rather remain just under carrying capacity. However, overshooting carrying capacity can be a valuable strategy as well, provided the population can introduce new individuals before it crashes.

Carrying capacity is an important regulator of population size and a powerful driver of evolution. Populations respond to carrying capacity by expanding their range or evolving adaptations, which relieve them of some of the restrictions of carrying capacity. No organism can indefinitely evade carrying capacity, and if it is overshot, high mortality results.

Mortality Patterns

In demography, predictions can ascertain the probability that an individual will die before their upcoming birthday based upon their age. The tool used to make these predictions is a *life table* (also *mortality table* or *actuarial table*). This information ultimately signifies the survivorship of certain age-based populations.

Region	1990	1995	2000	2005	2010	2012	MDG target 2015	Decline (percent) 1990–2012	Annual rate of reduction (percent)		
									1990–2012	1990–2000	2000–2012
Developed regions	15	11	10	8	7	6	5	57	3.8	3.9	3.8
Developing regions	99	93	83	69	57	53	33	47	2.9	1.8	3.8
Northern Africa	73	57	43	31	24	22	24	69	5.4	5.3	5.5
Sub-Saharan Africa	177	170	155	130	106	98	59	45	2.7	1.4	3.8
Latin America and the Caribbean	54	43	32	25	23	19	18	65	4.7	5.1	4.4
Caucasus and Central Asia	73	73	62	49	39	36	24	50	3.2	1.6	4.5
Eastern Asia	53	46	37	24	16	14	18	74	6.1	3.7	8.0
Excluding China	27	33	31	20	17	15	9	45	2.7	−1.2	5.9
Southern Asia	126	109	92	76	63	58	42	54	3.5	3.1	3.9
Excluding India	125	109	93	78	66	61	42	51	3.3	3.0	3.5
South-eastern Asia	71	58	48	38	33	30	24	57	3.9	3.9	3.8
Western Asia	65	54	42	34	26	25	22	62	4.4	4.4	4.5
Oceania	74	70	67	64	58	55	25	26	1.4	1.0	1.7
World	90	85	75	63	52	48	30	47	2.9	1.7	3.8

*This life table, developed by the United Nations, indicates
the mortality levels and trends for children under five years old worldwide.*

In actuarial science, two varieties of life tables are used. A *period table* is used to calculate mortality rates during a set period for a specified population. A *cohort life table* (generation life table) is used to represent a certain population's overall mortality rates.

Life tables track cohorts over their lifetime. A *cohort* is a group of individuals born at the same time that are aging together. The life table shows how members of the cohort die at various ages. *Survivorship* refers to how many individuals remain alive at a given point in time.

The three general types of survivorship curves are:

Type I survivorship curve shows a long curve with a relatively short drop-off near the end in which most individuals survive until they die of old age (e.g., the human population).

Type II survivorship curve, which is negative and linear, shows individuals dying at a constant rate over their lifespan (e.g., some birds and lizards).

Type III survivorship curve is when most individuals in the population die at an early age. Those that do survive, however, tend to live for a relatively long time. It is essentially the opposite of a Type I curve and is seen in many invertebrates, plants, and fish.

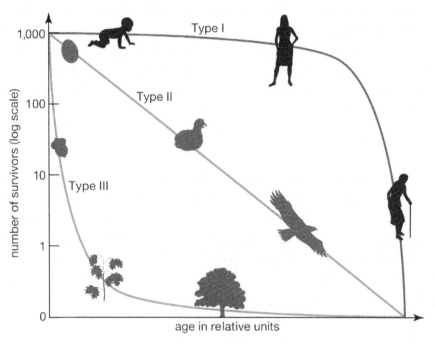

Survivorship curves comparing type I, type II and type III organisms

Regulation of population size

As previously discussed, populations are regulated by a number of density-dependent and independent factors. These may be *intrinsic* (i.e., within the population) or *extrinsic*. Intrinsic factors include the behavior and anatomy of the species, while extrinsic factors include climate, habitat and other organisms.

The exponential and logistic growth curve models are a straightforward view of population growth that only takes into account classic limiting factors. However, real populations may be affected by hundreds of complex and interrelated factors. These are usually intrinsic factors such as social behavior, which influence how competition proceeds and individuals immigrate or emigrate. For example, populations may actively recruit new members or exclude them due to territoriality.

Straightforward models have difficulty predicting randomness. Populations may deviate from the expectation because of chance or unpredictable events, like a natural disaster.

Life history patterns

Ecologists have historically divided organisms into two major life history patterns: *r-selection* and *K-selection*. However, most species are not strictly r-strategists or K-strategists; it is more common for a species to exhibit characteristics of both. They may be able to shift strategy in response to environmental factors.

r-Selection

The r-selected species attempt to maximize their rate of natural increase. They typically overshoot carrying capacity, causing the population to crash suddenly. Therefore, their population growth may show severe fluctuations. Typically, *opportunistic species*, r-strategists rapidly seize the opportunity to proliferate. They are often the first to colonize a new habitat and do well in unstable environments subject to density-independent factors. This is because they reproduce quickly and reach sexual maturity at a young age, maximizing the opportunity for reproduction before death. They may get the chance to reproduce once, making semelparity (single reproductive event) a common characteristic of r-strategists. The trade-off is that they must produce many offspring at one time because they cannot protect them from infant mortality. To survive, r-selected organisms have a short lifespan and must quickly adapt to new environments.

K-Selection

K-selected species attempt to maintain their rate of natural increase. They exist near the carrying capacity at a state of equilibrium, making them *equilibrium species*. Unlike r-strategists, K-strategists are specializers uniquely suited to their environment. This makes them successful but vulnerable to disturbances. They typically enter a new habitat after it has been colonized by r-strategists. To maintain their existence, K-selected species are typically large and invest considerable energy in caring for their offspring, of which they often produce one at a time. K-strategists reach sexual maturity slowly, but they can live for a long time. They can reproduce several times throughout their lifespan, making them *iteroparous* (multiple reproductive cycles during their lifetime).

Human population growth

The human population is in the exponential phase of a J-shaped growth curve. The global population is currently increasing by about 80 million people per year. This tremendous growth has been fueled by technological advances, an increase in food supply, reductions in disease and habitat expansion. Current estimates predict that the world population will level off sometime in this century between 8 and 10 billion. Some claim this number is a vast underestimate and that the human population may reach 14 billion by the end of the 21st century.

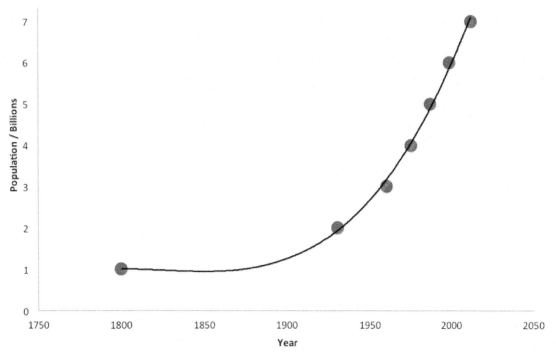

Human population growth with exponential population growth between 1800 and 2000

In the mid-20th century, the developed countries had a significant decline in mortality rate, soon followed by a decline in birth rate. Currently, the growth rate in first world nations is at about 0.1%. Their age structures are relatively stable, with some countries even exhibiting a declining population.

Nearly all population growth in the coming years will be seen in the less developed countries, especially in Africa, Asia, and Latin America. Even so, the growth rate in these countries is lower than it was at its peak of 2.5% in the 1960s. The way to level off population growth is an aggressive campaign of family planning, birth control, and encouragement to produce fewer children. However, due to cultural attitudes and a high infant mortality rate in underdeveloped world nations, it is difficult to convince people to have fewer children or delay childbearing until later years.

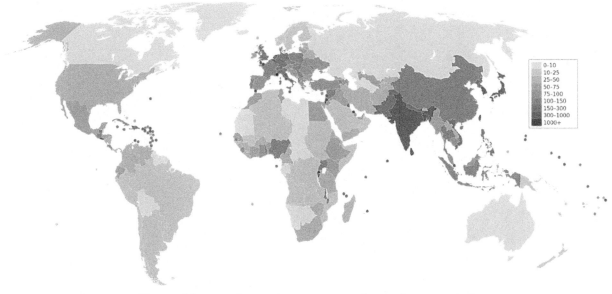

This world map indicates the average population density per km^2

The growing populations of the less developed countries and the high consumption of the more developed countries put stress on the environment. Currently, the *ecological footprint* of those in the United States and other developed nations is unsustainable. The ecological footprint is determined by the amount of land which is required to sustain an individual's lifestyle, including the area in which he or she lives, the farmland required to produce food, the factories required to produce material goods and the distances across which these products must travel to reach the individual. An average American family, regarding consumption and waste production, equates to the lifestyle habits of thirty people in India.

Developed countries account for one-fourth of the world population but provide 90% of the hazardous waste production. Intense resource consumption affects the cycling of chemicals and contributes to pollution and the extinction of species. Without drastic reductions in the collective ecological footprint, humans will overshoot carrying capacity and possibly experience catastrophic disease, famine, and other density-dependent factors.

Notes for active learning

Notes for active learning

Community Ecology

Community ecology is the study of the composition, diversity, interactions, and relationships between populations and how these characteristics change over time.

The concept of the community

A community includes all populations within a given environment that interact with one another. They may be large, as in an entire forest, or small, as in a bacterial community found in the gut of an animal. Because of this variability in scale, it can be difficult to delineate the boundaries of a community.

Studies show that the composition of a community is constantly in flux due to natural selection, migration, environmental changes, and random chance. Many communities fluctuate regularly with the seasons; for example, the tundra is inhospitable in winter but supports plant and animal life in the summer. Some communities may be transient, as with an animal corpse, which supports a community until decay is complete.

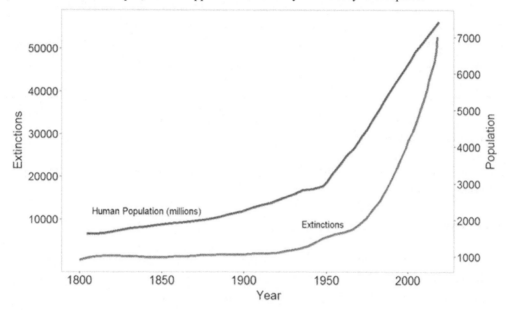

The correlation between human population levels and the number of species lost to extinction

Various models were proposed in the 20th century to outline the concept of a community. The American ecologist Frederic Clements described a *holistic theory,* in which the community acts together as a "superorganism." By contrast, his contemporary Henry Gleason proposed the *individualistic theory,* which states that each population can inhabit a community due to its unique adaptations. Under this model, the range of a species is due to its tolerance to physiological stressors and is independent of the distribution of other species. Finally, Stephen Hubbell's *neutral theory* proposes that at a basic level, all species have the same ability to adapt, grow and disperse. Their differences are negligible, and the variation seen in different communities is essentially due to randomness. Biodiversity is a product of chance and not of inherent characteristics of the species. Likely, none of these models are exactly correct. It seems that communities are affected by biotic and abiotic factors, as well as by random chance.

Structure of the community

Species composition, or *species richness,* is the number of different species within a community, without any further information as to their relative abundances. Relative abundance is *species evenness* or the relative size of each population found in the community; for example, a forest with 40 yellow poplars and 40 American elms has more species evenness than a forest with 70 poplars and 10 elms. Together, evenness and richness describe the *species diversity* of a community. The most diverse communities have a high level of both richness and evenness.

The structure of a community depends on abiotic factors along with complex interactions between populations. *Niche theory* is essential to understanding how organisms and populations fit into the community. The *ecological niche* is the role an organism plays in its community, including its habitat, resources consumed and interactions with other organisms. Two deer species may occupy the same geographic range but inhabit different niches because they feed on different species of plants.

The *fundamental niche* is the place which an organism occupies in the absence of competition from other species. However, organisms are usually limited to a *realized niche,* the more restricted niche which allows it to avoid overlap with other organisms. For example, one barnacle species may be able to live on rocks that are exposed to the full range of tides, making their fundamental niche the entire tidal area. However, a second barnacle species may be capable of out-competing the first, but can only live in the lower tidal region where desiccation is minimal. This forces the first species into a realized niche that includes only the higher tidal region. The two species typically have an area of niche overlap at the middle region where intense competition takes place.

Organisms have developed different strategies to maximize success under the constraints of niche theory. *Generalists,* such as humans, can occupy a variety of niches. They can quickly adapt to a new niche if the current one is threatened. *Specialists* become highly adapted to a single niche.

Interactions between populations can be complex and include competition for resources, predation, coevolution, and symbiotic relationships.

Competition between populations

Interspecific competition occurs when different species utilize a resource that is in limited supply. The *competitive exclusion principle* states that no two species can occupy the same niche at the same time. Over time, either one population replaces the other, or the two species evolve to occupy different niches.

Resource partitioning occurs when two species occupy the same habitat but pursue slightly different resources or secure their resources in different ways, minimizing competition and maximizing success. This is commonly observed in birds, which may inhabit the same tree but spend time in different tree zones to avoid competition. Another example is the mixed flocks of swallows, swifts, and martins, which fly together and eat the same insects but have different nesting sites. Studies show that when bird species are separated, they have intermediate beak sizes, but when forced together they begin to diversify and develop beaks of many different sizes. This is *character displacement,* or a *niche shift,* and is a powerful form of evolution. Natural selection favors adaptations which minimize competition.

Predator-prey interactions

Predation is a community interaction which occurs when one organism feeds on another. In a broad sense, this includes not only carnivores killing prey, but filter feeders which strain microorganisms from the water, parasites that feed on a host and herbivores which eat plants. Herbivores that are *grazers* (grass eaters) and *browsers* (leaf eaters) are examples of animals that eat part of their prey, weakening it in the process. This is similar to most parasitic relationships.

The predator-prey relationships of the food web may fluctuate over time. Predator-prey population densities show regular peaks and valleys with the predator population often lagging slightly behind the prey. This may occur because the predator can overconsume the prey, which causes the prey population to decline, followed by the predator population. It may be the opposite, in which the prey is unable to keep pace with the prey population, causing the prey to overshoot carrying capacity and then crash. In many cases, several scenarios affect predator-prey cycling. For example, the snowshoe hare and the Canadian lynx exhibit cycling, which is affected by both predation as well as the hare's food supply. The grouse population cycles, perhaps because the lynx switches to grouse when the hare populations decline, evidence that predators and prey do not normally exist as simple two-species systems.

Coevolution

Predator-prey interactions drive *coevolution*, in which one species evolves in response to the adaptation of another. Prey have evolved a variety of predator defenses.

Crypsis is a common adaptation which allows an organism to escape detection by predators. It may include camouflage, hiding behavior, or *mimicry* (imitation of another species). *Batesian mimicry* is when one defenseless species (the mimic) imitates another species (the model), which has successful antipredator defenses. For example, the harmless corn snake exhibits similar coloration to the venomous copperhead snake. *Mullerian mimicry* occurs when several different species, all with some defense mechanism, have coevolved to have similar coloration serving as a universal warning. This warning coloration is *aposematic coloration.* Aside from toxicity, prey may have other passive defenses that make the prey difficult, unpalatable or even fatal to eat. This may include a large body size, sharp spines, tough skin or shells and a foul odor.

Defenses against predation may be active, such as fleeing from, frightening or fighting back against a predator. Active defenses are more costly in energy but can be quickly adapted to a particular situation and may be effective.

Coevolution need not be competitive, as many beneficial relationships result from coevolution. Pollination, for example, is the result of millions of years of evolution between flowers and pollinators. Flowers have evolved energy-rich nectar along with coloration and pheromones which attract the pollinators. The pollinators have evolved anatomy which is well adapted for nectar consumption and pollen transfer. This coevolution is an example of a symbiotic relationship.

Symbiotic relationships

Symbiosis is an intimate, often permanent, association between members of two populations that may (or may not) be beneficial and may be *obligatory*, where one or both organisms cannot survive without the other.

Parasitism

Parasitism involves an organism that derives nourishment from the host. This relationship benefits the parasite at the expense of the host and allows the parasite to live with minimal expenditure of energy. Parasites may be *ectoparasites*, which cling to the exterior of the host using special appendages, or *endoparasites* that live within the host. Parasites occur in all kingdoms of life, and even viruses are classified as parasitic. Many parasites have several hosts. The primary host is the main source of nutrition, while the secondary host may serve as a vector to transport the parasite to other hosts. *Parasitoids* are organisms which invariably kill their host, unlike parasites, which usually permit the host to live.

Commensalism

In *commensalism*, one species benefits and the other is neither benefitted nor harmed. It is difficult to determine true commensalism because classification must determine that one organism is not affected. For example, barnacles on a whale could be considered commensalism, but because they slow the whale, this may be parasitism. However, some relationships which may be reasonably defined as commensalism include insects that land on other animals for transport and crustaceans that inhabit the discarded shells of other organisms. Some relationships are so loose that it is difficult to know if they exhibit true commensalism. Many ecologists argue that any relationship between the two species has some subtle degree of parasitism or commensalism.

Mutualism

Mutualism is a cooperative relationship which is essentially the opposite of competition. A mutualistic relationship benefits both individuals provided the relationship is balanced. The imbalance is commonly seen in mutualistic relationships, whereby one individual violates the terms of the relationship to gain an unfair advantage. For example, *mycorrhizae* of plant roots and fungi are common mutualists, in which the fungus provides inorganic minerals to the plant in exchange for organic nutrients. However, the fungus may continue to receive nutrients but refuse to supply the plant. When this happens, the mutualistic relationship becomes parasitic.

Plant-fungus mutualism is often not obligatory, because both organisms can survive without their relationship. By contrast, the relationship between ant colonies and the bullhorn acacia tree is necessary for the acacia's survival. The ants are protected within the tree and receive nutrients, while the ants defend against herbivores and other plants that might block light to the tree. If the ants are killed, the tree is quickly overrun and dies.

Cleaning symbiosis is another common mutualism; crustaceans, fish, and birds clean ectoparasites from other animals, improving the "client's" health while providing the cleaner with food. However, cleaners may feed on the client's tissues, turning this into a case of parasitism.

Mutualistic relationships may involve the exchange of resources (e.g., mycorrhizae), a service for a resource (e.g., cleaning symbiosis, pollination), or the exchange of services (e.g., sea anemone and clownfish protecting one another from their respective predators).

Community development

All communities experience *ecological succession* as they change over time. This process can be observed over years or vast periods of geologic time. *Primary succession* occurs after an event creates or exposes a substrate that has never previously supported life. This may be bare rock left behind after a glacier moves, or a lava flow after volcanic activity. *Pioneer species* are the organisms first to colonize a newly exposed habitat. They are opportunistic, r-selected species that can tolerate harsh conditions. In primary succession, moss and lichens are the pioneer species, which die and leave behind organic matter that accumulates into the soil. After the soil is built, grasses begin to grow, followed by shrubs and finally trees. Herbivores enter the community, followed by their predators. As succession progresses, many K-selected species outcompete the pioneers.

If an existing community is sufficiently disturbed, all life will be destroyed, and the habitat reverts to a barren state. Common events are forest fires or abandonment of farmland to cause this scenario. In this case, the habitat undergoes *secondary succession*. The soil is already present and does not need to be built. Unlike primary succession, secondary succession is strongly influenced by the previous conditions of the habitat.

Clements popularized the idea that species diversity and total biomass increase until a final equilibrium, or *climax community,* is reached. This is the stable state of the community, which remains relatively unchanged until a catastrophic event destroys it. Stability of communities is seen in three ways: persistence through time, resistance to change and recovery after a disturbance.

However, most modern ecologists recognize that true climax communities are rare. Realistically, disturbances are so frequent that most communities are succession and never truly reach a climax community. Furthermore, the "steady" state of a community is dynamic. Many ecologists refer to the steady state as the *mature community* or the *old growth community*. The transitional states are *seral community* or *sere*.

Clements' ideas are summarized under the *climatic climax theory*, where each region has one possible climax community, determined by the climate alone. Other factors are negligible compared to the climate. However, many ecologists subscribe to the *polyclimax theory*, which states that a region has multiple possible climax communities depending on the climate plus other environmental conditions such as topography and the nature of the disturbance. By contrast, the *climax pattern theory* proposes that there are multiple possible climax communities, but that they are influenced by both the environment *and* the species present. This theory places more emphasizes on how organisms respond to the changing environment and the way this shapes how succession proceeds. Finally, many ecologists believe that succession is cyclical, with a habitat passing through several alternating climax communities over time.

Three main models describe succession. The *facilitation model* applies to species which alter the environment to make it more hospitable to the next species. Soil building is an important example. The *inhibition model* describes species that attempt to hold on to their place in the community and make it more difficult for new species to succeed them. It assumes that each successional stage has a dominant species, which must be outcompeted or destroyed by a disturbance to allow the next species to establish itself. Finally, the *tolerance model* describes species that neither help nor hurt succeeding species. This model assumes that the climax community is made of species that can co-exist with one another.

All three models have been observed in nature, but it is difficult to predict which model a particular environment will experience.

Community biodiversity

The *intermediate disturbance hypothesis* states that a moderate level of disturbance yields the highest community diversity. Frequent disturbances may cause extinction, while few disturbances allow one species to grow dominant and outcompete others. Occasional disturbances, however, periodically inhibit dominant species and dampen competition to allow new species to enter, maximizing biodiversity. Disturbances may alter the physical environment to favor different species than before. Many communities rely on disturbances to keep them healthy, which is why forest management personnel set controlled forest fires.

Communities that experience widespread, frequent disturbances are dominated by r-strategists, while K-strategists, which outcompete others dominate undisturbed communities. Competition must be at moderate levels to maintain the most diverse communities. *Keystone predators* are essential species which regulate competition by controlling the population of species that would otherwise overrun a community. The starfish *Pisaster* is a classic example of a keystone predator that keeps the mussel *Mytilus* from outcompeting other invertebrates and algae for space.

The jaguar is an example of a keystone species that regulates competition

Biodiversity is best served by intermediate migration, i.e., emigration that is sufficient to offset mortality and immigration. Isolated communities have difficulty sustaining migration and may experience extinctions. *Insular biogeography* studies how isolation affects community structure. "Island communities" may be on islands or in an isolated region, such as a lake or patch of forest surrounded by cropland. Islands which are most distant from other communities have the lowest rates of migration and usually exhibit low diversity. They are more likely to experience extinction since new individuals cannot easily emigrate and replenish the population. Insular biogeography proposes that larger islands are more capable of supporting high diversity, especially because they can sustain keystone predators.

The *spatial heterogeneity model* is a concept in biogeography that explains why heterogeneous habitats can support higher diversity. The best habitats are patchy, or heterogeneous, creating a wider variety of niches. Heterogeneity may be seen in the topography, soil, and climate. Forests usually have vertical heterogeneity, or *stratification,* which creates drastically different habitats at different heights of the forest. Spatial heterogeneity is self-reinforcing since greater heterogeneity leads to greater biodiversity, and diversity in itself is a form of heterogeneity.

Global biodiversity has been on the decline for some time due to the effects of humans. Pollution, habitat destruction and hunting cause extinctions, which have a domino effect that can lead to the collapse of entire communities. Invasive species are rampant, which is a grave threat to diversity. Invasive species often have no natural predators in the environment they are introduced to, allowing them to outcompete other species rapidly. Many communities have become overrun by invasive species in a matter of decades and are now barren. The problem has been compounded by misguided efforts to introduce an even more invasive species to cull the original invader. In many cases, the new invaders take the place of the original ones. However, some efforts have successfully suppressed invasive species. Ecologists continue to research methods to minimize the effects of human disturbances and interventions, and preserve biodiversity.

Notes for active learning

Notes for active learning

Customer Satisfaction Guarantee

Your feedback is important because we strive to provide the highest quality prep materials. Email us comments or suggestions.

info@sterling–prep.com

We reply to emails – check your spam folder

Highest quality guarantee

Be the first to report a content error for a $10 reward
or a grammatical mistake to receive a $5 reward.

AP Biology Practice Questions provides high-yield practice questions covering topics tested on AP Biology exam. Develop the ability to apply your knowledge and quickly choose the correct answer to increase your test score.

Visit our Amazon store

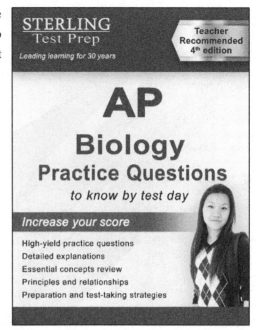

AP Chemistry, Biology and Physics online practice tests

Our advanced online testing platform allows you to take AP practice questions on your computer to generate a Diagnostic Report for each test.

By using our online AP tests and Diagnostic Reports, you will:

Assess your knowledge of subjects and topics to identify your areas of strength and weakness

Learn important scientific topics and concepts for comprehensive test preparation

Improve your test-taking skills

To access AP questions online
at special pricing for book owners, visit:
http://ap.sterling-prep.com/bookowner.htm

Advanced Placement (AP) prep books

Biology Practice Questions

Biology Review

Physics 1 Practice Questions

Physics 1 Review

Physics 2 Practice Questions

Physics 2 Review

Environmental Science

Psychology

U.S. History

World History

European History

U.S. Government and Politics

Comparative Government and Politics

Human Geography

Visit our Amazon store

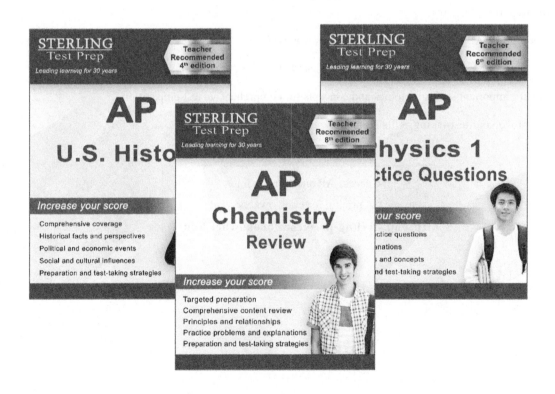

College Level Examination Program (CLEP)

Visit our Amazon store

College study aids

Cell and Molecular Biology Review

Organismal Biology Review

Cell and Molecular Biology Practice Questions

Organismal Biology Practice Questions

Physics Review

Physics Practice Questions

Organic Chemistry Practice Questions

United States History 101

American Government and Politics 101

Environmental Science 101

Visit our Amazon store

Made in the USA
Monee, IL
30 August 2023

41877521R00293